WEBSTER'S NEW WORLD®

ESSENTIAL
VOCABULARY

WEBSTER'S NEW WORLD®

ESSENTIAL VOCABULARY

by David A. Herzog

John Wiley & Sons, Inc.

Library of Congress Cataloging-in-Publication Data:

Herzog, David Alan.
 Webster's New World essential vocabulary / by David A. Herzog.
    p. cm.
  ISBN 0-7645-7165-6 (pbk.)
  1. Vocabulary. 2. Vocabulary—Problems, exercises, etc. 3. Vocabulary—Examinations—Study guides. I. Title: Essential vocabulary. II. Title.
  PE1449.H445 2005
  428.1—dc22

                                                       2004022068

Manufactured in the United States of America

10 9 8 7 6 5 4 3 2 1

Acknowledgments

The author would like to thank Willis, Gizmo, Lefty, and Archie for their furry invaluable assistance.

Dedication

This book is dedicated to the memories of Rose and George Herzog, Henry Smolinski, and Allan Shaw, and to their children, grandchildren, and great-grandchildren on four continents.

Contents

Introduction

How's your vocabulary? Is it okay, pretty good, or exceptional? Whatever your answer to these questions, this is the book for you. For those whose vocabulary ranges from okay to pretty good, here is the opportunity to improve it. The main content is grouped into sets of words that have been taken from the SAT and GRE examinations over the past 10 years. These approximately 1,500 words are expected by the examiners to be familiar in one form or another to college and graduate school applicants. They need to become familiar to you, too.

If your vocabulary is exceptional, this is the opportunity to see whether you really understand what the words you think you know mean and whether you can correctly use them in a sentence.

Each word comes complete with a label indicating its part of speech, at least one definition (often more), and usually at least two sentences using the word. Most entries also include synonyms and other forms of the word, such as past tense and gerund forms (for verbs) and adverbial and noun forms (for adjectives). Following each group of vocabulary words is a matching test so that you can check what you've just studied.

Check Appendix A for some very useful prefixes and suffixes that often affect the meanings of words. I also recommend you check Appendix B, which lists some foreign words that have insinuated themselves into the English language. These words are commonly used by the more literate among us — in addition to everyday words like *sandwich*, which reminds the author that he's getting hungry. Read on and have an enlightening and, hopefully, enjoyable experience.

PRONUNCIATION KEY

I've never much cared for the pronunciation keys used by most dictionaries because they use a whole different alphabet and set of symbols, which one must either memorize or keep referring to just to understand the sounds being represented. The key used here makes use of standard alphabet characters used in familiar words. The following is a list of the letters that are used and the sounds they make. These pronunciations are based on phonetic sounds. You might want to put a bookmark here so that you can get back to it quickly when needed. We indicate the stressed syllable of each word by using capital (KAP i tl) letters.

Letter(s)	Makes a Sound Like . . .	In the Word . . .
a	a	hat
ae	ai	hair
ah	o	on
aw	aw	saw
ay	a	day
ch	ch	chip
e	e	bed
ea	ea	ear
ee	ee	bee
g	g	go
i	i	bid
ing	ing	sing
oe	o	work
oh	o	go
oo	oo	moon
ow	ow	cow
oy	oy	toy
s	s	kiss
th	th	think
TH	th	that
u	oo	took
uh	u	rug
y	y	my
zh	s	measure

PARTS OF SPEECH

Parts of speech are indicated by italicized abbreviations: *adj.* (adjective), *adv.* (adverb), *conj.* (conjunction), *n.* (noun), *pn.* (pronoun), *pr.* (preposition), *vi.* (intransitive verb), and *vt.* (transitive verb). To review a little grammar very briefly, a noun is a person, place, or thing. An adjective modifies a noun. For example, a *pretty girl* gets more attention than a *plain girl.* In the preceding sentence, both *pretty* and *plain* are adjectives modifying two separate occurrences of the noun, *girl.*

A verb is an action word. If the verb is transitive, it carries the action to an object. Consider the following sentence: Peter *ate* a grape. In that sentence, the grape receives the action of the transitive verb, *to eat* (past tense, *ate*). The verb, *to eat,* can also be intransitive, if nothing is receiving the action. For example, when I go to dinner, I *eat.*

An adverb modifies a verb, another adverb, or an adjective. Look at the following sentence: The boat moved *quickly. Quickly* is an adverb modifying the verb, *moved.*

Part I

SAT® WORDS

Answers to Quick Review questions are found in Part III.

Words followed by an asterisk (*) also have appeared as vocabulary words on the Graduate Record Examinations® (GRE®).

A

abandon (uh BAN dn) *vt.* 1. to give up something forever; 2. to leave in a time of danger

- *Abandon* all hope of seeing your family again.
- We must *abandon* the boathouse until the storm is over.

  [-ed, -ing, abandonment *n.*] [Syn. quit, desert, forsake (Each of these has a slightly different emotion attached to it.)]

abbreviate (uh BREE vee ayt) *vt.* to shorten something by leaving a part, or parts, out

- We might *abbreviate* this word abbrev.
- The student *abbreviated* most of the words in his or her class notes to keep up with the teacher's lecture.

  [-d, abbreviating, abbreviation *n.*]

ability (uh BIL etee) *n.* 1. being able; having power to do something; 2. skill, expertise, power

- You have the *ability* to succeed at what you attempt.
- Einstein had exceptional mathematical *ability*.
- An automobile lacks the *ablility* to pull a freight train.

abridge (uh BRIJ) *vt.* 1. to reduce in scope; 2. to shorten while maintaining the essence

- Condensed books *abridge* the original to appeal to a less than scholarly audience.
- The 9-hour *Lord of the Rings* trilogy was *abridged* to 1 1/2 hours for its television broadcast.

  [-d, abridging]

abscond (ab SKAHND) *vi.* to run away and hide; especially to avoid capture by law enforcers

- Jesse James *absconded* just ahead of the sheriff.
- To *abscond* often results in a false sense of security.

  [-ed, -ing, absconder *n.*]

absolve (ab ZAHLV) *vt.* 1. to declare free from guilt; 2. to free from duty or a promise

- The Lord *absolved* the sinner and forgave him.
- The jury *absolved* the accused of any wrongdoing.
- Dad *absolved* Junior of his promise to wash the car.

  [-d, absolving, absolver *n.*] [Syn. pardon, forgive, acquit]

absorb (ab ZAWRB) *vt.* 1. to suck up; 2. to take up the full energy or attention of; engross; 3. to take in and incorporate; 4. to assume the full cost

- The sponge *absorbed* the entire spill.
- Learning fractions *absorbed* Hailee's full attention.
- If we fail to *absorb* the lessons of history, we are doomed to repeat them.
- I'll *absorb* the charge for the window replacement.

  [-ed, -ing, absorbant *adj.*]

abstain (ab STAYN) *vi.* to hold back (from); refrain from

- I shall *abstain* from smoking or drinking.
- Three voted for the bill, two against it, and one *abstained*.

  [-ed, -ing, abstention *n.*]

abstract (ab STRAKT *for adj.*, AB strakt *for n., v.*) *adj.* 1. not concrete; thought of apart from any material object; 2. not easily understood —*n.* a brief statement of the content of a book, court case, article, etc.; a summary —*vt.* to remove or take away; to summarize

- I had an *abstract* idea of what he meant, but nothing solid.
- Frankie's ideas were too *abstract* to fully comprehend.
- We knew about the case from having read the *abstract*.
- *Abstract* the story, stating only the relevant facts.

  [-ed, -ing, abstraction *n.*, abstractly *adv.*]

absurd (ab SOERD *or* ab ZOEHRD) *adj.* 1. so obviously untrue as to be laughable; 2. laughably different from what is reasonable

- The story that his arms were tired because he had just flown in from Los Angeles was *absurd*.
- The outfit that Gino wore with the red and white striped shirt and the green and yellow checked pants was *absurd*.

  [absurdly *adv.*, absurdity *n.*]

accentuate (ak SEN choo ayt) *vt.* 1. to pronounce or mark with a stress or accent; 2. emphasize

- When you tell people about your vacation, *accentuate* the high points and play down the low points.
- Wear clothing that *accentuates* your youthful looks.

  [-d, accentuating, accentuation *n.*]

acceptable (ak SEPT ibl) *adj.* adequate; tolerable; bearable; okay

- Eating peas at a restaurant using only your knife is not considered *acceptable* manners.
- Dressing in a toga is considered *acceptable* at certain fraternity parties.

QUICK REVIEW #1

Match the word from column 2 with the word from column 1 that means most nearly the same thing.

1. abandon	a. condense
2. abbreviated	b. refrain
3. ability	c. engross
4. abridge	d. theoretical
5. abscond	e. forsake
6. absolve	f. ridiculous
7. absorb	g. acquit
8. abstain	h. tolerable
9. abstract	i. emphasize
10. absurd	j. expertise
11. accentuate	k. shortened
12. acceptable	l. flee

acceptance (ak SEP tins) *n.* 1. being accepted; 2. an approval
- Jack's *acceptance* by Jill's family made him very happy.
- Ian's *acceptance* of full responsibility for the telephone charges got Kira off the hook (so to speak).

access (AK ses) *n.* 1. the act of coming near to; approach; 2. a way of approaching something; 3. the right to enter or use something —*vt.* to gain or have use of a database
- The *access* to the house was through the side door.
- Sebastian gained *access* to his car through the driver's window.
  [-ed, -ing]

accommodate (uh KOM uh dayt) *vt.* 1. to make fit; to adapt; adjust; 2. to reconcile; 3. to do a service or favor for; 4. to have room for
- An adapter is needed for your sink to *accommodate* the dishwasher hose.
- Even though I don't want to do it, I'll *accommodate* you.
- The hotel *accommodates* its guests with room service.
- The kitchen *accommodates* seating space for four.
  [-d, accommodating]

accommodation (uh kom uh DAY shun) *n.* 1. adjustment; adaptation to a certain use; 2. reconciliation of differences; 3. a convenience; 4. living or traveling space

- Myles made an *accommodation* to staying up all night and annoying his parents by sleeping most of the day.
- The employee and his former boss reached an *accommodation* over the matter of severance pay.
- Having coffeemakers in each room was an *accommodation* for motel guests.
- The train's compartment had sleeping *accommodations* for up to four passengers.

accomplice (uh KOM plis) *n.* a person who knowingly assists in committing a crime; partner in crime

- While Bob was robbing the bank, his *accomplice,* Louise, was behind the wheel of the getaway car.

  [Syn. associate]

accomplish (uh KOM plish) *vt.* 1. to do or succeed in doing; 2. to perfect; to complete

- Rocio *accomplished* her task of bathing the dog.
- The human fly never failed to *accomplish* its mission.

  [-ed, -ing, accomplishment *n.*] [Syn. perform, reach]

accord (uk AWRD) *vt.* 1. to make agree; to reconcile; 2. to grant or concede —*vi.* mutual agreement —*n.* 1. an informal agreement, as between two states or countries; 2. consent; permission

- Our objectives are in *accord.*
- I intend to *accord* you every courtesy.
- Jakob had his dad's *accord* to use the family car.

  [-ed, -ing, (in) accordance *n.*]

accost (uh KAWST) *vt.* to approach and greet first (often in an intrusive way)

- I wouldn't be so bold as to *accost* someone who did not greet me first.
- I was walking along, minding my own business, when I was *accosted* by a street peddler.

  [-ed, -ing]

account (uh KOWNT) *vt.* to tell, consider, or judge —*vi.* 1. to furnish a reckoning of money collected and/or payed out; 2. to make acceptable amends for; 3. to give acceptible reasons for —*n.* 1. a counting or calculation; 2. a record of monetary funds; 3. a bank account; 4. a record of transactions

- The detective asked Jim to *account* for his time on Sunday.
- The cashier had to *account* for her daily receipts.
- The criminal must *account* for his or her evil action.
- Karen *accounts* for her funds in her checkbook register.
- There's no *accounting* for people's tastes.
- Jason keeps track of what is due to him in his *accounts* receivable ledger.

  [-ed, -ing, accountable *n.*]

accuracy (AK yur isee) *n.* the quality of being correct or exact; exactness, preciseness

- Weather forecasts are not renowned for their *accuracy*.
- Robin Hood could shoot an arrow with great *accuracy*.

accurate (AK yur it) *adj.* 1. careful and precise; 2. free from errors; 3. sticking closely to a standard (like a scale)

- Ian made an *accurate* drawing of his pet pug Willis.
- Sarah had to be *accurate* in math to get a grade of 100%.
- Making candy requires a very *accurate* thermometer.

    [accurately *adv.*] [Syn. precise]

achieve (uh CHEEV) *vt.* 1. to succeed in doing; 2. to get somewhere; to attain; to gain —*vi.* to succeed

- Franklin Roosevelt *achieved* election to the U.S. presidency four separate times.
- It is difficult to *achieve* the lead in the Tour de France bicycle race.
- When Hillary tried to climb Everest, the goal was his to *achieve*.

    [-d, achieving, achievement *n.*] [Syn. reach, perform]

QUICK REVIEW #2

Match the word from column 2 with the word from column 1 that means most nearly the same thing.

1. acceptance	a. adjust
2. access	b. perform
3. accommodate	c. careful
4. accommodation	d. judge
5. accomplice	e. precision
6. accomplish	f. approach
7. accord	g. gain
8. accost	h. approval
9. account	i. associate
10. accuracy	j. consent
11. accurate	k. adaptation
12. achieve	l. intrude

acknowledge (ak NAH lidzh) *vt.* 1. to admit to be true; confess; 2. to recognize the claims or authority of; 3. to answer a greeter, respond to an introduction, etc.; 4. to express thanks for; 5. to affirm the reception of something

- Roxane *acknowledged* the charges against her.
- The insuror *acknowledged* the claims of the victim.
- The chair *acknowledges* the senator from Neverland.
- I'd like to *acknowledge* both my parents for the gift of life.

  [-d, acknowledging, acknowledgment *n.*]

acquire (ak WYR) *vt.* 1. to gain or get something; 2. to take possession of; obtain

- You would do well to *acquire* a good education.
- We all *acquire* some of our parents' traits by heredity.
- The United States *acquired* the Louisiana Territory by purchasing it from France.
- An appreciation for caviar is an *acquired* taste, unlike a love for creamed corn, which is, of course, innate.

  [-d, acquiring]

acquisition* (AK wuh zi shuhn) *n.* something or someone obtained

- A developer's *acquisition* of the old Bethlehem Corp.'s property is seen as a good thing for Easton.
- Tania's *acquisition* of a new PDA made her very happy.
- Ali's *acquisition* of a new chauffeur pleased her to no end.

  [acquisitive *adj.*, acquisitively *adv.*, acquisitiveness *n.*]

acrimony (AK ruh moh nee) *n.* bitterness, sharpness, or harshness of speech, manner, or temper

- The *acrimony* of the temper of a scorned woman is legendary both in literature and in life.
- Dylan greeted the news that his new DVD player did not work at all with considerable *acrimony* in his oaths.

  [acrimonious *adj.*, acrimoniously *adv.*] [Syn. asperity]

acute (uh KYOOT) *adj.* 1. sharply pointed; 2. shrewd; quick of mind; 3. sensitive to something (like acute hearing); 4. severe and sharp (like acute pain); 5. serious; severe

- An *acute* angle forms a sharp point.
- Geoffrey's *acute* mind made short work of the crossword.
- The eagle's *acute* eyesight can pick up a mouse on the ground from hundreds of meters in the air.
- Certain pains, like John, are *acute* but of short duration.
- There is an *acute* shortage of labor in some job categories.

  [-ly *adv.*, acuity *n.*] [Syn. sharp, keen, critical]

adapt* (uh DAPT) *vt.* 1. to make suitable or to make fit by changing; 2. to change oneself to fit new or changed conditions

- Jim thought it perfectly sensible to *adapt* his gas stove's IN line to connect to the hot water line from his sink.
- When Mary travels between Miami and Juneau, she *adapts* her wardrobe—especially outerwear—accordingly.

  [-ed, -ing, -able *adj.*, -ation, -er, adaptability *n.*]

adept (uh DEPT) *adj.* very skilled, expert —*n.* a person who is very skilled in some field of endeavor or knowledge

- George Jetson will be a very *adept* widget maker.
- When it comes to guarding those Academy Award winners, the accounting firm of Price Waterhouse has shown itself to be *adept*.

[adeptly *adv.*, adeptness *n.*] [Syn. expert]

adhere* (ad HEER) *vi.* 1. to stick to something; stick to a plan; 2. to stay firm in support of a leader or a plan

- Peanut butter will *adhere* to one's teeth almost every time.
- The candidate *adhered* to her promise to support the health plan, even after she was elected.
- The secretary *adhered* to his boss's story, even after the latter had changed it.

[-d, adhering, adherer, adherence *n.*] [Syn. stick]

adjudicate (uh JOO dik ayt) *vt.* to hear and decide a court case —*vi.* to serve as a judge to decide some dispute or problem

- Judge Judy *adjudicates* cases on television five days a week.
- Melissa agreed to *adjudicate* a dispute between two of her neighbors on how high to construct a fence between their backyards.

[-d, adjudicating]

admirable (AD muh ruh bl) *adj.* inspiring or deserving admiration or praise; excellent; splendid

- Melissa's success in totally renovating the house with limited available resources is *admirable*.
- The varsity hockey team did an *admirable* job defending against their opponent's star shooter.
- The orchestra performed *admirably* at last night's concert.

[admirably *adv.*]

admire (ad MYR) *vt.* 1. to look upon with approval, wonder, and delight; 2. to have a high regard for

- Any basketball fan has to *admire* the effortlessness with which Jason Kidd dishes the rock to his teammates.
- Students of the Korean police action of the 1950s *admire* General MacArthur's daring in landing his troops and equipment behind the enemy lines at Inchon.

[-d, admiring, admiration *n.*]

adorn (uh DAWRN) *vt.* 1. to be ornamental to; add beauty or distinction to; 2. put decorations on; ornament

- Many ornaments are hung on a Christmas tree to *adorn* it.
- Jewelry often *adorns* a woman's arms and neck.
- In summer, a house's lawn is often *adorned* by colorful flowers.

[-ed, -ing, adornment *n.*] [Syn. beautify, decorate, bedeck]

QUICK REVIEW #3

Match the word from column 2 with the word from column 1 that means most nearly the same thing.

1. acknowledge		a. harshness
2. acquire		b. bedeck
3. acquisition		c. decide
4. acrimony		d. approve
5. acute		e. stick
6. adapt		f. confess
7. adept		g. splendid
8. adhere		h. gain
9. adjudicate		i. change
10. admirable		j. hire
11. admire		k. expert
12. adorn		l. serious

adulate (AD joo let) *vt.* 1. to praise too highly or flatter in a servile manner; 2. to admire to an excessive degree

- In the king's presence, his subjects often *adulate* him.
- Ali always *adulates* her husband Joe when she's looking to get him to do something for her.

  [-d, adulating, adulation, adulator *n.*, adulatory *adj.*]

advantageous (AD van TAY juhss) *adj.* resulting in having an advantage; profitable; favorable

- The outbreak of war in Europe was quite *advantageous* for American industry.
- Because they get to bat last, the home team in a baseball game is in an *advantageous* position.

adversarial* (AD voer SER ee uhl) *adj.* of or characterized by disagreement, opposition, hostility, etc. (as would be the case between adversaries)

- A prosecutor and a defense attorney have an *adversarial* relationship—at least while they are in court.
- During the U.S. Civil War, the Union and the Confederacy were *adversarial*.

adversary (AD vuh SER ee) *n.* a person who fights against another; one who is in opposition to something

- Muhammad Ali was Joe Frasier's *adversary* in the boxing ring on three separate occasions.
- The New York Yankees and the Boston Red Sox are legendary *adversaries* in baseball's American League.
- In World War II, the U.S.'s Pacific *adversary* was Japan.

  [Syn. enemy, opponent]

adversity (ad VER si tee) *n.* a state of poverty and trouble; a condition of misfortune or wretchedness; an instance of calamity

- Those who lived through the Great Depression of the early 1930s learned how to triumph over *adversity.*
- The only solution to the *adversity* of those living in the Dust Bowl of Oklahoma in the 1930s was to move away.
- The Japanese automobile and electronics industries helped the country to recover from the *adversity* of defeat.

aerate (AER ayt) *vt.* 1. to open to air or to cause air to circulate through; 2. to get oxygen to the blood (as in respiration); 3. to charge a liquid with gas (such as making soda pop)

- To improve the taste of drinking water, huge plants *aerate* it before it is sent to your home.
- Your lungs *aerate* the blood that is brought there from your heart as part of your pulmonary circulation.
- Soft drink makers *aerate* their drinks by forcing carbon dioxide to dissolve under pressure.

  [-d, aerating, aeration *n.*]

aesthetic* (es the tik) *adj.* 1. of beauty; 2. sensitive to art and beauty; demonstrating good taste; being artistic

- Van Gogh's *Starry Night* has an *aesthetic* quality that defies being expressed in words.
- Aaron was touched by the *aesthetic* arrangement of the flowers blooming in the garden.

  [aesthetically *adv.*, aesthetical, aesthete *n.*]

affect (uh FEKT) *vt.* 1. to influence; to produce a change; 2. to move or cause an emotional response; 3. to pretend to be, have, feel, or like —*n.* an emotional response; an emotion or feeling attached to an idea

- Both crosswind and current *affect* our ability to row straight across to the other side of the river.
- Seeing the photos of the liberated concentration camp inmates *affects* many people.
- As the voice of Shrek, Mike Meyers *affects* the role of a lovable green ogre.

  [-ed, -ing, affectable *adj.*] [Syn. assume (sense 3)]

affront (uhf RUHNT) *vt.* 1. to openly or purposefully insult; offend; slight; 2. to confront in a defiant manner —*n.* an open or deliberate insult

- Don't *affront* Bill's mother by telling her the chicken she prepared tasted like the take-out chicken's bucket.
- When you tell your parents you'll do anything you want regardless of what they think, you *affront* them.
- Debbie's not inviting Sally to her birthday party was a deliberate *affront.*

  [-ed, -ing] [Syn. offend]

agenda* (uh JEN duh) *n.* a list of things to be done; especially, a program of things to be done at a meeting

- Jason wanted to settle down and have children, but his brother Dylan had a totally different *agenda*.
- "Old Business" was the second thing on the *agenda* for the meeting, just after the reading of the minutes from the last meeting.

agile (A juhl) *adj.* 1. able to move quickly and easily; deft and active of body or mind; 2. keen and lively (of mind)

- The ballerina showed how *agile* she was as she effortlessly danced and frolicked about the stage.
- The comedian was *agile* of mind as he moved from one quip seamlessly to the next.

   [agilely *adv.*, agility *n.*]

agrarian (uhg RAR ee uhn) *adj.* 1. relating to land in general; 2. relating to farms, farmers, and agriculture

- The *agrarian* laws of the late twentieth century had the government paying farmers to not grow certain crops.
- *Agrarian* schools teach farmers about crop rotation and how alternating certain crops replenishes soil nutrients.

QUICK REVIEW #4

Match the word from column 2 with the word from column 1 that means most nearly the same thing.

1. adulate	a. hostile
2. advantageous	b. carbonate
3. adversarial	c. list
4. adversary	d. offend
5. adversity	e. fawn
6. aerate	f. agricultural
7. aesthetic	g. keen
8. affect	h. artistic
9. affront	i. profitable
10. agenda	j. calamity
11. agile	k. assume
12. agrarian	l. opponent

agreement (uh GREE mnt) *n.* 1. being in harmony or accord; 2. an understanding between two parties; 3. a contract

- Tania and Ali came to an *agreement* on who'd bring what to the Cinco de Mayo party.
- Canada and the U.S. have an *agreement* concerning the openness of their shared border.
- Calling a strike would violate the union's *agreement* with the automaker.

ailment (AYL mnt) *n.* disease; illness; any mental or physical disorder, especially a mild but persistent one

- Marley walked with a limp as a result of a bout with rickets, an *ailment* that had affected him as a puppy.
- Delusions of grandeur describes an *ailment* that afflicts many teenaged boys.

alacrity (uh LAK ri tee) *n.* eager readiness or willingness, usually demonstrated by quick and lively action

- Consuela ate her dinner with *alacrity,* eager to leave to go to the movie theater.
- Willis wagged his tail rapidly indicating his *alacrity* to go for a walk when he heard Jim getting his leash.

alchemy (AL ku mee) *n.* 1. an early combination of magic, chemistry, and philosophy from the Middle Ages, the main purposes of which were to turn base metals into gold and to find the elixir for eternal youth; 2. a process or power for turning one thing into a better thing as if by miraculous means

- Four-year-old Francesco was positive that his grandfather could practice *alchemy* to change his pennies into quarters.
- Anyone who believes that a cottage sitting on a quarter acre of land can be turned into a mansion believes in the teachings of *alchemy.*

  [alchemical *adj.,* alchemically *adv.,* alchemist *n.*]

alienate (AY lee en ayt) *vt.* 1. to transfer land ownership to another; 2. to estrange; make unfriendly; 3. to cause to be detached or withdrawn; 4. to cause a change of affection

- That to sell a piece of property to another is to *alienate* it is a rarely used meaning of the word in the U.S.
- When you ask a friend's former girlfriend for a date, you're likely to *alienate* that friend. Ask a friend's current boyfriend for a date and you're certain to alienate her.
- Snatching a dog's food from his mouth is likely to *alienate* the dog—especially if it's not your own pet.
- Sally told Suzie stories about Cheryl's past dealings with her friends that were sure to *alienate* Suzie from Cheryl and, she hoped, gain Suzie's friendship for herself.

  [-d, alienation *n.*]

ally* (uh LY *for vt.*, A ly *for n.*) *vt.* 1. to unite or join with for a certain purpose; 2. to relate by similarity of purpose, structure, or other character —*n.* 1. a country, group, or individual joined with others for a common end; 2. plants or animals closely related by some characteristic

- A marriage was often used to *ally* two royal European families during the Middle Ages and beyond.
- The U.K. was our *ally* in both wars with Iraq.
- The lilly and the onion are two closely *allied* bulbs.

  [allied, allying, allies *pl.*, alliance *n.*] [Syn. associate]

alter (AWL ter) *vt.* 1. to cause to change in detail but not in substance; modify; 2. to take parts of a garment and resew them for a better fit; 3. to neuter (an animal) —*vi.* to change; become different

- Mike and Alice *altered* their plans for the evening.
- The tailor had to *alter* the gown to make it fit Jan better.
- *Alter* your pet to keep down an overpopulation of strays.
- The Fab Five *altered* Al's style of dress and his lifestyle.

  [-ed, -ing, alteration *n.*] [Syn. change, vary]

although (awl THOH) *conj.* despite the fact that; granting that; though

- Mike sat down to dinner, *although* he had eaten less than a half hour before.
- *Although* Mary claimed to not care for opera, she had to admit that the music from *Il Trovatore* was exceptional.

altruism (AL troo i zm) *n.* unselfish concern for others' well-being

- It had to be *altruism* as well as bravery that caused Maria to run into the burning house to rescue the crying child.
- It is uncommon to see a case of pure *altruism,* where there is no thought of personal gain.

  [altruist *n.*] [Syn. selflessness]

ambiguous* (am BIG yoo uhs) *adj.* 1. having more than one possible meaning; 2. unclear; vague; indefinite

- The third base coach's *ambiguous* signals left the batter not knowing whether to swing away or bunt.
- Roxane was *ambiguous* in her instructions for feeding the cat while she was away.

  [-ly *adv.*, -ness, ambiguity *n.*, ambiguities *pl.*] [Syn. obscure]

ambivalence (am BIV uh lens) *n.* having conflicting feelings about a person or thing at the same time, such as love and hate

- Karen had a real *ambivalence* about being invited to Uncle Bob's cabin; she loved visiting but hated the four-hour trip.
- David showed *ambivalence* about serving artichokes because, while they are delicious, they're a pain to prepare.

amenity (uh MEN i tee) *n.* 1. pleasing quality; attractiveness; 2. a pleasant or desirable feature; something that adds to one's comfort —*pl.* the courteous manners and pleasant acts of polite social behavior

- The tropical scenery is only one *amenity* of Hawaii.
- Hawaii's climate is an additional *amenity* of the place.
- The restaurant's servers and hostesses demonstrated all the *amenities* one would expect at those prices.

[amenities *pl.*]

QUICK REVIEW #5

Match the word from column 2 with the word from column 1 that means most nearly the same thing.

1. agreement	a. magic
2. ailment	b. vary
3. alacrity	c. selflessness
4. alchemy	d. despite
5. alienate	e. conflict
6. ally	f. contract
7. alter	g. unclear
8. although	h. pleasantness
9. altruism	i. estrange
10. ambiguous	j. illness
11. ambivalence	k. associate
12. amenity	l. eagerness

amicable (AM i kuh bl) *adj.* feeling friendly; demonstrating goodwill; peaceable

- Alice and her husband Ted had an *amicable* discussion about putting in a flower garden in the spring.
- Bob and Carol separated on *amicable* terms.

[amicably *adv.*, amicability *n.*]

among (uh MUHNG) *prep.* 1. In the midst of; surrounded by; included in a group of; 2. from place to place in; 3. in the number or group of; 4. by or with a lot of

- You are *among* friends.
- He passed *among* the crowd.
- Ralph is included *among* the supporters of the president.
- Machiavelli's work is popular *among* business executives.

amorphous (uh MAWR fuhs) *adj.* 1. lacking definite form; shapeless; 2. of no specific type; anomolous; 3. indefinite; vague

- Sulfur is a yellow, nonmetallic element that is found in crystal and *amorphous* forms.
- To one unfamiliar with the game of rugby, the game appears to be governed by *amorphous* rules.
- When Gino tried to pin Hailee down to a specific time, all he could get from her was an *amorphous* response.

  [amorphously *adv.*]

amphibian (am FIB ee en) *n.* 1. any one of a class of cold-blooded vertebrates without scales (including frogs, newts, salamanders, and toads) that starts life with gills, living in the water, and later develops lungs; 2. any plant or animal that is at home both on land and in water; 3. any aircraft or vehicle that can operate on land and in water

- It is not unusual to find *amphibians* in and around a pond.
- The early Pan American Airways Clippers were *amphibians* that loaded and unloaded their passengers on land but took off from and landed on water.

  [amphibious *adj.*]

amplify* (AMP li fy) *vt.* 1. to make bigger and stronger; increase or extend (power, authority, etc.); 2. to strengthen by adding details, examples, etc.; 3. (electronics) to strengthen an audio signal or electrical current

- Caesar Augustus *amplified* the reach of the Roman Empire.
- The robbery victim *amplified* his story by providing the license plate number of the felon's car and a thorough description of his height, build, and clothing.
- The sound of the lead singer's voice is almost inaudible, but the sound engineer will *amplify* it to make it stand out.

  [amplified, amplifying, amplification, amplifier *n.*]

amusement (uh MYOOZ mnt) *n.* 1. the condition of being entertained; 2. a thing or activity that amuses or entertains; entertainment

- Randy's *amusement* was Claire's main occupation.
- Marcia played solitaire for her own *amusement*.
- The antics of the dancing bears was a source of great *amusement* for the audience.

amusing (uh MYOOZ eeng) *adj.* 1. entertaining; diverting; 2. causing laughter or merriment

- The comedian's stand-up routine was very *amusing*.
- An *amusing* incident takes one's mind off his or her woes.
- Jose's *amusing* facial contortions made everyone laugh.

  [Syn. funny]

anachronism (un AK ron i zm) *n.* 1. the putting forth of something as having happened outside its appropriate time, especially earlier; 2. anything that seems to be out of its proper time frame in history

- The depiction in some movies of people interacting with dinosaurs is an often-portrayed *anachronism.*
- *Anachronism* is a frequently used tool of literature because it allows all sorts of interactions that would be otherwise impossible.
- Having a conversation with the founding fathers or interviewing Abe Lincoln or Marie Curie are but three literary uses for *anachronism.*

[anachronistic *adj.*, anachronistically *adv.*]

analogy (uh NAL uh gee) *n.* 1. a likeness in some ways between things that are otherwise not alike; 2. the likening of one thing to another based on some shared similarity

- There is an *analogy* between polar bears and humans, in that both are mammals and both live on earth.
- Mork's *analogy* convinced Mindy that her problem closely resembled the one Curtis had last month; the circumstances were the same although the names and locations differed.

[analogous *adj.*, analogously *adv.*] [Syn. likeness]

analysis* (uh NA lis is) *n.* 1. breaking up or separating a whole into its parts so that they can be inspected to determine their nature, proportions, functions, etc.; any detailed inspection; 2. a statement of the results of this process

- The statement is undergoing detailed *analysis* to determine its true meaning.
- The specimen was sent to the laboratory for *analysis.*
- The historian's *analysis* of the spaghetti company's battle for supremacy is available in his latest book, *Pasta for You.*

analytical (an uh LIT ik uhl) *adj.* 1. something that separates into constituent parts; 2. skilled at using analysis

- Greg's *analytical* mind breaks each problem into tiny parts and carefully examines each and every one.
- The more one practices *analytical* procedures, the more skilled at them he or she is likely to become.

[analytic, analytically *adv.*] [Antonym: synthetic]

analyze (AN i LYZ) *vt.* 1. to separate into constituent parts so as to determine their nature, proportion, interrelationship, etc.; 2. to examine in detail to find out the nature, tendencies, etc. of something; 3. to psychoanalyze

- Heat is often very handy as a tool to help *analyze* the composition of substances, because once vaporized the substances' unique light spectra can be recorded.
- A microscope is a useful tool to *analyze* things that are invisible to the naked eye.
- Some people need *analyzing* by a shrink.

[-d, analyzing, analyzer *n.*]

QUICK REVIEW #6

Match the word from column 2 with the word from column 1 that means most nearly the same thing.

1. amicable		a. entertainment
2. among		b. examine
3. amorphous		c. likeness
4. amphibian		d. examination
5. amplify		e. vague
6. amusement		f. untimely
7. amusing		g. separating
8. anachronistic		h. friendly
9. analogy		i. funny
10. analysis		j. within
11. analytical		k. increase
12. analyze		l. caecilian

anarchy (AN er kee) *n.* 1. a complete lack of government; 2. characterized by political disorder and violence; lawlessness; 3. disorder in any area of activity or endeavor

- With no government in power, *anarchy* reigned supreme.
- In the current state of *anarchy,* looting and violence were the everyday state of affairs.
- With no proven theory as to the mechanism of the Copelia virus, *anarchy* prevailed in the field of viral research.

  [anarchic, anarchical *adj.*, anarchist *n.*, anarchically *adv.*]

ancestor (AN ses toer) *n.* 1. someone from whom one is descended, especially one earlier than a grandparent; forefather; forebear; 2. an earlier kind of animal from which later types have evolved; 3. anything regarded as a forerunner of a thing that developed later

- My neighbor Bryan claims that Davey Crockett was his *ancestor.*
- The sabertooth tiger is thought to be an *ancestor* of today's big cats as well as domesticated cats.
- The British Morris Mini is considered the *ancestor* of all modern compact cars with sideways-mounted engines.

  [ancestral *adj.*]

ancient (AYN shent) *adj.* 1. belonging to the distant past, especially prior to the end of the Western Roman Empire (476 A.D.); 2. having been in existence a long time; very, very old; 3. antiquated; old-fashioned —*n.* 1. a person who lived in ancient times; 2. a very old person

- In *ancient* days, Athens and Sparta were great city-states.
- Baltimore's Fort McHenry is an *ancient* structure.
- Barbara thinks her mom's notions of proper behavior are totally *ancient,* dude.
- Julius Caesar was an *ancient;* so is my grandfather.

  [Syn. old]

ancillary (AN sil er ee) *adj.* 1. underling or subordinate, often used with *to;* 2. that serves as an aid; auxiliary

- On the *Minnow,* Gilligan was *ancillary* to the Skipper.
- While the main body of a news article imparts primary information, side-bars usually contain *ancillary* or related facts.

anecdote (AN ik doht) *n.* 1. a short, entertaining account of something that happened, usually personal or biographical; 2. (obsolete) a little-known amusing fact

- Jonah related the *anecdote* about himself and the whale.
- Many are unaware of the fact that some social studies books once con-tained the *anecdote* that Abraham Lincoln was born in a log cabin that he'd built with his own hands.

  [anecdotal *adj.,* anecdotally *adv.*] [Syn. story]

animate (AN i mayt) *vt.* 1. to bring to life; to give life to; 2. to cause to be ener-getic or spirited; 3. to move to action; inspire

- Skillful puppeteers are able to convincingly *animate* lifeless, wooden, marionettes.
- You can rely on Harold to join in a dull discussion and, by so doing, to immediately *animate* it.
- The group of soldiers sat around acting glum, until Sergeant Jones *animated* them to take action.

  [-d, animating, animation *n.*]

antagonist* (an TAG uh nisst) *n.* 1. a person who competes against or opposes another; adversary; opponent; 2. a muscle, drug, etc. that acts to opppose another

- The Boston Red Sox baseball team is the chief *antagonist* of the New York Yankees baseball team.
- For every muscle in your body that causes a body part to move in a certain direction, an *antagonist* muscle exists to return the part to its original position.

  [-ic *adj.,* -ically *adv.,* antagonism *n.*] [Syn. opponent]

anthology (an THOL i jee) *n.* a collection of short stories, songs, poems, excerpts, etc. compiled into a single book

- Every poetry collection is an *anthology* if more than a single poet's works are included.
- Almost every CD of popular music is an *anthology* of songs.

[-logies *pl.*, -logize *vt.*, -logizer, -logist *n.*, -logistic *adj.*]

antiquated (an tik WAY tid) *adj.* 1. no longer useful or used; obsolete; out of date; old fashioned; 2. very aged

- A very small part of this book was typed on an *antiquated* IBM Selectric typewriter—a very small part.
- I usually drive an *antiquated* Toyota from the mid-1980s.

[antiquate *vt.*] [Syn. old]

antiseptic (AN ti SEP tik) *adj.* 1. disallowing infection, decay, etc. by slowing the growth of microbes; 2. free from infectious agents or infection; 3. very clean; sterile; 4. untouched by life's problems, emotions, etc. —*n.* a cleaning agent meant to prevent the growth of bacteria and viruses

- When you get a cut, it's a good idea to use an *antiseptic* cream to prevent its becoming infected.
- An operating room should be in *antiseptic* condition.
- You need not keep your room *antiseptic;* just neat will do.
- The hermit led an *antiseptic* life, locked away in his penthouse apartment with no contact with the outside.

[-ally *adv.*]

anxiety (ang ZY i tee) *n.* 1. a state of uneasiness, apprehension, or worriedness about what the future might hold; 2. feeling powerless and unprepared to deal with threatening (usually imaginary) events; 3. an eager but often uneasy concern (to do well)

- Karen always felt *anxiety* about her investments in the stock market and was nervous about losing money.
- Lou's biggest *anxiety* concerned earthquakes, which was especially unusual because he lived in New York City.
- *Anxiety* hung heavily in the air of the SAT exam room.

[anxieties *pl.*] [Syn. care]

apathetic (AP uh THET ik) *adj.* 1. feeling emotionless; unmoved; 2. disinterested; listless

- That most Americans were *apathetic* to the election was evidenced by the very low turnout.
- Football fans are rarely *apathetic* to the fortunes of their home teams; they yell and cheer for them, even on TV.

[-ally *adv.*, apathy *n.*] [Syn. impassive]

QUICK REVIEW #7

Match the word from column 2 with the word from column 1 that means most nearly the same thing.

1. anarchy		a. auxiliary
2. ancestor		b. impassive
3. ancient		c. clean
4. ancillary		d. aged
5. anecdote		e. collection
6. animate		f. care
7. antagonist		g. lawlessness
8. anthology		h. inspire
9. antiquated		i. story
10. antiseptic		j. forebear
11. anxiety		k. opponent
12. apathetic		l. obsolete

appalling (uh PAWL ing) *adj.* creating horror, shock, or dismay

- The children's lack of attention while crossing the busy street was absolutely *appalling*.
- An *appallingly* large number of the general public have no notion of what March Madness means.

  [-ly *adv.*, appall *vt.* (appalled)] [Syn. dismaying]

apparent (uh PAR int) *adj.* 1. easily seen; visible; 2. readily understood or perceived; obvious; evident; 3. seeming (but not necessarily) true

- Your coat's location is *apparent;* I can see it on the rack.
- It was clearly *apparent* that when the judge decided the case, she did not have all the information.
- Ian has an *apparent* knowledge of the stock, but I don't think you should buy it until the research has been completed.

  [-ly *adv.*] [Syn. evident]

appearance (uh PEER enss) *n.* 1. a coming forth or becoming visible; 2. the outward look or aspect of a person or thing; 3. any thing or person seen; 4. an outward pretense; 5. how things seem to be (but are not necessarily)

- She made an *appearance* at the Oscar presentations.
- Gina's *appearance* was one of calm and stateliness.
- The groundhog's *appearance* was ever so brief, and it soon disappeared back into its burrow.
- Though only of middling means, Genghis and Sylvia Kahn liked to keep up an *appearance* of being well off.
- From all *appearances*, he's innocent.

appreciate (uh PREE shee AYT) *vt.* 1. to think well of; to understand or enjoy; esteem; 2. to recognize and be thankful for; 3. to estimate the quality or value of (especially favorably); 4. to be sensitively aware of; 5. to increase the price or value of

- We all *appreciate* how well mannered Shewana is.
- Many of her students *appreciate* the educational experience Mrs. Sheridan provides in her applied physics class.
- The connoisseur *appreciated* the fineness of the woodwork.
- The college entrance committee fully *appreciates* all the applicants' concern for its ethnic and racial blindness.
- The price of fine art continues to *appreciate* even as you are reading this sentence.

[-d, appreciating, appreciation *n.*] [Syn. treasure, cherish, pride]

approach (uh PROHch) *vt.* 1. to come close or closer to; 2. to be similar to; to approximate; 3. a proposal or request to; to make advances; 4. to start dealing with

- You may *approach* the rim of the Grand Canyon, but don't *approach* it too closely—for obvious reasons.
- Digital audiotape *approaches* the quality of CD sound.
- Do you have the nerve to *approach* your boss for a raise?
- It's time to *approach* the matter of clearing the flood waters' debris out of the basement.

[-es *pl.*, -ed, -ing, -able *adj.*, -ability *n.* (also approach *n.*)]

appropriate (uh PROH pree AYT *for v.,* uh PROH pree it *for adj.*) *vt.* 1. to take for one's exclusive use; 2. to take without permission or improperly; 3. to set aside for a certain use or particular person —*adj.* right for the purpose; suitable; fit; proper

- The Duchess has been known to *appropriate* the entire seating area of a town's only restaurant when she desires to have tea.
- Jane's mother overruled Jane's attempt to *appropriate* her neighbor's lawn chair.
- Farmer Jack had to *appropriate* the horse to draw the sleigh—at least until the snowmobile was fixed.
- A bathing suit is *appropriate* for the swimming pool but not at all appropriate for the igloo.

[-d, appropriating, -ness, appropriation *n.*] [Syn. fit]

aquarium (uh KWAER ee uhm) *n.* 1. a tank, usually having glass sides, or a pool, bowl, etc. for keeping live water plants, fish, and/or aquatic mammals; 2. a building used to put such collections on exhibit

- Margie had tropical fish in the 20-gallon *aquarium* that she kept against a wall of the living room.
- The National *Aquarium* in Baltimore, Maryland, is a major tourist attraction in that city's inner harbor.

arable (AR i bl) *adj.* appropriate for plowing and, therefore, for growing crops —*n.* cultivatable land

- A farm is only as useful as its *arable* land.
- Thomas bought the field on the basis of its *arability*.

  [arability *n.*]

arbitration (AHR bit RA shn) *n.* the act of settling a dispute by a person or group picked to hear both sides and make a decision [arbitrator *n.* the person(s) who so decide(s)]

- Jackie's dispute with the cable company was settled by binding *arbitration,* meaning that the arbitrator's decision was final and had to be abided by.
- Nonbinding *arbitration* is more like advice after a fair hearing because neither party has to follow that advice.

arboreal (ahr BAWR ee uhl) *adj.* 1. having to do with trees; 2. living in trees or adapted to living in trees

- A tropical rain forest is an *arboreal* habitat—full of trees.
- Certain monkeys and sloths are *arboreal* and spend their entire lives in the trees, while squirrels are equally at home on the ground and out on a limb.

architect (AHRK i tekt) *n.* 1. a person whose job is to design and draw up plans for buildings, bridges, etc.; 2. any similar designer in a specific field; 3. a planner or creator

- Frank Lloyd Wright's *architecture* is impressively displayed in New York City's Guggenheim Museum of Art, where visitors begin at the top and walk continuously downhill.
- Perhaps our most celebrated naval *architect* was Admiral Hyman Rickover, the father of the nuclear submarine.
- The men who wrote the U.S. Constitution were the *architects* of American democracy.

arena (uh REE nuh) *n.* 1. The central part of an ancient Roman amphitheater, where gladiators fought and shows were put on; 2. an area used for sporting and other events, usually surrounded by rows of seats; the building containing same; 3. any area of struggle or conflict

- In the *arenas* of Rome, gladiators' swords often clashed.
- Basketball is the most frequent conflict in today's sports *arenas,* like the Staples Center or Madison Square Garden.
- Both candidates rolled up their sleeves and joined combat in the political *arena,* just two weeks before election day.

QUICK REVIEW #8

Match the word from column 2 with the word from column 1 that means most nearly the same thing.

1. appalling	a. esteem
2. apparent	b. tank
3. appearance	c. creator
4. appreciate	d. plowable
5. approach	e. wooded
6. appropriate	f. shocking
7. aquarium	g. approximate
8. arable	h. evident
9. arbitration	i. theater
10. arboreal	j. look
11. architect	k. settlement
12. arena	l. fit

argument (AHR gyoo mint) *n.* 1. a reason or reasons offered for doing or not doing something; 2. the putting forth of such reasons; 3. a discussion containing disagreement; debate; dispute

- The *argument* for preserving our natural resources is that they are irreplaceable and in many cases unrenewable.
- Randi might make the *argument* that iced drinks, drunk too fast, make you feel like they're freezing your brain.
- The candidates had an *argument* about the pros and cons of trying to eat French toast through a straw.

arid* (AR id) *adj.* 1. absent enough water for things to grow; dry; barren; 2. dull; lifeless; of no interest

- Most of Nevada is *arid* desert, despite the Colorado River.
- Moesha's social life is as *arid* as a mouthful of unsalted, fat-free tortilla chips.

  [-ness, -ity *n.,* -ly *adv.*] [Syn. dry]

aristocratic (uh RIS tuh KRAT ik) *adj.* 1. of, characteristic of, or favoring rule by an elite group as a form of government; 2. of the upper class or nobility; 3. like a member of the upper class or nobility in manner and/or taste or carrying oneself (used favorably, as proud, distinguished, etc. or unfavorably as snobbish, haughty, etc.)

- During the French Revolution, *aristocratic* government was rejected by the revolutionaries, but it wasn't long until Napoleon changed all that.
- The *aristocratic* class in England sits in the House of Lords.
- William was much admired for his *aristocratic* demeanor.
- Elaine's *aristocratic* manner was loathed by most, who felt she was looking down her blue-blooded nose at them.

  [aristocratically *adv.*]

arrogant (AR uh gnt) *adj.* full of or due to undeserved pride and self-importance; overbearing; haughty

- The entertainer in the lounge seemed very *arrogant* for one who was not even close to being a headliner.
- The *arrogant* bearing of the heavyweight champion was justly rewarded when he was knocked out in round one.

  [-ly *adv.*, arrogance *n.*] [Syn. proud]

artist (AHRT ist) *n.* 1. a person who is skilled in or works in the techniques of fine arts, especially in drawing, painting, sculpture, etc.; 2. someone who does anything very well, imaginatively, and with a feeling for form, effect, etc.; 3. one in any of the performing arts (dance, theater, etc.)

- When asked how he'd managed to sculpt Muhammad Ali so realistically, the *artist* replied, "I used Cassius clay."
- Mark Twain was an *artist* with the spoken and written word.
- The Beatles were the most prolific recording *artists* of their day.

artistic (ahr TIS tik) *adj.* 1. of or by art or artist(s); 2. skillful and tasteful; aesthetically satisfying; 3. sensitive to artistic values

- Life in Tahiti was romanticized by the *artistic* touch of Paul Gaugin's paintings of the islanders' customs.
- Van Gogh's *Sunflowers* is very *artistic*, with a balanced composition that is very pleasing to the eye.
- Picasso's revulsion by the Spanish Civil War comes through in his *artistic* antiwar statement, *Guernica*.

  [-ally *adv.*]

artwork (AHRT woerk) *n.* a single work of art, or works of art, collectively

- Leonardo daVinci's *Mona Lisa* is an *artwork* that has withstood the test of time.
- If you get to Paris, don't miss the opportunity to check out the magnificent *artwork* that's housed in the Louvre.

ascetic (uh SET ik) *adj.* self-denying; austere —*n.* 1. a person who lives a life of rigorous self-denial for whatever purpose; 2. anyone living with strict self-discipline and renouncing the usual comforts and pleasures

- Gandhi led an *ascetic* life, permitting himself few comforts.
- The *ascetic* refused to buy chairs with any kind of cushions or padding, lest he be thought of as pampering himself.

  [-ally *adv.*, -ism *n.*] [Syn. severe]

ascribe (uhs KRYB) *vt.* 1. to credit to or blame something on a specific cause, event, person, etc.; 2. to regard something as being the work of or belonging to someone

- The falling of nuclear power plants into mistrust and disrepute is *ascribed* to events at Chernobyl in the USSR.
- *The Iliad* and *The Odyssey* are epics that were passed down over the centuries as part of oral tradition, until they were finally written down and *ascribed* to Homer.

  [-d, ascribing]

aspect (AS pekt)) *n.* 1. how a person appears or looks; 2. how something looks from a specific point of view; 3. any of the numerous ways in which a problem, idea, etc. can be looked at; 4. a certain part or quality; element; 5. a side facing in a certain direction

- Linda's *aspect* is bright, cheery, and happy-go-lucky.
- As viewed from my *aspect*, the writings of Geoffrey Chaucer are rather old-fashioned and stilted.
- In deciding whether to build a new water main, the problem must be viewed from the *aspect* of the contractor as well as that of the eventual consumer.
- How well a chess player uses his or her knights is just one *aspect* of the game.
- The northern *aspect* of Glenn's house never got sunlight.

assert* (uh SOERT) *vt.* 1. to declare; affirm; to state positively; 2. to defend or maintain (rights, claims, etc.); 3. to insist

- Harold had to *assert* that he was actually himself rather than the culprit who had stolen his identity.
- You must *assert* your right to vote by registering and then by showing up to cast your vote on election day.
- When summoned to court, Dolores *asserted* her right to be represented by counsel.
- Rodrigo *asserted* his innocence.

   [-ed, -ing, -ion *n.*]

assess (uh SES) *vt.* 1. to estimate the value of something (for example, property) for the purpose of taxing it; 2. to set the amount of (a tax, a fine, damages, etc.); 3. to impose a fine, tax, etc.; 4. to estimate or determine the significance, importance, or worth of something; to evaluate

- The city *assesses* each lot and its improvements to determine what the property owner must pay to city hall.
- For being late in paying her parking ticket, the judge *assessed* Eleanor a penalty of $40.
- The town decided to *assess* a 1% sales tax on top of the 6% already charged by the state.
- For purposes of insurance, the appraiser *assessed* the painting's value at $1,200 to $1,500.

   [-ed, -ing, -ment *n.*]

QUICK REVIEW #9

Match the word from column 2 with the word from column 1 that means most nearly the same thing.

1. argument	a. affirm
2. arid	b. painting
3. aristocratic	c. assign
4. arrogant	d. severe
5. artist	e. tasteful
6. artistic	f. evaluate
7. artwork	g. element
8. ascetic	h. debate
9. ascribe	i. proud
10. aspect	j. dry
11. assert	k. sculptor
12. assess	l. noble

assiduous (uh SID yoo uhss) *adj.* 1. gone about with constant and careful attention; 2. industrious; persevering

- Nuclear submarines must be built by *assiduous* workers.
- To learn algebra well, you must be *assiduous* in doing your homework assignments.
- The difference between a mediocre potter and an exceptional craftsman is that the latter is *assiduous*.

    [-ly *adv.*, -ness *n.*] [Syn. busy]

assist (uh SIST) *vt.* 1. to aid; give help to; 2. to work as a helper —*n.* helping someone to do something

- Dawn likes to *assist* her parents with the laundry; she dirties it.
- Freddie *assists* at the school library by reshelving returns.
- May I give you an *assist* with starting your car?

    [-ed, -ing] [Syn. help]

associate (uh SOH shee ayt *for vt.,* uh soh SHEE it *for n. and adj.*) *vt.* 1. to connect; combine; join together; 2. to bring a person into a relationship (friendship, partnership, etc.); 3. to connect mentally —*n.* 1. somebody with whom one is connected, such as a partner, friend, fellow worker, etc.; 2. a member of some group, firm, society, etc. with less than full status; 3. anything joined to some other thing —*adj.* 1. joined with others in some kind of work; 2. of less than full status; 3. connected; accompanying

- Barry and Bob have chosen to *associate* and form The Killer Bees—a company that will make buzzers.
- For their advertising needs, The Killer Bees have decided to *associate* with Bell Star and *Associates.*
- I often *associate* peanut butter with jelly; don't you?
- The non–chief justices of the U.S. Supreme Court are *associate* justices.
- Betty and Veronica are *associates* in a certain comic book.
- Jim earned an *associate* degree from County College.
- Barry is a sales *associate* at a major appliance store.

  [-d, -ciating]

assume (uh SOOM *or* uh SYOOM) *vt.* 1. to put on or take on the appearance, job, form, etc. of; 2. to grab; usurp; 3. to personally undertake; 4. to take for granted; 5. to feign; pretend to have

- When Jodi put on the costume, she *assumed* the appearance of a human-sized mouse.
- After a coup, Napoleon *assumed* the power to rule France.
- Marty will *assume* the task of providing refreshments.
- I *assumed* that Geri had bought tickets, and I was wrong.
- You may *assume* the role of the nuclear scientist, even though you failed to pass arithmetic.

  [-d, assuming]

assumption (uh SUHMP shn) *n.* 1. (religious) the taking up of a person into heaven; a Roman Catholic holiday celebrating the Virgin Mary's being taken up; 2. a taking upon one's self, taking over, or taking up; an assuming; 3. anything taken for granted; a supposing

- The Feast of the *Assumption* is a Roman Catholic holiday.
- The First Bank just completed the *assumption* of Harry and Peter's mortgage loan, so from now on, the monthly checks should be made out to First Bank.
- Napoleon's *assumption* of the title of emperor gave the rest of Europe something to be concerned about.
- The *assumption* that you were going to get a B or better in chemistry does not appear to have been well founded.

astute (ast OOT, ast YOOT) *adj.* being clever or shrewd of mind; cunning; crafty; wily

- Getting out of the dot.com stocks just before they crashed was an *astute* move on Jerry's part.
- A fox is a very *astute* animal, often referred to as cunning.
- If Hal were *astute,* he'd pick up on Lynn's hint to call her.

  [-ly *adv.,* -ness *n.*] [Syn. shrewd]

athlete (ATH leet) *n.* someone trained in exercises, games, or contests requiring physical strength, speed, skill, stamina, etc.

- It takes a trained *athlete* to perform on the parallel bars.
- Tammy proved her ability as an *athlete* when she ran the 100-meter sprint in less than 11 seconds.

  [athletic *adj.*, athletically *adv.*]

attain (uh TAYN) *vt.* 1. to gain; accomplish; achieve; 2. to reach or come to; arrive at

- Sherry worked very hard to *attain* a B+ average.
- It took Lillian and Bob the better part of two days' worth of climbing to *attain* the peak of Mount Hood.

  [-ed, -ing, -able *adj.*, -ability *n.*] [Syn. reach]

attention (uh TEN shn) *n.* 1. the act of keeping one's mind on something or the ability to do that; concentration; mental readiness for such concentration; 2. observation or notice; 3. care or consideration; 4. thoughtfulness for the needs of others; courtesy; 5. the military command to come to erect posture

- Debbie had to pay *attention* to navigate the treacherous winding road.
- Mike's *attention* wasn't always on his work.
- Farah's smile caught Todd's *attention*.
- This matter will receive our immediate *attention*.
- Smart congressmen always pay careful *attention* to the needs of their constituents.
- The sergeant barked the order to come to *attention*.

attitude (AT i tood) *n.* 1. the position or posture assumed by the body in connection with an action, feeling, mood, etc.; 2. a manner of acting, thinking, or feeling that shows one's disposition, opinion, etc.; 3. one's disposition, opinion, mental set, etc.; 4. the position of an air- or spacecraft with respect to a given line or plane, such as the horizon

- Victor assumed a humble *attitude* as he prayed.
- Phyllis made it clear that she was not impressed by Wilma's haughty *attitude* of self-righteousness.
- The coach was impressed by Joe's positive *attitude*.
- The plane's *attitude* changed as it banked 45° to port.

  [attitudinal *adj.*] [Syn. posture]

attribute (at TRIB yoot *for vt.*, AT rib YOOT *for n.*) *vt.* 1. to think of as belonging to, produced by, resulting from, or originating in; assign; ascribe to; 2. assign as a characteristic or quality —*n.* 1. a characteristic or quality of a person or thing; 2. a thing in art or literature used as a symbol for a person, office, etc.

- Scholars *attribute* many sonnets to Shakespeare without having any real evidence that he wrote them.
- The motion picture *Gentle Ben attributes* the quality of gentleness to a bear.
- The *attribute* of winged sandals is often used to represent the Greek god Hermes, or Roman Mercury.

  [-d, attributing, attributable *adj.*, attribution *n.*] [Syn. ascribe, quality]

atypical (ay TIP i kl) *adj.* not usual; not characteristic; abnormal
- Failing to run away when people came near was *atypical* behavior on the part of the raccoon.
- It was *atypical* for Ryan to display poor manners.

[(also atypic), -ly *adv.*]

QUICK REVIEW #10

Match the word from column 2 with the word from column 1 that means most nearly the same thing.

1. assiduous	a. feign
2. assist	b. posture
3. associate	c. crafty
4. assume	d. reach
5. assumption	e. quality
6. astute	f. combine
7. athlete	g. courtesy
8. attain	h. unusual
9. attention	i. attentive
10. attitude	j. supposition
11. attribute	k. skilled one
12. atypical	l. aid

audacious* (aw DAY shuhs) *adj.* 1. bold or daring; fearless; 2. not restrained by a feeling of shame or impropriety; rudely bold; brazen
- Severely outnumbered, the platoon's *audacious* attack caught the enemy by surprise.
- After Sonya had had one drink too many, her *audacious* behavior toward the host got her ejected from the party.

[-ness *n.*, -ly *adv.*] [Syn. bold]

audience (AW dee ens) *n.* 1. a group of people assembled to see and hear a speaker, play, concert, etc.; 2. everybody who is tuned in to a particular TV or radio show; 3. everybody who hears what one says or who reads what one writes; one's public; 4. a chance to have one's ideas heard; 5. a formal interview with a person in a high position
- The *audience* completely filled the theater to see *Aida*.
- The Superbowl always draws a large TV *audience*.
- Stephen King has a ready *audience* for whatever he writes.
- The TV networks all gave the candidates an *audience* so that the public might hear their positions.
- Very few are fortunate enough to get an *audience* with the president of the United States.

augment* (awg MENT) *vt.* to increase in quantity, strength, size, etc.; enlarge —*vi.* to become larger; increase

- Sam worked nights to *augment* his income.
- The chili's heat was *augmented* by adding canned jalapenos.

  [-ed, -ing, -ation *n.*]

authentic (awth EN tik) *adj.* 1. trustworthy; believable; reliable; 2. real; in fact; genuine; 3. legally executed, as a deed

- The news report from the Middle East seemed *authentic*.
- That is an *authentic* diamond ring that Jill is wearing.
- The raised seal on the document proves that it's *authentic*.

  [-ally *adv.*]

authenticate (awth EN tik AYT) *vt.* 1. to valididate or make authentic; 2. to verify; establish the truth of; 3. to prove to be real, genuine, or as represented or advertised

- The immigration agent *authenticated* the passport with a raised seal.
- The painting was *authenticated* by the art expert to be an actual work of Lambrou Mourioti.
- The maker's hallmark on the silver vase was used to *authenticate* it as having been made around 1870.

  [-d, authenticating, authentication *n.*] [Syn. confirm]

avarice (A voer is) *n.* greed; too great a desire for wealth

- Many pirates were driven by *avarice*.
- *Avarice* drives certain CEOs to cheat their stockholders.

  [avaricious *adj.*, avariciously *adv.*, avariciousness *n.*]

aversion (uh VER zhin) *n.* 1. an intense or decided dislike; repugnance; 2. whatever is causing that dislike

- Many children have an *aversion* to seeing a doctor for shots.
- Barry, who had a fear of heights, was made to go to high places as a form of *aversion* therapy.

avoid (uh VOYD) *vt.* 1. to stay away from; evade; shun; 2. to not let happen; 3. to turn away from

- As part of her weight-loss diet, Maria tries to *avoid* people who are eating as well as commercials for food.
- Driving carefully helps to *avoid* accidents.
- Being shy, Vance tries to *avoid* the eyes of others.

  [-able *adj.*, -ably *adv.*] [Syn. escape]

aware (uh WAER) *adj.* realizing or knowing; informed; conscious

- Fran was well *aware* of the No Parking sign.
- Bill was not *aware* that he kept clicking his teeth together.
- Maribel was made *aware* of the restriction on eating peas by picking them up with one's knife.

  [-ness *n.*]

awe (AW) *n.* a mixed feeling of fear, respect, and wonder brought on by something majestic, sacred, sublime, etc.

- The first time Ron saw Mt. Kilamanjaro, he was filled with *awe*.
- Ruth stood in *awe* of her older brother David, the rocket scientist.

QUICK REVIEW #11

Match the word from column 2 with the word from column 1 that means most nearly the same thing.

1. audacious	a. confirm
2. audience	b. wonder
3. augment	c. shun
4. authentic	d. antipathy
5. authenticate	e. conscious
6. avarice	f. enlarge
7. aversion	g. bold
8. avoid	h. greed
9. aware	i. public
10. awe	j. reliable

B

barricade (BAR I kayd) *n.* 1. a defense barrier hastily thrown up, as in street fighting; 2. any obstacle or barrier —*vt.* to keep out or in by use of a barrier; to obstruct

- Police put up *barricades* to keep the crowd off the parade route.
- *Barricades* consisting of piled-up rubble were used for defense by soldiers in the cities of post–D-day Europe during World War II.
- The people of Stalingrad *barricaded* the streets to keep out the invading Germans.

  [-d, barricading]

barter (BAHR toer) *vi.* to trade goods or services without the use of money —*vt.* to swap goods or services in return for other goods and services; trade —*n.* 1. the act of swapping; 2. anything swapped

- In colonial days it was common for settlers to *barter* knives and hatchets to Native Americans for beaver pelts.
- *Barter* that hat for two pairs of socks and a Hershey bar.
- Al and Frank often do business by *barter*.
- This hat cost me nothing; I got it from Alice by *barter*.

  [-ed, -ing, -er *n.*]

basic (BAY sik) *adj.* 1. of or at the beginning; fundamental; essential; 2. making or being a support or introduction; elementary

- A *basic* course in weaving might be helpful to rug makers.
- A knowledge of mathematics is *basic* to learning physics.
- Honesty is a *basic* principle to live by.

basis (BAY sis) *n.* 1. the start, foundation, or main support of anything; 2. the main ingredient of anything; 3. the underlying philosophy; 4. a timed plan or procedure; 5. a certain attitude

- "What is the *basis* for your accusing me of eating on the job?" Gail asked, quickly swallowing what was in her mouth.
- That all men are created equal is the *basis* of the U.S. Constitution.
- We pay for cable TV on a monthly *basis*.
- Mark and Louise are on a friendly *basis* these days.

battle (BA tl) *n.* 1. a fight—as that between armed units on the sea, land, or in the air; 2. war or armed combat; fighting; 3. any conflict or fight —*vt.* to oppose; fight —*vi.* 1. to participate in a fight or struggle; 2. to fight

- One of the most intense *battles* in the Pacific during WWII was for the island of Iwo Jima.
- There was a street *battle* between two rival gangs.
- The landlord and tenant had an ongoing *battle* over upkeep.
- Nemo's father *battled* the move to expel him from school.
- Geoffrey was in the *battle* for human rights in El Salvador.
- Oscar de la Hoya and Ray Mancini were in a real ring *battle*.

  [-d, battling]

behalf (be HAF) *n.* on (or in) behalf of; in the interest of; speaking for; representing

- Harriet spoke in *behalf* of the truth's being known.
- The lawyer appeared on *behalf* of his client, Mr. Jones.

behavior (be HAYV yoer) *n.* 1. how anybody acts; conduct; deportment; 2. any organism's reaction to stimulus—especially a recordable response; 3. noticeable actions or responses of any person, animal, or machine

- Nora's *behavior* seemed perfectly normal to Dennis.
- Juanita thought Ted's *behavior* to be rather strange when she saw him hit his finger with a hammer and laugh.
- Amy was disturbed by her car engine's rough *behavior.*

being (BEE eeng) *n.* 1. existing or living; life; existence; 2. basic or essential nature; 3. someone or thing that is alive or exists; 4. all the qualities, physical and mental, that make up a person; personality

- Any living thing is in a state of *being.*
- Any plant or animal can be thought of as a *being.*
- Very few people acknowedge a fly as a *being,* but it is one.
- Most religions believe in the existence of a Higher *Being.*

belie (bee LY) *vt.* 1. to disguise; misrepresent; 2. to disappoint or leave unful-filled; 3. to prove false or show to be untrue

- Al's good-natured smile *belies* his evil intentions.
- Sally hated to *belie* her customer by telling her the cake she had ordered was not yet ready.
- It is a debunker's job to *belie* the tricks of charlatans.

  [-d, belying]

belief (bee LEEF) *n.* 1. a conviction that some things are true or real; 2. faith, especially in a religious sense; 3. confidence in; trust in; 4. something accepted as true; 5. an opinion; an expectation; a judgment

- Geoffrey's *belief* that there is a tooth fairy is based on a chapter from his book of bedtime stories.
- Maribel's *beliefs* are between her and her pastor—and are none of our business.
- Valerie had complete *belief* in Harper's honesty.
- It was her *belief* that Santa would show up later.
- Your accomplishments are totally beyond *belief.*

belligerent* (bel IDG oer ent) *adj.* 1. at war; 2. relating to war; of fighting; 3. showing an eagerness to fight; spoiling for a fight

- During World War I, the *belligerents* engaged in four years of unmoving trench warfare.
- The *belligerent* adversaries duked it out in the ring.
- Veronica's attitude was always *belligerent,* as if she were seeking to get into an argument.

  [belligerently *adv.*] [Syn. bellicose]

beneficial (BEN e FISH uhl) *adj.* 1. to the advantage of; helpful; 2. getting bene-fit; 3. in one's best interest

- Mary's friendship turned out to be *beneficial* to Evelyn around holiday time.
- Having auto insurance proved quite *beneficial* for Tania when a reckless driver ignored the stop sign and hit her car.
- It is *beneficial* for you to have an individual retirement plan.

    [-ly *adv.*]

benefit (BEN e fit) *n.* 1. a helpful, charitable act; 2. an advantage; a gain —*vt.* to help; aid —*vi.* to gain; to profit from

- The singer sang at a *benefit* to raise money for the group.
- The cab waited an additional 10 minutes for Bob's *benefit.*
- My singing publicly *benefited* the business of all ear doctors in the neighborhood.
- A playwright *benefits* from each performance of her play.

    [-ed, -ing]

berate (be RAYT) *vt.* to scold or strongly rebuke (with wagging finger)

- Don't *berate* me for acting the way you act.
- Audrey *berated* Robert for driving after having had a drink.

    [-d, berating] [Syn. scold]

QUICK REVIEW #12

Match the word from column 2 with the word from column 1 that means most nearly the same thing.

1. barricade	a. disguise
2. barter	b. conduct
3. basic	c. opinion
4. basis	d. profit
5. battle	e. quarrelsome
6. behalf	f. helpful
7. behavior	g. conflict
8. being	h. existence
9. belie	i. scold
10. belief	j. elementary
11. belligerent	k. representing
12. beneficial	l. procedure
13. benefit	m. trade
14. berate	n. obstruct

bereft (bi REFT) *adj.* 1. without; devoid (of); deprived; 2. bereaved

- For his crime, the criminal was *bereft* of his freedom.
- The crime victim was *bereft* of her feeling of security.
- The *bereft* twins mourned the death of their uncle.

betray (bit RAY) *vt.* 1. to aid the enemy, or make vulnerable to the enemy in a traitorous way; 2. to break faith with; to not act up to expectations; 3. to deceive; 4. to give away secret information

- Benedict Arnold *betrayed* his defenses to the British.
- Bill went to the broker so as not to *betray* Anne's faith in his ability to get tickets for *Cats*.
- Nan got Sue to join the team, convincing her that they'd have fun together; then she *betrayed* her by quitting.
- During the game, Sue *betrayed* Hal's hiding place to Jim.

   [-d, -ing, -al, -er *n.*] [Syn. deceive, reveal]

between (bit WEEN) *prep.* 1. in or through the area separating two things; 2. in the time separating two things; 3. along a path that connects two things —*adv.* 1. in a middle location, time, space, or function; 2. in the midst of; 3. in confidence

- The gate is *between* the third and fourth fence posts.
- Lunchtime comes *between* breakfast and dinner times.
- That color is *between* blue and green.
- Second gear is *between* first and third gears.
- In *between* jobs, Hannah and her sisters took a vacation.
- Let's keep this *between* you and me.

bewilder (bee WIL der) *vt.* to thoroughly confuse, as by something very involved and complicated; befuddle; puzzle

- Jose was *bewildered* by the *Times'* crossword puzzle.
- Alice's disappearing coin trick served to *bewilder* Francine.
- On Ian's visit to the art supply store, he was faced with a *bewildering* selection of brushes and palette knives.

   [-ed, -ing] [Syn. puzzle]

bias (BY uhs) *n.* 1. a line cut or sewn on the diagonal to the weave of a cloth; 2. a mental partiality or slant; bent; partiality; inclination —*vt.* to have a prejudice; to influence

- The seamstress sewed the hem on a *bias*.
- As Jason aged, his childhood *bias* in favor of dark-meat chicken had changed to one for white meat; go figure.
- The attorney feared that the judge might be unduly *biased* by his client's unsavory reputation.
- Kira's wallpaper choice is *biased* by her love of earth tones.

   [-ed, -ing]

bicker (BI kuhr) *vi.* 1. to quarrel in a petty manner; to squabble; 2. (rare) to move with quick, rippling noises —*n.* 1. a little quarrel; 2. a rippling or a pattering sound

- Carl and Violet *bicker* all the time about everything.
- The brook *bickers* in the breeze.
- Carl and Violet just had another minor *bicker.*
- One can barely hear the *bicker* of a snake coming down the path.

    [-ed, -ing]

bilk (BILK) *vt.* 1. to thwart; 2. to swindle; cheat; defraud; 3. to escape or flee leaving unpaid debts; 4. to elude

- The raccoon *bilked* all attempts to catch him.
- The investors were *bilked* out of millions by crooked management.
- Nate *bilked* the bank by his failure to make payments.
- The crook *bilked* the police.

    [-ed, -ing]

biological (BY uh LAH gzhi kl) *adj.* 1. of or connected to living things; 2. related genetically, in contrast to by adoption

- A botanist is only interested in the plant part of the *biological* sciences.
- Mark's scientific interests are purely *biological.*
- Your *biological* parents are your real mother and father.

    [-ly *adv.* (also biologic)]

blueprint (BLOO print) *n.* 1. a plan drawn in white on a blue background and used by architects or engineers; 2. any exact or detailed plan

- The contractor checked the *blueprint* of the house to see what materials he would need to order.
- With its adoption in 1789, the U.S. Constitution became the *blueprint* for American democracy.

bog (BAHG) *n.* wet, spongy area of ground, noted for smelly decaying mosses that form peat —*vi.*, *vt.* to get stuck in; mired (usually with down)

- For organic matter, Martha used peat from the nearby *bog* to enrich her garden soil.
- The Medicare revisions got *bogged* down in committee.

    [-ged, -ging]

bore (BAWR) *vt.* 1. to make a hole with a drill; 2. to dig a well, tunnel, etc. with a turning helical tool; 3. to push one's way (through) —*vi.* to tire of or lose interest in —*n.* 1. a hole made by a drill; 2. the interior of a hollow tube

- Before hanging the door, I must *bore* holes for the hinges.
- Gino *bored* holes for the deck's concrete footings.
- Gracie *bored* through the rush-hour crowd.
- Go away; you *bore* me.
- The plot was very predictable, and therefore very *boring.*
- The hole in the wall was a very shallow *bore.*
- Shotgun barrels come in various *bores.*

    [-d, boring, -dom *n.*]

brain (BRAYN) *n.* 1. the mass of tissue inside the skull of vertebrates; the organ that is the destination for the spinal cord, the main center of reasoning and interpreter of senses, as well as the director of motor functions; 2. a comparable organ in an invertebrate; 3. (often *pl.*) mental capacity; intelligence; 4. (usually *pl.*) the chief organizer or planner of a group event; head director —*vt.* to hit hard on the head

- No computer can yet equal the human *brain*.
- A flea's *brain* is not very complex.
- You don't need instructions; just use your *brains*.
- When it comes to planning, Kevin's the *brains* of this outfit.
- Roger got *brained* by the baseball bat.

    [-ed, -ing]

brandish (BRAEN dish) *vt.* to wave about or shake, in a threatening or challenging way; flourish

- When you *brandish* that saber, everyone ducks for cover.
- Helen *brandished* the fireplace poker as if she wanted to strike someone with it.

    [-ed, -ing]

burden (BOER din) *n.* 1. a load; anything carried; 2. something one has to put up with; a heavy load; hard work; sorrow or responsibility —*vt.* to weigh down; to oppress

- The drywall was a heavy *burden* for the roof of the car.
- When Jill sat on the jury, she had the *burden* of deciding the guilt or innocence of the defendant.
- Certain trucks are classified by the *burden* they can carry.
- I hate to *burden* you with the job of deciding what to wear.

    [-ed, -ing]

burrow (BOER o) *n.* 1. a hole dug by an animal or a tunnel in the ground; 2. any hole or passage serving as a shelter, refuge, etc. —*vi.* 1. to dig (into, under, etc.); 2. search as if by digging —*vt.* to make burrows in the ground

- Groundhogs live in *burrows* of their own making.
- Some animals often find shelter in *burrows* dug by others.
- *Burrowing* through old files led to finding the real murderer.
- Construction crews *burrowed* beneath the English Channel to build the Chunnel, connecting the U.K. and France.

    [-ed, -ing]

buttress* (BUH tris) *n.* a brace, usually of brick or stone, built against a wall to support or reinforce it; a prop —*vt.* 1. to support or reinforce with such a structure; 2. to prop up; bolster

- Many Gothic buildings sport *buttresses* to reinforce them.
- Flash cards can be thought of as *buttresses* for rote learning of facts.
- *Buttress* your argument against the tax hike by having the documentation concerning the results of previous hikes.

    [-ed, -ing]

QUICK REVIEW #13

Match the word from column 2 with the word from column 1 that means most nearly the same thing.

1. bereft   a. influence

2. betray   b. elude

3. between   c. planner

4. bewilder   d. related

5. bias   e. plan

6. bicker   f. mire

7. bilk   g. devoid

8. biological   h. drill

9. blueprint   i. deceive

10. bog   j. puzzle

11. bore   k. squabble

12. brain   l. amidst

13. brandish   m. threaten

14. burden   n. search

15. burrow   o. oppress

16. buttress   p. reinforce

C

cajole (kuh JOHL) *vt.* to coax with insincere talk; to flatter in hopes of getting one's way; to wheedle

- Maxine tried to *cajole* her husband into going to the movies.
- Barney *cajoled* Lois to accompany him to the book sale.

[-d, cajoling, -ry *n.*, cajolingly *adv.*] [Syn. coax]

calamity (kuh LAM i tee) *n.* 1. deep trouble; misery; 2. any great misfortune entailing sorrow and loss; disaster

- The loss of a loved one is always a *calamity.*
- The attack on the World Trade Center ranks with Pearl Harbor among the U.S.A.'s greatest *calamities.*

[calamitous *adj.*, calamitously *adv.*] [Syn. disaster]

camaraderie (kam uh RAD oer ee) *n.* warm, friendly feelings of loyalty among comrades; comradeship

- *Camaraderie* is most likely to develop among military comrades who have been through some combat together.
- A general feeling of *camaraderie* pervaded the air as the business associates gathered in the tavern to relax and share their tales on a Friday afternoon.

campaign (kam PAYN) *n.* 1. a sequence of military operations aimed at a certain objective; 2. a series of organized actions for some specific purpose —*vi.* to be involved in a campaign

- The Second World War's European *campaign* was fought to liberate the captive nations and to defeat Germany.
- Andrea was involved in the presidential election *campaign.*
- She *campaigned* enthusiastically for (then) Senator Kerry.

[-ed, -ing, -er *n.*] [Syn. battle]

canvass (KAV vuhs) *vt.* 1. to look over carefully; 2. to go to or among (people) to seek votes, orders, etc. —*vi.* to try to get votes, orders, etc.; solicit —*n.* the act of asking a targeted group of people questions such as who they voted for, what brands they use, etc., especially in an attempt to estimate the outcome of an election, sales campaign, etc.

- Charlie *canvassed* the canvas with the art appraiser to determine the insurance value of the painting.
- Samantha *canvassed* the mothers at the soccer game, trying to get some orders for Daryl's school fund-raiser.
- *Canvassing* potential voters was how the paper was able to predict the outcome of the election.

[**Alert** Do not confuse with *canvas*, the cloth.] [-ed, -ing, -er *n.*]

captive (KAP tiv) *n.* 1. one captured and held prisoner; 2. a person enthralled, as by love or beauty —*adj.* 1. taken or held prisoner; 2. unable to act independently; 3. made to watch/listen (as in a captive audience)

- The *captive* was behind bars.
- The first time Iris saw San Francisco, she became *captive* to its charm.
- A babysitter is *captive* to his or her charge.
- For many years, Poland was a *captive* nation of the USSR.
- Ian loves to play his guitar before a *captive* audience.

career (kuh RIR) *n.* 1. one's way of earning a living; lifework; 2. a profession or occupation for which one trains and which one pursues for life —*adj.* adapting a normally temporary activity as a lifework

- One's *career* is not always the one prepared for.
- Some veterinarians pursue that *career* deliberately, while for others it is a booby prize for failing medical school.
- Herbert decided to become a *career* soldier.

carnivore* (KAHR ni VAWR) *n.* 1. any of a number of fanged, flesh-eating mammals, like lions and tigers and bears; 2. an animal that eats other animals; 3. a plant that eats small animals—especially insects.

- Unlike herbivores, who eat plants, and omnivores, who eat both plants and animals, a *carnivore* prefers a diet of meat.
- The Venus flytrap is a plant that can be categorized a *carnivore*.

    [carnivorous *adj.*, carnivorously *adv.*]

QUICK REVIEW #14

Match the word from column 2 with the word from column 1 that means most nearly the same thing.

1. cajole		a. solicit
2. calamity		b. wheedle
3. camaraderie		c. battle
4. campaign		d. friendliness
5. canvass		e. lifework
6. captive		f. dependent
7. career		g. flesh eater
8. carnivore		h. disaster

carnivorous (kahr NIV oer uhs) *adj.* 1. flesh eating (as opposed to herbivorous); 2. insect eating (applying to some plants); 3. of the carnivores

- Wolves hunt mostly mammalian prey because they are *carnivorous.*
- The sundew represents a class of *carnivorous* plants.
- Having canine teeth, or fangs, is a *carnivorous* trait.

cartographer (kahr TOG ruh fuhr) *n.* a person who designs and makes maps or charts

- Mercator is the name of the man who is probably the best-known *cartographer* who ever lived.
- Robinson is another well-known *cartographer.*

castigate* (KAS ti gayt) *vt.* to punish or bawl out, especially by using harsh public criticism

- The police chief proceeded to *castigate* the officers for showing poor judgment dealing with the demonstrators.
- The nine-year-old *castigated* the president for not being able to pronounce "nuclear."

  [-d, castigating, castigation, castigator *n.,* castigatory *adj.*] [Syn. punish]

catalyst* (KAT uh list) *n.* 1. an agent in a chemical reaction that causes the reaction to speed up, but does not itself undergo any permanent change; 2. a person or thing that speeds up a result

- During the process of photosynthesis, chlorophyll is the *catalyst* for plants combining water and carbon dioxide to manufacture sugar and oxygen in the presence of light.
- The *catalyst* for Karen and David giving their realtor an immediate deposit on the house was another couple's interest in it.

catnap (KAT nap) *n.* a doze; a short, light sleep —*vi.* to take a snooze

- The watchman often takes two- or three-minute *catnaps.*
- Karen often *catnaps* while watching TV at night.

  [-ped, -ping]

cautious (KAW shus) *adj.* very careful; trying to avoid danger; wary; circumspect

- The bomb-squad member was very *cautious* in his approach to the mysterious package.
- *Cautious* people regret less later.

  [-ness *n.,* -ly *adv.*] [Syn. careful]

celebrate (SEL eb RAYT) *vt.* 1. to perform some kind of public and formal ritual; 2. to mark an anniversary, a holiday, etc. with ceremony or festiveness; 3. to praise or honor publicly; 4. to perform cheerful activity to mark an occasion

- Melissa and Gino invited 200 people to *celebrate* their wedding.
- Let's *celebrate* Arbor Day with a tree-planting ceremony.
- We join with Timmy to *celebrate* Lassie's heroics yet again.
- Get out the noisemakers and funny hats so that we can *celebrate* the ringing in of the New Year.

  [-d, celebrating, celebration *n.*] [Syn. commemorate, observe]

censor (SEN soer) *n.* 1. an official with the power to examine books, movies, TV programs, etc. and to remove anything objectionable; 2. an official in times of war who reads mail, news articles, etc. and removes anything he/she thinks might help the enemy —*vt.* to put a book, writer, etc. to such treatment as just described

- Comic George Carlin made a living from parodying the TV *censor* with his routine about seven words you can't say on TV.
- During the Second World War, people at home received mail from their relatives in the armed forces that had whole paragraphs blacked out by the *censors.*
- In the Soviet Union, every newspaper article was *censored.*

[-ed, -ing, -ship *n.*]

century (SEN che ree) *n.* 1. any span of 100 years; 2. a specific period of 100 years dating from the beginning of the Christian (or Common) Era; 3. a series, group, or subdivision of 100

- A *century* passed between the beginnings of the American Civil War and our involvement in Vietnam.
- Alexander the Great lived in the fourth *century* B.C.
- Roman legions were divided into *centuries,* each of which consisted of 100 men.

cerebral (SIR ib ril *or* sir EEB ril) *adj.* 1. concerning the brain or the cerebrum; 2. appealing to the intellect—not the emotions; intellectual

- A *cerebral* hemorrhage is not a pleasant prospect.
- The *cerebral* cortex is where higher brain functions occur.
- Tchaikovsky's music is more emotional than *cerebral.*

certain (SOER tin) *adj.* 1. fixed, settled, or specific; 2. certain to occur; inevitable; 3. undoubtable; unquestionable; 4. reliable; dependable; 5. an amount, but not very much

- We'll get a *certain* trade-in allowance for the old car.
- The sun is *certain* to rise tomorrow.
- It is *certain* that Gary committed the robbery.
- You can be *certain* of a fair hearing.
- A *certain* number of people will believe anything.

[-ty *n.*] [Syn. sure]

challenge (CHA linj) *n.* 1. a demand for identification; 2. questioning; a demand for proof or for an explanation; 3. a dare or an urge to participate; 4. any job that requires special effort; 5. a questioning of a vote or one's right to vote —*vt.* to do any of the preceding things

- The sentry gave the *challenge* to the incoming patrol.
- It's a *challenge* to explain Tom's behaving so strangely.
- The Count answered the Marquis' *challenge* to a duel.
- Getting the dog to behave properly is quite a *challenge.*
- The committee member *challenged* the visitor's right to take part in the group's vote.
- I was *challenged* to show my ticket at the theater door.

[-d, challenging]

QUICK REVIEW #15

Match the word from column 2 with the word from column 1 that means most nearly the same thing.

1. carnivorous	a. sure
2. cartographer	b. intellectual
3. castigate	c. doze
4. catalyst	d. hundred
5. catnap	e. evaluator
6. cautious	f. demand
7. celebrate	g. mapmaker
8. censor	h. expediter
9. century	i. meat eating
10. cerebral	j. wary
11. certain	k. punish
12. challenge	l. observe

character (KAR ik tir) *n.* 1. a special mark; 2. any symbol or letter that's used in writing and printing; 3. style of printing or handwriting; 4. a magical symbol or mystic emblem; a code or cipher; 5. a distinctive quality or trait; an attribute; a characteristic; 6. essential quality; nature; 7. the personality of an individual or group; 8. status; position; 9. a part in a play, movie, etc.

- The cabinetmaker marked the drawer bottom with his own *character* to identify it as having been made by him.
- Omega is the final *character* of the Greek alphabet.
- Arabic *characters* are used in our system of numerals.
- Philip's handwriting has a great deal of *character*.
- A pyramid with an eye is a *character* on the Great Seal of the United States of America.
- It is the *character* of the scorpion to sting indiscriminately.
- I recommend Edith as having *character* of the highest sort.
- Sheep have the *character* of flocking together.
- The *character* of the presidency is one of great power.
- Don't always take the advice of an actor, just because the *character* he plays is that of a doctor on TV.

[Syn. disposition, quality]

circumstance (SIR kuhm STAENS) *n.* 1. a fact or event that goes with another, as an essential factor or incidentally; 2. any situation; event; 3. conditions affecting a person

- When there is thunder, the presence of lightning is an inescapable *circumstance.*
- A *circumstance* for buying cotton candy is a circus visit.
- Charles was in difficult financial *circumstances.*

cite (SYT) *vt.* 1. to demand an appearance before a court; 2. to quote (a passage, book, writer, speech, etc.); 3. to refer to or bring up (as precedent)

- Henry was *cited* to appear in traffic court next Wednesday.
- Mary always *cites* some classical composer as the inspiration for her musical compositions.
- *Brown v. Board of Education* is a case lawyers often *cite* when arguing for equal educational opportunities in court.
  [-d, citing, citation *n.*]

civil (SI vil) *adj.* 1. of a citizen or citizens; 2. of a community of citizens or their interactions; 3. cultured; 4. courteous or polite

- All citizens are entitled to certain *civil* rights.
- *Civil* war is an oxymoron, like military intelligence.
- *Civil* people should develop an appreciation for the arts.
- It is important to be *civil,* rather than rude, to one another.

clarifiy (KLA ri fy) *vi., vt.* 1. to make or become clear (especially liquids); 2. to make or become easier to comprehend

- The chef passed the chicken soup through a strainer to *clarify* the broth.
- Jane *clarified* the point she was trying to get across.
- Often a map will serve to *clarify* the directions to a place.
  [clarifies, clarified, -ing, clarification* *n.*]

classical (KLAS i kl) *adj.* 1. of the highest class; excellent; 2. having a balanced and simple style; restrained; the name of an era bestowed by historians, such as the Classical Era in music history, which preceded the Romantic Era; 3. typical of or based on the literary works of ancient Greece and Rome; 4. well versed in Greek and Roman literature and culture; 5. music in the European style, as distinct from folk, popular, or jazz

- The Rolex watch is *classical* and worth every thousand.
- The Jaguar XJ6 has absolutely *classical* (or classic) lines.
- Shakespeare's tragedies followed those of Sophocles and Euripides as being both *classical* and timeless.
- Until the 1950s, the college graduates of modern Europe and those from Ivy League colleges were given *classical* educations, with a knowledge of Latin being essential.
- Mozart, Haydn, and Beethoven are generally considered the greatest *classical* composers, although Beethoven bridges the Classical and Romantic eras.
  [-ly *adv.,* -ity *n.*]

clique (KLEEK *or* KLIK) *n.* a small, exclusive circle of people; snobbish or narrow coterie (Common interest and snobbery are implied.)

- The cheerleaders kept together in their own *clique*.
- The Obscure Poets Society was a self-important, highbrow *clique* that generally looked down on others.

[-ish or cliquish *adj.*, cliquishly *adv.*, cliquishness *n.*] [Syn. coterie]

cloying (KLOY ing) *adj.* 1. displeasing or distasteful due to excess; 2. excessively sweet, sentimental, etc.

- The romance novel was *cloying* in its sentimentality.
- The date can have a *cloying* sweetness that causes many people to avoid eating that fruit unless it is only one of several ingredients, as in date-nut bread.

[-ly *adv.*, (to) cloy *vt.*]

cohere (koh HEER) *vi.* 1. to stick together; 2. to be connected naturally or logically, as by some common idea or principle; 3. to become or stay united in action; be in accord

- Grapes appear to *cohere* until you notice the tiny stems.
- Freedoms of religion and press seem to logically *cohere*.
- The U.S. and U.K. *cohered* from 1941 through 1945 in their fight against the Nazis.

[-d, cohering, -nt *adj.*, -nce, cohesion, cohesiveness *n.*] [Syn. stick]

colleague (KAH leeg) *n.* a fellow worker; one in the same profession

- Matt and Louise were *colleagues* at the electric company.
- Dr. Lang and Dr. Griffith were *colleagues* at Lehigh Hospital.

[Syn. associate]

collect (kuh LEKT) *vt.* 1. to bring together; assemble; 2. to call for and receive (for example, taxes); 3. to regain control (of oneself); 4. to pick up; go get —*vi.* to gather; assemble —*adj.*, *adv.* to be payed for by the recipient

- Libby *collects* bottle caps as a hobby.
- The news boy *collects* fees weekly from his patrons.
- You need to *collect* your wits before reading another word.
- June *collects* aluminum cans to turn in for the 10¢ deposit.
- The crowd *collected* outside the ballpark.
- When you get there, call *collect*.

[-ed, -ing] [Syn. gather]

collection (kuh LEK shin) *n.* 1. the act or process of accumulating; 2. the things collected; 3. a pile; an accumulation; 4. money collected, as by a fund-raiser

- A weekly *collection* of garbage is essential for urban living.
- Laurie has quite an extensive stamp *collection*.
- Ian has some *collection* of dirty clothes in his room.
- After the religious service, a *collection* plate was passed.

QUICK REVIEW #16

Match the word from column 2 with the word from column 1 that means most nearly the same thing.

1. character	a. stick
2. circumstance	b. coterie
3. cite	c. accumulation
4. civil	d. excessive
5. clarify	e. assemble
6. classical	f. associate
7. clique	g. quote
8. cloying	h. clear
9. cohere	i. situation
10. colleague	j. polite
11. collect	k. nature
12. collection	l. restrained

collector (kuh LEK toer) *n.* a person or thing that accumulates (for example, a person whose job is to collect overdue bills, taxes, etc. or a person whose hobby is collecting stamps, books, etc.)

- The tax *collector* has very few friends in town.
- When told that everyone should collect something, Allan replied that he is a *collector* of dust.

colloquial (kuh LOH kwee il) *adj.* 1. normal conversational style; 2. used to describe words, phrases, etc. that are used in everyday speech; informal

- *It ain't necessarily so* is all right to use as a *colloquial* expression, but it would be improper in formal speech or writing.
- Personally, hearing a person say, "How are youse today?" (meaning the two of you), hurts my ears, yet the phrase is in widespread *colloquial* use.
  [-ly *adv.*]

collusion (kuh LOO zhin) *n.* a secret agreement for illegal or fraudulent purpose; conspiracy

- The court found that there was *collusion* between Daniel and Joy to defraud the royal family.
- *Collusion* to commit robbery is a felony punishable by jail.
  [collusive *adj.*, collusively *adv.*]

comedic (kuh MEE dik) *adj.* of or having to do with comedy; humorous

- John Cleese had a *comedic* walk in Monty Python's Ministry of Silly Walks routine.
- Mike Meyers' *comedic* portrayals appeal to some people more than they do to others.

[-ally *adv.*]

commencement (kuh MENS mint) *n.* 1. the beginning or start; the time of same; 2. the school or college ceremonies at which degrees or diplomas are awarded; 3. the day upon which this takes place

- The *commencement* of the show will be at 8 P.M.
- Lafayette High School's *commencement* will be held at the field house.
- Yale's *commencement* is often on a Thursday.

comment (KOM ent) *n.* 1. a note that explains, criticizes, or illustrates something written or said; annotation; 2. a remark or observation made to express criticism or opinion; 3. talk; chatter; gossip —*vi.* to comment on; to make remarks

- George just had to make a *comment* on Paul's theories.
- When Sue remarked that it was hot in the room, Pam felt it necessary to *comment* in her support.
- With gossips, it's just one *comment* after another.
- Some people find it necessary to *comment* on practically anything and everything.

[-ed, -ing] [Syn. remark]

commercial (kuh MER shil) *adj.* 1. of or connected to trade; 2. of or having to do with stores, office buildings, etc.; 3. of a lower grade or for use in large amounts in industry —*n.* paid radio or TV advertisement

- The ship was engaged in international *commercial* trade.
- Beth's neighborhood was zoned for *commercial* use, so she had no recourse when the grocery opened next door.
- The warehouse club sells mayonnaise in gallon jars, suitable for *commercial* use but kind of large for use at home.
- Some of the most entertaining television these days is to be found in soft-drink *commercials*.

commitment (kuh MIT mint) *n.* 1. a delivering for safekeeping; 2. official internment of a person to a prison or a mental institution; 3. a promise to do something; 4. dedication to a long-term involvement; 5. a financial liability

- A burial service accompanied the *commitment* of the naval officer's body to the ocean depths.
- It'll take a court order to affect the *commitment* of this book's author to the booby hatch.

- The Heart Association is looking for a *commitment* to contribute and for you to encourage your neighbors to do so, too.
- The U.S. has a *commitment* to defend the Americas.
- Getting a mortgage is a long-term financial *commitment*.

communication (kuhm YOO ni KAY shuhn) *n.* 1. a giving or exchanging of information, messages, etc.; 2. the information so exchanged; 3. a medium for exchanging information; 4. the art of expressing ideas; 5. the science of transmitting information

- There was good *communication* among the jury members.
- The *communication* received from the spy satellite held obsolete plans for a Spacely sprocket.
- Satellites permit almost instant *communication* by electronic signals anywhere on earth.
- Vera has less-than-admirable *communication* skills.
- The armed forces *communication* system is constantly being upgraded with the latest bells and whistles.

comparative (kuhm PA ruh tiv) *adj.* 1. estimated by relating it to something else; relative; 2. comparing one thing to another —*n.* 1. in grammar, the comparative degree (words ending in *er*); 2. a word or form in this degree

- Height is one *comparative* way to relate buildings.
- *Comparative* linguistics notes similarities and differences between languages, both in grammar and vocabulary.
- The *comparative* degree in grammer goes from tall to taller, as opposed to the superlative, which is tallest.
- Bigger, smaller, newer, and older are all *comparatives*.

   [-ly *adv.*]

comparison (kuhm PAR is uhn) *n.* 1. estimation of similarities and differences; 2. sufficiently similar in likeness to make a relating of one to the other possible

- Apples and watermelons are two fruits with seeds, but any further *comparison* might prove fruitless.
- A *comparison* of lemons and limes might be made with respect to their colors, tartness, and climatic habitats.

compassion (kuhm PA shin) *n.* sorrow for the suffering or problems of another or others, often accompanied by an urge to help; deep sympathy; pity

- Tina had great *compassion* for the families of the victims of the earthquake.
- Rosita was driven by her *compassion* for the homeless to volunteer twice weekly at the local shelter.

   [-ate *adj.*, -ately *adv.*] [Syn. pity]

QUICK REVIEW #17

Match the word from column 2 with the word from column 1 that means most nearly the same thing.

1. collector	a. humorous
2. colloquial	b. annotation
3. collusion	c. exchange of ideas
4. comedic	d. sympathy
5. commencement	e. pledge
6. comment	f. relation
7. commercial	g. relative
8. commitment	h. conspiracy
9. communication	i. acquirer
10. comparative	j. beginning
11. comparison	k. informal
12. compassion	l. advertisement

compel (kuhm PEL) *vt.* 1. to force; constrain; 2. to get or cause by force

- Eve had to *compel* Adam to try her applesauce.
- Iraq used its army to *compel* Kuwait to share its oil income.

    [-led, -ling, -lable *adj.*, -ler *n.*] [Syn. force]

competent (KOM pit int) *adj.* 1. well qualified; capable; fit (sometimes used with *to*); 2. sufficient; adequate; 3. permissible or properly belonging

- Vi's M.A. made her quite *competent* academically to apply for the teaching position.
- One doesn't need to be an electrician to have *competent* credentials to change a lightbulb.
- The judge ruled Jack *competent* to stand trial for murder.

    [-ly *adv.*] [Syn. able]

competition (kom pet ISH in) *n.* 1. the act of competing; rivalry; 2. a contest or match; 3. official participation in an organized sport; 4. the opposition in a contest; 5. the person or persons against whom one competes

- Jimmy Connors and Andre Agassi were often *competition* for one another on the tennis courts.
- The 100-meter hurdles *competition* will start at 2 P.M.
- To paticipate in the *competition,* an application form must be filed, and an entry fee must be paid.

- The New York Yankees have been the Boston Red Sox's fiercest *competition* over the years for the AL crown.
- Lucy was always Desi's *competition* when it came to getting attention from an audience.

competitive* (kuhm PET it iv) *adj.* 1. of, involving, or based on competing; 2. having a chance in a competition

- When it comes to job opportunities, quarterback is the most highly *competitive* field.
- Jerri was always *competitive* with her twin sister, Merri.
- The Pacers basketball team's eight-foot-tall center gave them a *competitive* edge over all their likely opponents.

[-ness *n.*, -ly *adv.*]

complain (kuhm PLAYN) *vi.* 1. to announce or express pain, displeasure, etc.; 2. to find fault; state annoyance; 3. to make an accusation; make formal objection; bring charges

- Frank's mom loves hearing Frank *complain* how his toe hurts where he stubbed it; just ask her.
- Barb's neighbors often *complain* about her loud stereo.
- Betty *complained* to the police that Archie had damaged her front lawn when he and Reggie trespassed on it.

[-ed, -ing, -er, -t *n.*]

complex (kuhm PLEKS *for adj.*, KOM pleks *for n.*) *adj.* 1. made up of two or more related parts; 2. not simple; 3. involved or complicated —*n.* 1. a collection of interrelated ideas, activities, etc. that form a single whole; 2. a group of units, such as buildings or roads, that together form a single whole; 3. an unconscious psychological condition related to a particular thing or activity

- A *complex* sentence has at least two clauses, one of which is independent and one or more of which is subordinate.
- A camera is too *complex* an instrument to repair yourself.
- The interrelationship of characters in a Shakespearean play is usually quite *complex*.
- The vitamin-B *complex* consists of at least 12 parts.
- A housing *complex* might contain a few storefronts for the convenience of the tenants.
- The fact that April suffered from an inferiority *complex* did not necessarily mean that she was not inferior.

[-ity *adv.*]

composure* (kum POH zhur) *n.* a calmness of mind or manner; tranquillity; self-possession; one's togetherness

- Though all about him were rife with excitement or dismay, Winston Churchill seldom lost his *composure*.
- *Composure* is one of the most important conditions to retain to behave rationally in an emergency.

[Syn. equanimity]

comprehensive (KOM pri HEN siv) *adj.* 1. dealing with all or many of the relevant details; inclusive; 2. able to understand fully; 3. a type of property insurance covering many risks in the same policy

- A *comprehensive* survey should test the mood of the voters on many different issues.
- Hailee has a *comprehensive* mind, which allows her to grasp ideas in their entirety.
- Carrying *comprehensive* insurance that will cover scratches and malicious mischief on your car is rarely recommended for older vehicles.

[-ly *adv.*, -ness *n.*]

compromise (KOM pri MYZ) *n.* 1. a settlement in which each side gives up something to reach a middle ground; 2. an adjustment of opposing principles, systems, etc. by modifying some aspects of each; the result of such an adjustment; 3. something midway between two others in quality, position, etc.; 4. a baring of one's reputation to danger, suspicion, or disrepute —*vt.* 1. to settle or adjust by concessions on both sides; 2. to lay open to danger, suspicion, or disrepute; 3. to weaken one's principles, ideals, etc. to expedite things

- The Missouri *Compromise* permitted Missouri to enter the Union as a slave state and Maine to enter as a free state.
- A *compromise* is the result of two sides coming together to close the distance between them.
- Joe was on the extreme right, Debbie was on the extreme left, and Mike *compromised*, midway between them.
- Being seen with you might cause my reputation to be *compromised*.
- If we all *compromise*, we'll be out of here a lot sooner.
- Do you expect me to *compromise* my principles just to get us out of here in a shorter time?

[-d, compromising]

compulsion (kuhm PUHL shin) *n.* 1. being forced; being coerced; constraint; 2. something that forces; 3. an irresistible irrational impulse to perform an act

- Jane felt a *compulsion* to seek out chocolate ice cream, despite the rather late hour.
- The subpoena was *compulsion* enough for Bill to show up.
- The news junkie watched one news broadcast after another, unable to shake the *compulsion* to stay informed.

[compulsive, compulsory *adj.*, compulsorily *adv.*]

concept (KON sept) *n.* 1. an idea or thought, especially one of an abstract nature; 2. an original idea, design, or concept; 3. a central unifying idea or theme

- The automaker had a *concept* of what the car of the future should look like and be able to do.
- Given the job to create a perfect building for milking cows, the architect sketched out a few *concepts*.
- The décor was in keeping with the *concept* of a Vietnamese theme restaurant and lounge.

[Syn. idea]

concern (kuhn SOERN) *vt.* 1. to be about or to involve; 2. to draw in; engage or involve; 3. to cause to feel uneasy or anxious —*n.* 1. a matter of interest or importance to one; 2. interest in or regard for a person or thing; 3. relation; reference; 4. worry; anxiety

- *The Iliad concerns* a war between Greece and Troy.
- A good teacher tries to *concern* parents with their children's day-to-day school experiences.
- It *concerns* Lois that she has not yet heard from her tax preparation person.
- Mark's well-being is a *concern* of Diane's.
- Sandy has a financial *concern* in the company's health.
- The stock market's fall was a great *concern* of those nearing retirement.

    [-ed, -ing; also -ed *adj.* and -ing *prep.*] [Syn. care]

QUICK REVIEW #18

Match the word from column 2 with the word from column 1 that means most nearly the same thing.

1. compel	a. opponent
2. competent	b. inclusive
3. competition	c. care
4. competitive	d. calmness
5. complain	e. modify
6. complex	f. idea
7. composure	g. accuse
8. comprehensive	h. urge
9. compromise	i. force
10. compulsion	j. contested
11. concept	k. intricate
12. concern	l. able

concert (KON soert) *n.* 1. mutual agreement; concord; togetherness of action; 2. a music program in which a number of musicians perform together

- Pete and Andy were careful to paddle the canoe in *concert*.
- Getting the car out of the snow took a *concerted* effort.
- Five singing groups performed at the April *concert*.

    [-ed *adj.* (in) concert]

conclusion (kuhn KLOO zhn) *n.* 1. the end or final part; 2. the result of the reasoning process; judgment; decision; an opinion reached after investigating; the last in a chain of events

- The coda is the *conclusion* of many musical pieces and is used to reinforce the main idea.
- After thinking it through thoroughly, the *conclusion* that the butler had done it was unavoidable.
- Scotland Yard's investigator reached the same *conclusion*.
- The "Waltz of the Flowers" is the *conclusion* to Tchaikowsky's *The Nutcracker Suite.*

condemn (kuhn DEM) *vt.* 1. to blame; strongly disapprove of; censure; 2. to declare guilty of wrongdoing; to doom; pronounce penalty on; 3. to claim private property for public use by using the power of eminent domain; expropriate; 4. to declare unfit for service

- We all *condemn* the actions of the 9/11 hijackers.
- Let us *condemn* the serial killer to a life in jail.
- The city *condemned* five private homes to make room for the football stadium's parking lot.
- The run-down tenement will be *condemned* and demolished.

    [-ed, -ing, -er *n.*] [Syn. criticize]

condescend (KON dis END) *vi.* 1. to lower oneself to the level of the person one is dealing with; to graciously and willing do something regarded as beneath one's dignity; deign; 2. to deal with others in a proud or haughty way

- The judge may *condescend* to explain his decision to the convicted felon, even though the law does not require it.
- Our cat *condescends* to hang out with the dog from time to time, even though she makes it abundantly clear that she occupies a much higher social level than he does.
- The elite castes in traditional India would not *condescend* to speak with an untouchable.

    [-ed, -ing] [Syn. stoop]

condition (kuhn DISH uhn) *n.* 1. anything that's a requirement before performing or doing something else; 2. any prerequisite to the happening of another thing, event, etc.; 3. something that modifies or restricts the nature, existence, or occurrence of something else; 4. state of being; health; 5. social position; rank; station —*vt.* 1. to set as a requirement; to stipulate; 2. to impose rules on; 3. to affect, modify, or influence; 4. to bring to a desired state

- Being paid in advance is a *condition* of my not singing at charity concerts; if you heard me sing, you'd know why.
- Fertile soil is one *condition* of good crop growth.
- Lack of sun is a *condition* preventing my having a nice lawn.
- Alex's *condition* has improved since he saw the doctor.
- The vice president's *condition* keeps him in close touch with the pulse of the Senate.

- Sarah's mom *conditioned* her going to the party on her being home by 10 P.M. at the latest.
- Ulie's outer garb is *conditioned* on the weather report.
- After shampooing, it helps to *condition* one's hair.

  [-ed, -ing] [Syn. state]

conduct (KON duhct *for n.,* kuhn DUHCT *for vt.*) *n.* 1. the process or way of managing or directing; 2. how one acts; behavior —*vt.* 1. to show the way to; to lead; to guide; to escort; 2. to manage, control, or direct; 3. to behave; 4. to be able to transmit, convey, or carry

- Hands-on *conduct* is how Rocio handles her investments.
- Richard has never been sent to the office for bad *conduct.*
- The tour guide *conducts* a new group every half hour.
- While Leonard Bernstien was music director of the New York Philharmonic, he frequently *conducted* his own works.
- Children should *conduct* themselves properly in public.
- Aluminum *conducts* heat better than steel but not as well as copper.

  [-ed, -ing, -ible *adj.,* -ibility *adv.*]

confirm (kuhn FIRM) *vt.* 1. to strengthen; establish; encourage; 2. to make valid by formal approval; to ratify; 3. to prove truth, validity, or authenticity of; 4. to cause to go through the religious ceremony of confirmation

- We should *confirm* our reservations to make sure they hold our spaces on tomorrow morning's flight.
- The appointment of a Supreme Court justice must be *confirmed* by a two-thirds vote of the Senate to be valid.
- Ruth contacted the manufacturer to *confirm* that the model on sale was the latest one.
- Ray's parents arranged for him to be *confirmed.*

  [-ed, -ing, -ation *n.*] [Syn. verify, validate]

confiscate (KON fis kayt) *vt.* 1. to seize (private property) for the public treasury, usually as a penalty; 2. to seize by or as by authority; appropriate —*adj.* 1. taken away; 2. having property seized

- In some states, automobiles driven while under the influence of an intoxicant are *confiscated.*
- A counterfeit bill is always *confiscated* by the bank teller who spots it, on authority of the Treasury Department.
- Vera sued the city, trying to recover her *confiscated* car.
- Bill hadn't yet delivered his *confiscated* handgun.

  [confiscated, confiscating, confiscator, confiscation *n.*]

conflate (kuhnf LAYT) *vt.* to combine or mix (for example, two different readings into a single text); to bring together; to fuse; to join or meld

- There is a tendency in some corners to *conflate* all drug use into a single dreadful statistic.
- Ralph's film *conflates* the the past and present through skillful use of flashbacks.

conflict (kuhn FLIKT *for vi.*, KON flikt *for n.*) *vi.* to be contradictory; be in opposition; clash —*n.* 1. a fight or struggle, especially a lengthy one; war; 2. sharp disagreement or opposition; clash; 3. emotional disturbance resulting from a clash of impulses

- Sometimes Fran's emotions *conflict* with her brain, her heart pulling one way and her head pulling the other.
- The Hundred Years' War was a very lengthy *conflict*.
- Todd's sweet tooth is in a *conflict* with his need to diet.
- Emotional *conflict* can often result from a desire to do two or more things at the same time.

  [-ed, -ing] [Syn. fight, struggle]

confront (kon FRUHNT) *vt.* 1. to stand or meet face-to-face; 2. to face or oppose boldly or defiantly; 3. bring face-to-face with

- The boxers first *confronted* each other over a couple of Philadelphia cheese-steak sandwiches.
- Two fencers *confront* each other with staple guns drawn.
- Eric learned to *confront* his fear of pussycats by getting his very own kitten.

  [-ed, -ing, -ation *n.*, -ational *adj.*]

confuse (kuhn FYOOZ) *vt.* 1. to mix up; put in disorder; 2. to mix up mentally; perplex; bewilder; 3. to fail to distinguish between; err in identifying

- To *confuse* Gino, Jim walked backward with his arms extended in front of him.
- Anna *confused* real events with imaginary ones.
- Charlie *confused* a Chevrolet with an Oldsmobile.

  [-d, confusing, confusion *n.*] [Syn. puzzle]

QUICK REVIEW #19

Match the word from column 2 with the word from column 1 that means most nearly the same thing.

1. concert	a. face
2. conclusion	b. meld
3. condemn	c. state
4. condescend	d. together
5. condition	e. clash
6. conduct	f. seize
7. confirm	g. perplex
8. confiscate	h. verify
9. conflate	i. stoop
10. conflict	j. result
11. confront	k. behavior
12. confuse	l. doom

congruous (KON groo uhs) *adj.* 1. congruent; 2. fitting; suitable; appropriate
- *Congruous* figures are exactly the same shape and size.
- When appearing in public, a member of Congress is expected to demonstrate *congruous* behavior at all times.

[-ly *adv.*, -ness *n.*]

connection (kuhn NEK shuhn) *n.* 1. a coupling, a joining or unifying; a unification 2. a means of joining; 3. a relationship; 4. a business associate; 5. the means of changing from one train, bus, etc. en route to somewhere; 6. a circuit in electricity; a line of communication between two points in telegraphy, telephony, etc.
- A *connection* is made between two pipes by means of some type of coupling.
- *Connection* from car engine to radiator is by rubber hose.
- You can just sense that Ted and Alice have a *connection*.
- Bill was looking for an MP3 player, and he thought his *connection* with the appliance store worker might help him to get one at a good price.
- When Juanita flew from New York to Miami, she had to make a *connection* at Atlanta.
- Most electrical *connections* are made by sticking a plug into a wall outlet.

consciousness* (KON shuhs nes) *n.* 1. the state of being aware; awareness of one's own feelings or one's surroundings; 2. the totality of one's thoughts, feelings, etc.
- Having been out cold, Ali gradually regained *consciousness*.
- Stream of *consciousness* entails saying or writing whatever pops into your head in the order that it does.
- *Consciousness* implies both an awareness of and an inclination to interact with the world around you.

consensus (kuhn SEN suhs) *n.* 1. an opinion held by all or most; 2. general agreement of opinion
- There is a *consensus* among Americans that democracy is a superior form of government to autocracy.
- There is a *consensus* among men that male drivers are superior to female drivers.
- Amazingly, the exact opposite *consensus* exists among women and, astonishingly, is supported by statistical data.

consequence (KON si KWENS) *n.* 1. a result of an action; outcome; effect; 2. a logical conclusion; 3. the relation of effect to cause; 4. importance
- A *consequence* of buying a new pen is a handwritten note.
- Having the correct time can be a *consequence* of keeping a fresh battery in your wristwatch.
- The *consequence* of consuming a lot of dairy products as a child will be strong teeth and bones as an adult.
- The Emperor Maximillian's presence in Mexico during the American Civil War was of no *consequence* in the war's outcome.

[consequent *adj.*, consequently *adv.*] [Syn. effect, importance]

consider (kuhn SID uhr) *vt.* 1. to think about; ponder; 2. to keep in mind; take into account; 3. to be thoughtful of others

- In studying World War I, one must *consider* the alliances that had been formed among the nations of Europe.
- Her health is really very good, if you *consider* her age.
- We cannot give our security contract to a new provider without *considering* its effect on our current provider.

  [-ed, -ing, -ation *n.*] [Syn. contemplate, weigh]

consist (kuhn SIST) *vi.* 1. to be made up of; 2. to be contained or inherent in; 3. to be characterized by

- Water *consists* of two hydrogen atoms and one oxygen atom.
- Wisdom *consists* of more than just knowing facts.
- Her cultural pursuits *consist* of watching television.

construct (kuhn STRUHKT *for v.*, KAHN strukt *for n.*) *vt.* 1. to create; 2. to draw a figure to meet specifications —*n.* 1. something built or put together systematically; 2. a concept or theory devised to unify diverse data

- Some children love to *construct* buidings with interlocking plastic blocks, and so do I.
- Suzanne was asked to *construct* an isosceles triangle congruent to the one in her geometry book.
- The plan for the new field house was a *construct* that had taken two years and hundreds of meetings to achieve.
- The big-bang theory is a *construct* to explain discoveries and observations of astronomers over the last century.

contaminate (kuhn TAM in AYT) *vt.* to corrupt, make impure, infect, etc. by adding something that shouldn't be there; pollute; defile; taint

- Truck exhaust fumes *contaminate* the air we all breathe.
- Salt *contaminates* seawater, making it undrinkable for us.
- The nuclear accident at Chernobyl *contaminated* much of northern Europe's pasturelands.

  [-d, contaminating, contaminator *n.*] [Syn. defile, taint, corrupt]

contemplate (KON tem PLAYT) *vt.* 1. to stare at intently; 2. to think about carefully; study intently; 3. to keep in mind as a possibile plan of action

- Jerry *contemplated* the telephone bill, studying the total charges in disbelief.
- The coach *contemplated* whom to put into the starting lineup for the next day's game.
- To improve our property value, please *contemplate* running away from home (please).

  [-d, contemplating, contemplation *n.*] [Syn. consider]

contemporary* (kuhn TEM poer ery) *adj.* 1. living or occurring in the same time frame; 2. around the same age; 3. from recent times; modern —*n.* a person who lived at the same time as another/others; the same age as another/others

- The first Super Bowl was *contemporary* with the Dodgers and Giants moving from New York to California.
- Willis is Francesco's *contemporary,* both of them having been born about six years ago.
- Michael Schelle's compositions are exemplary of *contemporary* serious music.
- Composer Franz Joseph Haydn was a *contemporary* of George Washington but outlived him by 10 years.

  [contemporaneous *adj.*]

contemptuous (kuhn TEMP choo uhs) *adj.* full of scorn; full of contempt; disdainful

- Ramses II was *contemptuous* of Moses' attempt to free his people (at least in the Charlton Heston version of *The Ten Commandments*).
- Marie Antoinette was *contemptuous* of the French peasants' being unable to afford bread when she remarked, ". . . then let them eat cake."

  [-ly *adv.,* -ness *n.*]

QUICK REVIEW #20

Match the word from column 2 with the word from column 1 that means most nearly the same thing.

1. congruous	a. composed
2. connection	b. effect
3. consciousness	c. scornful
4. consensus	d. simultaneous
5. consequence	e. build
6. consider	f. stare at
7. consist	g. taint
8. construct	h. suitable
9. contaminate	i. awareness
10. contemplate	j. agreement
11. contemporary	k. join
12. contemptuous	l. weigh

contentment (kuhn TENT mint) *n.* a feeling of being satisfied; a feeling of well-being

- Dinner having been finished, Gerald felt total *contentment.*
- Her life being one of complete *contentment,* Susan had no desire for anything she did not already have.

context (KON tekst) *n.* 1. the spoken or written information immediately around a certain word or passage that helps to determine its meaning; 2. the entirety of the situation in which an event occurs

- Quoting her out of *context,* one might believe that Margaret had found a dress to be particularly lovely, while what she had actually said was "I don't find that dress to be particularly lovely."
- To appreciate the significance of the latest explorations of Mars, we must look at it in the *context* of our exploration of the entire solar system.

    [-ual *adj.,* -ually *adv.*]

contract (KON trakt *for n. and sometimes v.,* kuhn TRAKT *for most v.*) *n.* 1. an agreement between two or more parties to do something in exchange for something else; 2. a formal agreement of marriage or engagement; 3. the document detailing the terms of the agreement —*vt.* 1. to arrange or agree to do something; 2. to get or incur (a debt, an illness, etc.); 3. to get or make smaller; to shorten; to narrow; to shrink; 4. to restrict

- I just made a *contract* with a flooring company to replace that seedy looking living-room floor.
- Wedding *contracts* are really obsolete in the twenty-first century.
- Keep a copy of the *contract* in your desk or filing cabinet.
- Lynn's going to *contract* for new kitchen cabinets.
- Olga seems to have *contracted* a nasty case of the flu.
- It would be good to *contract* the size of your debt.
- Regulations have *contracted* the number of people allowed to be in airline waiting rooms.

    [Syn. shrink, deflate, reduce]

contrary (KON tre ree) *adj.* 1. opposed to; against; 2. opposite in nature, order, direction, etc.; completely different; 3. posturing oneself to consistently disagree; perverse —*n.* the opposite

- Democrats and Republicans have *contrary* positions on many issues.
- *Contrary* to popular opinion, Calbert can dance quite well.
- Carla is disagreeing with everything just to be *contrary.*
- George often says one thing and then does the *contrary.*

contrast (KON trast *for n.,* kun TRAST *for v.*) *vt.* to compare so as to notice or point out the differences; to make a side-by-side comparison —*vi.* to show differences when compared —*n.* 1. a difference, especially a striking one, between two things; 2. showing a striking difference, in color or tone, between different parts of a painting, photograph, or video image

- It's easy to *contrast* Hal's easygoing mannerisms with R. Lee's drill-sergeant demeanor.
- *Contrast* the appearance of a 10-karat-yellow gold ring to a 14-karat one, and the difference is immediately obvious.

- Look at a rectangle next to another parallelogram, and you will immediately recognize the *contrast.*
- Adjusting the *contrast* on a television will soften or harden the way objects next to each other are differentiated.

[-ed, -ing] [Syn. compare]

contribute (kun TRIB yoot) *vt.* 1. to give to a common fund or cause; 2. to write and give or sell a piece of writing to a magazine, newspaper, or other publication; 3. to furnish or donate knowledge, ideas, expertise, etc.

- Pat always *contributes* to cancer-fighting organizations.
- James Thurber *contributed* many humorous cartoons and short stories to various editors during his lifetime.
- Many scientists of the Manhattan Project *contributed* the ideas and calculations that led to Robert Oppenheimer's becoming the father of the atomic bomb.

[-d, contributing, contribution *n.*]

contrite (kun TRYT) *adj.* 1. feeling sorrow; remorse; 2. showing or resulting from repentance; regretting having done wrong

- Kathy was *contrite* for having taken Rhoda's car without first having gotten permission.
- Bob's avoiding meeting Gary's eyes after having damaged his boat was the result of his feeling *contrite.*

[-ly *adv.*, contrition *n.*] [Syn. penitent]

controversial (KON truh VER shee uhl) *adj.* subject to or likely to cause disagreement; debatable

- The question of whether or not to build a new parking garage was the most *controversial* subject on the agenda.
- *Controversial* topics are often the subject of public debate and can polarize opinions.

[-ly *adv.*, controversy *n.*]

controvert (KON truh voert) *vt.* 1. to argue against; dispute; deny; contradict; 2. to argue about; debate; discuss

- It is becoming increasingly difficult to *controvert* the notion that life might have once existed on Mars.
- Magellan's voyage should have been enough to *controvert* all notions of the world's being flat.

[-ed, -ing, -ible *adj.*, -ibly *adv.*] [Syn. disprove]

conundrum (kuh NUHN drm) *n.* 1. a riddle in which the answer contains a pun (play on words); 2. any puzzling question or problem

A *conundrum's* sense #1 is illustrated in the following Q & A:

Q. **What's the difference between a jeweler and a jailer?**

A. **One sells watches, and the other watches cells.**

- Having been invited to three different New Year's Eve parties, and not wanting to hurt anyone's feelings, Olive felt that deciding how to act was a *conundrum.*

convergence* (kuhn VOER jins) *n.* 1. a coming together; 2. the point at which things come together

- The *convergence* of Donna's and Flo's musical interests convinced them that they might make it as a duo.
- There is a *convergence* of two roads into a single road that takes place at the fork.

[convergency *n.*, convergent *adj.*]

conversation (KON ver SAY shin) *n.* 1. the act or a case of talking together; familiar talk; verbal interchange of ideas, opinions, etc.; 2. an informal discussion on an area of common interest by two governments

- Ned and Fred had a *conversation* over coffee, discussing where to get their motorcycles serviced.
- It was customary at Vanessa's workplace to discuss plans for the weekend during the water-cooler *conversations*.
- Representatives of Russia and Japan have *conversations* now and again over Russia's returning Sakhalin to Japan.

[-al *adj.*, -ally *adv.*]

QUICK REVIEW #21

Match the word from column 2 with the word from column 1 that means most nearly the same thing.

1. contentment	a. disprove
2. context	b. penitent
3. contract	c. meeting
4. contrary	d. debatable
5. contrast	e. satisfaction
6. contribute	f. discussion
7. contrite	g. puzzle
8. controversial	h. deflate
9. controvert	i. compare
10. conundrum	j. framework
11. convergence	k. furnish
12. conversation	l. opposed

convey (kuhn VAY) *vt.* 1. to carry from one place to another; transport; 2. to act as a channel or medium for; 3. to make known; 4. to transfer (property) from one person to another

- The van *conveyed* Gerri's furniture to her new home.
- Kaj asked Al to *convey* his condolences to Cindy.
- Lisa *conveyed* her displeasure to Michael with a scowl.
- The deed *conveyed* title to the lot from Sally to Harry.

[-ed, -ing, -able *adj.*] [Syn. carry]

conviction* (kuhn VIK shin) *n.* 1. the finding that a person is guilty of a crime; 2. the appearance or reality of being convinced; 3. a strong belief

- The criminal's *conviction* was for shoplifting.
- Jill told with *conviction* of her and Jack's tumble on the hill.
- The mayor expressed belief in his programs for urban renewal with *conviction*.

[Syn. certainty, opinion]

coop* (KOOP) *n.* 1. a small cage, pen, or building for keeping poultry; 2. any place of confinement; (slang) a jail —*vt.* to confine as in a coop (usually with *up*) —*vi.* (slang) to sleep on the job; (slang) to get away, as from a jail (as in *fly the coop*)

- Some of the chickens have gotten out of the *coop*.
- Because she was grounded, Olivia felt like she was in a *coop*.
- Keep the puppies *cooped* up in your room so that they don't get into mischief.
- Night watchmen need to punch time clocks periodically so that their supervisors know they haven't been *cooping*.

[-ed, -ing]

corroborate* (kur AHB ir AYT) *vt.* to back up the correctness of; to confirm; to support; to bolster

- Willa *corroborated* Kim's location at the time in question.
- A second expert will *corroborate* the authenticity of the Picasso lithograph.

[-d, corroborating, corroborative *adj.*, corroboratory *adj.*] [Syn. confirm]

cosmopolitan (KAHZ muh PAH li tn) *adj.* 1. representative of a wide area of the world; not local or provincial; 2. not bound by local habits, likes, or dislikes; 3. embodying worldly sophistication; fashionable; urbane

- Max's world travels have given him a *cosmopolitan* outlook.
- A taste for Maryland crab cakes has had a *cosmopolitan* impact, drawing orders from all over the world to packers on the Chesapeake Bay.
- The typical European capital city dweller is likely to have a more *cosmopolitan* view of things than his or her compatriot farmer.

couch (KOWCH) *vt.* 1. to lower or bring down, especially to lower (a spear, lance, etc.) to attack position; 2. to put in certain or specific words or phrases; express

- The knight *couched* his lance as he prepared to enter the lists and join the joust. (There's a sentence you'll use every day!)
- The general's warning was *couched* in barely veiled threats.
- The poet's images were *couched* in flowery language.

[-ed, -ing]

counterfeit (KOWN toer fit) *adj.* 1. imitation of something real to deceive or defraud; 2. not genuine; sham; feigned —*n.* a copy made to purposely deceive; forgery; —*vt.* 1. to make an imitation of (money, pictures, etc.) usually to deceive or defraud; 2. to pretend; feign

- The *counterfeit* Van Gogh you bought yesterday for $40 is very well done but definitely not rare.
- *Counterfeit* money in circulation is a danger to everyone in the country— including the counterfeiter.
- That *counterfeit* was made to deceive you into believing it was a Tiffany lamp. (Just trying to throw some light on it.)
- It is not a good idea to *counterfeit* U.S. currency.
- One *counterfeit* most people are familiar with is alligator tears, produced when someone pretends to cry.

    [-ed, -ing, counterfeiter *n.*] [Syn. false, artificial]

courage (KUR ij) *n.* the attitude of confronting something acknowledged as difficult, painful, or dangerous, rather than running or hiding from it; the quality of bravery; fearlessness; valor

- Having the *courage* of one's convictions means being brave enough to do what one believes is the right thing.
- When faced with a potential attack by the vicious cat, Willis the Pug exhibited great *courage*.

    [-ous *adj.*, -ously *adv.*, -ousness *n.*]

creation (kree AY shin) *n.* 1. a coming into existence or a causing to come into existence; 2. the whole universe; all the world; 3. anything created, especially something original created by the imagination; invention, design, etc.

- Gino is the *creation* of his parents, Melissa and Gennaro.
- One's *creation* can be figured from the time of conception.
- You are the most important person in all *creation*.
- The *creations* of DaVinci's mind were ahead of their time.

creative (kree AY tiv) *adj.* 1. able to invent or discover; 2. possessing or showing artistic or intellectual inventiveness or imagination; 3. stimulating the imagination and inventiveness; 4. imaginatively deceptive

- The plan was the result of the general's *creative* powers.
- The architect made a very *creative* use of available space.
- The music of Mozart often helps to get one's *creative* juices flowing.
- The deception was accomplished through the firm's use of *creative* accounting.

creature (KREE chir) *n.* 1. anything created, whether animate or inanimate; 2. a living thing; a human being (often used in a patronizing, demeaning, or endearing manner); 3. one totally dominated by or depending on another

- Muppets are *creatures* animated by puppeteers.
- A *creature* widely admired for its beauty is the wild horse.
- Danielle was predictable, being a *creature* of habit.
- Henry is such a sweet *creature,* one can't help but like him.
- Drug addicts are *creatures* of their addictions.

crisis (KRY sis) *n.* 1. the turning point of an illness for better or for worse; 2. a very painful attack of illness; 3. a decisive, crucial time in the course of anything; a turning point; 4. a time of great danger or trouble

- Alessandra's fever declined after the *crisis* had passed.
- The doctor could tell that Dylan was in *crisis* by the pained expression on his face.
- The battle's *crisis* came when the enemy turned and fled.
- September 11 has played a significant role in more than one *crisis*.
  [crises *pl.*] [Syn. emergency]

QUICK REVIEW #22

Match the word from column 2 with the word from column 1 that means most nearly the same thing.

1. convey	a. dependent
2. conviction	b. invention
3. coop	c. urbane
4. corroborate	d. artistic
5. cosmopolitan	e. valor
6. couch	f. emergency
7. counterfeit	g. confine
8. courage	h. express
9. creation	i. transport
10. creative	j. confirm
11. creature	k. certainty
12. crisis	l. sham

critic (KRIT ik) *n.* 1. someone who makes judgments of people or things based on certain standards; 2. such a person whose occupation is to write or broadcast such judgments of books, music, paintings, etc.; 3. a person who indulges in finding fault with everything

- *Critics* help to maintain high standards in many fields.
- Checking what trusted movie *critics* have to say is one way to keep from wasting hard-earned money on fluff.
- My mother was a *critic,* finding fault with almost everything I ever did— but she meant well.

critical (KRI ti kuhl) *adj.* 1. inclined to find fault; censorious; 2. characterized by close dissection, analysis, and judgment; 3. of critics or criticism; 4. decisive; 5. dangerous or risky

- A teacher's job is to be *critical* of his/her students' work.
- A *critical* study of the factory plans found flaws in them.
- The *critical* community was wowed by your performance.
- This military situation calls for immediate *critical* action.
- Following the surgery, Miranda was in *critical* condition.

    [-ly *adv.*]

criticism (KRIT I si zim) *n.* 1. the act of judging; analyzing qualities and comparing relative worth; 2. a review, comment, article, etc. expressing an evaluation; 3. the act of finding fault; censure; disapproval

- *Criticism* of the merits of the two teams left no doubt that the Yankees were superior to the 7th Grade Allstars.
- A *criticism* of current investment strategies appeared in yesterday's *Wall Street Journal*.
- Judge Maxine's ruling in the dog-bite case drew much *criticism*.

criticize (KRIT i SYZ) *vi., vt.* 1. to evaluate as a critic; 2. to judge disapprovingly; to find fault with

- Reporters from all media came early to get the opportunity to view and to *criticize* the new Egyptology exhibit.
- Given the ballplayer's haughty attitude, it was not surprising that the local fans took the opportunity to *criticize* every imperfect move that he made.

    [-d, criticizing]

crucial (KROO shil) *adj.* 1. of extreme importance; decisive; critical; 2. (medicine) in the form of a cross

    At the first sign of a tick, Lois made the *crucial* decision to take her German shepherd, Libby, to the vet.

    Vince's appendectomy scar was *crucial,* like the letter *x*.

    [-ly *adv.*] [Syn. acute]

cultural* (KUL choer il) *adj.* 1. relating to culture (developing, improving, and refining the arts, intellect, interests, tastes, skills, etc.); 2. pertaining to a certain culture; 3. gotten by breeding or cultivation

- Gracie decided to get tickets to the Philharmonic as part of her concerted effort at *cultural* self-improvement.
- A fondness for drinking ouzo is a Greek *cultural* thing.
- The "jug" is a *cultural* phenomenon obtained by crossing a pug with a Jack Russell terrier.

curator* (KYUR ay ter) *n.* 1. someone in charge of a museum, library, etc.; 2. a guardian or caretaker, as of a minor

- The *curator* of documents is in charge of the archives.
- Bruce Wayne is Dick Grayson's *curator,* in an artful way.

curiosity (KYUR ee ahs i tee) *n.* 1. a wanting to learn or know; 2. a wish to learn about things that don't normally concern one; inquisitiveness; 3. anything curious, strange, rare, or novel

- Children often show *curiosity* about where they came from.
- Spies tried not to openly show *curiosity* about factories.
- The armadillo is certainly as much of a *curiosity* as the duck-billed platypus.

current (KOER int) *adj.* 1. taking place now; at the present time; contemporary; 2. passing from person to person; 3. commonly used, known, or accepted —*n.* 1. a flow of water or air in a certain direction; 2. a general flow or drift; course

- The *current* weather report is for a pleasant, sunny day.
- The *current* rumor has Anne and Fred romantically linked.
- To call something cool is no longer *current,* and I'm cool with that.
- The river's *current* carried the swimmer rapidly along.
- When it comes to whom to invite to a party, I go with the *current* of this year's crop.

curtail (KOER tayl) *vt.* to cut short; reduce; abridge

- The urgent call caused me to *curtail* my visit to the park.
- You must *curtail* your planned two-hour welcoming speech.

  [-ed, -ing, -ment *n.*] [Syn. shorten]

custom (KUHS tim) *n.* 1. a usual practice or accepted way of behaving; habit; 2. a social tradition passed on through generations and upheld by social disapproval; those traditions, collectively; 3. duties and taxes imposed on imports —*adj.* 1. made, cooked, or done to order; 2. making things to order or dealing in things that are made to order

- It is Neal's *custom* to always shower before shaving.
- Not eating bread is one *custom* of the Passover holiday.
- Not eating during daytime is a *custom* during Ramadan.
- When we impose *customs* on imports, reciprocal taxes usually follow on our exports.
- I'm going to buy a *custom* luxury car next month or as soon as I have a half-million dollars to spare—whichever comes last.
- *Custom* kitchens are Gloria and Jeff's specialty.

cynical (SIN ik uhl) *adj.* 1. believing that all personal actions are motivated by selfishness; 2. sarcastic, sneering, etc.

- When Geraldine heard that the car company had donated 30 uniforms to her soccer team, she was *cynical,* and she was proven correct when each donated uniform had the car company's logo sewn onto it.
- Max had a *cynical* view toward all apparent good deeds, just like his mother did.

  [-ly *adv.*]

cynicism (SIN i SI zm) *n.* 1. attitudes or beliefs of a cynical person; 2. a cynical remark, idea, or action

- Karl greeted the ad for a complete oil change for $10 with considerable *cynicism*, wondering what the catch was.
- *Cynicism* is a lot like skepticism, which means that if something sounds too good to be true, the odds are that it is.

QUICK REVIEW #23

Match the word from column 2 with the word from column 1 that means most nearly the same thing.

1. critic		a. disapprove
2. critical		b. sarcastic
3. criticism		c. rarity
4. criticize		d. abridge
5. crucial		e. contemporary
6. cultural		f. judge
7. curator		g. habit
8. curiosity		h. decisive
9. current		i. guardian
10. curtail		j. acute
11. custom		k. tasteful
12. cynical		l. disapproval
13. cynicism		m. doubt

D

damage (DAM ij) *n.* 1. injury or harm, resulting in a loss of soundness or value; 2. (*pl.*) (law) money claimed by or ordered paid to a person to compensate for injury or loss —*vt.* to do harm to —*vi.* to incur harm

- Marla received *damage* to her neck when she skied off the main slope and into a nearby compost heap.
- Claiming that the compost heap should not have been so close to the slope, Marla sued the ski lodge for *damages*.
- When he hit the lamppost, Jakob *damaged* his tricycle.
- Freddy's ear was *damaged* when the newspaper carrier hit it with the Sunday paper.

  [-d, damaging] [Syn. injure]

daze (DAYZ) *vt.* 1. to stun, stupefy, or bewilder as by a shock or blow to the head; 2. to dazzle —*n.* a stunned condition

- The bright headlamps *dazed* the deer as she momentarily froze in her tracks.
- Bumping his head *dazed* Ian just long enough to permit his prisoner to slip away unnoticed.
- After having survived frightful conditions while marooned on the island, the newly rescued sailor wandered around in a *daze*.

  [-dly *adv.*]

debacle (di BAK il) *n.* 1. a torrent of debris-filled waters; 2. an overwhelming defeat or route; 3. a total, often ludicrous, collapse or failure

- After the dam burst, a *debacle* descended on the farms and villages below.
- Napoleon never recovered from his Battle of Waterloo *debacle*.
- The Bible tells of the *debacle* that resulted from man's attempt to build the Tower of Babel.

debatable (di BAYT i bl) *adj.* 1. arguable, having pros and cons on both sides; 2. something that can be questioned or disputed; 3. in dispute, as land claimed by two countries

- Whether the country's economy does better under Republicans or Democrats is highly *debatable*.
- Whether the next Oscar really will go to the best picture of this year is *debatable*.
- The ownership of Kashmir is *debatable* because it is claimed by both India and Pakistan.

debunk (di BUHNK) *vt.* to expose the false or exaggerated claims, pretensions, glamour, etc. of con artists and charlatans

- Some people take it as their life's work to *debunk* the schemes of con artists.
- The self-proclaimed Great Randi has *debunked* many so-called mentalists by revealing their deceptions.

  [-ed, -ing, -er *n.*]

73

deceive (di SEEV) *vt.* to cause (a person) to believe what is not true; delude; mislead —*vi.* to use deceit; lie

- Flattery is a time-tested device to *deceive* one into thinking he or she is hotter than is actually the case.
- The Flyby Knight Furniture Company tried to *deceive* people into believing that their $298 sofa was real leather.
- False advertising is intended to *deceive*.

[-d, deceiving, deceivable *adj.*, deceivingly *adv.*, -r *n.*]

decibel (DE si bil) *n.* 1. (acoustics) a numerical expression of the relative loudness of a sound; 2. (electronics, radio) a numerical expression of relative power levels of electronic signals (In both cases the decibel level [dB] is related to common logarithms, so small differences in decibels denote large differences in levels.)

- A 115-*decibel* sound level at a rock concert is enough to cause permanent hearing damage, while a 130-*decibel* sound can cause actual physical pain.
- Loss of electromagnetic energy as it passes through transmission lines is measured in *decibels,* with a loss of 3 dBs equal to half the strength.

decline (di KLYN) *vt., vi.* 1. to slope downward or aside; 2. to sink; wane; near the end; 3. to lessen in force, health, value, etc.; 4. to sink to behavior that is base or immoral; 5. to refuse to accept

- The graph of violent crimes per capita in New York during the 1990s *declines* as it moves from left to right.
- As it approaches the loading platform, the speed of the roller coaster *declines*.
- The value of the dollar against the Euro *declined* in 2003.
- In dealing with a monkey, you need not *decline* to its level.
- Karen *declined* payment from Barney for having baby-sat.

[-d, declining] [Syn. refuse]

decorous (di KAW ris) *adj.* characterized by or showing propriety in behavior, dress, etc.; demonstrating good taste

- Tom behaved in a very *decorous* manner at the graduation, never raising his voice or wiping his mouth on his sleeve.
- The ettiquette consultant was hired by Maxine's mother to supervise the *decorous* behavior of all the servers at the wedding reception.

[-ly *adv.*]

defend (dif END) *vt.* 1. to protect from attack; keep from harm or danger; 2. to support, maintain, or justify; 3. (law) to oppose (an action); to plead (one's case)

- Though the door is unlocked, a German shepherd in the living room is usually adequate to *defend* a home from theft.
- I don't need to *defend* my conduct in this case.
- The corporation had more than one attorney to *defend* it against liability actions.

[-ed, -ing, defense *n.*, *adj.*]

deferment (di FOER mint) *n.* a postponement; a putting off to a later time

- In the bad old days of the draft, college students were able to get *deferments* until after graduation.
- *Deferment* of jury duty is often obtainable by mothers of preschool children.

[(to) defer *vt.*]

QUICK REVIEW #24

Match the word from column 2 with the word from column 1 that means most nearly the same thing.

1. damage	a. refuse
2. daze	b. protect
3. debacle	c. mislead
4. debatable	d. appropriate
5. debunk	e. loudness
6. deceive	f. postponement
7. decibel	g. injure
8. decline	h. arguable
9. decorous	i. failure
10. defend	j. expose
11. deferment	k. stupor

defiant (di FY int) *adj.* full of angry resistance; openly and boldly resisting (in spite of opposition)

- The men defending the Alamo were *defiant* in the face of Santa Ana's overwhelmingly superior numbers.
- Rosa Parks sparked civil rights awareness by being *defiant* of the "Blacks ride in the back" convention of the day.

  [-ly *adv.*, defiance *n.*]

deficit (DEF i sit) *n.* the amount of money less than the necessary amount; having more liabilities than assets, losses than profits, or expenditures than income

- The U.S. government almost always has a financial *deficit*.
- Those in the high-tech sector of the stock market experienced a severe *deficit* at the opening of the twenty-first century.

define (di FYN) *vt.* 1. to state or set down the boundaries of; to delineate; 2. to determine or state the nature or extent of; 3. to differentiate; 4. to state the meaning or meanings of a word (like we're doing here)

- A couple needs to *define* what will be expected of each before rushing blindly into a marriage.
- Mr. Smedley, our head of sales, will now *define* what your job here will be.
- Never *define* a word by using that word in the definition.

  [-d, defining, definition *n.*]

deleterious (DEL it ir ee uhss) *adj.* bad for health or well-being; injurious; harmful

- Smoking cigarettes is *deleterious* to everyone's health, not just the smoker's.
- An infestation of locusts can have a *deleterious* effect on a farmer's crops.

  [-ly *adv.*, -ness *n.*] [Syn. pernicious]

demagogue (DEM uh GOG) *n.* one who tries to rouse the people by appealing to emotion, prejudice, etc. to win them over and attain (political) power

- Hitler was the most infamous *demagogue* of the twentieth century.
- Stalin was a terrible dictator, but he does not qualify as a *demagogue* because he gained power by brute force alone.

  [demagogy, -ry *n.*]

demeanor (di MEEN oer) *n.* outward manner; carriage; the way one behaves

- Princess Diana had a regal *demeanor* and a gentle one.
- Between a Rottweiler and a Doberman pinscher, the Rottie has the meaner *demeanor.*

  [*Brit. sp.* demeanour] [Syn. bearing]

democracy (di MAHK ri see) *n.* 1. government by the people, with the populace holding the reins of power, either directly or through elected representatives; power in the hands of the ruled; 2. a country, state, etc. with that type of government; 3. majority rule; 4. the principle of equal rights and opportunities for all, and equal treatment by the legal system; the practice of these principles

- Athens had the first experiment in *democracy* we know of.
- American *democracy* was not viewed kindly by the crowned heads of eighteenth- and nineteenth-century Europe.
- India is the world's largest *democracy* in terms of population.
- Schoolchildren learn the principles of *democracy* by voting for class officers (who have little to no power).
- The U.S. Constitution is the primary legal document that assures the principles of *democracy* be followed.

demonstrate (DEM uhn STRAYT) *vt.* 1. to prove; show by reasoning; 2. to make clear or explain through examples, experiments, etc.; 3. to show how a product works or what it tastes like in order to sell it; 4. to show feelings plainly

- Descartes was the first philosopher to *demonstrate* his existence by the dictum, "I think, therefore I am."
- The operation of the steam engine is often *demonstrated* in classes using a cutaway working model.
- There are often people *demonstrating* certain foods at the warehouse club by offering free samples in small cups.
- Tears on her cheek *demonstrated* Patricia's sadness.

  [-d, demonstrating]

denounce* (di NOWNS) *vt.* 1. to condemn publicly; inform against; 2. to accuse of being evil; 3. to give formal notice of the termination of (a treaty, armistice, etc.)

- American loyalists *denounced* Washington as a traitor to the British Crown.
- The French patriots *denounced* Louis XVI as a tyrant.
- The Japanese government did not *denounce* the naval treaty that limited the size and number of warships they could build; they just disregarded it.

  [-d, denouncing] [Syn. criticize]

deny (di NY) *vt.* 1. to declare something untrue; contradict; 2. to not accept as factual; to reject as unfounded, unreal, etc.; 3. to disown; to refuse to acknowledge as one's own; rerepudiate; 4. to not allow the use of or access to; 5. refuse to grant or give; 6. to refuse a person's request

- Cara *denied* the charge that she had cheated on her diet.
- Evan did not *deny* having cheated on Mary but claimed that she had cheated on him first.
- Ian *denied* having painted the big mural outside the store.
- Ryan was forced to *deny* Sophie use of the handicapped parking space on the grounds that she wasn't handicapped.
- I *deny* all of you access to the ice cream in my freezer.
- I also must *deny* your request for parole.

    [denied, -ing, denial *n*.]

depict (di PIKT) *vt.* 1. to portray; to represent in a painting, drawing, sculpture, etc.; 2. to describe; to picture in words

- Leonardo DaVinci's *Last Supper depicts* a Passover seder.
- A portrait artist will *depict* a likeness of you, for a fee.
- The sports section of today's newspaper *depicts* a detailed account of yesterday's games, artfully drawn in words.

    [-ed, -ing, -ion *n*.]

deplore (di PLAWR) *vt.* 1. to be sorry about; to regret; lament; 2. to regard as unfortunate or awful; 3. to disapprove of; to condemn as wrong

- My neighbor's mother *deplores* the day he was born.
- Any feeling individual must *deplore* the conditions in which the urban homeless are condemned to live.
- The whole world *deplores* the lack of safety measures that were in place at Chernobyl's nuclear power plant.

    [-d, deploring]

QUICK REVIEW #25

Match the word from column 2 with the word from column 1 that means most nearly the same thing.

1. defiant	a. prove
2. deficit	b. lament
3. define	c. bearing
4. deleterious	d. reject
5. demagogue	e. criticize
6. demeanor	f. portray
7. democracy	g. lack
8. demonstrate	h. pernicious
9. denounce	i. popular rule
10. deny	j. rebellious
11. depict	k. rabble-rouser
12. deplore	l. delineate

deride (di RYD) *vt.* to laugh at contemptuously or scornfully; to make fun of; ridicule

- Jack *derided* his sister for having trouble riding the bicycle.
- It is poor form to *deride* anyone for his or her handicaps or inabilities.
   [-d, deriding, derision *n.*, derisive *adj.*, deridingly *adv.*] [Syn. ridicule]

derivative* (di RIV a TIV) *adj.* 1. using or taken from other sources; 2. not original —*n.* something derived

- Many modern medicines are tropical plant *derivatives.*
- *The Lord of the Rings* movies were *derivative* films, having been taken from Tolkein's writings.
- Chocolate is a *derivative* of the cacao bean.
   [-ly *adv.*]

derive (di RYV) *vt.* 1. to get, take, or receive something from a source; 2. to arrive at by reasoning; deduce or infer; 3. to trace to or from its source; show the origin and development of

- Alice *derived* most of her term paper from Web sources.
- Pythagoras *derived* his famous theorem by drawing squares on the sides of a right triangle and relating their areas.
- The ancestry of many immigrants may be *derived* from the archives at Ellis Island.
   [-d, deriving, derivation *n.*]

descent (dee SENT) *n.* 1. a coming or going down; 2. lineage; ancestry; 3. a downward slope; 4. a sudden attack or raid (on or upon); 5. a decline; fall

- Wally's *descent* down the banister was much faster than it would have been had he used the stairs.
- Jack could trace his *descent* from a long line of no-good Nicks.
- The ski trail made a steep *descent* before leveling off.
- The Mongols' *descent* upon the caravan came swiftly and without warning.
- The power of the Egyptian pharoahs was in *descent* long before the reign of the last pharoah, Cleopatra.

describe (di SKRYB) *vt.* 1. to give a detailed account of; 2. to make a word picture of; 3. to trace or outline

- Lewis Carrol *describes* Alice's adventures in Wonderland as growing "curiouser and curiouser."
- Ernest Hemingway was able to *describe* places in words so that exotic, detailed pictures formed in his readers' minds.
- Valerie used her compass to *describe* a 3 cm radius circle.
   [-d, describing]

description (dis KRIP shin) *n.* 1. the process of picturing in words; describing; 2. a statement or passage that describes; 3. sort, kind, or variety of; 4. the act of tracing or outlining

- James Michener's *description* of the islands of the South Pacific were vivid enough to transport the reader there.
- Write a brief *description* of the accident and how you caused it to happen.

- There are coffee beans of every *description* that are grown in South America, Africa, and other places.
- Hal's arm swept through the *description* of a 90° arc.

design (di ZYN) *vt.* 1. to make creative sketches of; to plan; 2. to plan and carry out; 3. to form (plans) in the mind; to contrive; 4. to intend; purpose —*n.* 1. a plan, scheme, or project; 2. an aim or purpose; 3. a thing planned for or a result aimed at; 4. the organization of parts, details, form, color, etc. to get an artistic result

- The architect *designed* the floor plan on a large sketch pad.
- It is hard to *design* a foolproof bank holdup, and he or she who thinks otherwise is a fool.
- Martha tried to *design* a plan of study that would help her get ready for the math examination.
- Bob *designed* to work straight through until dinner.
- The *design* of the house was Tara's own.
- Jason built the plane from a commercial *design*.
- The wedding reception went off according to *design*.
- We should lay out the *design* for the painting before actually working on the canvas.

  [-ed, -ing] [Syn. intend, plan]

desolate (DES uh lit *for adj.*, DES uh LAYT *for v.*) *adj.* 1. isolated; lonely; solitary; 2. uninhabited; deserted; 3. made uninhabitable; in a ruined condition; 4. forlorn; wretched —*vt.* 1. to rid of inhabitants; 2. to make uninhabitable; to devastate; 3. to forsake; abandon; 4. to make wretched, forlorn, etc.

- Ed has been *desolate* since Trixie took his teddy bear.
- The desert island was a *desolate* place.
- The nuclear tests had left the land in a *desolate* state.
- The naval gunnery practice range was *desolated* by its almost constant bombardment.
- You'll *desolate* me if you run away with my best friend without giving me at least 10 days' notice so that I can replace you.

  [-d, desolating, -ly *adv.*]

despise (dis PYZ) *vt.* 1. to detest; to look on with contempt and scorn; 2. to regard with dislike or repugnance

- The cowboys learned to *despise* the scorpions that crawled into their boots at night.
- They also *despised* eating pork and beans night after night.

  [-d, despising] [Syn. scorn, disdain]

destitution (DES ti TOO shin) *n.* the state of being very poor; being without; lacking the necessities of life; abject poverty

- *Destitution* is a condition in which it is unenviable to find oneself.
- Do not confuse *destitution,* a state of abject poverty, with restitution, a paying back for injuries caused.

  [Syn. poverty]

destruction (dis TRUHK shin) *n.* 1. demolition; the act of destroying; slaughter; 2. the fact or state of being demolished; 3. the cause or means of demolition

- Peter's task was to effect the *destruction* of the old ballpark so that it could be replaced with a new one.
- The tornado had caused almost complete *destruction* where it had touched down.
- *Destruction* is a good thing, when practiced in moderation.

  [Syn. ruin]

detachment (di TACH mint) *n.* 1. a separating; 2. a unit of troops separated from a larger unit for special duty; a small permanent unit organized for special service; 3. the state of being disinterested, impartial, or aloof

- The shipping container was a *detachment* from a long-haul tractor-trailer's bed.
- A *detatchment* of marines was sent in to reconnoiter before the main landing was to take place.
- The cat watched the dog being bathed with complete *detachment,* having no clue that she was to be next.

QUICK REVIEW #26

Match the word from column 2 with the word from column 1 that means most nearly the same thing.

1. deride	a. poverty
2. derivative	b. impartiality
3. derive	c. ridicule
4. descent	d. scorn
5. describe	e. unoriginal
6. description	f. ruin
7. design	g. deduce
8. desolate	h. scheme
9. despise	i. sudden attack
10. destitution	j. forsake
11. destruction	k. picture
12. detachment	l. tracing

determine (di TOER min) *vt.* 1. to set limits to; to bound; define; 2. to settle a dispute, question, etc.; to decide; 3. to come to a conclusion; 4. to assign direction to

- A chain-link fence *determines* the boundaries of many city playgrounds.
- A meeting between the two contenders should *determine* once and for all the true heavyweight champion.
- The jury has to *determine* whether the defendant is innocent, or guilty as charged.
- The prevailing winds will *determine* where the balloon goes.

  [-d, determining] [Syn. decide, learn]

detract (dee TRAKT) *vt.* 1. to take or draw away (from); 2. to belittle; disparage —*vi.* to remove something desirable (from)

- We must not *detract* strength from his argument.
- Do not *detract* the importance of following one's heart.
- Frowning *detracts* from her beauty.

  [-ed, -ing, -or *n.*]

development (di VEL uhp mint) *n.* 1. a growing or expanding (in size, strength, etc.); 2. a step or stage in growth, advancement, etc.; 3. an event or an occurence; 4. a number of buildings on a large tract of land

- Ned's *development* of his muscles is impressive.
- *Development* of the Polaroid picture is easy to see, as the image gains in definition before your eyes.
- What a revolting *development* this is!
- The new housing *development* will occupy 40 acres.

  [-al *adj.*, -ally *adv.*]

diagnosis (DY uhg NOH sis) *n.* 1. the act of finding or classifying a condition by means of medical examination, lab tests, etc.; 2. a careful studying and analyzing of the facts to understand or explain something; 3. a decision or opinion based on such an analysis

- The *diagnosis* of strep infection came after the throat culture returned from the lab.
- Before we can *diagnose* your business's problems, we must analyze your clientele, your expenditures, and your suntan.
- Steve's *diagnosis* of the cause of the computer's strange graphics was the Rhino virus, which put a horn on every image's nose.

digression* (dy GRESH in) *n.* 1. an act of straying from the main theme or idea when talking or writing; 2. a temporary straying from the main theme

- During Bill's discussion of bridge designing came a 10-minute-long *digression* about his love of chocolate milk.
- Laura's *digression* on her childhood was barely noticed by her art history students, most of whom were already asleep.

  [(to) digress *vi.*, -al *adj.*]

dingy (DIN gee) *adj.* 1. yucky; dull; not clean; grimy; 2. ragged; gloomy

- If you don't use chlorine bleach on your cotton whites, you're likely to have them come out a *dingy* yellow.
- Jane's attempt to wangle an invitation to the party was rather *dingy*.

  [dingily *adv.*, dinginess *n.*]

discern (dis OERN) *vt.* 1. to clearly distinguish one thing from another or others; to recognize as distinct or separate; 2. to clearly make out

- It was not hard to *discern* the difference between the hearts and the spades in the deck of cards.
- Terry *discerned* a feeling of approval rising from her captive audience.

  [-ed, -ing, -able *adj.*, -ably *adv.*] [Syn. perceive, distinguish]

discordant* (dis KAWR dint) *adj.* 1. not in agreement; conflicting; 2. out of harmony; clashing; dissonant

- The unhappy incoming news was *discordant* with the recipient's more uplifting expectations.
- A *discordant* note was struck by the politician addressing the labor union leadership.

  [discordance or discordancy *n.*, -ly *adv.*]

discount (DIS cownt *for n.*, dis COWNT *for v.*) *n.* 1. money off the usual price; 2. a deduction from a debt allowed for paying it early or in cash; 3. the interest rate charged —*vt.* 1. to pay or get the present value of a note less the interest; 2. to subtract an amount or percent from (a bill, price, etc.); 3. to sell at less than the usual price; 4. to take a story, statement, opinion, etc. at less than face value, or to totally disregard it as exaggeration

- Everything in the store was *discounted* 15%.
- Many Treasury bonds are sold at a *discounted* rate to allow for the interest that will accrue between purchase and maturity.
- Corporate bonds are often sold at a *discount* rate so that the purchaser pays less than the face value.
- In certain furniture stores, the pieces are marked so that the customer can *discount* 50% to get the selling price.
- The police officer *discounted* most of Denise's story, which made her role look better than it actually was.

  [-ed, -ing] [Syn. reduction]

discourse* (DIS kawrs) *n.* 1. exchange of ideas, information, etc. usually through talking; conversation; 2. a long, formal speech or essay on a subject; lecture; treatise; dissertation —*vi.* 1. to carry on a talk; confer; 2. to speak or write formally and at some length

- The secretary of state gave a *discourse* on foreign policy.
- The doctoral candidate's dissertation was a *discourse* on the number of seeds that one might expect to find on various breeds of strawberries and why.
- The two musicians *discoursed* with each other about the meaning of Beethoven's notations in the margins of his pieces.
- The president *discoursed* at some length about not knowing how the terrible economy could be fixed and about how it wasn't his fault anyway.

  [-d, discoursing] [Syn. speak]

discovery (dis KUH vir ee) *n.* 1. finding out about, seeing, or knowing about first; 2. making famous; bringing to the public's attention; 3. pretrial procedures for compelling the disclosure of certain facts

- Jonas Salk's *discovery* of a vaccine against polio put an end to the most feared infectious disease of the twentieth century.
- The *discovery* of Lana Turner in Schwab's drug store in Los Angeles is the stuff of which fairy tales are made.
- All the evidence the prosecution has must be revealed to the defense during the *discovery* process.

    [discoveries *pl.*] [Syn. learning]

discredit* (dis KRED it) *vt.* 1. to reject as not true; to disbelieve; 2. to be a cause for disbelief or distrust; to cast doubt on; 3. to damage the reputation or credibility of; disgrace

- The authorities *discredited* Marsha's story about how she was abducted by little green creatures in a flying saucer.
- The fact that he had been caught lying in three previous incidents *discredited* any further testimony he would give.
- The story of how he had turned and run in a previous emergency *discredited* his standing as a local hero.

    [-ed, -ing]

QUICK REVIEW #27

Match the word from column 2 with the word from column 1 that means most nearly the same thing.

1. determine	a. reduction
2. detract	b. learning
3. development	c. grimy
4. diagnosis	d. dissonant
5. digression	e. doubt
6. dingy	f. lecture
7. discern	g. disparage
8. discordant	h. straying
9. discount	i. analysis
10. discourse	j. decide
11. discovery	k. distinguish
12. discredit	l. expansion

discretion (dis KRE shin) *n.* 1. the ability to decide or to choose; power to judge or act; 2. the quality of being careful about what one does or says; prudence

- You may pay by check or by cash, at your own *discretion*.
- Karen snuck the chips and dip into her bedroom with *discretion,* so nobody could see she was deviating from her diet.

discriminate (dis KRIM in ayt *for v.,* dis KRIM in it *for adj.*) *vt.* 1. to recognize a difference between; differentiate; 2. to notice the difference between; to distinguish —*vi.* 1. to be discerning; 2. to treat differently; show partiality —*adj.* involving making distinctions; distinguishing carefully

- Tax rates *discriminate* between married and single payers.
- Ralph's fingers were sensitive enough to *discriminate* between apples and pears by just touching their skins.
- While shopping for credit terms, it pays to *discriminate* by comparing the terms very carefully.
- The law *discriminates* between keeping domestic and wild animals as pets, generally prohibiting the latter.
- When it comes to wine, Judy has very *discriminating* taste (among bottles costing $6 or less).

    [-d, discriminating] [Syn. distinguish]

discussion (dis KUSH in) *n.* talking or writing in which the pros and cons and/or various aspects of a subject are considered

- If you want to see the complete *discussion* that preceeded the passage of a law, read *The Congressional Record.*
- It is important that you participate in a thorough *discussion* of current events before you decide for whom to vote.

disdain* (dis DAYN) *vt.* to regard or treat someone/thing as beneath one's dignity; to refuse or reject with aloofness and scorn; to show contempt for —*n.* the feeling, attitude, or expression of scornfulness; aloof contempt

- The cat totally *disdained* the dog, who was content to lie on the hard floor rather than on the soft pile of laundry.
- Gandhi might have *disdained* walking among the lowest caste of the Indian people, but he did not.
- In some industries the white-collar workers foolishly look upon the blue-collar workers with *disdain*.

    [-ed, -ing] [Syn. despise]

disease (diz EEZ) *n.* 1. any varying from healthiness; illness in general; 2. a certain destructive process in an organ or organism rooted in a particular cause; ailment; 3. any harmful or destructive social condition

- At the first sign of *disease,* a doctor's visit is a good idea.
- Jaundice is only one of many *diseases* of the liver.
- High unemployment is a *disease* that can cripple society.

disguise (dis GYZ) *vt.* 1. to make look, sound, etc. different from usual so as to be unrecognizable; 2. to hide or obscure the real nature of —*n.* 1. anything used to change one's appearance, voice, etc.; 2. the state of being disguised; 3. the act or practice of disguising

- Red Chief's kidnappers *disguised* their voices when they made ransom demands, never dreaming that the child's parents would not want him back.
- While *disguised* as a ghost, Shaila kept bumping into walls.
- The bank robber was incorrect when he thought the Groucho Marx *disguise* would prevent his being recognized.

[-d, disguising]

disheveled (dis SHEV ild) *adj.* sloppily dressed and untidy; sloppy; not neatly groomed; having wrinkled clothing, etc.

- Donna's hair was quite *disheveled,* as if she had gotten up after a night's tossing and turning and not brushed it.
- Howard looked *disheveled,* as if he were wearing the clothes he had slept in.

disingenuous (DIS in JEN yoo uhs) *adj.* not straightforward; not candid or frank; insincere

- Carrie was *disingenuous,* telling Kaj what she thought he wanted to hear just to get rid of him.
- When Harry asked Sally why she had been late, her *disingenuous* answer included a story about a jacknifed tractor-trailer truck.

[-ness *n.,* -ly *adv.*]

disparage* (dis PA ridzh) *vt.* 1. to discredit; 2. to speak ill of; show disrespect for; to belittle

- Walter *disparaged* his own reputation when he told the story of the time he had spent behind bars.
- Don't *disparage* me by talking about me behind my back.

[-d, disparaging *vt.* or *adj.,* disparagingly *adv.*]

disparate (dis PA rit) *adj.* not alike; distinct or different in kind; unequal

- When Diane interviewed the brother and sister for the job, she spent a *disparate* amount of time with the brother.
- Marty said the twins were as alike as peas in a pod, but to Jill they seemed as *disparate* as green beans and cantaloupes.

disparity* (dis PA ri tee) *n.* 1. difference or inequality, as in rank, amount, quality, etc.; 2. unlikeness; incongruity

- There is a *disparity* between a private's and a general's paycheck commensurate with that of their ranks.
- There is a *disparity* in the areas of a triangle and a rectangle of equal base and height.

dispel (dis PEL) *vt.* to drive away; scatter; make vanish; disperse

- When Kate saw Julio stand on his head while spinning two rings on each ankle, it was enough to *dispel* any doubt that he was the man for her.
- The policemen's presence helped to *dispel* the crowd.

[-led, -ling] [Syn. scatter]

QUICK REVIEW #28

Match the word from column 2 with the word from column 1 that means most nearly the same thing.

1. discretion	a. belittle
2. discriminate	b. incongruity
3. discussion	c. toussled
4. disdain	d. scatter
5. disease	e. insincere
6. disguise	f. different
7. disheveled	g. prudence
8. disingenuous	h. despise
9. disparage	i. consideration
10. disparate	j. alter
11. disparity	k. distinguish
12. dispel	l. illness

dispersal* (dis POER sil) *n.* 1. a scattering; a spreading about; 2. a breaking up of light into its component colored rays (by use of a triangular prism)

- The spreader assured that the grass seeds would get a thorough *dispersal*.
- When white light is passed through a prism, a *dispersal* occurs and the rays form the colors of the rainbow.
- In fact, a real rainbow is caused by the *dispersal* of the sun's rays by the water in the air.

  [Syn. scattering]

disregard (DIS ri GAHRD) *vt.* 1. to pay little or no attention to; 2. to not respect; slight —*n.* 1. lack of attention; neglect; 2. lack of respect

- *Disregard* that little man behind the curtain! (Where have we heard something like that before?)
- It is important to never *disregard* the feelings of others.
- When Frank painted his room, he treated his wife's dislike of red with total *disregard*.

  [-ed, -ing] [Syn. neglect]

dissemble (dis EM bl) *vt.* to hide beneath a false appearance; to disguise —*vi.* to hide the truth, or one's true feelings, motives, etc. by pretending; to behave hypocritically

- Some guests feel it proper to *dissemble* their displeasure so as not to upset the host or hostess.
- You want the truth? We have to *dissemble* our facts, for fear that you can't handle the truth.
- Gary *dissembled* his dislike for chocolate by asking for a second piece.

  [-d, dissembling]

disseminate (dis EM in AYT) *vt.* to scatter far and wide; spread about, as if sowing seed; make known widely

- The newspaper's purpose was to *disseminate* the ideas of its editorial staff over a wide region.
- Maple seeds have sails so that they can be *disseminated* by air currents over a wide area.

[-d, disseminating] [Syn. broadcast, promulgate]

dissent (dis ENT) *vi.* 1. to have a different belief or opinion; disagree, often with *from;* 2. to reject the doctrine of an established religion —*n.* the act of disagreeing, specifically a legal opinion against the majority's; religious nonconformity

- Bulls and bears *dissent* from one another in their stock purchase plans.
- Henry VIII's *dissent* with the pope caused the formation of the Anglican Church.
- Oliver Wendell Holmes Jr. wrote some very famous *dissents* during his term on the Supreme Court.

[-ed, -ing]

dissimilar (dis SIM i loer) *adj.* not alike; different

- Cats and dogs have very *dissimilar* personality traits, with the dog trying to please you and the cat believing it's your job to please it.
- Twins Bob and Ray have *dissimilar* jobs at the phone company; Bob's in operations, and Ray's an operator.

[-ity *n.,* -ly *adv.*] [Syn. different]

dissipate (DIS i PAYT) *vt.* 1. to break up and scatter; dispel; disperse; 2. to drive completely away; make disappear; 3. to waste or squander

- The rising sun will help to *dissipate* the fog.
- Of course, it won't completely *dissipate* until the sun's rays have had a chance to dry up all the water droplets.
- Don't *dissipate* all your energy looking for a leprechaun.

[-d, dissipating] [Syn. scatter]

distinct* (dis TEENKT) *adj.* 1. not alike; different; 2. not the same; individual; separate; 3. clearly sensed or marked off; clear; plain; 4. well defined; unmistakable; definite

- Each ballplayer is a *distinct* entity.
- Every puppy in the litter has a *distinct* personality.
- Every school bus has a *distinct* serial number.
- Our effort brought a *distinct* success.

[Syn. different]

distinguish (dis TING wish) *vt.* 1. to tell apart; to sense or show the difference in; to differentiate; 2. to be an essential feature of; characterize; 3. to separate and classify; 4. to make famous or prominent; give distinction to

- Rubies and sapphires can be easily *distinguished* from each other by color.
- Hardness *distinguishes* real diamonds from fake ones.
- The Dewey Decimal System helps us to *distinguish* a book by its cover.
- "The *distinguished* senator from (your state)" is a title of rank and respect.

[-ed, -ing, -able *adj.,* -ably *adv.*] [Syn. discriminate]

distort (dis TAWRT) *vt.* 1. to twist out of shape; change the normal shape, form, or appearance of; 2. to misrepresent; misstate; pervert

- Rubber dolls and action figures are easy to *distort.*
- Martin's report on Korea seriously *distorts* the facts.

  [-ed, -ing, -er *n.*] [Syn. deform]

diversion* (di VER zhuhn) *n.* 1. a turning aside; 2. distraction of attention; 3. anything that distracts the attention, such as a pastime or an amusement

- *Diversion* of the Colorado River through tunnels allowed the Hoover Dam to be built near Las Vegas.
- The Japanese attacked the Aleutians in World War II as a *diversion* to draw America's attention away from Midway.
- Six Flags provides *diversion* at several amusement parks.

divination (DIV i NAY shun) *n.* 1. a trying to predict the future or examine the unknown by means beyond human understanding; 2. a prophecy; prediction; foreknowing; 3. a correct guess or good intuition

- *Divination* was often used in the Old West to decide where to dig wells for water.
- Nostradamus's stock and trade was *divination.*
- One who succeeds in *divination* is often referred to as a lucky guesser.
- *Divination* is ESP (not ESPN).

QUICK REVIEW #29

Match the word from column 2 with the word from column 1 that means most nearly the same thing.

1. dispersal	a. different
2. disregard	b. deform
3. dissemble	c. unmistakable
4. disseminate	d. foretelling
5. dissent	e. characterize
6. dissimilar	f. distraction
7. dissipate	g. disagree
8. distinct	h. squander
9. distinguish	i. neglect
10. distort	j. promulgate
11. diversion	k. scattering
12. divination	l. pretend

divisive (di VYS iv *or* di VIS iv) *adj.* causing division, especially causing disagreement or dissension

- Whether or not to get a second dog was a *divisive* issue for Lois and Jeremy.
- Which bills should be paid first is often a *divisive* matter for newlyweds and longtime couples alike.

divulge (div UHLDZH) *vt.* to make known; disclose; unveil; reveal

- The newspaper reporter was obliged to not *divulge* the source of his highly sensitive information.
- If I were to *divulge* to you the secret processes that were involved in the making of this product, I'd have to shoot you.

[-d, divulging] [Syn. reveal]

domestic (duh MES tik) *adj.* 1. having to do with the home, housekeeping, or family; 2. of one's own country, or the country referred to; 3. made or produced in the home country; 4. tame —*n.* 1. a houseworker such as a maid, housekeeper, or butler; 2. blankets, linens, towels, etc.

- *Domestic* tasks, which used to be exclusively a woman's, are shared by both men and women in modern homes.
- *Domestic* receipts for many Hollywood movies are exceeded by overseas receipts.
- Some very fine *domestic* wines are produced in California, Washington, and New York.
- Nora worked as a *domestic* in the home of a Hollywood actress.
- The cardboard box in the attic contained old sheets, towels, blankets, canning jars, and other *domestics*.

[domestically *adv.*]

dominance* (DAHM in ins) *n.* controlling or being in control; authority

- About 90% of all people show *dominance* of the right hand.
- In a pride of lions, *dominance* is usually exhibited by the largest male member of the group.

dominant (DAHM in uhnt) *adj.* exercising authority or influence; ruling; prevailing; controlling

- While it was a close call, the *dominant* political party in twentieth-century U.S. presidential politics was Republican.
- The *dominant* grape variety in the Bordeaux region of France is the cabernet sauvignon.
- The New York Yankees is the *dominant* professional baseball team of all time.

[Syn. preeminent]

donation (doh NAY shin) *n.* 1. the act of giving; 2. a gift or contribution to a charitable organization

- *Donations* of usable clothing are always helpful.
- Maribel always makes a *donation* to the Lung Association.
- *Donations* to the March of Dimes led to a vaccine for polio.

[Syn. present]

draft (DRAFT) *n.* 1. a drawing or pulling of a vehicle or load; 2. a taking of liquid into the mouth; drinking; 3. a rough or preliminary sketch of an artwork or a piece of writing; 4. an air current in a room; 5. the choosing of an individual for some specific purpose —*vt.* to do any of the above —*adj.* used for any of the above

- Clydesdale horses are used for *draft,* not for riding.
- Nora took a *draft* from her glass of root beer.
- Shakespeare wrote *drafts* of all his plays, over and over.
- Do you feel a *draft* in here?
- George answered his party's *draft* to run for office.

  [-ed, -ing; draught, British spelling]

drub (DRUHB) *vt.* 1. to beat, as with a stick or club; thrash; 2. to defeat soundly in a fight, contest, etc.

- The tried-and-true way of cleaning a rug in the nineteenth century was to hang it over a rope and *drub* it with all your might.
- The Mets were given an eight-to-one *drubbing* by the Braves.

  [-bed, -bing] [Syn. thrash]

duplicity (doo PLIS i tee) *n.* double-dealing; hypocritical cunning or deception

- The Greek army was able to take Troy by the *duplicity* of hiding soldiers in the statue of a horse.
- Most dictators stay in power through *duplicity,* making their people believe they're doing other than they are.

  [duplicitous *adj.,* duplicitously *adv.*]

dwelling (DWEL ing) *n.* residence; house; abode

- Some Native Americans lived in cliff *dwellings*.
- Many southwestern *dwellings* are made of adobe—a kind of clay readily available there.

QUICK REVIEW #30

Match the word from column 2 with the word from column 1 that means most nearly the same thing.

1. divisive		a. beat
2. divulge		b. drink
3. domestic		c. abode
4. dominance		d. deception
5. dominant		e. homegrown
6. donation		f. gift
7. draft		g. separating
8. drub		h. authority
9. duplicity		i. controlling
10. dwelling		j. reveal

E

eccentric* (ek SEN trik) *adj.* 1. not having the same center; 2. not exactly circular in shape or motion; 3. deviating from the norm, as in behavior; odd; unconventional

- If one circle is drawn inside another and they are not concentric, they must be *eccentric*.
- A football is of an *eccentric* shape.
- Unless one who dresses in a red wig with matching suspenders and over-sized shoes is a clown, he or she would have to be called more than a bit *eccentric*.

eclectic (ek LEK tik) *adj.* 1. taken from various sources, systems, or doctrines; 2. made up of materials gathered from many different sources, systems, etc.

- A good historian gathers his or her information from *eclectic* sources rather than just one.
- *Eclectic* is the only way to describe the earliest computers, which were made from vacuum tubes and a variety of condensers and resistors.

ecological* (ek uh LAH ji kl) *adj.* having to do with the relations between living things and their environment or a certain organism and its environment

- The plants and animals that live in and around a pond have their own intertwined *ecological* subsystem.
- Urban sprawl's *ecological* impact can be clearly seen in the presence of deer and bears on suburban roadways.

economic (ek uh NAH mik) *adj.* 1. dealing with the management of income, expenditures, etc. of a household, business, community, or government; 2. concerning the production, distribution, and consumption of wealth; 3. concerned with the material needs of people; —*pl.* the social science that is concerned with the preceding

- The *economic* well-being of his or her household is a major concern to the head of any family.
- The indices of *economic* indicators give a reading of how well the country's economy is doing.
- People's main *economic* needs are as much as it takes for them to live comfortably.
- *Economics* is the social science devoted to the study of supply and demand.

  [-ally *adv.*]

ecstatic (ek STA tik) *adj.* 1. having the nature of being overpowered by joy, happiness, or rapture; 2. causing or caused by ecstasy

- Morissa was absolutely *ecstatic* over the raise in salary that she had received.
- It was an *ecstatic* day for the world champions.

  [-ally *adv.*]

effect (uh FEKT) *n.* 1. something resulting from a cause; a result; 2. the ability to bring about results; 3. an influence or action on something —*vt.* to bring about; to produce as a result; to cause; to accomplish

- When someone tickles you, the *effect* is that you laugh.
- Drinking too much can have the *effect* of making you light-headed.
- The Kid has the talent and quickness to *effect* a knockout in three rounds.

  [-ed, -ing] [Syn. consequence, outcome; Ant. cause]

effective* (uh FEK tiv) *adj.* 1. creating a result; 2. creating a definite or desired result; efficient; 3. in effect; operative; active; 4. actual, rather than potential or theoretical; 5. equipped and ready for combat

- Winston Churchill was a very *effective* speaker.
- Certain bug sprays are more *effective* than others.
- The order to report is *effective* within 24 hours.
- We will have an *effective* solution within the week.
- The marines will have an *effective* force on the ground by the first of next month.

  [-ly *adv.*]

efficacious* (EF I KAY shis) *adj.* capable of creating the desired result; actually creating that result; effective

- Aspirin is an *efficacious* medication with many uses.

  [-ly *adv.*] [Syn. effective]

efficient (ef FISH int) *adj.* using a minimum of effort, expense, or waste to cause a desired result with

- A diesel engine is much more *efficient* than a steam engine, even though diesel fuel is not clean burning.
- When your desk is organized in an *efficient* manner, those things you use most often are the most accessible.

egregious (e GREE juhs) *adj.* terrible; filled with undesirable qualities; amazingly bad; flagrant

- When the American people elected [you fill in the name], they made an *egregious* error.
- The dinner served on our flight from St. Louis was absolutely *egregious*.

  [-ly *adv.*]

elated* (ee LAY tid) *adj.* very happy; joyful; filled with elation; high spirited

- Terry was *elated* when he saw that his family had come to watch him play baseball.
- Ian was *elated* at the sight of his grandma's chocolate cream pies.

  [-ly *adv.*]

element (EL i mint) *n.* 1. the most basic (as-small-as-it-gets) part or principle of anything, whether concrete or abstract; 2. a component; a constituent; an ingredient; a factor; a building block

- There are 106 known chemical *elements,* of which 96 occur in nature.
- Your argument seems to contain an *element* of truth.
- *Elements* of the Eighth Army neared Baghdad.

elicit (el IS it) *vt.* 1. to draw out; evoke; 2. to cause to be revealed

- Perry's quiet manner was meant to *elicit* a confession.
- She hoped to *elicit* a hint as to what her present might be.
- The pitch was made to *elicit* enough sympathy to get a monetary contribution.
    [-ed, -ing, -able *adj.*, -ation *n.*]

elite (e LEET) *n.* 1. those selected or regarded as the finest, best, most distinguished, etc.; 2. a size of type for typewriters (remember them?) measuring 12 characters per inch —*adj.* of, forming, or suitable for elites

- The SEALS are the *elite* of the U.S. Navy.
- The *elite* of the feline family is the Siberian tiger.
- My old IBM Selectric II used courier (10 characters per inch) and *elite* (12 characters per inch) interchangable type balls.
- The British Commandos are an *elite* group.

QUICK REVIEW #31

Match the word from column 2 with the word from column 1 that means most nearly the same thing.

1. eccentric	a. extract
2. eclectic	b. best
3. ecological	c. joyful
4. economic	d. finest
5. ecstatic	e. horrible
6. effect	f. component
7. effective	g. interrelated
8. efficacious	h. actual
9. efficient	i. rapturous
10. egregious	j. working
11. elated	k. outcome
12. element	l. of money
13. elicit	m. hodgepodge
14. elite	n. unconventional

elocution (EL i KYOO shin) *n.* 1. vocalizing words distinctly when speaking in public; 2. the art of public speaking or declaiming (now usually associated with a studied or artificial style)

- Cicero was well known for his *elocution* in the Senate of ancient Rome.
- Proper *elocution* requires one to project from the diaphragm rather than just speaking with one's voice.
- Opera singers are often taught *elocution.*

    [-ary *adj.,* -ist *n.*]

eloquent* (EL uh kwint) *adj.* 1. having a vivid, forceful, fluent, graceful, and persuasive quality of writing or speech; 2. vividly expressive

- Mark Twain was an *eloquent* speaker as well as a humorous one.
- Rachel shrugged and sighed an *eloquent* sigh.

    [-ly *adv.*]

elude (il OOD) *vt.* 1. to use quickness, cunning, etc. to avoid being captured; evade; 2. to escape detection, notice, or understanding

- The fox does not often *elude* detection by the hounds.
- The prisoner *eluded* the guards by hiding in the laundry bin.
- I recognize her face, but her name *eludes* me.

    [-d, eluding] [Syn. escape]

embellishment* (em BEL ish mint) *n.* 1. fancying up; 2. something that adorns, as an ornament, or a bit of fancifulness added to a factual account; a fancy musical phrase

- Tree lights and icicles are often added as *embellishments.*
- A good storyteller often adds a few *embellishments,* just to make his (or someone else's) role appear more important.
- William F. Cody's (Buffalo Bill's) autobiography has often been called one big *embellishment* from start to finish.
- A rimshot on a snare drum accompanying a TV talk-show host's punch line is an *embellishment.*

embitter (em BIT ir) *vt.* 1. to anger; make resentful or morose; 2. to make more bitter; exacerbate; aggravate

- Ignore his cynicism; he's just an *embittered* old grouch.
- Pulling her hair is bound to *embitter* her even further.

    [-ed, -ing, -ment *n.*]

embrace (em BRAYS) *vt.* 1. to enfold in the arms, usually as an expression of affection or desire; to hug; 2. to accept readily; to avail oneself of; 3. to take up or adopt (especially eagerly or seriously); 4. to include; contain

- The homecoming sailor happily *embraced* his wife and child.
- Phyllis *embraced* Cathy's offer to help her with math.
- Mr. Jones eagerly *embraced* his new profession.
- The science of biology *embraces* zoology and botany.

    [-d, embracing] [Syn. include]

embroil (em BROYL) *vt.* 1. to mix things up; bungle; jumble; 2. to lure into a battle or fight; get into trouble

- His waffling on the subject served only to *embroil* matters.
- The North and South were *embroiled* in the bloody Civil War.

  [-ed, -ing, -ment *n.*]

emend (ee MEND) *vt.* 1. to make scholarly corrections or improvements to a text; 2. (rare) to correct or improve

- Loren had to *emend* the manuscript to take into account the latest information on the subject.
- After finding errors, the author *emended* the text.

  [-ed, -ing]

emergence* (ee MOER jins) *n.* 1. a becoming visible; coming forth into view; a coming out; 2. an outgrowth from beneath the outer layer of a plant

- The sudden *emergence* of the beluga whale from beneath the surface caught all the whale watchers by surprise.
- The *emergence* of the sun from below the horizon is well worth getting up early to watch.
- It took a few weeks before the *emergence* of the prickles on the rosebush.

emigrate (EM i grayt) *vt.* to leave one country to settle down in another

- During the potato famine, many people *emigrated* from Ireland and came to the United States.
- Albert Einstein *emigrated* to the United States from Germany.

  [-d, emigrating] [Syn. migrate; Ant. immigrate]

eminent (EM in int) *adj.* 1. rising above other things or places, both literally and figuratively; high; lofty; 2. projecting; prominent; protruding; 3. standing high when compared to others, as in rank or achievement; renowned; exalted; distinguished

- The Matterhorn is an *eminent* peak in the Swiss Alps.
- The office of U.S. senator is an *eminent* position.
- George Patton was a general with *eminent* achievements.

  [-ly *adv.*, eminence *n.*] [Syn. famous]

emissary (EM is ery) *n.* an agent of a government, a company, or an individual sent on a certain mission

- The Italian ambassador to the United Nations was sent as an *emissary* to the peace talks.
- Although the United States was never a member of the League of Nations, our government sent an *emissary* there to look out for American interests.

  [emissaries *pl.*]

QUICK REVIEW #32

Match the word from column 2 with the word from column 1 that means most nearly the same thing.

1. elocution	a. leave
2. eloquent	b. anger
3. elude	c. appearance
4. embellishment	d. declaiming
5. embitter	e. famous
6. embrace	f. ornamentation
7. embroil	g. include
8. emend	h. fluent
9. emergence	i. jumble
10. emigrate	j. agent
11. eminent	k. edit
12. emissary	l. evade

emollient (i MAHL yint) *n.* something with a softening or soothing effect, especially a medicinal lotion applied to the skin of the body

- After a day outside, an *emollient* is helpful in combating the drying effect of the wind.
- Women are more likely to use an *emollient* than men because the former care more about maintaining their appearance.

emotional (i MOH shin uhl) *adj.* 1. of dealing with strong feelings; 2. showing feelings, especially strong ones; 3. easily or quick to weep, be angry, etc.; 4. appealing to the emotions; moving people to tears, anger, etc.

- Karen always gets very *emotional* at weddings.
- Victor's return from overseas was an *emotional* time for his whole family.
- Films that cause *emotional* reactions with lots of tears and "awws!" are often classified as "chick flicks."

    [-ly *adv.*]

emphasize (EM fuh SYZ) *vt.* to give special force and importance to; to stress

- When dealing with heart disease, doctors *emphasize* that speed in getting treatment is urgent.
- Using eyeliner *emphasizes* the beauty of your eyes.

    [-d, emphasizing] [Syn. stress]

emphatic (em FA tik) *adj*. 1. expressed or done with force of expression or stress; 2. using emphasis (stressing) while speaking or expressing oneself; 3. very striking; forcible; definite

- George was *emphatic* in his dislike for broccoli.
- When scheduling the students versus teachers basketball game, Mr. Hilson was *emphatic* that it would be played come rain or shine.
- At Waterloo, Napoleon received an *emphatic* defeat.

  [-ally *adv*.]

emulate* (EM yoo LAYT) *vt*. 1. to try to equal or surpass, often by copying; 2. to imitate (a person one admires); 3. to rival in success

- Jason learned to do plumbing and wiring by attempting to *emulate* what he had seen his dad do.
- Many successful comedians *emulate* the timing of the late Jack Benny.
- Some companies have become very successful by *emulating* others.

  [-d, emulating]

encompass* (en KAHM pis) *vt*. 1. to close in all around; surround; encircle; 2. to contain; include; 3. to bring about; achieve

- The Galley restaurant was completely *encompassed* by the boat basin.
- The resident pass program *encompasses* our efforts to deal with the parking problem around the college.
- The new athletic complex, when completed, will *encompass* the complete revitalization of the neighborhood.

  [-ed, -ing]

encourage (in KOER ij) *vt*. 1. to give braveness, hope, or confidence; to embolden; hearten; 2. to give support to; to be favorable to; to foster; to help

- When Ian first put on ice skates, everyone tried to *encourage* him—not an easy task because he spent as much time on his belly as on his feet.
- All voters should *encourage* their senators and representatives to support legislation to improve the environment.

  [-d, encouraging, -ment *n*.]

endorse (in DAWRS) *vt*. 1. to sign one's name on the back of a check; 2. to write a note, title, etc. on a document; 3. to give approval to; support; sanction

- One must *endorse* a check before it can be cashed.
- Jack's teacher *endorsed* his essay with remarks in red ink.
- It is with great pleasure that I *endorse* that great American icon, Mickey Mouse, for president of the United States.

  [-d, endorsing, -ment *n*.] [Syn. approve]

endure (in DUR *or* ind YUR) *vt.* 1. to hold up under (pain, fatigue, etc.); to stand; bear; undergo; 2. to put up with; tolerate —*vi.* 1. to continue in existence; last; survive; 2. to bear pain, fatigue, etc. without flinching; hold out

- It is reputedly well documented that women can *endure* pain better than men.
- Jane *endured* the cat hair on the rug for as long as she could, before she bought the boa constrictor.
- The United States has *endured* for more than 200 years.
- He's holding a 25-pound weight in his left hand; let's see how long he can *endure*.

  [-d, enduring, endurance *n.*] [Syn. bear, continue]

energy (EN oer JEE) *n.* 1. potential force; inherent power; capacity for vigorous action; 2. such forces in action; 3. strength or power efficiently exerted; 4. various resources such as coal, gas, or petroleum from which heat or electrical energy can be produced; 5. (physics) the capacity to do work

- Myles's mom hoped that he'd use up all his *energy* in the playground so that he'd be ready for a nap.
- Running around and around in circles uses a lot of *energy*.
- It took a good deal of *energy* to knock home railroad spikes with a sledgehammer.
- Electrical *energy* is most efficiently produced by converting the *energy* contained in sunlight.
- In physics, work is the amount of *energy* used multiplied by the distance an object is moved and is measured in foot-pounds.

  [Syn. strength]

enervate* (EN oer VAYT) *vt.* to sap of strength, life, vigor, etc.; to weaken in some way, physically or otherwise; to devitalize; to —*adj.* weakened

- A long commute to work each morning is enough to *enervate* some people.
- Many were *enervated* by the sight of the fall of the World Trade Center before being angered to strike back.
- A home team's losing streak can be an *enervating* thing.

  [-d, enervating, enervation *n.*] [Syn. unnerve, weaken]

enhance (in HAENS) *vt.* 1. to make greater (in cost, value, beauty, etc.); heighten; augment; 2. to improve the quality or condition of; 3. to electronically improve the clarity of an image, photo, etc. by means of a computer

- Planting shade trees often *enhances* the value of a home.
- A trip to the salon *enhanced* Audrey's appearance.
- Digital photos can often readily be *enhanced* by the machines at your photo processor's counter.

  [-d, enhancing, -ment *n.*] [Syn. intensify]

QUICK REVIEW #33

Match the word from column 2 with the word from column 1 that means most nearly the same thing.

1. emollient	a. approve
2. emotional	b. improve
3. emphasize	c. softener
4. emphatic	d. imitate
5. emulate	e. strength
6. encompass	f. moving
7. encourage	g. encircle
8. endorse	h. devitalize
9. endure	i. stress
10. energy	j. foster
11. enervate	k. continue
12. enhance	l. forcible

enigmatic* (EN ig MAT ik) *adj.* of or like a puzzle; perplexing; baffling

- Don's expression was *enigmatic;* we could not even imagine what he was thinking.
- How the giant snowball appeared on the baseball field in the middle of June was *enigmatic.*

[-ally* *adv.*] [Syn. obscure]

enjoy (en JOY) *vt.* 1. to experience pleasure; get pleasure from; relish; 2. to have the benefit or advantage of

- Margo *enjoys* listening to a Beethoven symphony.
- Steven *enjoyed* his song's receiving a large measure of radio and TV airtime.

[-ed, -ing]

enlighten (en LY tin) *vt.* 1. to free from ignorance, prejudice, or superstition; 2. to inform; make clear to; educate

- Years of experience with the electorate had served to *enlighten* the senator about the folly of favoring one group over another.
- Please *enlighten* me as to the time you got home last night.

[-ed, -ing] [Syn. inform]

enmity (EN mi tee) *n.* the bitter anger or feeling of an enemy, or of mutual enemies toward one another; hostility; antagonism

- The Romans and the Scots had great *enmity* toward one another.
- Considerable *enmity* characterized rival gangs of Chicago during Prohibition.

[Syn. hostility, animosity, antagonism]

ensemble (on SOM bil) *n.* 1. all parts taken together; the total effect; 2. a complete costume, especially one having matching articles of clothing, like a suit; 3. a group of actors, dancers, etc., who perform together; 4. a musical group

- The success of the debating team does not rest on the shoulders of one member but falls on the *ensemble*.
- With two pairs of pants, two blouses, and two jackets, you can make eight different *ensembles*.
- This is a theatrical *ensemble*, with no single star.
- The string quartet was a very talented *ensemble*.

epidemiology (EP i DEEM ee OL uh jee) *n.* 1. the branch of medicine that investigates the causes and control of epidemics; 2. all of the elements that combine to cause or prevent a disease in a population; ecology of a disease

- The *epidemiology* of the outbreak of the Ebola virus in Africa has been studied very carefully.
- The *epidemiology* of West Nile virus and its outbreak in the eastern United States is under close scrutiny.

  [epidemiological *adj.*, epidemiologist *n.*]

epilogue (EP i LOG) *n.* 1. a closing section added to a novel, play, etc. providing extra comment, interpretation, or information; 2. a short speech or poem read by an actor to the audience at the end of a play

- An *epilogue* is to the end of a story what a prologue is to the beginning.
- After his opera *Don Giovanni* ended with the lead character's going to hell, Mozart felt obliged to add an *epilogue* that said the Don's departure left the world a happier place.
- Douglas MacArthur's "Old Soldiers Never Die" speech to Congress may be looked upon as the *epilogue* to his career.

epitaph (EP it AF) *n.* 1. words written on a tomb or gravestone in memory of the person buried there; 2. a short piece in prose or verse, written as a tribute to a dead person, past event, etc.

- W. C. Fields proposed the following *epitaph* for himself: "Here lies W. C. Fields. I would rather be living in Philadelphia." (It is not on his tombstone.)
- When World War II ended, its *epitaph* was splashed across newspaper front pages in every city.

epitomize* (i PIT uh MYZ) *vt.* 1. to summarize the main points of a book, report, incident, etc.; 2. showing all the particular qualities of something

- A good book report should critique as well as *epitomize* the story of the book.
- Actor Michael Douglas *epitomizes* most of the qualities of his father, Kirk.

  [-d, epitomizing] [Syn. summarize]

eradicate (ir AD ik AYT) *vt.* 1. to tear out by the roots; uproot; 2. get rid of; wipe out; destroy

- Marge tried to *eradicate* the dandelions in her lawn.
- It was not so easy to *eradicate* the nest of hornets that took up lodgings on the front porch.

  [-d, eradicating, eradication *n.*] [Syn. exterminate]

erratic (ir AT ik) *adj.* 1. without fixed course or purpose; irregular; random; meandering; 2. deviating from the usual course; eccentric; odd

- A moth's *erratic* flight is one adaptation to its survival.
- Billionaire Howard Hughes's reclusive behavior during his final years can easily be called *erratic*.

  [-ly *adv.*]

erroneous (ir OH nee uhs) *adj.* based on or containing error; mistaken; wrong

- The report of your beheading was apparently *erroneous*.
- *Erroneous* information is commonly on the front page of supermarket tabloids.

  [-ly *adv.*]

QUICK REVIEW #34

Match the word from column 2 with the word from column 1 that means most nearly the same thing.

1. enigmatic	a. exterminate
2. enjoy	b. tribute
3. enlighten	c. hostility
4. enmity	d. summarize
5. ensemble	e. wrong
6. epidemiology	f. afterthought
7. epilogue	g. inform
8. epitaph	h. eccentric
9. epitomize	i. medicine
10. eradicate	j. relish
11. erratic	k. whole
12. erroneous	l. obscure

especially (es PESH uh lee) *adj.* particularly; mainly; to a great degree; unusually

- Chinese is an *especially* difficult language for Occidentals to master.
- This sentence is for Bill, Bob, and Marcia, and *especially* for Suzanne.
- *Especially* is not an *especially* unusual word; you probably hear it every day—*especially* from TV news programs.

espouse (es POWZ) *vt.* 1. to take as a spouse; marry; 2. to take up, support, or advocate some cause, idea, etc.

- Diana and Charles were *espoused*.
- Dick and Jane will *espouse* at 1:30 P.M.
- Consumer advisors *espouse* shopping for a car and for financing separately.
- Teddy Roosevelt often *espoused* speaking softly and carrying a big stick.

  [-d, espousing] [Syn. advocate]

essence (ES ins) *n*. 1. something existing; entity; 2. vital characteristic; intrinsic, fundamental nature; most important quality; 3. a substance that keeps (in concentrated form) the flavor, fragrance, or other properties of the plant, food, etc. from which it is extracted

- International law is something that exists in *essence*, although it is not codified.
- Humor is the *essence* of satire and of satirical pieces.
- Oddly, a certain nastiness is the *essence* of satirists.
- Vanilla extract contains all the *essence* of a vanilla bean's flavor but none of the grittiness of the seeds.

essential (is EN shil) *adj*. 1. of the intrinsic nature of something; basic; inherent; 2. necessary; requisite; indispensible

- A happy wagging tail is *essential* to a golden retriever.
- It is *essential* to bring your driver's license when you go to cash a check.

  [-ly *adv*.] [Syn. vital, important, crucial]

establish (es TAB lish) *vt*. 1. to make stable; to make firm; 2. to permanently order, ordain, or enact (for example, a law); 3. to set up (a government, business, organization, etc.); found; institute; 4. to cause to happen or to be; bring about

- The sheriffs *established* law and order in the Old West.
- Congress *establishes* the laws by which we live.
- Johnny *established* his law office in New York City.
- Rose and Dorothy *established* a lifelong friendship.

  [-ed, -ing, -ment *n*.] [Syn. launch, create]

esteem (es TEEM) *vt*. 1. to have great regard for; to value highly; 2. to hold to be; —*n*. favorable opinion; high regard; respect

- Val *esteemed* Bert's help in selecting colleges to apply to.
- I *esteem* your aid in installing the storm door correctly to have been invaluable.
- Do you hold your dog's opinion of people in high *esteem*?

  [-ed, -ing] [Syn. appreciate, admire]

ethical (ETH ik l) *adj*. 1. concerned with ethics or morality; of or conforming to moral standards; 2. conforming to the standards of a particular profession or group

- The Geneva Conventions deal with the *ethical* treatment of prisoners of war.
- Many consider the testing of cosmetics on animals to be less than *ethical*.
- The legal profession's *ethical* code calls for not divulging any communication between client and attorney.

  [-ly *adv*.] [Syn. principled]

ethicist (ETH is IST) *n*. someone devoted to ethical ideas; one very well versed in moral issues and considerations

- An *ethicist* was consulted to help the hospital form a policy on treatment of those without medical insurance.
- *Ethicists* are often consulted about genetic engineering projects.

  [ethnician *n*.] [Syn. moralist]

ethnicity* (eth NIS i tee) *n.* classification of a cultural subgroup with a common cultural heritage or nationality

- Being of Ethiopian descent is an *ethnicity.*
- Having a Lithuanian heritage is an *ethnicity.*
- Speaking Spanish or English is a commonality of language but is not an *ethnicity.*

evaluate (ee VAL yoo AYT) *vt.* 1. to find the value or amount of; 2. to judge the worth or quality of something; appraise; 3. (math) to find the numerical value of

- The appraiser *evaluated* Kim's oil painting as being worth between $1,500 and $2,000.
- Jorge *evaluated* the parcel of land as being too small for raising cattle.
- By solving the equation, Millie *evaluated* x to be 45.

  [-d, evaluating, evaluation *n.*] [Syn. estimate]

evanescent (EV in ES int) *adj.* tending to be transitory; having the tendency to pass or fade from sight; ephemeral

- The *evanescent* mist soon began to dissipate from the heat of the sun.
- The *evanescent* smoke from the cannon's muzzle vanished within minutes.

  [-ly *adv.*] [Syn. transient]

eventually (ee VENT yoo i lee) *adv.* finally; in the end; ultimately

- All things, good or bad, *eventually* come to an end.
- A trip around the world will *eventually* bring you back to your starting point.

  [eventual *adj.*]

QUICK REVIEW #35

Match the word from column 2 with the word from column 1 that means most nearly the same thing.

1. especially	a. requisite
2. espouse	b. moral
3. essence	c. transient
4. essential	d. heritage
5. establish	e. unusually
6. esteem	f. ultimately
7. ethical	g. estimate
8. ethicist	h. advocate
9. ethnicity	i. found
10. evaluate	j. moralist
11. evanescent	k. entity
12. eventually	l. appreciate

evidence (EV id ins) *n.* 1. something that makes another thing easy to see; a sign; an indication; 2. something that proves (something else); grounds to believe that something is so

- Juan's momentary blurriness of vision was *evidence* of the eye problems that were to come.
- Carrie's eyewitness testimony was the *evidence* that made Eddie's conviction almost certain.
- Karl's fingerprints on the machete were powerful *evidence* of his coconut poaching.

[Syn. proof]

evident (EV id int) *adj.* easily seen; clear; obvious; plain

- It is *evident* that you have no knowledge of how to raise mangoes.
- That the window had not been cleaned in a long time was *evident* from a single glance at it.

[-ly *adv.*] [Syn. manifest]

evitable (EV it uh bl) *adj.* avoidable (Think about it; *inevitable* means unavoidable.)

- The automobile accident was definitely *evitable*.
- Getting your foot stepped upon by an elephant is a very *evitable* event.

exacerbate (eg ZAS ir bayt) *vt.* 1. to increase in intensity; to sharpen; aggravate; 2. to irritate or annoy; exaggerate

- Tweaking her only *exacerbates* her embarrassment.
- Putting weight on your twisted ankle will *exacerbate* your discomfort.
- Showing a hungry person pictures of food serves only to *exacerbate* his hunger.

[-d, exacerbating]

exasperation (eg ZAS pir ay shun) *n.* great irritation or annoyance; vexation

- Flora's inability to hit the high notes in the song led to her eventual feeling of *exasperation*.
- *Exasperation* usually comes from considerable effort met with little or no success.

exception (ek SEP shin) *n.* 1. an omission; a leaving out; 2. a situation or case in which a rule, order, etc. is not applicable; 3. an objection or disagreement

- Everyone, without *exception,* is responsible for washing his or her own dishes.
- The No Parking signs are applicable to almost every vehicle, but a police car is an *exception*.
- The senator took *exception* to the ruling of the chairman and raised a point of order.

excessive (eks ES iv) *adj.* too much; too great; inappropriately large

- In subduing the perpetrator, many felt that the police had used *excessive* force.
- *Excessive* anything is always too much.
- Americans are generally overweight because we consume *excessive* quantities of food.

[excessively *adv.*] [Syn. inordinate, extravagant]

exclude (eks KLOOD) *vt.* 1. to keep out; shut out; refuse to admit; bar; 2. to expel; to put out

- The doorman at the entrance to the club is there to *exclude* all but members and their honored guests.
- The bride-to-be was *excluded* from the group planning her bridal shower.
- Victor *excluded* Emanuel by giving him the boot.

[-d, excluding] [Syn. eliminate]

exclusive (eks KLOO siv) *adv.* 1. eliminating all others; shutting out everyone else; 2. keeping out all but those indicated or specified; 3. not shared; sole right to; 4. snobbish

- One's spouse shoud be one's *exclusive* soul mate.
- The golf course is for the *exclusive* use of its members.
- Sandy Hook's beach is for the *exclusive* use of people named Sandy.
- The country club's *exclusive* membership committee refuses to accept an application from anyone whose net worth is less than $10,000,000.

[-ly *adv.*, -ness *n.*]

exculpate (EKS kul payt) *vt.* 1. to prove to be without blame or guilt; 2. to declare to be guiltless

- Verifying Laura's alibi served to *exculpate* her from the potential charges.
- The DNA results had absolutely nothing to do with *exculpating* the dog in the case of the disappearing sandwich.

[-d, exculpating, exculpatory *adj.*] [Syn. absolve]

excursion (eks KUR zhin) *n.* 1. a short trip with intent to return relatively soon to the point of origin; a pleasure jaunt; 2. a round trip on a train, plane, etc., usually with certain provisions, sold at bargain rates; 3. a group taking such a trip; 4. a digression from the main point, journey, etc.

- The Circle Line specializes in waterborne *excursions* around the island of Manhattan.
- A Saturday night stay-over and traveling on Tuesday or Thursday are usual conditions of special rates for airline *excursions*.
- An *excursion* to the Pyramids was part of the Egyptian group package.
- A two-day *excursion* to Paris was a part of our London trip.

exemplary (eg ZEM plir ee) *adj.* 1. (*from example*) a model; worthy of imitation; 2. serving as a warning; 3. acting as a sample, illustration, etc.

- Roxane's behavior at the restaurant was *exemplary*.
- The judge's severe punishment was an *exemplary* one and served as a notice to potential wrongdoers.
- Charlie brought an *exemplary* brownie so that the custom baker would know what he wanted made.

[exemplarily *adv.*, exemplariness *n.*]

QUICK REVIEW #36

Match the word from column 2 with the word from column 1 that means most nearly the same thing.

1. evidence	a. omission
2. evident	b. model
3. evitable	c. snobbish
4. exacerbate	d. absolve
5. exasperation	e. avoidable
6. exception	f. eliminate
7. excessive	g. jaunt
8. exclude	h. proof
9. exclusive	i. inordinate
10. exculpate	j. manifest
11. excursion	k. vexation
12. exemplary	l. aggravate

exemplify (eg ZEM pli FY) *vt.* 1. to serve as an example; 2. to show by example

- Gloria's behavior at the solemn memorial service *exemplifies* the proper way to behave at such an event.
- Peter's essay should *exemplify* what Mrs. Jones is looking for in a book report.

[exemplified, -ing]

exhibit (eg ZIB it) *vt.* 1. to show or display; 2. to open to public view; 3. to give evidence of

- Rhea *exhibited* her school artwork for her parents to admire.
- The Guggenheim collection is *exhibited* daily in a museum designed by Frank Lloyd Wright.
- Lawrence is *exhibiting* a good deal of irritation with the automobile cleaning service.

[-ed, -ing] [Syn. prove, reveal]

existence (eg ZIST ins) *n.* 1. state of being; act of living; 2. taking place; occurrence; 3. manner of living

- According to DesCartes, one's *existence* is proven by the fact that one thinks—at least I think it is.
- The *existence* of a circus at Madison Square Garden is made evident by the odors that meet the noses of passersby.
- Homeless persons live a rather wretched *existence*.

exorbitant (eg ZAWR bit int) *adj.* above and beyond what is reasonable; immodest; excessive; extravagant

- Would you say that William Randolph Hearst lived a rather *exorbitant* lifestyle at San Simeon?
- Some (myself included) consider $8 movie theater tickets to be *exorbitant*.

expect (eks PEKT) *vt.* 1. to look for or look forward to as likely to happen or appear; 2. to look for as if it were due; 3. to suppose

- Gizmo, the dog, sits by the front door each evening at 6:00 *expecting* his master at any moment.
- After retrieving the customer's car, the valet held out his hand as if a gratuity was *expected*.
- Diane *expects* to have a late supper after the theater.

  [-ed, -ing] [Syn. anticipate, presume]

expedite (EKS pid YT) *vt.* 1. to speed up, hasten, or facilitate something's happening; 2. to do quickly

- Preheating the oven will *expedite* dinner after mom brings the frozen pizza home.
- Paying for overnight delivery will *expedite* your receiving the new software package.

  [-d, expediting]

experience (eks PIR ee ens) *n.* 1. having had personal involvement in events as they occurred; 2. anything lived through or observed; 3. all that has occurred in one's life to that point in time being considered; 4. the effect of everything that has happened to a person or that the person has observed —*vt.* to personally encounter; to undergo

- After her third child, Melissa had ambivalent feelings surrounding the *experience* of childbirth.
- About 20 million people *experienced* the Northeast electrical blackout of 1977.
- Karen's total *experience* through the first 53 years of her life made her an optimistic person.
- David's urban life *experiences* gave him a cynical outlook.
- Try to *experience* as many new things as possible.

  [-d, experiencing]

experiment (eks PER im int) *n.* 1. a test to find something not yet known or to confirm or demonstrate something; 2. the performing of such tests —*vi.* to do experiments

- It took many *experiments* to find a vaccine for polio.
- Daphne's *experiments* with different versions of an uppercase *D* took place over several months before she settled on a signature that she was pleased with.
- Jake's mom *experimented* with many combinations of peanut butter and jelly before finding one he liked.

  [-al *adj.*, -ally *adv.*] [Syn. trial]

expertise (EKS poer TEEZ) *n.* the knowledge and capability of one who is highly skilled and trained in some particular field

- Jason demonstrated considerable *expertise* in building the deck in back of his house.
- Uncle Bob's botched repair job on the porch door attested to his complete lack of *expertise*.

explicit (eks PLIS it) *adj.* 1. distinctly and clearly stated; 2. plain and easily understandable or observable

- Helene left *explicit* instructions on how the cat and houseplants were to be cared for during her absence.
- The store's return policy is *explicit* about no refunds and is clearly posted behind the counter in plain view.

    [-ly* *adv.*] [Syn. distinct; Ant. vague, ambiguous]

exploitation* (EKS ploy TAY shin) *n.* 1. a using of something or someone in an unethical manner for one's own benefit or profit; 2. a use of the labor of others for profit without appropriate compensation

- Sweatshops in the garment industry are largely *exploitation* of undocumented workers.
- The United Farmworkers union was built to stop the *exploitation* of Mexican and other migratory workers by large corporate farmers.

express (eks PRES) *vt.* 1. to squeeze out; 2. to put into words; state; 3. to reveal; to show; 4. to represent in artistic or musical form —*adj.* 1. explicit as opposed to implied; 2. made for a special purpose; 3. high speed

- *Express* a cut lemon to get juice from it.
- Norma has difficulty *expressing* herself in writing.
- Don chose tonight to *express* his love of key lime pie.
- Beethoven *expresses* great joy in his ninth symphony.
- Steven gave Leonard *express* permission to use his tools.
- *Express* regulations govern the registration of handguns.
- The *express* train skips many of the local stops.

    [-ed, -ing, -ly *adv.*] [Syn. convey, utter]

QUICK REVIEW #37

Match the word from column 2 with the word from column 1 that means most nearly the same thing.

1. exemplify	a. excessive
2. exhibit	b. utter
3. existence	c. distinct
4. exorbitant	d. skillfulness
5. expect	e. trial
6. expedite	f. unethical use of
7. experience	g. typify
8. experiment	h. hasten
9. expertise	i. anticipate
10. explicit	j. show
11. exploitation	k. undergo
12. express	l. occurrence

expression (eks PRE shuhn) *n.* 1. a pressing out, like making juice; 2. putting something into words; 3. a representation in art, in music, etc.; 4. a manner of speaking; intonation; 5. an idiomatic phrase; 6. a facial contortion or showing of emotion

- *Expression* of grape juice from grapes is now accomplished by giant machines rather than peasant feet.
- Evan wrote an *expression* of his thanks for the gift.
- Picasso's *Guernica* was an *expression* of the horrors brought on by the Spanish Civil War.
- An *expression* of discomfort was evident from the hesitating mannerisms characterizing Jill's voice.
- "Another day, another dollar" is just an *expression*.
- Evelyn's *expression* went from none to a big smile.

extent* (eks TENT) *adj.* 1. length; width; distance covered; 2. the scope or limits of anything; 3. a vast area

- The *extent* of the cat's run was about the length of a football field.
- The *extent* of the pathologist's range of interest extends beyond microbes into the realm of human behavior.
- The Sahara Desert is of considerable *extent*.

extenuate* (eks TEN yoo AYT) *vt.* to lessen or seem to lessen in seriousness by excuses

- Elliot believed that his having felt threatened by the rabbit should *extenuate* his guilt at having slammed the door on it.
- Caroline believed that Jack would be less upset about her lateness after he had heard the *extenuating* circumstances.

[-d, extenuating* *vt., adj.,* extenuation *n.*]

extinct* (eks TEENKT) *adj.* 1. dead; no longer active; 2. no longer in existence

- Many volcanoes, although they have not erupted in generations, are considered dormant rather than *extinct*.
- The *Tyrannosaurus rex* is definitely *extinct*.
- The saber-toothed tiger is an *extinct* feline ancestor.

  [Syn. vanished]

extol* (eks TOHL) *vt.* to sing the praises of; laud

- Laurie could not help but *extol* the flavor of her mother's fudge brownies.
- Jonathan's jumping into the lake and rescuing the toddler was *extolled* on all the evening news shows.

  [-led, -ling] [Syn. praise]

extravagant (eks TRAV i gint) *adj.* 1. excessive; beyond reasonable boundaries; 2. too fancy; 3. too expensive

- Ali's 15-karat diamond earrings could certainly be called *extravagant*.
- Most of those present at Thursday's PTA meeting felt it was *extravagant* of Principal Smith to have worn a tuxedo.
- It was very *extravagant* of the Department of Defense to have spent $300 on a hammer.

  [-ly *adv.*] [Syn. profligate, profuse]

extricate (EKS trik AYT) *vt.* to set free; to release; to disentangle

- The boat's skipper fought hard to *extricate* it from the path of the oncoming storm.
- The activist *extricated* the beaver from the trap.
- The dolphin wriggled in its struggle to *extricate* itself from the commercial fishing net.

  [-d, extricating, extrication *n.*, extricable *adj.*]

QUICK REVIEW #38

Match the word from column 2 with the word from column 1 that means most nearly the same thing.

1. expression	a. dead
2. extent	b. disentangle
3. extenuate	c. representation
4. extinct	d. praise
5. extol	e. scope
6. extravagant	f. lessen
7. extricate	g. excessive

F

fabrication (FAB ri KAY shuhn) *n.* 1. something being constructed or manufactured; 2. a made-up thing, especially a falsehood; false excuse; lie

- The *fabrication* was completed on-site and would serve as office space for the workers.
- The new cabinets were the *fabrication* of a fine craftsman.
- Archie's story about having been asked out by Veronica was a *fabrication*.

factor (FAK tir) *n.* 1. any of the conditions, circumstances, etc. that bring on a certain result; 2. (math) any of two or more quantities that are multiplied together to form a product —*vt.* (math) to resolve an expression into its component factors

- Weather is one *factor* that might cause the postponement of tomorrow's picnic.
- Multiplying the *factors* 2 and 6 always produces 12.
- When dealing with a trinomial of the form $ax^2 + bx + c$, it always pays to try to *factor* out an *a*.

  [-ed, -ing] [Syn. element, agent]

fallacious* (fuh LAY shus) *adj.* 1. containing an error; mistaken; 2. misleading or deceptive

- Your logic in this matter is *fallacious*.
- It is *fallacious* to think that putting insect-repelling candles by the edge of a marsh will prevent mosquito bites.

  [-ly *adv.*]

fallible (FAL i bl) adj. 1. capable of making a mistake; 2. apt to be erroneous or less than accurate

- One person is too *fallible* to be trusted to make all the important decisions.
- A pencil-and-paper calculation of a difficult problem is likely to be more *fallible* than one made using a calculator or computer.

  [fallibly *adv.*, fallibility *n.*]

falsification* (FAWL si fi KAY shun) *n.* 1. a deliberately misleading account; misrepresentation; 2. a fraudulently altered record; something proven untrue

- A *falsification* of the account of the Battle of the Little Bighorn had Custer's forces winning the day.
- Some people are mistakenly spending time in prison for crimes they did not commit, because of *falsifications* on the part of certain witnesses.

  [falsity *n.*, falsify *vi.*]

fathom (FA thim) *vt.* 1. to measure the depth (of water); 2. to understand completely; comprehend —*n.* a unit of length equal to 6 feet, primarily used to measure water depth

- Keep *fathoming* the water beneath our keel.
- You must make sure that you completely *fathom* the directions before you proceed.
- The *fathom* was originally the measure from middle fingertip to middle fingertip of a man with his arms spread wide.

    [-ed, -ing]

feasible* (FEE zi bl) *adj.* 1. doable; practicable; 2. reasonable; suitable

- It is not always *feasible* to change one's automobile oil at the specified intervals.
- We'll need a study to decide whether putting a skating rink into West Park is *feasible*.

    [feasibly *adv.*, feasability *n.*] [Syn. possible]

felicitous (fel IS it is) *adj.* 1. appropriate; used in a way suitable to the occasion; 2. having the knack to pleasingly express

- A tuxedo is a *felicitous* outfit to wear to a formal wedding.
- Melissa is careful to be *felicitous* in all her public doings.
- Ariel writes in a *felicitous* manner.

    [-ly *adv.*]

fiction (FIK shin) *n.* 1. something made up or feigned; 2. something imagined; 3. a literary story using imaginary characters and/or events

- Rachel's proclaiming that she was having a heart attack was pure *fiction*, meant to attract attention.
- The monster that lives in your closet is no *fiction!*
- *The Legend of Sleepy Hollow* was a work of *fiction* that came from the pen of Washington Irving.

figurative (FIG yoer uh TIV) *adj.* 1. representing by likeness, picture, or figure; 2. having to do with drawing, painting, etc.; 3. not in the usual or exact sense; analagous to; metaphoric

- Some artists have *figurative* talents, while others do better with landscapes.
- When you say that he's caused you a million heartaches, we presume that you mean that in a *figurative* sense.

    [figuratively *adv.*]

financial (fy NAN shuhl) *adj.* 1. dealing with money resources, income, etc.; 2. concerning managing money, credit, etc.

- A corporation's chief *financial* officer is responsible for overseeing all income and expenditures.
- One unavoidable *financial* report that we all must deal with each year is our income tax return.

    [-ly *adv.*] [Syn. pecuniary, fiscal]

firebrand (FYR brand) *n.* 1. a piece of burning wood; 2. a person who stirs up a revolution, strife, or trouble

- Keep the *firebrands* well isolated in the fireplace so that they don't ignite flammable curtains or furniture.
- Samuel Adams was a real *firebrand,* always ready to incite the crowd.

flammable (FLA muh bl) *adj.* easily burnable; quick to catch fire; readily ignited

- Laws now restrict the *flammability* of children's pajamas.
- What is now known as *flammable* used to be "inflammable," or how readily something would go up in flame.

  [flammability *n.*]

flippancy (FLIP uhn see) *n.* 1. the quality or state of being frivolous and disrespectful; sauciness; impertinence; 2. such a remark

- Some of the most effective stand-up comedians have built a carreer on *flippancy.*
- One of the late Hennie Youngman's most famous *flippancies* was the line "Now, take my wife—please!"

  [flippancies *pl.*]

florid (FLAW rid) *adj.* 1. pink; rosy or ruddy in complexion; 2. highly showy; decorated

- After three hours in the wind, Anna's cheeks were *florid.*
- Cadenzas are *florid* passages in solo instrument parts that allow the soloist to show his or her virtuosity.
- Many homes become *florid* with holiday lights in December.

  [-ly *adv.*] [Syn. ornate]

flout (FLOWT) *vt.* 1. to show contempt or scorn for; mock; 2. to disregard openly; to defy; ignore

- Teenage boys are infamous for *flouting* their father figures' authority.
- Those Texans and Texacanos holed up in the Alamo *flouted* General Santa Ana's demands for surrender.

  [-ed, -ing]

fluent (FLOO int) *adj.* 1. flowing or smoothly moving along; 2. able to read or write smoothly and clearly in a foreign language or technical terminology

- The horse's motion was *fluent* as he unhesitatingly galloped down the home stretch.
- Quentin is *fluent* in French, but he should be because his parents were born there and speak it at home.
- To get along in today's world, you need to be *fluent* in technical terms, like WYSIWYG.

  [-ly *adv.*]

QUICK REVIEW #39

Match the word from column 2 with the word from column 1 that means most nearly the same thing.

1. fabrication		a. metaphoric
2. factor		b. burnable
3. fallacious		c. defy
4. fallibile		d. possible
5. falsification		e. pecuniary
6. fathom		f. lie
7. feasible		g. rabble-rouser
8. felicitous		h. flowing
9. fiction		i. impertinence
10. figurative		j. ornate
11. financial		k. comprehend
12. firebrand		l. imaginary
13. flammable		m. element
14. flippancy		n. erroneous
15. florid		o. error-prone
16. flout		p. misrepresentation
17. fluent		q. fortunate

focus (FOH kus) *n.* 1. the point at which waves (light, heat, sound) come together, or from which they seem to be generated; 2. an adjustmant of a lens to create a sharp image; 3. any center of attention, activity, etc. —*vt.* 1. to bring into clarity; 2. to adjust the focal length of a lens, the eye, etc. to make clear; 3. to concentrate on one thing

- The *focus* of a lens or mirror is also better known as the focal point.
- An image seen through a lens can be brought into *focus* by moving the lens, the object, or the person viewing it.
- The person who is the *focus* of all the other people's attention at a party might be the life or death of the party.
- When moving from a dark room to a well-lit room, it takes the eyes a moment or so to *focus* and adjust to the difference.
- Most adjustable cameras use a ring to *focus* the lens and make your viewfinder image sharp and clear.
- Sometimes the only way to get a job done is to *focus* on one task at a time.
  [-ed, -ing]

foolhardy (FOOL hahr dee) *adj.* rash; reckless; bold or daring in a foolish way

- Sid's rushing into the burning building to rescue the cat was both heroic and *foolhardy.*
- Sometimes *foolhardy* acts are rewarded by thankful people; most times they're rewarded by disaster.

foreboding (fawr BOH ding) *n.* a prescience or portent, especially of something bad to come

- When Nan and Suzie stepped into the haunted house, they each had a feeling of *foreboding.*
- Audrey's *foreboding* caused her to exit the tunnel, just moments before it collapsed.

forgery (FAWR joer ee) *n.* the act of imitating artworks, money, signatures, etc. with the intent to deceive

- Elmyr de Hory sold hundreds of pieces of art *forgery* to the galleries and museums of the world.
- His story was originally told in the book *Fake,* by Clifford Irving, who later wrote the *forgery* of Howard Hughes's autobiography.
- The Secret Service's main task is to stop *forgery* of U.S. currency.

  [forgeries *pl.*]

forlorn (fawr LAWRN) *adj.* 1. deserted or abandoned; 2. unhappy and lonely

- Being marooned on a desert island would tend to make one feel *forlorn.*
- Left standing at the altar, Harold heaved a *forlorn* sigh.

  [-ly *adv.,* -ness *n.*]

forsake (fawr SAYK) *vt.* 1. to give up; abandon (a habit, ideal, etc.); 2. to leave; renounce

- Having decided to *forsake* his 1971 Chevy, Gerald left it by the side of the road in Timbuktu.
- It behooves anyone who has started smoking cigarettes to *forsake* that practice forthwith.
- Janet vowed to *forsake* her life of crime and to become a doer of good deeds.

  [forsook, -n, forsaking]

fortitude (FAWR ti tood) *n.* the strength to withstand pain and misfortune calmly and patiently

- Although the fire's consumption of their home was a great loss to Malcom and his family, they withstood it with *fortitude.*
- It is not easy to display *fortitude* in the face of tragedy, but by definition, that's the only way one can do it.

  [Syn. grit, courage]

fortunate (FAWR tyoo nit) *adj.* 1. lucky; having good luck; having good fortune; 2. favorable; auspicious

- Roger was *fortunate* to have taken the plane just before the flight that crashed.
- Sarah was very *fortunate* when she picked the winning lottery numbers.
  [fortunately *adv.*]

foster (FAW stir) *vt.* 1. to carefully raise; rear; 2. to nourish; help grow or develop; promote —*adj.* being treated as a certain member of the family, although neither related nor adopted

- Mickey *fostered* the colt as if it were his own child.
- Dairy farmers *foster* a national campaign to promote milk drinking.
- Dorothy and Al are *foster* parents to three *foster* children.
  [-ed, -ing]

fracture (FRAK chir) *vt.* 1. to break or split; to crack; 2. to disrupt; to break up —*n.* 1. a break or cleft; 2. a broken-off part; fragment; 3. a broken bone

- The 2003 invasion of Iraq helped to *fracture* the Franco-American alliance.
- Alice's shriek *fractured* the near-complete silence.
- Matt *fractured* his ulna playing ice hockey.
- The doctor set Mike's *fractured* finger with a splint.
- Flint knives were made by hitting two pieces of flint together in hopes of *fracturing* a chip off one to form the blade.
  [-d, fracturing] [Syn. break]

freedom (FREE dim) *n.* 1. the state or quality of being free from the control of other persons, or certain laws or regulations; 2. a right or privilege

- The nations of the Americas value their *freedom* from their former European colonizers.
- Police cars on duty enjoy *freedom* from the parking regulations in the city.
- *Freedom* of speech and *freedom* of religion are just two of the rights Americans are supposed to enjoy.

frequency (FREE kwin see) *n.* 1. the number of times something is repeated within a certain specified time frame; number of oscillations per time period; 2. a repeated or repeating occurrence

- When something vibrates between about 30 and 16,000 times per second, its *frequency* is within the range of normal human hearing.
- Supersonic *frequencies* are above the range of human hearing, while subsonic *frequencies* are below that range.
- The *frequency* of car horn honkings in Amanda's neighborhood is about five per hour.

frugal (FROO gil) *adj.* 1. economical; thrifty; not wasteful; 2. inexpensive; not costly

- *Frugal* shoppers consider house brands when buying food.
- Cars with good gas mileage are built with the *frugal* in mind.
- *Frugal* watches tell time as well as those in gold cases.

    [-ly *adv.*, -ity *n.*] [Syn. thrifty]

frustrate (FRUH strayt) *vt.* 1. to cause to not have an effect; nullify; 2. to block; to prevent from attaining an objective

- Burglar alarms are designed to *frustrate* those who would hope to break and enter without detection.
- The large number of false alarms from automotive burglar alarms could *frustrate* the reason they were installed.
- Destroyers and antisubmarine bombers *frustrated* the U-boat captains of Germany's Kriegsmarine.

    [-d, frustrating, frustration *n.*] [Syn. thwart, baffle, foil]

function (FUHNK shin) *vi.* 1. to act in the usual or expected way; 2. to serve or be used (as) —*n.* 1. the usual action or use of something; 2. a special use or action of something; 3. one's job; 4. something that depends on and changes with something else

- Fred's bicycle *functions* just the way a bicycle should.
- The doorman *functions* as both greeter and gatekeeper.
- It is the *function* of a bottle opener to (duh!) open bottles.
- When jacking up a car for a tire change, a brick or block of wood should *function* as a cross block for its diagonally opposite tire.
- Joanne's *function* at the office is public relations.
- In graphing an algebraic *function,* or equation, the value of the dependent variable, y, changes with the value of the independent variable, x.

    [-ed, -ing] [Syn. capacity, use]

fundamental (FUHN di MENT il) *adj.* 1. basic; at the root of; essential; 2. radical; 3. chief; most important —*n.* 1. a principle, theory, etc.; 2. an essential

- The *fundamental* rights of all humans are the rights to life, liberty, and the pursuit of happiness.
- The new law makes *fundamental* changes in the tax rates.
- The *fundamental* principle of America is that all men are created equal.
- The *fundamentals* of safe operation of the tool are in the owners' manual.
- Getting a license is a *fundamental* of driving an automobile.

    [-ly *adv.*]

QUICK REVIEW #40

Match the word from column 2 with the word from column 1 that means most nearly the same thing.

1. focus	a. counterfeit
2. foolhardy	b. break
3. foreboding	c. abandon
4. forgery	d. lucky
5. forlorn	e. liberty
6. forsake	f. warning
7. fortitude	g. rapidity
8. fortunate	h. concentrate
9. foster	i. promote
10. fracture	j. abandoned
11. freedom	k. courage
12. frequency	l. reckless
13. frugal	m. principle
14. frustrate	n. thwart
15. function	o. thrifty
16. fundamental	p. use

G – H

gargantuan (gahr GAN tyoo uhn) *adj.* huge; gigantic (from Rabelais's 1552 satire, *Gargantua and Pantagruel*)

- There was a *gargantuan* traffic jam at the in-bound George Washington Bridge.

garish (GAI rish) *adj.* 1. very showy; very bright and gaudy; 2. showily dressed, written, or decorated

- The outfit she chose, with the hot pink top and the chartreuse bottom, can only be described as *garish*.
- The decorations were a *garish* blend of Peter Max, Andy Warhol, and Dollywood, with a liberal sprinkling of Sgt. Pepper's Lonely Hearts Club Band.

  [-ly *adv.*]

genealogy (JEE nee AH li jee) *n.* 1. a chart showing the ancestry of a person or family; 2. the study of family descent

- Gloria's *genealogy* was spread out on the dining room table.
- Rick could trace his *genealogy* back to late-nineteenth-century Russia, but no farther back than that.

  [geneological *adj.*, genealogically *adv.*]

generalize (JEN er il YZ) *vt.* to put into nonspecific terms; to infer from —*vi.* 1. to talk in generalities; 2. to create principles from known events; 3. to spread

- It is easy to *generalize* about the benefits of voting for one over the other, but a lot harder to get down to specifics.
- Most politicians find it easier to *generalize* than to take a fast stand for which they might later be called to task.
- Newton *generalized* from the things he observed every day to ultimately develop his laws of motion.
- The local custom of buttering one's plate and then rubbing bread on it is unlikely to *generalize* to the nation at large.

  [-d, generalizing, generalization *n.*]

generation (JEN er AY shun) *n.* 1. the act of producing something; 2. the specific act of producing offspring; procreation; 3. a single stage in the life cycle of a species; time between birth and procreation (in humans about 25 years); 4. a group of people born around the same time period

- The *generation* of electricity is a high priority for western states, which are growing in population density.
- Henry VIII's desire for the *generation* of a male heir was the main reason the Church of England separated from Rome.
- Fruit flies are much better subjects for studying genetics than humans because there can be a new *generation* every few days.
- If you were born after 1970, you are part of the computer *generation*.

genetics (jen ET iks) *adj.* 1. the branch of science that deals with heredity; 2. the traits of an individual, group, or type

- As branches of biology go, *genetics* is a rather young science but one that has yielded great returns.
- DNA research and identification is only one of the benefits brought about by *genetics*.
- Look at parent and child next to one another, and often the common *genetics* are obvious.

glacial (GLAY shil) *adj.* 1. of or like ice; of or like glaciers; 2. produced by a glacier or during a glacial age; 3. freezing; very cold; 4. unfriendly; 5. very, very slow, like the progress of a glacier

- The surface of Antarctica is quite *glacial* in texture, except where it is snow covered.
- Many mountain streams of today are of *glacial* production.
- Brrr! The weather outside is *glacial* in feel.
- Annette froze Hiram with a *glacial* glare.
- William had such a fear of calculus that his progress in the subject could only be described as *glacial*.

  [-ly *adv.*]

glissade (gli SAHD) *n.* 1. a mountain climber's deliberate slide down a snow-covered hill; 2. a gliding ballet step

- While descending the slopes of Everest, Hillary welcomed every *glissade* he had the chance to take.
- Ballerinas frequently do *glissades* when not on point (on their toes).

QUICK REVIEW #41

Match the word from column 2 with the word from column 1 that means most nearly the same thing.

1. gargantuan	a. slide
2. garish	b. enormous
3. genealogy	c. heredity
4. generalize	d. poularize
5. generation	e. pedigree
6. genetics	f. unfriendly
7. glacial	g. procreation
8. glissade	h. gaudy

glutton (GLUH tin) *n.* 1. a person who can eat a copious amount (like a pig); 2. someone capable of a great amount of something

- The *glutton* consumed such mass quantities of food that his dining companion feared that he might explode.
- Although Blossom had rejected his advances seven times before, being a *glutton* for punishment, Karl had to try just one more time.

[Syn. epicure]

gracious (GRAY shis) *adj.* 1. showing kindness, courtesy, charm, etc.; 2. compassionate; merciful; 3. showing kindness toward those in inferior positions; 4. showing taste and luxuriousness appropriate to the well-to-do and well educated

- Catherine was very *gracious* in her acceptance of the gifts.
- Francine listened to the prisoners' complaints about the quality of the food in a very *gracious* manner.
- The prince was *gracious* as he was introduced to the members of the regiment.
- Though sumptuous, the appointments of the manor were *gracious* so as to afford comfort to all who might visit.

[-ly *adv.*]

grandiose (GRAN dee ohs) *adj.* 1. imposing; impressive; magnificent; having grandeur; 2. seeming important, pompous, and showy, or trying to so seem

- The Breakers (built as a summer home by the Vanderbilts in Newport, Rhode Island) can only be described as *grandiose*.
- Napoleon had *grandiose* plans for a French empire.
- The court of Louis XVI was so *grandiose* as to show the commoners how unimportant they were.

gratuity (gra TOO i tee) *n.* a sum of money, often based on a percentage of the total bill, paid to a server or other service person; tip; present

- An appropriate *gratuity* for the waitperson at a restaurant is 15–20%, depending on the quality of service.
- A *gratuity* should rarely be left at a European restaurant because the cost of service is already reflected on the bill.
- Twenty percent is the appropriate *gratuity* for taxicab drivers.

[gratuities *pl.*] [Syn. tip]

greed (GREED) *n.* a desire for more than one needs or deserves; cupidity

- *Greed* is not always about money, although it often is.
- Monarchs and dictators through history have shown *greed* for land and/or power.
- *Greed* for more land also fueled the nineteenth-century American doctrine of Manifest Destiny.

[-iness *n.*] [Syn. avarice]

grudging (GRUD jing) *adj.* reluctant; with envy and resentment

- The company's outgoing CEO gave a *grudging* acknowledgment to his successor at the board meeting.
- Henry's ex-wife said a *grudging* hello to his new wife when they came to take the children for the weekend.

[-ly *adv.*]

hackneyed (HAK need) *adj.* made commonplace or trite through overuse

- "Been there, done that" is one example of a *hackneyed* expression.
- "We're going to give it 110%" is both *hackneyed* and impossible.

[Syn. trite]

harangue (hoer ANG) *n.* a long, loud, scolding speech; a blustering tirade —*vt.* to speak or address one in such a manner

- The sergeant gave the patrol a 20-minute *harangue* when they failed to be in the first two to finish their exercise.
- The coach *harangued* the kicker for 15 minutes for having missed the field goal.

[-d, haranguing] [Syn. tirade]

harass (HAR ris, hoer AS) *vt.* 1. to bother or torment as with worries, bills, repeated questions, etc.; 2. to trouble by repeatedly attacking

- Bill collectors *harass* their debtors with phone calls at all hours of the day and night.
- Viola's ex-boyfriend, Ted, kept *harassing* her about why they couldn't give it a second try.
- The attack helicopters kept *harassing* the retreating enemy with repeated sorties against their rear guard.

[-ed, -ing]

harvest (HAHR vist) *n.* 1. the time of year when ripe crops are reaped; 2. a season's yield of crops or of a particular crop —*vt., vi.* 1. to gather in the ripe crop(s); 2. to trap, shoot, or catch game, usually for commercial purposes; 3. to get something as the result of some action; 4. to collect organs for transplant

- Autumn is the time for the cranberry *harvest*.
- There was a plentiful *harvest* of all crops last year.
- We need some migrant labor to help *harvest* the grapes.
- Salmon farms *harvest* only salmon of a certain age after breeding is finished.
- How much goodwill you can *harvest* depends on how much your speech is believed.
- Surgeons *harvest* hearts, lungs, livers, kidneys, and corneas from donors for transplant.

[-ed, -ing, -er *n.*]

heckle (HEK il) *vt.* to annoy or harrass a speaker by taunting or interrupting with annoying questions

- It's not unusual for comedians in a nightclub to be *heckled* by one or more inebriated audience members.
- When the prime minister of England speaks to Parliament, he can expect members of the opposition to heckle him.

[-d, heckling, -r* *n.*] [Syn. bait]

hedonism (HEED 'n IZ m) *n.* 1. (philosophy) the belief that the happiness of the individual or the society is of paramount importance; 2. (psychology) the theory that a person always acts to seek pleasure and avoid pain; 3. a self-indulgence in seeking one's own pleasure as a way of life

- The philosophy of *hedonism* is most closely associated with the ancient Greek philosopher, Epicurus (342–270 B.C.E.), who taught that all our actions should maximize pleasure and minimize pain.
- Psychological *hedonism* views humans as built or programmed to exclusively desire pleasure.
- Spending one's entire life on a luxury cruise ship in the Caribbean is probably the ultimate goal of modern *hedonism*.

  [hedonistic *adj.,* hedonistically *adv.,* hedonist *n.*]

QUICK REVIEW #42

Match the word from column 2 with the word from column 1 that means most nearly the same thing.

1. glutton	a. trite
2. gracious	b. avarice
3. grandiose	c. tirade
4. gratuity	d. annoy
5. greed	e. torment
6. grudging	f. reap
7. hackneyed	g. magnificent
8. harangue	h. reluctant
9. harass	i. self-indulgence
10. harvest	j. epicure
11. heckle	k. tip
12. hedonism	l. kind

heed (HEED) *vt.* pay close attention to; to take careful notice of; obey

- A mother expects her child to *heed* her—at least until he turns 18.
- Ice skaters may be ejected if they do not *heed* the skating rink's regulations.
- Before going into the theater, make sure to *heed* the rules regarding bringing in outside food.

  [-ed, -ing, -ful *adj.,* -fully *adv.*]

heighten (HY tin) *vt.* 1. to take to a higher position; raise; rise; 2. to make better, greater, stronger, etc.; increase; intensify

- Alexis hoped that by taking evening classes, she would *heighten* her value to the firm.
- Regular periods of exercise can only *heighten* one's fitness.
- Having been picked on as a child served to *heighten* Paul's awareness of the sensitivities of others.

    [-ed, -ing] [Syn. intensify]

heinous (HAY nuhs) *adj.* terribly evil; wicked; abominable; totally awful

- The treatment of Iraqi Kurds by Saddam Hussein's government can only be described as *heinous*.
- It is *heinous* of anyone to attempt to deny that the Holocaust of World War II actually took place.

    [-ly *adv.*] [Syn. outrageous]

heritage (HER i tij) *n.* 1. any property that has been or will be inherited; 2. the rights, status, or duties attached to having been born of a certain status or at a specific time or place; birthright

- Aunt Dora's lamp with the reverse-painted shade is Karen and Bob's *heritage* (along with a load of crackle glass).
- Freedoms of speech, press, and religion are the *heritage* of every American citizen.
- It is also every American citizen's *heritage* to defend those freedoms.

    [Syn. inheritance, birthright]

hierarchy (HY ir AHR kee) *n.* 1. a group of officials, persons, or things arranged by rank, class, grade, etc.; a group of church officials so arranged; 2. the highest officials in such a group

- The *heirarchy* of commissioned officers in the army is easy to see because the ranks are arranged from the low rank of lieutenant to the top rank of general.
- The *hierarchy* of the Roman Catholic Church begins with the pastor, travels up through the bishops, archbishops, and cardinals, and ends with the pope.
- From municipality to county to state to federal is the *hierarchy* of U.S. government.

    [hierarchical *adj.*, hierarchically *adv.*]

hinder (HIN doer) *vt.* 1. to restrain; hold back; prevent; 2. to impede; make difficult for —*vi.* to get in the way of

- Police barriers are used at parades to *hinder* the public's physical access to the marchers.
- Jaamal's sore ankle *hindered* his ability to play basketball.
- A lightning storm would definitely *hinder* any action taking place at the golf tournament.

    [-ed, -ing] [Syn. obstruct, impede]

hindrance (HIN drins) *n.* 1. the act of preventing; 2. obstacle; impediment; obstruction

- *Hindrance* of the bill's coming to a vote was the intended purpose of the senator's filibuster.
- A Jersey Barrier is a deliberate *hindrance* to keep traffic moving in opposite directions from crashing into one another.
- Being a woman was a considerable *hindrance* to Jennifer's attempt to join the men's baseball team.

  [Syn. obstacle]

hostility (hahs TIL i tee) *n.* 1. a feeling of antagonism, ill will, unfriendliness, etc.; enmity; 2. hostile acts; an expression of enmity or ill will

- A general feeling of *hostility* toward Japan permeated America after the attack on Pearl Harbor.
- *Hostility* between members of rival gangs has made it difficult to live in some parts of certain U.S. cities.
- *Hostility* of the people toward the regime was the ultimate cause of the storming of the Bastille that began the French Revolution.

  [Syn. enmity]

humanity (yoo MAN i tee) *n.* 1. human nature; the act or quality of being of the species *Homo sapien;* 2. (*pl.*) human qualities, especially the desirable ones; 3. kindness, caring, mercy, sympathy, etc.; 4. mankind; people; 5. (*pl.*) the branches of learning dealing with social sciences

- All *humanity* is confined to the surface of the earth.
- Studying the *humanities* usually results in a Bachelor of Arts degree.
- In times of stress or hardship, it falls on all of us to display our *humanity* to one another.
- A natural disaster on any part of this planet impacts all *humanity*.

  [humanities *pl.*]

humorous (YOO mer uhs) *adj.* funny; amusing; comical; showing humor

- If one did not take a *humorous* view of life's happenings, he or she would be doomed to constant tears.
- Being *humorous* for a living is a difficult task that very few people manage to accomplish.
- Sebastian, who is two years old, thinks that rolling the sleeping dog off the sofa is *humorous*.

  [Syn. witty, droll, funny]

hypocrite (HIP uh krit) *n.* someone who pretends to be pious, virtuous, etc. without really being so; one who feigns being what he or she is not; a fake; pretender; sham

- Although Lloyd makes a big show of his piety at church on Sundays, he is really a *hypocrite* because he drinks, cusses, and chases loose women the rest of the week.
- Used-car salespersons have a well-deserved reputation for being *hypocrites,* guaranteeing you the world until you've signed the contract, then not taking your phone calls.

  [hypocritical *adj.*, hypocritically *adv.*]

hypothesis* (hy PAH thi sis) *n.* an unproved theory, supposition, presumption, etc. often used to provide a jumping-off point for exploring further

- An apple's falling from a tree, the story goes, inspired Newton's *hypothesis* that led to his laws of gravitation.
- The *hypothesis* that heat travels from warmer bodies to cooler bodies gave rise to the science of thermodynamics.
- The *hypothesis* that base metals could be turned into precious metals proved untrue, and so chemistry came to replace alchemy.

  [hypotheses* *pl.*]

QUICK REVIEW #43

Match the word from column 2 with the word from column 1 that means most nearly the same thing.

1. heed	a. ordering
2. heighten	b. obstacle
3. heinous	c. presumption
4. heritage	d. enmity
5. hierarchy	e. kindness
6. hinder	f. droll
7. hindrance	g. obey
8. hostility	h. pretender
9. humanity	i. intensify
10. humorous	j. birthright
11. hypocrite	k. obstruct
12. hypothesis	l. outrageous

I

idiosyncrasy (ID ee yoh SEENK ruh see) *n.* 1. a personal, peculiar mannerism or affectation; 2. an individual reaction to a food, drug, etc. that is different from other peoples' normal reaction to the same

- Robert's *idiosyncrasy* is touching food to his chin before putting it into his mouth.
- An *idiosyncrasy* of Aren's was triggered by her eating strawberries, following which blue smoke would issue forth from both her ears.

  [idiosyncrasies *pl.*, idiosyncratic *adj.*, idiosyncratically *adv.*]

ignore (ig NAWR) *vt.* 1. to intentionally disregard; 2. to pay no attention to; 3. to refuse to consider

- A sure way to cause an accident is to *ignore* a stop sign.
- Frieda often *ignores* the cat's meowing by the front door.
- The judge *ignored* Jeff's excuse that he hadn't known his act was against the law.

  [-d, ignoring, ignorance *n.*] [Syn. neglect]

illusory (il YOO sir ee) *adj.* unreal or deceptive; having the characteristics of an illusion

- Sue's guitar-playing talent was *illusory,* her best work having been achieved on air guitar.
- Custer's superiority over the Sioux at the Little Bighorn proved to be purely *illusory.*

illustrate (IL uhs TRAYT) *vt.* 1. to explain; to make clear; 2. to exemplify; 3. to provide pictures, drawings, diagrams, etc. —*vi.* to offer an example for the purpose of making something clear

- A schematic diagram can easily *illustrate* how an electrical circuit works.
- The story of Jackie Robinson's career *illustrates* the ideal role model that some major leaguers have been.
- Children's books are often *illustrated* because a child can appreciate pictures far more easily than written words.
- Accentuating the positive is *illustrated* by Jonah in the whale or Noah in the ark, says the song.

  [-d, illustrating, illustration *n.*]

imagine (im A jin) *vt.* 1. to conceive in the mind; form a mental picture; 2. to guess; to think; to suppose —*vi.* to use the imagination

- From the sound of her voice on the phone, Jonathan could *imagine* what Daphne looked like.
- Jerry could not even *imagine* how he'd have reacted had he been in George's shoes.
- Kareem *imagined* he was on a magic carpet ride.

  [-d, imagining, imagination *n.*]

imitate (IM i TAYT) *vt.* 1. to copy; to mimic; 2. to emulate; attempt to follow the example of; 3. to duplicate; reproduce; 4. to resemble

- Ian's drawings *imitated* those of his older brother and dealt with senseless violence and gore—artfully, of course.
- Frankie's attempt to *imitate* Uncle Jimmy made everyone laugh, as he smacked himself in the forehead with his palm.
- Marcy's pictures *imitate* Valerie's so closely that she might as well have used a duplicating machine.
- Some of Harry's paintings *imitate* those of Mondrian.

  [-d, imitating, imitation, imitator *n.*] [Syn. ape, mimic, emulate]

immerse (i MOERS) *vt.* 1. to plunge, drop, or dip into a liquid, or as if into a liquid; 2. to submerge in water; 3. to thoroughly absorb oneself in some activity; engross

- Some Christian denominations baptize their members by totally *immersing* them; others baptize by sprinkling water on their members' heads.
- *Immerse* your nonstick cookware in soapy water and season it with oil before using it for the first time.
- I was so *immersed* in the *Times* crossword puzzle that I didn't notice the phone until the third or fourth ring.

  [-d*, immersing, immersion *n.*]

immoderate (i MAH doer it) *adj.* excessive; without restraint

- Eighty miles per hour is an *immoderate* speed to drive at, as well as an illegal one in most states.
- An *immoderate* amount of sunlight can cause skin cancer.

  [-ly *adv.*, immoderation *n.*] [Syn. excessive]

impact (IM pakt) *vt.* 1. to force together; to tightly pack; 2. to affect —*n.* 1. a collision; violent contact; 2. the power of an event to change feelings, bring about changes, etc.; shock

- *Impact* the head of a nail enough times with the head of a hammer and you'll drive it home, unless you've bent it.
- The news of her sister's accident *impacted* Allison deeply.
- The bumpers of the two cars were involved in the *impact*.
- News of the president's assassination had a great *impact* on nearly everybody.

  [-ed, -ing] [Syn. shock]

impart (im PAHRT) *vt.* 1. to make known; tell; reveal; 2. to give a share in or of something

- When lecturing his son the on birds and bees, Mr. Brown *imparted* far more information than the boy wanted to know.
- If a teacher is a good one, he or she will *impart* an intellectual curiosity to his or her students.

  [-ed, -ing] [Syn. reveal]

impassioned (im PASH ind) *adj.* filled with, feeling, or showing very strong feeling; passionate; ardent; fiery

- The father made an *impassioned* plea to the kidnappers to release his daughter unharmed.
- The governor was *impassioned* in his appeal for people to donate blood to help the accident victims.

[-ly *adv.*]

imperceptible (IM poer SEP ti bl) *adj.* barely noticeable; not clearly distinct to the mind or the senses; very subtle

- The difference in flavors between the two brands of cola is almost *imperceptible*.
- Though *imperceptible* to some, there are differences in the sound quality of a bassoon's high register and an oboe's low one.

[imperceptibly* *adv.*]

QUICK REVIEW #44

Match the word from column 2 with the word from column 1 that means most nearly the same thing.

1. idiosyncrasy	a. shock
2. ignore	b. suppose
3. illusory	c. excessive
4. illustrate	d. engross
5. imagine	e. ardent
6. imitate	f. peculiarity
7. immerse	g. reveal
8. immoderate	h. subtle
9. impact	i. clarify
10. impart	j. neglect
11. impassioned	k. emulate
12. imperceptible	l. unreal

impermanent (im POER mi nint) *adj.* not lasting; temporary; fleeting

- A snowman is a rather *impermanent* type of statuary—especially in Maryland.
- Weather differs from climate in that the former is an *impermanent* condition.

[-ly *adv.*, impermanence *n.*]

impetuous* (im PET you is) *adj.* acting or done suddenly, with little thought; sudden; rash; impulsive

- Janet's volunteering to join the posse was an *impetuous* act on her part and took everyone by surprise.
- Buddy was *impetuous* when he suddenly joined the army, and he had two years to reflect on the act.

[-ly *adv.*, -ness *n.*] [Syn. sudden]

impious (IM pee uhs) *adj.* 1. lacking reverence for God; 2. lacking respect or sense of obligation toward one's parents

- When Bill made *impious* remarks, he was rebuked by Sister Kathleen.
- It was *impious* of Cara to abandon her father to a state-run nursing facility and wash her hands of him.

[-ly *adv.*, -ness *n.*]

implement (IM pli MINT) *vt.* 1. to put into effect; to fulfill; accomplish; 2. to give the means of carrying out something —*n.* 1. a tool, utensil, or device used to accomplish some task; 2. any tool or person used to accomplish some end

- It took some restaurateurs weeks to *implement* the ban on smoking in restaurants.
- Airline pilots will be trained in the use of firearms to *implement* the new aircraft security policy.
- A spade is only one *implement* used in gardening.
- An electric drill is the preferred hole-boring woodworking *implement*.

[-ed, -ing, -ation* *n.*]

implication (IM pli KAY shn) *n.* 1. an involvement or connection with something, such as a crime; 2. a showing to be involved with something; 3. something implied, from which an inference can be made

- Charlie's lawyer agreed to his client's giving testimony in exchange for the prosecution's dropping any *implication* that Charlie had been involved in the crime.
- I resent your *implication* that I had any connection to your home's having been vandalized.
- The seller made no *implication* that could be construed as a warranty, other than that provided by the manufacturer.

imply (im PLY) *vt.* 1. to suggest; indicate indirectly; hint; intimate; 2. to involve naturally; to have as a needed condition or part

- Jack did not mean to *imply* that you lacked intelligence.
- Your having taken the bicycle from the park *implies* that the bicycle was in the park in the first place.

[implied, -ing, implies *pl.*] [Syn. suggest]

impound (im POWND) *vt.* 1. to take and hold or shut up (an animal) in a pound; 2. to take and hold (a vehicle, money, papers, etc.) in legal custody

- The pug was *impounded* for seven days to make sure that he had no dangerous illnesses.
- Francine's car was *impounded* until $435 in overdue parking tickets were paid.

  [-ed, -ing]

impression (im PRESH in) *n.* 1. a mark or imprint caused by physical pressure; 2. an effect formed in the mind or senses by some force or activity; 3. a vague notion, feeling, or recollection

- When you sit on the sofa, your derriere makes an *impression* in the cushion.
- Rosa's demeanor gave Pietro the *impression* that she would welcome an invitation from him to the prom.
- Howard had the *impression* that he'd seen all this before.

  [Syn. idea]

impressive (im PRES iv) *adj.* tending to have or having a significant effect on the mind; wondrous; causing admiration

- Irwin's ability to lift 350 lbs. can only be called *impressive.*
- Marjory displayed an *impressive* command of spelling at the national spelling bee.

  [-ly *adv.*, -ness *n.*]

improve (im PROOV) *vt.* 1. to make better; improve the condition or quality of; 2. to make more valuable (as in by cultivating or building on land)

- New spark plugs *improve* the way some cars run.
- Keeping the amount of salt low *improves* the healthfulness of soup.
- When Virginia *improved* her property by building the boathouse, she was not surprised to see her taxes go up.

  [-d, improving] [Syn. better]

impugn (im PYOON) *vt.* to criticize or challenge as false or questionable in nature

- The defense witness was called to *impugn* the testimony of an earlier prosecution witness.
- The interview with Ari's eighth-grade teacher was enough to *impugn* Ari's reputation for honesty.

  [-ed, -ing] [Syn. deny]

impulse (IM puhls) *n.* 1. a driving force; push; impetus; thrust; sudden urge; 2. an inclination to act, without premeditation; a motive coming from within

- An *impulse* caused by the forced ejection of hot gases drives a jet engine.
- The *impulse* of his push made her fall from the cliff.
- Around midnight, Barbara had a sudden *impulse* to eat a pistachio ice-cream cone.

  [impulsive *adj.*, impulsively *adv.*] [Syn. thrust]

QUICK REVIEW #45

Match the word from column 2 with the word from column 1 that means most nearly the same thing.

1. impermanent	a. deny
2. impetuous	b. better
3. impious	c. involvement
4. implement	d. wondrous
5. implication	e. idea
6. imply	f. thrust
7. impound	g. sudden
8. impression	h. utensil
9. impressive	i. temporary
10. improve	j. suggest
11. impugn	k. irreverent
12. impulse	l. seize

impute (im PYOOT) *vt.* to ascribe; to attribute (especially a fault or bad deed) to someone; to charge with

- Film historians *impute* the phrase "Never give a sucker an even break" to W. C. Fields.
- Bugsy Seagal is *imputed* with being the first to recognize Las Vegas as a potential vacation destination.
- Chicago's bloody gang wars of the early twentieth century are often *imputed* to Al Capone.

  [-d, imputing] [Syn. ascribe]

incinerator* (in SIN oer AY tir) *n.* someone or thing (especially a high-temperature furnace) that is used to burn things (from the verb, *incinerate*)

- The man or woman burning the fallen leaves in a garbage can to get rid of them is probably the most universally known *incinerator*.
- Commercial *incinerators* are today required to meet standards to limit pollutants escaping into the air.

incompatible (IN kuhm PAT i bil) *adj.* 1. not able to exist in harmony; not getting along well together; inharmonious; 2. two or more jobs that cannot be held at the same time by the same person; 3. contradictory tenets or positions

- A 220V air conditioner's plug is *incompatible* with a 115V electrical outlet, grounded or otherwise.
- The jobs of prosecutor and judge are totally *incompatible*—you can't do both simultaneously.
- Contrary to popular myth, cats are far from *incompatible* with dogs.

  [incompatibly *adv.*, incompatibility *n.*]

incompetent (in KAHM pit int) *adj.* 1. lacking adequate ability, fitness, etc.; incapable; 2. not meeting legal qualifications

- The 240-pound, 45-year-old Anna was proclaimed *incompetent* to become an astronaut.
- Warren demonstrated his *incompetent* driving skills by parking his car in the grocery store's soda aisle.
- Although he had received 6 years of medical training, without a license, Dr. Pepper was *incompetent* to practice medicine in New York.

  [-ly *adv.,* incompetence, incompetency *n.*]

incomprehensible (IN kahm pri HEN si bil) *adj.* not capable of being understood; unintelligible; obscure

- When Julianna mumbled, what she had to say was completely *incomprehensible.*
- The *incomprehensible* plan for the democratization of Xanadu was not understood by anybody.

  [incomprehensibly *adv.,* incomprehensibility *n.*]

inconsequential (in KAHN si KWEN chil) *adj.* unimportant; trivial; of no consequence

- When compared to the Allies' landing at Normandy in 1944, Gino's landing at Palmer Mall in 2004 was *inconsequential.*
- Although considered a great invention in its own day, when balanced against the microcomputer, sliced bread seems *inconsequential.*

  [-ly *adv.*]

inconsistent (IN kuhn SIS tint) *adj.* not in agreement; not uniform; self-contradictory; changeable

- Given the facts that the police already knew, Arnold's story could only be described as *inconsistent.*
- Fishermen's tales tend to be *inconsistent,* with the size of the fish growing in each retelling.

  [-ly *adv.*]

incorporate (in KAWR pir AYT) *vt.* 1. to join with something already there; to combine; to embody; to include; 2. to merge or bring together to form a single entity; 3. to form into a legally organized group that acts as a single entity

- When the batter is well mixed, it's time to add the egg yolks, one at a time until each is *incorporated.*
- Many smaller single-purpose companies *incorporate* the multimeda giants of today.
- By *incorporating,* a company is able to protect its officers from personal liability for its misdeeds.

  [-d, incorporating] [Syn. embody, include]

indecorous (in DEK oer is) *adj.* lacking propriety; lacking correctness; not in good taste; unseemly

- Arthur's *indecorous* display of foul language at the ballpark indicated that he'd had a few too many beers.
- The army frowns upon *indecorous* behavior by anyone in uniform—this is the main reason it employs MPs.

  [-ly *adv.*] [Syn. improper]

indicate (IN di KAYT) *vt.* 1. to point to or point out; direct attention to; 2. to be or to give a sign or token of; signify

- The dashboard light *indicates* that a door is open.
- Uncle Sam's pointing finger in the old recruitment signs served to *indicate* that the one he wanted was you.
- An engagement ring is usually a good way to *indicate* that one is serious about another.

[-d, indicating]

indifference* (in DIFF oer ens) *n.* a lack of concern, interest, or feeling; apathy; the condition of being indifferent

- The parking valet's *indifference* toward the wishes of his clients was reflected in the paucity of his tips.
- Tania's concerns about her sister's well-being were met with *indifference* by the part-time night nurse.
- *Indifference* is the last reaction that a concerned person wishes to encounter.

indignation (IN dig NAY shin) *n.* righteous anger; anger at injustice, unfairness, or ingratitude

- Rhonda expressed her *indignation* at the shabby way her father was treated by the car dealer.
- The attentive waiter expressed his *indignation* to his boss at the paltry size of the gratuity the last diner had left.

[Syn. anger]

QUICK REVIEW #46

Match the word from column 2 with the word from column 1 that means most nearly the same thing.

1. impute	a. unseemly
2. incinerator	b. unreliable
3. incompatible	c. anger
4. incompetent	d. include
5. incomprehensible	e. apathy
6. inconsequential	f. signify
7. inconsistent	g. inharmonious
8. incorporate	h. unintelligible
9. indecorous	i. burner
10. indicate	j. unfit
11. indifference	k. ascribe
12. indignation	l. trivial

indomitable (in DAHM it i bil) *adj.* not easily discouraged or subdued; unbeatable; not conquerable

- Jim's *indomitable* spirit kept him in the race against all odds.
- Nancy's determination to reach her goal was *indomitable*.

  [indomitably *adv.*]

ineffable (in EF i bil) *adj.* 1. overwhelming; too great to be described in words; 2. too awesome or sacred to be spoken

- The orchid's *ineffable* beauty defied Sue's ability to describe it.
- The parishioner could not bring himself to speak the *ineffable* name of the Lord.

  [ineffably *adv.*]

inefficacious (in EF i KAY shuhs) *adj.* unable to bring about the desired result; not efficacious

- The special vitamins given to the horse to make it run faster proved to be *inefficacious*.
- It was obvious that the lawn treatment had been *inefficacious* when the new crop of dandelions appeared.

  [-ly *adv.*]

inefficient (IN if ISH int) *adj.* failing to give the desired result with a minimum use of energy, time, etc.; not suited to perform the desired task; incapable

- The engine was *inefficient* because it used a lot of fuel to accomplish the job.
- A fork, while excellent for eating steak, is quite *inefficient* when it comes to eating soup.

  [-ly *adv.*, inefficiency *n.*]

inexorable (in EGZ oer IB il) *adj.* 1. unmovable by persuasion, argument, or entreaty; unrelenting; 2. unchangeable; unstoppable

- Steven was *inexorable* in his support for universal medical coverage, despite all who argued against it.
- Undeterred by dire weather reports and unrelenting cold, Amundsen pursued his *inexorable* trek to the South Pole.

  [inexorably *adv.*]

infer (in FOER) *vt.* 1. to decide or conclude something from something that is known or assumed; to derive by reasoning; 2. to indicate indirectly; to lead to a conclusion; indicate

- From your knowledge of human behavior and that of Fred in particular, you should be able to *infer* whether he deliberately misled Wilma and Pebbles.
- The fact that Barney had both motive and opportunity might lead one to *infer* that he had something to do with the doughnut's disappearance.

  [-red*, -ring, -ence *n.*] [Syn. deduce, conclude]

infinite (IN fin it) *adj.* 1. lacking in boundaries or limits; without beginning or end; 2. very great; vast; immense

- The realm of natural numbers is *infinite*, with neither beginning nor end.
- Do you think people are destined to explore the *infinite* vastness of intergalactic space?

  [-ly *adj.*] [Syn. immense, endless]

inflammatory (in FLAM uh TAW ree) *adj.* 1. causing or likely to cause anger, excitement, violence, etc.; 2. of or characterized by redness as a reaction by the body to some irritant

- The revolutionary's speech was *inflammatory* and was calculated to incite the crowd to action.
- Poison ivy is *inflammatory* to the skin of anyone who is allergic to it.

  [inflammatorily *adv.*]

influence (IN floo INS) *n.* 1. the ability of a person(s) or thing(s) to affect others as evidenced by the effect; 2. the power of persons of wealth or high status to cause immediate change —*vt.* to effect the behavior, development, nature, etc. of others

- Harold's *influence* was evident in Marcy's choice of chocolate layer cake.
- Billionaire Vilo Kvetch used his *influence* to get a No Parking sign installed in front of his Park Avenue mansion.
- It is easy to see sunlight *influence* the direction in which day lilies face as they follow it across the sky.

  [-d, influencing] [Syn. power]

information (IN foer MAY shin) *n.* 1. a telling of or being told something; 2. something learned; news; intelligence; 3. facts; data; lore

- Iris just got the latest *information* from the travel agent.
- The more *information* you have on a subject, the easier it is to make an intelligent choice.
- Telephone *information* can be obtained (for a fee) by dialing one of several sources.

inhibit* (in HIB it) *vt.* 1. to restrain or hold back from some action; 2. to keep back; keep in check

- Smoking cigarettes tends to *inhibit* one's ability to participate in strenuous sports.
- Fear of needles *inhibits* many people from volunteering to donate blood.

  [-ed, -ing, -ion *n.*] [Syn. restrain, retard]

innocuous (in AHK yoo is) *adj.* 1. that does no harm or injury; harmless; 2. not controversial or oppressive; innocent; uninspiring and dull

- The butterfly is an *innocuous* insect that hurts neither plant nor animal.
- The president's speech was *innocuous,* treading on nobody's toes and generally boring the audience to sleep.

QUICK REVIEW #47

Match the word from column 2 with the word from column 1 that means most nearly the same thing.

1. indomitable	a. incapable
2. ineffable	b. indicate
3. inefficacious	c. power
4. inefficient	d. innocent
5. inexorable	e. provocative
6. infer	f. retard
7. infinite	g. intelligence
8. inflammatory	h. ineffective
9. influence	i. unbeatable
10. information	j. unrelenting
11. inhibit	k. overwhelming
12. innocuous	l. endless

innovative (IN OH vay tiv) *adj.* 1. the act or process of finding new methods; 2. a new method, custom, device, etc.

- Luther Burbank was an *innovative* person who bred many new varieties of fruits, vegetables, and flowers.
- Freeze-drying is an *innovative* way of preserving foods, invented in the second half of the twentieth century.

  [-ly *adv.*]

inordinate (in AWR din it) *adj.* 1. not regulated or orderly; 2. lacking in moderation; too great

- There are an *inordinate* number of bakeries throughout the United States.
- An *inordinate* number of students are not up-to-date on completing their homework assignments.

  [-ly *adv.*] [Syn. excessive]

inquiry (IN kwir ee *or* in KWY ree) *n.* 1. the act of seeking information; 2. an investigation or looking at something; 3. a question or questioning

- Marshall made an *inquiry* among his new neighbors before deciding on where to bank.
- An *inquiry* by the NHTSA followed the oil truck accident.
- The grocery cashier made an *inquiry* of each of her customers as to whether (s)he had found everything (s)he came to buy.

insight (IN syt) *n.* 1. the ability to intuitively grasp the inner nature of things; 2. a clear understanding of the inner nature of a certain thing

- Henry's *insight* made it possible for him to tell the quality of any cabinet's construction.
- Lois's long experience with cats and dogs gave her *insight* into why Libby was whining and whether to call the vet.

　[-ful *adj.*, -fully *adv.*]

insipid (in SIP id) *adj.* 1. tasteless; unflavored; 2. dull; lifeless; lacking tang or zest

- The lukewarm cup of weak tea was absolutely *insipid* without lemon or sugar.
- Byron had an *insipid* personality, sort of like a piece of wet toast.
- Last night's *insipid* party's most exciting moment was its ending.

　[-ly *adv.*] [Syn. banal, vapid, flat; Ant. zestful, spicy]

insolent (IN suh lint) *adj.* strongly disrespectful; impertinent; impudent in speech and behavior

- Jack was expelled from school for being *insolent* with his teachers and with the school administrators.
- *Insolent* behavior while in the armed services is a sure ticket to the brig.

　[-ly *adv.*, insolence *n.*] [Syn. impertinent, proud]

instill (ins TIL) *vt.* to put in little by little, or drop by drop; to impart a thought, idea, principle, etc. gradually

- It takes many lessons to *instill* a child with the proper way to treat other people.
- Farah was not quick to grasp the principles of driving a car, and it took her instructor 25 lessons to *instill* the skills she needed to pass her licensing exam.

　[-ed, -ing, -ment *n.*]

institution (IN sti TOO shin) *n.* 1. an established law, custom, etc.; 2. an instituting establishment; 3. an organization having a public character, such as a school, church, bank, etc.; 4. the building housing such an organization

- The Bill of Rights is an *institution* that has survived many assaults by lawmakers over the years.
- The *institution* of daylight saving time is not observed in all the contiguous 48 states.
- An *institution* of higher learning is ideally a place for a free exchange of ideas.
- The savings and loan *institution* is on the corner of Third and Main streets.

instrument (IN struh mint) *n.* 1. a tool; something or someone used to do something; 2. any of many kinds of devices used to measure (temperature, wind, electricity, etc.); 3. a device that produces a musical sound; 4. a legal document

- A spading fork might well be the most versatile garden *instrument*.
- A pilot's *instruments* tell the speed and altitude of the aircraft as well as the plane's attitude.
- When asked to choose an *instrument* to play, Benny picked the clarinet.
- A letter of credit is a financial *instrument*.

　[-al *adj.*, -ally *adv.*] [Syn. implement]

integrate (IN te GRAYT) *vt.* 1. to make whole or complete by bringing parts together; 2. to unify; 3. to remove the social barriers of racial segregation; 4. (math) to calculate the integrals of an equation

- A laptop computer *integrates* monitor, CPU, and keyboard into a single compact package.
- The European Union *integrates* the economic power of Europe into a formidable force.
- To racially *integrate* the South was a great undertaking of the 1960s.
- To learn to *integrate* equations, study calculus.

[-d, integrating, integration *n.*]

integrity* (in TEG ri tee) *n.* 1. wholeness; entirety; 2. the quality of being in perfect condition; soundness; 3. the quality of being morally sound; uprightness; honesty; sincerity

- The fuel tank's *integrity* survived the car crash.
- A plumber checks the *integrity* of a gas line by spraying it with a soapy solution and watching for bubbles.
- A person's *integrity* can often be measured by the trust of others.

intellectual (IN ti LEK tyoo il) *adj.* 1. pertaining or appealing to the ability to reason (intellect); 2. activities of the intellect; 3. having or showing superior reasoning powers —*n.* a person of intellect and learning

- The game of chess has often been looked at (incorrectly) as an *intellectual* training ground.
- Karen has demonstrated particularly keen *intellectual* powers when it comes to solving a mystery.

[-ly *adv.*] [Syn. intelligent]

QUICK REVIEW #48

Match the word from column 2 with the word from column 1 that means most nearly the same thing.

1. innovative	a. investigation
2. inordinate	b. establishment
3. inquiry	c. intelligent
4. insight	d. drip
5. insipid	e. implement
6. insolent	f. uprightness
7. instill	g. vapid
8. institution	h. unify
9. instrument	i. novel
10. integrate	j. intuition
11. integrity	k. impertinent
12. intellectual	l. excesssive

intemperate (in TEM per uht) *adj.* 1. not moderate; lacking in restraint; excessive or severe; violent; 2. consuming too large a quantity of beer, wine, liquor, etc.

- Lloyd was *intemperate* in his gambling, never missing an opportunity to place a bet.
- Diane's disposition was *intemperate,* being quick to anger at the slightest perceived slight.
- Rocco is an *intemperate* drinker, often ending up sloshed.

    [-ly *adv.*]

intense (in TENS) *adj.* 1. very strong; extreme; sharp; vivid; 2. strenuous; fervent; strained very hard; 3. showing or having strong emotion; being very serious

- The poet's words created an *intense* image of warfare.
- The effort he put into pulling on the rope was *intense.*
- Paula had an *intense* desire to become a professional musician.

    [-ly *adv.*]

interest (IN toer EST) *n.* 1. a claim to or share of something; 2. an involvement; 3. a concern

- Charlie had an *interest* in a bicycle repair shop on Elm St.
- Vicki's calling Bob upset Anne, who had her own *interest* in him.
- A good teacher always takes an *interest* in the welfare of his or her students.

intermission (IN toer MISH in) *n.* 1. a time period between acts in a play or half innings in a baseball game; 2. any pause between periods of activity

- The *intermission* between play acts, or *entre acte,* is a good time to stretch one's legs.
- In the *intermission* between halves of the seventh inning comes baseball's traditional seventh-inning stretch.
- An *intermission* between periods of fighting is always a welcome time during any war.

interpretation (in TOER pri TAY shin) *n.* 1. the meaning, expression, or explanation of something; 2. one person's take on the meaning of some work (of art, literature, etc.); artistic expression

- The *interpretation* of *The Iliad* from its ancient Greek has happened many times over.
- Freud's forte was the *interpretation* of the meanings of dreams.
- Two violinists' *interpretations* of a Beethoven sonata might differ greatly.

intervention (IN toer VEN shin) *n.* 1. the act of coming between; 2. any interference in the affairs of others, whether people, companies, or countries

- It often takes the *intervention* of a third party to keep two boxers apart at the weigh-in.
- The United States has gained a reputation for its frequent *intervention* in the affairs of Central American countries.
- The confrontation of a drug user by his friends to get him into rehab is known as an *intervention.*

intimidate (in TIM id ayt) *vt.* 1. to make afraid; daunt; 2. to deter or compel with threats of violence; cow

- It is easy to *intimidate* little children, but it's not very sporting.
- Mobsters have been known to *intimidate* potential witnesses against them to deter them from testifying.

    [-d, intimidating, intimidation, intimidator *n.*]

intrepid (in TRE pid) *adj.* not afraid; bold; fearless; very brave

- Actors who play Roman gladiators appear to be *intrepid*.
- The Marines who fought on Iwo Jima were *intrepid* indeed.
- Are you *intrepid* enough to ride a big roller coaster?

    [Syn. brave]

intrigue (in TREEG) *vt.* 1. to bring on by secret plotting; 2. to excite the curiosity; fascinate —*n.* 1. a secret or underhanded plotting; 2. a secret plot; 3. a love affair

- Brutus and Cassius *intrigue* to kill Julius Caesar in Shakespeare's take on the subject.
- A cliff-hanger *intrigues* one to find out what will come next.
- The *intrigue* of Quisling's fifth column betrayed Norway.
- Many believe the death of JFK was the result of *intrigue*.
- Tracy and Hepburn's *intrigue* lasted many years.

    [-d, intriguing] [Syn. plot]

intrinsic (in TRIN sik) *adj.* essential nature; not depending on outside sources; inherent

- Gold has always had an *intrinsic* value as a precious metal.
- Some, but not all, believe that good is *intrinsic* to all people.
- The *intrinsic* nature of children is innocence.

    [-ally* *adv.*]

intrusion (in TROO zhin) *n.* 1. the act of forcing one's self or ideas on another who has not asked for and/or does not welcome them; 2. (law) the illegal entry onto another's land; 3. (geology) the squeezing of magma between layers of solid rock; the actual solidified rock so created

- Eric's *intrusion* into the girl's locker room was not greeted with amusement.
- Tresspassing is one form of illegal *intrusion;* burglary is another.
- Volcanic *intrusions* can be found in some museums' geological exhibits.

intuitive (in TOO it iv) *adj.* 1. having to do with intuition (a direct and immediate understanding or learning of something without use of reasoning); 2. learning or knowing by such a feeling

- Ginny seemed to have been born with an *intuitive* grasp of how to ride a horse.
- Alan found driving an automobile to be *intuitive* and was driving like an old-timer the first time he took the wheel.

    [-ly *adv.*]

QUICK REVIEW #49

Match the word from column 2 with the word from column 1 that means most nearly the same thing.

1. intemperate	a. tresspass
2. intense	b. fascinate
3. interest	c. explanation
4. intermission	d. excessive
5. interpretation	e. inherent
6. intervention	f. brave
7. intimidate	g. feeling
8. intrepid	h. cow
9. intrigue	i. pause
10. intrinsic	j. severe
11. intrusion	k. interference
12. intuitive	l. involvement

inundate (IN uhn DAYT) *vt.* 1. to cover with flood water; to engulf; 2. to over-run with a rush or copious amount of anything

- As the dam burst, the town below it was *inundated* by a raging torrent of water.
- Business has been so busy that the work is beginning to *inundate* our employees.

[-d, inundating, -s* *pl.*]

invaluable (in VAL yoo UH bl) *adj.* priceless; too valuable to measure

- Joy's babysitting help during our recent emergency was absolutely *invaluable*.
- Taking the PSAT exam last year was an *invaluable* warm-up for this year's SAT test.

[Syn. costly]

investigative (in VES ti GAY tiv) *adj.* 1. of or inclined to look into the facts to find an answer; 2. inclined to investigate

- *Investigative* reporters spend most of their time doing research and a much smaller portion reporting.
- A branch of medicine is devoted to *investigative* research to discover how certain drugs work to cure illnesses.

[-ly *adv.*]

investigator (in VEST i GAY tir) *n.* a person who gathers information, confidential and otherwise, for an individual, a company, or an organization (governmental or other)

- When someone has an auto accident, the insurance *investigator's* job is to find out what or who caused the accident.
- Many detective stories have been written about fictional private *investigators* who are for hire.

invigorate (in VIG uh RAYT) *vt.* to fill with energy or vigor; to enliven

- A brisk walk after dinner often serves to *invigorate* one.
- Sailors claim that nothing *invigorates* like a sea breeze.

[-d, invigorating*] [Syn. animate]

inviolable (in VY uh li bl) *adj.* 1. not to be profaned, injured, or violated; sacred; 2. unable to be violated; indestructible

- The Geneva Conventions contain certain *inviolable* rules for the humane treatment of prisoners of war.
- The laws of nature are the only rules on earth that are truly *inviolable*.

iridescent (I rid ES int) *adj.* having or showing a rainbow of colors that shift as it is looked at from different angles

- An abalone shell lying on the beach seems to have an *iridescent* gleam when struck by a bright light.
- Metallic car finishes often appear *iridescent* in sunlight.

ironic (ay RAH nik) *adj.* 1. meaning the opposite of what is said; 2. given to saying the opposite of what one means

- Isn't it *ironic* how Kenny always does the opposite of what he says he's going to do?
- Reverse psychology is *ironic* in that one tells the child to do the exact opposite of the desired behavior.

[-ally *adv.*]

irrational (i RASH in uhl) *adj.* 1. lacking the power to reason; 2. unreasonable; absurd; senseless

- There is no point in arguing with two-year-olds because they are almost always *irrational*.
- Adele's *irrational* behavior led to her being taken to the psychiatrist for examination.

[-ly *adv.*, -ity *n.*] [Syn. unreasonable]

irrelevant (i REL iv ent) *adj.* not relating to the subject; not pertinent; not to the point

- When the doctor asked you whether you had any allergies, your reply about what your grandmother used to cook was completely *irrelevant*.
- When purchasing a sport jacket, the size of your feet is *irrelevant*.

[-ly *adv.*, irrelevance *n.*]

irresponsible (I ris PAHN si bl) *adj.* not liable for certain actions; unreliable; shiftless

- The judge ruled that Dorothy was *irresponsible* for Rose's broken eyeglasses.
- Driving an automobile after having a few alcoholic beverages is an *irresponsible* act.
- I would never hire the guy who installed my sink again; he's just too *irresponsible*.

[irresponsibly *adv.*]

irreverence (i REV er rins) *n.* 1. lack of respect or reverence; 2. an act showing lack of respect; 3. a person's being treated with same

- Some comedians' stock in trade is speaking of serious matters with *irreverence*.
- It is not a good idea to show *irreverence* for the power of a chain saw—especially when using it.
- Very few parents appreciate their teenaged children's *irreverence* toward their wishes.

isolate (AY suh LAYT *for vt., adj.,* AY suh lit *for n.*) *vt.* to set apart from others; to cause to be alone —*adj.* of or relating to something that has been set apart —*n.* a person or group that has been set apart

- If you are a chess player, the last thing you want is for your opponent to *isolate* your king from his protection.
- Accidentally leaving a child home alone is one *isolated* instance (in more ways than one).
- When a solid is precipitated out of a solution or suspension, that solid is called the *isolate*.

[-d, isolating]

isolation (AY suh LAY shin) *n.* the condition of having been set apart; being alone

- To prevent the spread of infection, a carrier of an infectious disease is often placed in *isolation*.
- *Isolation* is often the best place for an inmate who is a danger to others.

[Syn. solitude]

QUICK REVIEW #50

Match the word from column 2 with the word from column 1 that means most nearly the same thing.

1. inundate	a. colorful
2. invaluable	b. animate
3. investigative	c. disrespect
4. investigator	d. unreliable
5. invigorate	e. opposite
6. inviolable	f. impertinent
7. iridescent	g. unreasonable
8. ironic	h. engulf
9. irrational	i. curious
10. irrelevant	j. snoop
11. irresponsible	k. costly
12. irreverence	l. sacred
13. isolate	m. solitude
14. isolation	n. separate

J – K

jaded (JAY did) *adj.* 1. worn out; weary; tired; 2. satiated or dulled from overindulging

- After having studied all night, Amber was *jaded* by morning.
- Having handled hundreds of homicide cases over the years, the detective's view of humanity has become rather *jaded*.
- The social worker tried not to be *jaded* at each new family abuse case she encountered, but it was difficult.

  [-ly *adv.*]

journal (JOER nil) *n.* 1. a daily record of events; diary; 2. the records of an organization's transactions; ledger; 3. a newspaper, daily or otherwise

- Daniel Dafoe's *Robinson Crusoe* is in the form of a *journal* kept by a castaway on a desert island.
- The treasurer of any corporation must keep a *journal* of all the financial transactions.
- Many local newspapers contain the word *journal* in their names, like New York City's lamented *Journal-American*.

judge (JUHJ) *vt.* 1. to hear arguments and decide the outcome; 2. to decide the outcome of a contest; 3. to form an opinion; to estimate; 4. to criticize —*n.* 1. a public official elected or appointed for purposes of *vt.* #1 and #3; 2. a contest decider; 3. one qualified to form an opinion or to criticize; 4. a critic

- In most civil cases, a jury is not used, and a single person must *judge* the merits of the case.
- Would you like to *judge* a contest to determine the most beautiful pig?
- You *judge* which of the two chairs is more comfortable.
- Do you *judge* the new automobiles as being of higher or lower quality than last year's models?
- The position of *judge* is considered one of great trust.
- The *judge* will decide which pie is tastiest.
- Years of experience are required to refine one's taste buds to the point where (s)he can qualify as a *judge* of fine wines.
- When it comes to movies, everyone's a *judge*.

  [-d, judging, -ment *n.*] [Syn. decide]

judicial (joo DISH il) *adj.* 1. pertaining to judges, courts, or their functions; 2. enforced or set by order of a court or judge; 3. suitable to or like a judge; 4. fair and unbiased

- Laws are passed and signed subject to *judicial* review.
- For a search warrant to be valid, it must bear a *judicial* signature.
- Strict codes of behavior govern *judicial* proceedings.
- A court must follow *judicial* procedures evenhandedly.

justice (JUHS tis) *n.* 1. impartiality and fairness; 2. the quality of being correct; right; 3. sound reason; validity; 4. deserved results; reward or penalty for good or bad deeds, respectively; 5. procedure of a court of law; 6. a judge

- *Justice* must be meted out equally to all; anything else is unjust.
- *Justice* must allow no favoritism of any kind.
- *Justice* requires that the good be rewarded and the evil be punished.
- The courts of law in this country are charged with administering *justice*.
- A *justice* of the peace has the power to perform weddings.

justify (JUHS ti fy) *vt.* 1. to show to be right; vindicate; 2. to supply lawful grounds for; warrant —*vi.* 1. to show sufficient reason for doing something; prove; 2. to align a row or rows of type on a page

- The town cited the fire hazard caused by old wiring to *justify* upgrading its electrical code.
- Law officers must present a judge with some evidence of wrongdoing to *justify* getting a wiretap warrant.
- Mr. Jones must *justify* his having cut down Mrs. Smith's oak tree.
- The lines of type on most papers that you submit in school are *justified* on the left.

  [justified, -ing, justification *n.*]

juxtaposition (JUHX tuh puh ZISH in) *n.* placed side by side or close together

- Words that modify other words should be placed in *juxtaposition* to the words they modify.
- When returning home after grocery shopping, it is preferable to place the trunk of the car in *juxtaposition* with the door to your house nearest the kitchen.

knowledge (NAH lij) *n.* 1. information; awareness; understanding; 2. acquaintance with the facts; 3. the complete body of information; enlightenment

- Do you have any *knowledge* of the whereabouts of Waldo?
- It is important to have a thorough *knowledge* of the facts before reaching any conclusion about them.
- An encyclopedia attempts to catalog all the *knowledge* of mankind, and it does it alphabetically for convenience.

QUICK REVIEW #51

Match the word from column 2 with the word from column 1 that means most nearly the same thing.

1. jaded		a. nearby	
2. journal		b. fairness	
3. judge		c. vindicate	
4. judicial		d. information	
5. justice		e. wearied	
6. justify		f. evaluate	
7. juxtaposition		g. unbiased	
8. knowledge		h. diary	

L

lame (LAYM) *adj.* 1. disabled or crippled, especially in one or both legs; 2. stiff and painful; 3. weak; unconvincing; ineffectual

- When Lucy fell off the horse and hurt her leg, there was a danger that she might be *lame* for life.
- While running the bases, Sebbie came up *lame* and had to limp off the field.
- "The dog ate my homework" is universally recognized as a very *lame* excuse.

[lamer, lamest, lamely *adv.*]

languid (LANG wid) *adj.* 1. lacking vitality; drooping; weak; 2. lacking interest; 3. indifferent; sluggish

- After his bout with mononucleosis, Jim was *languid* for a number of weeks.
- Ian's interest in mathematics is lacking and can best be described as *languid*.
- Kathy was unprepared for her trip to Quebec because of her *languid* attempts to learn enough French.

[languidly *adv.*, languidness *n.*]

latent (LAY tint) *adj.* hidden; present but not visible; inactive —*n.* a fingerprint left at a crime scene

- Brown-eyed Jose carries a *latent* blue eye color gene.
- Ali has a *latent* desire to dress like a fireman.

[-ly *adv.*, latency *n.*] [Syn. potential, quiescent]

lavish (LA vish) *adj.* 1. very generous in spending or giving; 2. more than enough; abundant —*vt.* to give or spend abundantly on

- A *lavish* amount of green paint was used to cover the brown front lawn.
- Jim's friend Shaila was *lavish* in her gifts to him.
- All the wedding guests *lavished* attention on the new bride.

[-ed, -ing, -ly *adv.*, -ness *n.*] [Syn. profuse]

legislation (LEJ is LAY shin) *n.* 1. the act or process of making a law; 2. the law itself

- Congress is currently considering *legislation* to require all citizens to keep physically fit.
- The process of *legislation* usually takes a fairly lengthy amount of time.
- There is no *legislation* requiring that all children be fed ice cream for dessert, but that doesn't mean it's a bad idea.

legislator (LEJ is LAY tir) *n.* one who makes laws; a member of a legislative body, such as an assemblyman, a congressman, or a senator

- *Legislators* are elected for a specific length of time.
- A U.S. senator has the longest term of any American *legislator,* namely 6 years.

[Syn. lawmaker]

legitimacy (li JIT im is ee) *n.* the quality of being legally correct; lawful; sanctioned by law or custom; reasonable and just

- Don't give anybody your personal information online, unless you're 100% certain of that person's *legitimacy*.
- The *legitimacy* of backroom poker games is doubtful.
- The *legitimacy* of Virgil's tracing Rome's history back to the Trojan War is questionable but artful.

  [Syn. lawfulness]

levee* (LEV ee) *n.* 1. a retaining wall built beside a river to prevent flooding; a dike; 2. a landing place on the riverbank; 3. a ridge of earth built around a field that is to be irrigated

- *Levees* are common sights on the lower Mississippi River.
- If you're planning to take a riverboat, you just might find yourself on the *levee,* waiting for the *Robert E. Lee.*

liberal (LIB ir el) *adj.* 1. not restricted; 2. generous; 3. plentiful; ample; abundant; 4. not limited to the literal meaning; 5. tolerant of views other than one's own

- A loose-fitting sweatshirt allows one a *liberal* amount of arm movement.
- The mayor was *liberal* in his praise for the fire department.
- Tina put a *liberal* amount of strawberry jam on her roll.
- Some judges have a *liberal* interpretation of the meaning of the law.
- A university is a place for a *liberal* exchange of viewpoints.

  [-ly *adv.*] [Syn. progressive (in the political sense)]

library (LY bre ree) *n.* 1. a collection of books, films, magazines, CDs, etc., especially a large one that is systematically arranged; 2. a public or private institution in charge of such a collection; 3. the building in which the aforementioned is housed

- The *Library* of Congress is one serious collection.
- One of the greatest losses to Western civilization was the burning of the *Library* at Alexandria (Egypt, not Virginia).
- Helene and Judy met to do some reading at the public *library*.

linchpin (LINCH pin) *n.* 1. a pin that goes through the outer end of an axle to prevent the wheel from falling off; 2. anything that holds the parts of a whole together

- Most automobiles use cotter pins as their *linchpins*.
- Evers was the *linchpin* of the Cubs great double-play trio, Tinkers to Evers to Chance.
- The keystone is the *linchpin* or the true arch.

literal (LIT oer il) *adj.* 1. having to do with letters of the alphabet; 2. word for word; following the exact words or meaning of the original; 3. interpreting things according to their precise meaning

- Placing something in *literal* order is another way of saying alphabetizing.
- Ben was very *literal,* so when his girlfriend told him to "go jump in the lake," he went looking for a lake to jump into.
- Only a few sects nowadays live their lives according to a *literal* interpretation of Holy Scripture.

  [-ly *adv.*]

literary (LIT oer ER ee) *adj.* 1. having to do with books or writing; 2. tending toward the more formal, polished language of writing rather than that of everyday speech; 3. familiar with or well versed in literature (the classics)

- A library can be thought of as a living museum of *literary* works.
- It is doubtful that anyone ever spoke in the *literary* language that characterizes Shakespeare's plays.
- A *literary* critic must have enough experience to be able to judge a work against many other examples.

literature (LIT er uh TYUR) *n.* 1. all writings in prose or poetry, especially of an imaginative nature, without regard to their merit, distinguished from those of scientific writing, reporting of news, etc.; 2. those writings considered to have lasting merit, either because of their excellence of form or the value of their examples; 3. printed matter of any kind

- The *literature* of the late twentieth century runs the gamut from the philosophy of the existentialists to the adventures of Harry Potter.
- The classics of *literature* comprise a number of books that have survived for centuries and are still being reproduced.
- Among the less lasting *literature* of recent years, we must count the billboards extolling the merits of certain drinks.

QUICK REVIEW #52

Match the word from column 2 with the word from column 1 that means most nearly the same thing.

1. lame	a. lettered
2. languid	b. glue
3. latent	c. legality
4. lavish	d. precise
5. legislation	e. collection
6. legislator	f. writings
7. legitimacy	g. laws
8. levee	h. dike
9. liberal	i. potential
10. library	j. lawmaker
11. linchpin	k. profuse
12. literal	l. generous
13. literary	m. ineffectual
14. literature	n. sluggish

litigant (LIT i gnt) *n.* a party to a lawsuit

- The two *litigants* entered the courtroom to plead their cases before Judge Judy.
- The first *litigant* was a bride, suing the dress alterer for having ruined her wedding.

livid (LIV id) *adj.* 1. discolored by a bruise; 2. lead colored often taken to mean whitish or pale; 3. very angry; enraged

- Lori's elbow was *livid* where she had bumped it.
- Barney's face went *livid,* as if he had seen a ghost.
- When Joe saw that he had been charged for the use of the limousine that had not shown up, he became *livid* with rage.

  [-ity, -ness *n.*] [Syn. pale]

loathe (LOHTH) *vt.* to feel intense disgust or distaste for; detest; despise

- Dina absolutely *loathed* the combination of green and pink.
- Don't you just *loathe* being asked where you'd like to eat and then ending up at your friend's choice of restaurant?
- As a general rule, country-and-western music lovers *loathe* hip-hop.

  [-d, loathing] [Syn. hate]

lobbyist (LAHB ee ist) *n.* a person in the employ of a special interest group who tries to persuade legislators or government administrators to act in the interest of his/her employers

- It used to be very difficult to get antismoking bills passed because of the strength of the tobacco *lobbyists.*
- The word *lobbyist* is peculiarly American and originated with people buttonholing legislators in the lobby of the Capitol building on their way to vote on or debate a bill.

logo (LOH goh) *n.* a distinctive company symbol, trademark, etc. that is designed to be associated with that company only and to get instant recognition for that company

- A good *logo* evokes the name of the company without the need to spell it out.
- The dog listening to the gramophone horn with the words "his master's voice" remains a *logo* of RCA.
- Another well-recognized *logo* is the stylized "3M" of the Minnesota Mining and Manufacturing Corp.

longevity (lawn JEV i tee) *n.* 1. long life span; length or duration of lives; 2. length of time spent employed or in service to a single company or individual

- The normal *longevity* of a dog is about 15 years but is shorter for larger dogs.
- The *longevity* of a running back's career in the NFL is less than 5 years.

lubricant (LOOB ri kint) *n.* a substance for reducing friction by being spread on one or both of the moving parts to form a film between them; grease, oil, or graphite

- The use of axle grease as a *lubricant* in wheel hubs greatly extends the longevity of both wheel and axle.
- If left uncorrected, the loss of *lubricant* from a car engine will surely doom the engine.

lubricate (LOOB ri kayt) *vt.* 1. to make slippery or smooth; 2. to put a lubricant onto or into —*vi.* to act as a lubricant

- It used to be standard practice at each oil change to *lubricate* the car's ball joints.
- This practice is no longer followed because most automotive ball joints these days are self-*lubricating*.

    [-d, lubricating]

lurid (LU rid) *adj.* harsh or shocking; vivid; sensational; shocking

- Tabloids love to feature *lurid* stories on their front pages to attract the attention of impulse-buying shoppers.
- Nothing is as welcome at the box office as a *lurid* story about an ax murderer or a cannibalistic doctor.

QUICK REVIEW #53

Match the word from column 2 with the word from column 1 that means most nearly the same thing.

1. litigant	a. persuader
2. livid	b. grease
3. loathe	c. shocking
4. lobbyist	d. suer
5. logo	e. pale
6. longevity	f. graphite
7. lubricant	g. symbol
8. lubricate	h. duration
9. lurid	i. detest

machination (MAK in AY shin) *n.* a secret or artful plot, usually one having evil intention (usually plural)

- The *machinations* of the KGB have made for some pretty exciting spy novels.
- The *Odessa File* tells of the *machinations* of an organization designed to further the cause of the Nazis after the war.

  [Syn. plot]

malediction (MAL I DIK shin) *n.* 1. a curse or the calling down of an evil spell on someone; 2. evil talk about someone; slander

- Giving one the evil eye is one form of *malediction* popular among some European cultures.
- Certain Caribbean cultures carry out their *maledictions* through the use of effigies called voodoo dolls.
- The newspaper story about Henry's drug misuse was a *malediction* worthy of a healthy sized lawsuit.

malinger* (muh LING oer) *vt.* to feign illness or injury to avoid work; to shirk

- They have a name for *malingering* in the army; it's goldbricking.
- One who *malingers* and gets a reputation for so doing is not likely to remain employed for very long, unless, of course, his/her employer is his/her parent.

  [-ed, -ing, -er *n.*]

mallet (MAL it) *n.* 1. a kind of hammer usually with a head of wood (used to drive a chisel) or of hard rubber (used to bang out dents in sheet metal); 2. a long-handled hammer with a cylinder-shaped head used for playing croquet or one with an even longer handle used for playing polo; 3. a small, wooden hammer with a round head used to play xylophone, marimba, glockenspiel, bells, etc.

- The body-shop worker uses a rubber *mallet* to hammer out small dents.
- A polo *mallet* has a very long handle because each player must strike the ball while seated on a horse.
- Wooden *mallets* with ball-shaped heads are used to strike the keys on a xylophone.

mandate* (MAN dayt) *n.* 1. an authoritative order, usually in writing; 2. the overwhelming wishes of an elected official's constituents, regarded as an order —*vt.* to require, as by law

- As a result of World War I, *mandates* to rule certain areas that used to be parts of the Ottoman Empire were issued by the League of Nations.
- The shop foreman has a *mandate* from ownership to require each worker to put in 16 hours of overtime.
- Senator Strong's overwhelming victory is a *mandate* for him to pursue equal rights for women.
- The new law *mandates* a $300 fine for overtime parking.

  [-d,* mandating]

manual (MAN yoo il) *adj.* 1. of or having to do with the hands; 2. without electrical or other power assist; 3. not automatic (as in an automotive transmission) —*n.* 1. a book of facts or instructions; 2. any of several organ keyboards; 3. a drill for handling certain weapons

- A carpenter needs good *manual* dexterity.
- Most old-fashioned wells have a *manual* crank that lifts a bucket on the end of a rope.
- To drive a car with a *manual* transmission, you must learn how to use the clutch.
- Don't throw out your DVD *manual;* you never know. . . .
- The fingers operate the *manual* on an organ, while the feet play the pedals.
- A good soldier must learn the *manual* of arms.

manuscript (MAN yoo skript) *adj.* 1. handwritten or typed, but not printed; 2. writing consisting of unconnected letters; not cursive —*n.* 1. a book or document written by hand; 2. a copy of an author's work submitted to a printer or publisher; 3. writing, as apart from printing

- Your report needs to be at least four pages of *manuscript,* double-spaced if typed.
- *Manuscript* is the style of writing we first learn, before we are taught to write in cursive.
- Until the printing press was invented, all books were *manuscripts.*
- Any *manuscript* submitted to a publisher should be accompanied by an SASE (self-adressed stamped envelope).

mar (MAHR) *vt.* to injure or damage so as to disfigure; spoil; impair; hurt the appearance

- With her key, Joan *marred* the finish on Bud's car.
- The cries of protesters *marred* the president's appearance at the convention.

  [-red, -ring]

mastery (MAS tir ee) *n.* 1. control; rule; 2. the upper hand in a struggle; victory; 3. expert skill or knowledge; 4. accomplishing success in understanding something

- Agassi had complete *mastery* on the tennis court.
- In the battle between the sexes, women achieve *mastery* about 60% of the time.
- Glenn's lack of *mastery* of the guitar is what caused his audience to leave the recital during the intermission.
- Kim's years of practice had led to *mastery* of the art of karate.

materialism (muh TIR ee uhl i zm) *n.* 1. the philosophical doctrine that everything in the world is matter, and even thought, will, and feeling can be connected to matter (the opposite of idealism); 2. the notion that possessions, wealth, and comfort are the most important things in the world; 3. the tendency to be more concerned with material things than with the intellectual or spiritual

- The philosophy of *materialism* enjoyed some popularity in the nineteenth century.
- The idea of *materialism* permeates some of the work of pop singer Madonna—especially in her song "Material Girl."
- When a person pursues someone of the opposite sex because of the latter's wealth, that is a display of *materialism*.

  [materialistic *adj.*, materialistically *adv.*]

mathematical (MATH i MAT i kl) *adj.* 1. of, concerned with, or about mathematics; 2. precise; rigorously exact

We all need some sort of *mathematical* education.

A high-quality diamond must be cut with *mathematical* precision.

maverick (MAV rik) *n.* 1. a stray calf; any unbranded livestock; 2. a person who takes an independent stand or a position different from that of the rest of his group

- One of the jobs of a cowboy on a drive is rounding up *mavericks*.
- A *maverick* politician often votes against the official position of his party's leadership.

maxim (MAX im) *n.* a concisely worded statement of truth or rule of conduct

- "A stitch in time saves nine" is a well-known *maxim*.
- "Do unto others as you would have others do unto you" is a *maxim* we should all live by.

  [Syn. saying]

meaning (MEE ning) *n.* significance; import; what is intended to be conveyed, signified, or indicated —*adj.* 1. intending; having purpose; 2. significance

- Only time will tell us the *meaning* of today's world events.
- Sally was *meaning* to tell Harry how much she cared.
- Barbara's locket's *meaning* was a reminder of her mother.

  [-ly *adv.*]

means (MEENZ) *n.* 1. the way in which something is done; agency; 2. available wealth; resources; 3. great wealth

- He had the *means* to get over the top of the fence.
- Margie had the *means* to buy the very best silver.
- The CEO of the software company is a woman of great *means*.

QUICK REVIEW #54

Match the word from column 2 with the word from column 1 that means most nearly the same thing.

1. machination	a. stray
2. malediction	b. intent
3. malinger	c. greediness
4. mallet	d. saying
5. mandate	e. precise
6. manual	f. wealth
7. manuscript	g. order
8. mar	h. spoil
9. mastery	i. handwritten
10. materialism	j. hammer
11. mathematical	k. control
12. maverick	l. instructions
13. maxim	m. curse
14. meaning	n. shirk
15. means	o. plot

media (MEE dee uh) *n.* all means of communication, such as radio, television, cinema, and print matter that provide the public with news and entertainment

- Most of the *media* in the United States are driven by advertising dollars.
- Since the advent of television, the roles played by the print *media* have tended to become more specialized.

mediocre (MEE dee OH kir) *adj.* 1. of average quality; not too good, not too bad; 2. inferior; not good enough

- The quality of prime-time TV shows has, over the years, been *mediocre,* with the best shows airing after 10 P.M.
- For the most part, packaged supermarket baked goods are *mediocre* when compared with freshly baked goods.

melee (MAY lay) *n.* 1. a noisy or confused struggle or brawl among a number of people; 2. a confused mixture

- After the first half of watching the football game at the tavern, a *melee* broke out among the patrons.
- Sangria is a *melee* of citrus fruits and red wine served over ice.

melodrama (MEL uh DRAH muh) *n.* 1. a play or film concerned with exaggerated conflict and sensational overacting stereotypical characters; 2. any sensational hyperemotional acting, utterance, etc.

- *Melodrama* is typical of daytime soap operas, with lots of gesticulating and grand gestures.
- Silent films were filled with *melodrama* in contrived scenes such as the heroine's being tied to the tracks as the train approaches.

  [-tic *adj.*, -tically *adv.*]

memorable (MEM uh ri bl) *adj.* worth remembering; notable

- Lou Gehrig's farewell address was a *memorable* moment in sports history, as was Jackie Robinson's breaking baseball's color line.
- September 11, 2001, is probably as *memorable* a date for today's generation as was December 7, 1941, for the World War II generation.

  [memorably *adv.*, memorability *n.*]

mentor (MEN tir) *n.* 1. a wise advisor; 2. a teacher, coach, or active role model —*vi.*, *vt.* to act as an advisor or teacher

- Athenian philosopher Aristotle was a *mentor* to Alexander of Macedon, also know as Alexander the Great.
- Julius Caesar was a *mentor* to Octavian, who later became the first Roman emperor, Caesar Augustus.

merely (MEER lee) *adv.* no more than; only; and nothing else

- Fishing is thought by some to be *merely* a blood sport rather than a form of relaxation.
- Mighty Mouse is *merely* a muscular mouse in yellow and red tights and cape.

metamorphose* (met uh MAWR fohz) *vt.* to change in form or in nature; to transform; to undergo metamorphosis

- The caterpillar can be seen to *metamorphose* into a moth or butterfly.
- A tadpole will *metamorphose* into a frog or toad.
- Now *metamorphose* your frown into a smile; it uses fewer muscles.

  [-d, metamorphosing] [Syn. transform]

metaphor* (MET uh fawr) *n.* a figure of speech containing an implied comparison, but not using *like* or *as* (which would make it a simile), for example, "raining cats and dogs," but not "that pepper is as hot as fire"

- *Metaphor* is skillfully used by Shakespeare, although it is sometimes mixed as in ". . . to take arms against a sea of troubles and by opposing drown them."
- A *metaphor* is like a simile, which is what the first part of this sentence is.

methodical (meth AH dik uhl) *adj.* orderly and systematic

- The surgeon proceeded with the operation in a *methodical* manner.
- The floor waxer was *methodical,* making sure that he got every square inch of the room.

  [methodic *adj.*, -ly *adv.*]

meticulous* (mi TIK you luhs) *adj.* extremely careful about detail; paying careful attention; scrupulous

- The model builder was *meticulous* in his attention to getting the rigging just right.
- The chef was *meticulous* in making sure that no raw meat came in contact with ingredients meant for the salad.

miffed (MIFT) *vt.* (past) offended; put out of good humor
- Walter was *miffed* at his shoddy treatment by the produce supplier.
- Audrey went to school in a good humor but was soon *miffed* at what she heard.

  [miffing, (to) miff *vi., vt.*]

QUICK REVIEW #55

Match the word from column 2 with the word from column 1 that means most nearly the same thing.

1. media		a. transform
2. mediocre		b. offended
3. melee		c. teacher
4. melodrama		d. systematic
5. memorable		e. comparison
6. mentor		f. scrupulous
7. merely		g. average
8. metamorphose		h. sensationalism
9. metaphor		i. only
10. methodical		j. television
11. meticulous		k. notable
12. miffed		l. donnybrook

mimicry* (MIM ik REE) *n.* 1. the practice, art, instance, or way of imitating; 2. a close resemblance in color, form, or behavior of one organism to another, or of an organism to an inanimate object in its environment (for the purpose of concealment)
- Many great comedians have developed their comic senses of timing through *mimicry* of the late Jack Benny.
- For the chameleon, *mimicry* of the color of its environment is the way in which it protects itself, keeping it hidden from potential predators.

mineral (MIN oer il) *n.* 1. an inorganic substance in nature with certain physical and/or chemical properties; such a substance that is organic in origin, such as coal; 2. ore; 3. anything not animal or vegetable; 4. any element needed by plants or animals for growth, like oxygen, nitrogen, phosphorous, iron, etc.
- It's odd to consider coal to be a *mineral* because millions of years ago it was alive.
- Veins of *minerals* like gold and silver can be chipped from surrounding rocks.
- Ocean water is rich in *minerals* as well as in animal and plant life.
- The *mineral* most necessary for all existing life is oxygen.

misgiving (mis GIV ing) *n.* qualm; doubt; apprehension; disturbed feeling of doubt

- Did you ever have *misgivings* about going to a certain place or event?
- Richard had no *misgivings* about having been to the Rock Festival at Woodstock.

  [Syn. qualm]

mishap (MIS hap) *n.* accident; an unlucky or unfortunate occurrence

- Running into the lamppost was just a *mishap.*
- When you're dressed up, it's a good idea to drink nothing but colorless liquids, in case a *mishap* causes your drink to land on your clothes.

  [Syn. accident]

misleading (mis LEED ing) *adj.* leading in the wrong direction; deceptive —*vt.* 1. leading to error; deceiving; deluding; 2. influencing badly; leading to wrongdoing; leading astray

- When the electronics clerk said he'd have the part in by the next morning, he was being *misleading.*
- The directions included with the invitation were *misleading* because they omitted the mention of one turn.
- Jackie's mom wanted her to avoid having friends with poor study habits, worrying they might be *misleading* her with their careless ways.

  [(to) mislead *vt.,* misled *p.,* -ly *adv.*] [Syn. deceive]

missing (MIS ing) *adj.* absent; lost; lacking; missing after combat but not known to be dead or captured

- The *missing*-man formation is used by combat pilots to honor a lost comrade.
- Frank was *missing* at his class's morning roll call.

mitigate (MIT i GAYT) *vt.* to lessen; to make or become less severe; to moderate; to make or become less rigorous or painful

- The doctor told Gail to take aspirin to *mitigate* the pain.
- The severe weather of the past week will *mitigate* as the cold front comes through.
- Repeated exercise will *mitigate* the stiffness in your joints.

  [-d, mitgating] [Syn. relieve]

mock (MAHK) *vt.* 1. to ridicule or expose to scorn; 2. to imitate as in having fun or deriding; to make fun of; 3. to defy and lead to futility —*n.* an imitation or counterfeit —*adj.* false; imitation; sham

- It's traditional for teenagers to *mock* each others' actions.
- Dottie *mocked* Dan by putting on a baseball cap at a cocked angle and speaking in her lowest vocal range.
- The castle *mocked* the invading army's attempts to storm its walls.
- Most New York street scenes seen in older movies are *mock,* having been shot on a studio back lot.
- *Mock* turtle soup does not harm any turtles, *mock* or otherwise.

  [-ed, -ing] [Syn. imitate, ridicule]

moderation (MAH doer AY shin) *n.* 1. bringing within bounds; 2. avoiding excesses or extremes; 3. calmness; absence of violence

- Everything should be done in *moderation,* including *moderation* itself.
- Partying in *moderation* means that you're likely to have a good time and to remember it the next day.
- Both parties to the dispute acted with *moderation* so that no fighting erupted.

modicum (MAH di kim) *n.* a small amount; a bit (with *of*)

- Grandpa likes to tell tall tales, so take everything he tells you with a *modicum* of salt.
- You need not use a lot of ground pepper when seasoning your roast; usually just a *modicum* is needed.

modulate (MAHD yoo LAYT) *vt.* 1. to adjust or to regulate to the appropriate degree; 2. change the pitch or intensity, usually to a lower level; 3. (radio) to vary the amplitude or frequency of a wave's oscillation in accordance with some signal

- One must *modulate* what to expect from a child in accordance with the child's age.
- A great opera singer is one with the ability to *modulate* his or her voice.
- AM radio is amplitude *modulated,* while FM is frequency *modulated.*

    [-d, modulating, modulator *n.*]

momentous* (moh MEN tis) *adj.* very important; of great moment

- The Wright Brothers' first powered flight, in 1903, was a *momentous* occasion for human travel.
- Deciding whether or not to apply to college is a *momentous* decision.

    [-ly *adv.*]

QUICK REVIEW #56

Match the word from column 2 with the word from column 1 that means most nearly the same thing.

1. mimicry	a. bit
2. mineral	b. important
3. misgiving	c. imitation
4. mishap	d. calmness
5. misleading	e. element
6. missing	f. regulate
7. mitigate	g. qualm
8. mock	h. lessen
9. moderation	i. accident
10. modicum	j. ridicule
11. modulate	k. deceiving
12. momentous	l. absent

monarch (MAH nahrk) *n.* 1. hereditary ruler, such as a king or queen; 2. the best; 3. the top performer in a certain field

- Henry VIII and Edward VIII were the highest numbered *monarchs* of England.
- Elvis Presley is called the king, which makes him the *monarch* of rock.
- Wal-Mart is the *monarch* of retail sales.

monopoly (muh NAH pi lee) *n.* 1. exclusive control of a type of product or service; 2. exclusive possession of something

- Before its being broken up into the so-called "Baby Bells," AT&T had a *monopoly* in the telecommunications business.
- Under President Teddy Roosevelt, antitrust legislation was passed to prohibit *monopolies* from getting a strangle hold on any one industry.
- Two-year-olds Jakob and Myles have a *monopoly* of their mothers' time.
  [monopolies *pl.*] [Syn. trust, cartel]

morality (maw RAL i tee) *n.* 1. code of proper behavior according to traditions, religious laws, etc.; 2. the property of rightness in conduct or ethics

- The code of *morality* in the Western world is based on the Judaeo-Christian tradition.
- The treatment of certain prisoners in Iraq violated the dictates of *morality*.

morose (maw ROHS) *adj.* 1. bad tempered; sullen; gloomy; 2. distinguished by gloom

- A *morose* comic character walks around with a dark cloud over his head wherever he goes.
- When asked what the probability was of staying out of the course of the storm, the pilot's facial expression was *morose*.

motivation (MOH ti VAY shin) *n.* an incitement or impelling; the cause that makes someone do something

- Looking down the barrel of a gun is usually an adequate *motivation* to hand over your money.
- A method actor needs some sort of *motivation* to get into the role of the character he's playing.

motive (MOH tiv) *n.* an inner drive that causes a person to do something, or to act in a certain way; goal

- Greed is often a good *motive* for robbery.
- The *motive* for Arnold's saving every nickel he earned was his desire to purchase an automobile.

muffle (MUH fil) *vt.* 1. to dull a sound; stifle; 2. to wrap in a shawl or blanket to deaden a sound

- Each motor vehicle contains a special part designed to *muffle* the roar that the engine makes, but we won't tell you its name.
- A scarf wrapped around someone's mouth and lower face is often referred to as a muffler, in that it *muffles* any speech coming from the wearer's mouth.
- Murderers on TV often use silencers to *muffle* the sound of the gunshot.
  [-d. muffling]

mundane (muhn DAYN) *adj*. 1. earthly, as distinguished from heavenly or spiritual; 2. ordinary; everyday

- The clergy of the Middle Ages lived much more *mundane* lives than their calling might have led one to expect.
- The peacock is an outstandingly beautiful bird, while the pigeon is considerably more *mundane*.

  [-ly *adv*.] [Syn. earthly]

munificent (myoo NIF is int) *adj*. 1. very generous; giving lavishly; 2. distinguished for great generosity

- Andrew Carnegie was noted for his *munificent* donations to artistic causes.
- John D. Rockefeller's descendants have proven very *munificent* in trying to distribute some of the wealth that the family's patriarch amassed from his businesses.

  [-ly *adv*, munificence *n*.]

museum (myoo ZEE im) *n*. a room, institution, or building for displaying and/or showcasing artifacts, works of art, or items associated with a person, activity, etc.

- *Museums* can be as different as the District of Columbia's Air and Space Museum and its National Museum of Natural History.
- The Baseball Hall of Fame in Cooperstown, New York, is a *museum* devoted exclusively to the sport of baseball.

musing (MYOO zing) *adj*. meditative; pondering —*n*. meditation; reflection

- Yolanda was in a *musing* frame of mind as she thought over the day's events.
- Yoga teaches the benefits of *musing* for a set amount of time each day.

  [-ly *adv*.]

muskrat (MUHS krat) *n*. 1. any of the various glossy, brown-furred American rodents with a musky odor that are adapted by webbed hind feet for living in water; 2. such an animal's fur

- *Muskrats* have been known, as have other rodents, to carry disease.
- Imitation mink coats are usually made of *muskrat*.

QUICK REVIEW #57

Match the word from column 2 with the word from column 1 that means most nearly the same thing.

1. monarch		a. generous
2. monopoly		b. pondering
3. morality		c. goal
4. morose		d. earthly
5. motivation		e. rodent
6. motive		f. showcase
7. muffle		g. exclusive
8. mundane		h. incitement
9. munificent		i. gloomy
10. museum		j. queen
11. musing		k. stifle
12. muskrat		l. rightness

mutter* (MUH dir) *vi.* 1. to speak in a low, indistinct voice; 2. to complain —*vt.* to say something in low, often angry tones

- Neil tended to *mutter,* and it was necessary to pay very close attention to make out what he was saying.
- Laura *muttered* to the floor cleaners about what a shabby job they had done.
- When Sebastian saw what he owed in income taxes for the year, he began to *mutter* profanities.

[-ed, -ing] [Syn. murmur]

myriad (MI ree uhd) *n.* a very large number; countless; innumerable; a great number of persons or things

- Look up in the sky on a clear night away from city lights, and you'll find a *myriad* of stars and other glowing bodies.
- *Myriads* of ocean worshippers flock to the seaside each summer.

mystifying (MIS ti FY ing) *adj.* 1. puzzling; bewildering; perplexing; 2. made obscure or difficult to understand

- There is something *mystifying* about a man wearing a cape and carrying a walking stick.
- Many claim that the income tax code is *mystifying* by design rather than circumstance.

[-ly *adv.*, mystification *n.*]

mythical (MITH i kil) *adj.* 1. imaginary; fictitious; not scientifically proven; 2. existing only in myths

- The fact that the refrigerator's light goes out when the door is closed is considered *mythical* by some children (and by some adults).
- A dragon is a *mythical* creature, which never really existed.

naive (nah EEV) *adj.* 1. innocent; unworldly; childlike; unsophisticated; 2. unsuspicious; credulous

- Lara was too *naive* to know what to order at the French restaurant, so she trusted Buddy to order for her.
- Vic left his portable DVD player on the front seat of his open convertible and was *naive* enough to expect that it would still be there when he returned.

narcissistic (NAHR si SIS tik) *adj.* loving one's self; having an excessive interest in one's own appearance, comfort, importance, etc.

- Nancy is *narcissistic* enough to spend 6 hours every day in front of a full-length mirror.
- Hector is wealthy enough to be able to afford his *narcissistic* nature, having hired six full-time servants to see to his every need.

[-ally *adv.*, narcissism *n.*]

narrative (NA ruh TIV) *adj.* 1. in story form; taking the nature of a narration; 2. occupied with narration —*n.* a story; tale

- H. G. Wells's *The Time Machine* is a *narrative* told from the vantage point of the machine's inventor.
- "Call me Ishmael" is the opening sentence of Melville's *Moby Dick* and introduces the reader to the identity of the *narrative's* teller.
- In Hemingway's *The Old Man and the Sea*, it is unclear whose *narrative* the tale is.

[Syn. story]

nefarious (ni FAER ee uhs) *adj.* very wicked; underhanded; most villainous; iniquitous

- The Spanish Inquisition used *nefarious* means to identify so-called heretics.
- Joseph McCarthy was *nefarious* in his "red baiting" tactics during the 1950s communist witch hunts.

[-ly *adv.*, -ness *n.*]

negligible (NEG li jib il) *adj.* small enough to be disregarded; hardly noticeable; trifling

- The difference between a 30-gram and a 29-gram portion of flour is *negligible* to the naked eye.
- The ineffective diet that Shaila was on for 7 weeks had a *negligible* influence on her weight.

[negligibly *adv.*]

nitpicker (NIT pik oer) *n.* one who finds fault with petty details; one who pays too much attention to little things that shouldn't ordinarily matter; one who is petty or overly finicky

- Mrs. Higgins was a real *nitpicker* and would deduct points from an essay for every undotted *j* or *i* in a handwritten creative paper.
- To *nitpick* originally meant to pick tiny nits (lice eggs) out of someone's hair by using a comb or tweezers; it's not too hard to see how *nitpicker* today describes someone who obsesses over tiny details.

[nitpick *vi.*]

nomenclature (NOH min KLAY chir) *n.* 1. a set of names that is peculiar to a particular field (for example, ROM and RAM in computers) or terms exclusive to biology or another science; 2. the act or system of naming

- In the *nomenclature* of computers, ROM is read-only memory, while RAM is random-access memory.
- A dele is a deletion, parens are parentheses, and a graph is a paragraph in the *nomenclature* of proofreading.

nonchalance (NAHN shuh LAHNS) *n.* the state or quality of not showing warmth or interest in something; coolness; showing a lack of concern

- Beth greeted the news of Amy's marrying her old boyfriend, John, with *nonchalance.*
- There was an air of *nonchalance* on the face of the killer as he mowed down the nest of termites with his spray gun.

[Syn. equanimity]

nondescript (NAHN dis KRIPT) *adj.* 1. hard to classify because of a lack of recognizable qualities; 2. dull; uninteresting

- Kenny drove a *nondescript* car from the mid to late '60s.
- The only way Jim could describe Edna's neighborhood was shabby, but as for any particular features, it was just *nondescript.*

novel (NAH vil) *adj.* new; unusual —*n.* a relatively long piece of fictional prose with a complicated plot

- The Fosbury Flop was a rather *novel* approach to the high jump track-and-field event.
- When it comes to recreational reading, Marianne finds a *novel* much more satisfying than a book of short stories.

QUICK REVIEW #58

Match the word from column 2 with the word from column 1 that means most nearly the same thing.

1. mutter	a. trifling
2. myriad	b. names
3. mystifying	c. story
4. mythical	d. equanimity
5. naive	e. iniquitous
6. narcissistic	f. petty
7. narrative	g. murmur
8. nefarious	h. fictional
9. negligible	i. obscure
10. nitpicker	j. self-concerned
11. nomenclature	k. innumerable
12. nonchalance	l. unsophisticated
13. nondescript	m. unique
14. novel	n. uninteresting

O

obdurate (AHB dyoo RAYT) *adj.* 1. not easily moved to feeling empathy; 2. not readily giving in; stubborn; inflexible

- Despite his tenants' having a difficult time coming up with the rent, Simon Legree was *obdurate* in his intention to evict them.
- Although Susan tried to get her employer to allow her to work flexible hours so that she could take some courses, the manager remained *obdurate* in insisting she stick to a fixed schedule.

[-ly *adv.*] [Syn. inflexible]

oblique (oh BLEEK) *adj.* 1. Neither vertical, nor horizontal, but slanting; 2. indirect rather than to the point; 3. evasive and underhanded

- The hypotenuse of a right triangle is always *oblique* to both of the triangle's legs.
- Despite Joe's trying to get a direct answer from his supervisor as to whether his taking vacation time would impair his chances of promotion, the supervisor's answers remained *oblique*.
- The lawyer tried to pin Alice down on how much of the conversation she had overheard, but she was *oblique* in most of her responses.

[-ly *adv.*, -ness *n.*]

obscurity* (ahb SKYUR i tee) *n.* the condition or quality of being difficult to perceive, hard to see, not well known, vague, or ambiguous

- Because the soldier had taken care to completely camouflage his position, despite the enemy's closeness, his presence remained in *obscurity*.
- Elvis's presence at the top of the pop music scene elevated him to the limelight from near *obscurity*.
- The *obscurity* of the wording of the contract made it difficult to determine what was expected from either party.

[obscurities *pl.*]

observation (AHB zir VAY shin) *n.* 1. the following or keeping a law, custom, principle, etc.; 2. a noticing of something; 3. being seen or noticed; 4. the noting and recording of facts; 5. a comment or remark

- The *observation* of the Sabbath was a key part of Allan's upbringing.
- Helen's *observation* of a stranger near her car made her suspicious.
- The burglar kept low to the ground, hoping to elude everyone's *observation*.
- Kenny's *observations* during the chemical experiment were kept in his chemistry notebook.
- Rosa noticed the mismatch of Pedro's socks and could not help making an *observation* to him.

[Syn. remark]

obsessiveness (ahb SES iv nis) *n.* 1. having the nature of being haunted by something; 2. a being preoccupied by some emotion, thought, desire, etc. in defiance of reason

- His *obsessiveness* with being right all the time has driven away all his friends.
- Xavier has pursued excellence in the field of motorsports with an *obsessiveness* that can only be described as being driven (no pun intended).

obstacle (AHB stik il) *n.* anything that gets in the way or hinders; impediment; obstacle; barrier

- Police barriers are *obstacles* meant to keep fans back from parades during festive occasions.
- Lack of a high school diploma or equivalency diploma can be a real *obstacle* to getting a college degree.

obstreperous (ahb STRE pir us) *adj.* noisy, unruly, or boisterous, especially in one's opposition to something

- College students at a fraternity party generally turn *obstreperous* after a couple of hours.
- The opposition party member was *obstreperous* in his outcry against the position of the prime minister.

  [Syn. vociferous]

offensive (aw FEN siv) *adj.* 1. attacking; 2. designating the side that is seeking to score in a contest; 3. aggressive; 4. unpleasant; disgusting; repugnant

- In the game of chess, white always starts out on the *offensive,* even though it doesn't always remain such.
- In volleyball, the *offensive* side is the one with the serve.
- *Offensive* action is needed to clean up toxic waste sites.
- A skunk's odor is extremely *offensive* to most.

office (AWF is) *n.* 1. a function or duty assigned to someone; 2. a post or position of trust and/or authority; 3. any government branch; 4. the room, suite, or building occupied by people in definition #2 or #3

- Seeing to it that packages were shipped out on time was the *office* assigned to Stanley.
- It was Hillary's desire to change things that caused her to run for *office.*
- The post *office* sees to the delivery of the mail six days a week and rests on the seventh.
- The senators' offices are for the most part, unsurprisingly, in the Senate *Office* Building.

  [Syn. position, function]

onerous (OH nir is) *adj.* 1. laborious; burdensome; 2. more burdensome than rewarding

- The *onerous* task of cutting wood for the winter is tedious as well as difficult; that's what makes it *onerous.*
- A job that requires a great amount of energy and pays a very small return is *onerous.*
- Slave labor is the perfect example of *onerous* work.

opponent (uh POH nint) *n.* a person against one in a fight, argument, debate, etc.

- The navy will carry the fight to our *opponent*.
- The *opponents* sat across the chess board from each other.
- Sometimes we must sit down with our *opponents* and try to work things out.
  [Syn. adversary, enemy, foe]

opportunity (AHP oer TOO ni tee *or* AHP oer TYOO ni tee) *n.* 1. a good chance; 2. a set of circumstances favorable to

- Every person deserves an *opportunity* to succeed.
- Billy is looking for an *opportunity* for advancement.
- The United States has been called the land of *opportunity*.
  [opportunities *pl.*]

QUICK REVIEW #59

Match the word from column 2 with the word from column 1 that means most nearly the same thing.

1. obdurate	a. remark
2. oblique	b. repugnant
3. obscurity	c. barrier
4. observation	d. burdensome
5. obsessiveness	e. vociferous
6. obstacle	f. position
7. obstreperous	g. vagueness
8. offensive	h. preoccupation
9. office	i. adversary
10. onerous	j. slanted
11. opponent	k. chance
12. opportunity	l. stubborn

oppression* (uh PRESH in) *n.* 1. a weighing heavily on the mind, spirit, or soul; worry; troubling; 2. a keeping down by cruel or unjust use of power; 3. a feeling of being weighed down as with worries or problems

- *Oppression* can have a paralyzing effect on a person's ability to act.
- The *oppression* of slavery was a terrible weight on many Americans prior to the Civil War.
- The *oppression* of separate-but-equal educational opportunities that were inherently unequal was not legally terminated until almost a century after the Civil War.
  [oppressive *adj.*, oppressively *adv.*]

optimism (AHP ti mi zm) *n.* 1. the belief that good triumphs over evil; 2. the tendency to take the most cheerful point of view or hope for the best possible outcome

- If you believe that bad will be vanquished and good will win in the end, then you are a practitioner of *optimism.*
- *Optimism* permits one to look at a half empty container of chocolate milk and see it as half full.

  [optimistic *adj.*, optimistically *adv.*]

orator (AW ruh tir) *n.* 1. a person who delivers a formal public speech; 2. an eloquent public speaker

- An *orator* was a person who impressed and swayed his listeners before the days of telecommunication.
- Cicero was perhaps the *orator* of greatest fame to emerge from the senate of ancient Rome.

  [oration *n.*] [Syn. declaimer]

orchard (AWR chird) *n.* 1. an area of land set aside for the raising of fruit-bearing trees; 2. such a stand of trees; a grove of fruit trees

- Peach *orchards* dot the countryside in certain parts of Georgia.
- In New York's southern Catskill Mountains, it is common to find roads lined by apple *orchards.*

orchestra (AWR kes truh) *n.* 1. the main floor of a theater; 2. a large musical ensemble, specifically a symphony orchestra; 3. the instruments of definition 2

- As a general rule, the most expensive seats in the theater are the front and center *orchestra* seats.
- The United States is fortunate to have at least five world-class symphony *orchestras.*
- The instruments of the *orchestra* are divided into strings, brass, woodwinds, and percussion.

ordain (awr DAYN) *vt.* 1. to order; establish; decree; 2. to predestine; predetermine; 3. to invest with the office of a rabbi, minister, or priest

- In 1789, the framers *ordained* the U.S. Constitution to be the law of the country.
- Some people believe that the future is *ordained,* and no matter what we do, we can't change it.
- New clergypersons are *ordained,* usually from among the ranks of the seminarians.

  [-ed, -ing, -ment, ordination *n.*]

origin (AWR i jin) *n.* 1. a beginning; a coming into existence; 2. the birth; lineage; parenthood; 3. that in which something has its root, source, cause, etc.

- The Nile River's *origin* is in Lake Victoria.
- The *origin* of the practical home computer can be traced to Steve Wozniak's garage.
- Musical drama with fixed songs and story lines had its *origin* with the operas of Giuseppi Verdi.

  [Syn. source, inception]

originality (uh RIJ in AL i tee) *n.* 1. the quality or condition of never having occurred before; 2. the ability to be creative or inventive

- The person who wrote "Roses are red, violets are blue, monkeys are hairy, and so are you" can hardly lay claim to having any *originality.*
- When it comes to cooking contests, *originality* in use of seasonings usually plays a large part in determining the winner.

ornate (awr NAYT) *adj.* 1. heavily adorned, often to excess; 2. showy or flowery, as in some musical or literary styles

- Corinthian capitals (column tops) are known for their exceptionally *ornate* decoration.
- Paganini was an exceptionally gifted violinist, and some of his compositions are so *ornate* that nobody else can play them.

orthodox (AWR thuh DAHKS) *n.* 1. conforming to the established beliefs and doctrines (as in religion, politics, etc.); 2. designating any of the churches of the Eastern Orthodox Church

- The *orthodox* politician makes it a point not to offend any potential voters.
- Admiral Yamamoto's *unorthodox* reliance on aircraft carriers was the main reason for early Japanese successes in World War II.
- The Catholic Church celebrates Easter at a different time from the *Orthodox* Church.

  [-y* *n.*] [Ant. unorthodox]

ostensible (ahs TEN sib il) *adj.* apparent; seeming; professed

- There was an *ostensible* misunderstanding between the valet parking attendant and his client.
- An *ostensible* difference of opinion exists between those voting for one candidate and those supporting the other.

  [ostensibly *adv.*]

ostentatious* (AHS tin TAY shuhs) *adj.* showy display of wealth or learning; pretentious

- The lobby of the Ritz Carlton Hotel can only be described as slightly *ostentatious,* as one would expect.
- As a Harvard graduate, Andrew felt it necessary to place his diploma in an *ostentatious* frame in his law office.

  [-ly *adv.*, ostentation *n.*]

ostracism (AHS truh sizm) *n.* barring; banishment; excluding (from the ancient Greek word *ostra,* for a shard of pottery)

- In ancient Athens, a man's name might be written on a broken piece of pottery, and if enough ostra had his name on it, an *ostracism* took place; that is, he was banished.
- *Ostracism* is a rather cruel form of social punishment.

  [ostracize *v.*, ostracized, ostracizing] [Syn. banish]

outcast (OWT kast) *n.* one cast out; a person or thing rejected by society

- One who has been ostracized is an *outcast.*
- Persons serving jail time for having committed crimes can be considered social *outcasts.*

outcome (OWT kuhm) *n.* result; consequence
- When a coin is tossed, there are two possible *outcomes*.
- The *outcome* of a day at the beach is too often a sunburn.
  [Syn. effect]

QUICK REVIEW #60

Match the word from column 2 with the word from column 1 that means most nearly the same thing.

1. oppression	a. decree
2. optimism	b. traditional
3. orator	c. ensemble
4. orchard	d. creativity
5. orchestra	e. source
6. ordain	f. fancy
7. origin	g. weighing down
8. originality	h. grove
9. ornate	i. apparent
10. orthodox	j. cheerfulness
11. ostensible	k. declaimer
12. ostentatious	l. pretentious
13. ostracism	m. banishment
14. outcast	n. result
15. outcome	o. rejected

P – Q

palette (PAL it) *n.* 1. a thin board, usually with a thumbhole, on which an artist mixes paint colors; 2. the colors used by a certain artist for a certain painting or paintings

- An artist's *palette* usually contains only the colors that he is using to make a particular painting.
- During Picasso's blue period, his *palette* was heavily tilted in the direction of that color.

pallid (PAL id) *adj.* pale; wan; faint in color

- Margaret had been out of the sun for so long that her face had taken on an unhealthy, *pallid* color.

  [Syn. pale]

pantomime (PAN tuh MYM) *vt.* 1. a play or presentation wherein the characters perform actions and gesticulate, but speak no words; 2. an actor or actress who performs in this way; 3. actions and gestures without words used as a means of expression

- It is customary in Japanese Kabuki theater for characters to *pantomime* while made up in whiteface.
- In Mel Brooks's *Silent Movie,* everyone *pantomimed* except for the famous mime Marcel Marceau, who spoke the only word.
- *Pantomiming* is a way of conveying information to one's teammates in the game of charades.

  [-d, pantomiming]

paramount (PA ruh mownt) *adj.* ranking above all others; utmost; chief; supreme

- A child's education, both intellectually and socially, is of *paramount* importance to society.
- The meaning of what they say is not *paramount* for the French; rather, it's how they pronounce it.

  [-ly *adv.*] [Syn. dominant]

parasite (PA ruh syt) *n.* 1. one who lives at the expense of others and contributes nothing in return; 2. an organism that lives on or in another, getting nourishment from the host but contributing nothing useful and sometimes causing harm, for example, a leech

- Sometimes their maternal instincts cause women to take in *parasites* who prey upon their better nature.
- Tapeworms are *parasites* that can live inside a person's intestines and take all the nourishment ingested for themselves.

  [parasitic *adj.*, parasitically *adv.*]

parboil (PAR boyl) *vt.* 1. partially boil to cut down on final cooking time, usually as a precursor to roasting; 2. to make uncomfortably hot; overheat

- Frozen vegetables are *parboiled* for a minute or more before freezing—a process known as blanching.
- Saunas are excellent places for *parboiling* people.

[-ed, -ing]

parch (PARCH) *vi.* 1. to expose to great heat; 2. to dry up from heat; make hot and dry; 3. to make or be very thirsty

- The peppers were *parched* by their stint on the grate of the charcoal grill.
- Tomatoes are often *parched* by sun-drying, which both wrinkles them up and intensifies their flavor.
- After two hours in the boat, Roxane was *parched* and reached for a bottle of iced tea.

[-ed, -ing]

parenthetical (PAR in THE ti kl) *adj.* 1. contained in parentheses; 2. interjected as explanatory or qualifying information; 3. using or containing parentheses

- The source of the article was *parenthetical.*
- Hailee was a very talented artist, and the *parenthetical* inclusion of her age, five, was just for the viewers' information.
- Often, as in the last sentence and in this one, *parenthetical* information is enclosed between commas.

pariah (puh RY uh) *n.* 1. an undesirable; one despised and rejected by others; an outcast; 2. a member of the lowest social caste in India

- The *pariahs* in India comprise a caste known as "the untouchables."
- The soldiers returning home from the Vietnam War were treated as *pariahs* by much of the American public.

parish (PA rish) *n.* 1. an administrative district of many churches; 2. the members of the congregation of any church; 3. in Louisiana, the equivalent of a county in any other state

- A British local government's territory is often identical with the size of the original church *parish.*
- On any given Sunday, about half the members of the *parish* show up for church.
- In Louisiana, the state is carved into local *parishes* that are equivalent to counties in all the other states.

QUICK REVIEW #61

Match the word from column 2 with the word from column 1 that means most nearly the same thing.

1. palette		a. overheat
2. pallid		b. pale
3. pantomime		c. dominant
4. paramount		d. dry
5. parasite		e. gesticulate
6. parboil		f. leech
7. parch		g. congregation
8. parenthetical		h. dry
9. pariah		i. interjected
10. parish		j. colors

partisan* (PAHR ti zin) *n.* 1. a person who takes one side or the other in a contest or dispute; 2. any of a group of guerrilla fighters —*adj.* 1. like or characteristic of a partisan; 2. blindly loyal

- In the argument between Stan and Gilda, Fred was a *partisan* of Gilda.
- Armed *partisans* have been common over the years in much of Central America.
- *Partisan* politics tends to get in the way of Congress ever doing very much.
- No matter what Carolina does, Rocio is *partisan* and follows her lead.
  [Syn. follower]

passive (PAS iv) *adj.* 1. acted upon without acting back; 2. yielding; submissive; patient; 3. taking no active part

- When sanding a block of wood, the sander is the active participant, while the wood is *passive*.
- Boxing is not a sport for a *passive* person.
- In pleading not guilty to the charge of robbery, Bonnie insisted that she had been *passive,* driving the car but having no idea that a robbery had even taken place until the police pulled her over.
  [-ly *adv.*]

paternal (puh TER nil) *adj.* 1. like or typical of a father; fatherly; 2. inherited from or related on the father's side

- Willis, the pug, acted *paternally* toward both kittens.
- Lois had inherited her hairy legs from her *paternal* side.
- Natalie was a *paternal* aunt, being a sister of the child's father.
  [-ly *adv.*]

pellagra (pil AG ruh) *n.* a vitamin deficiency disease caused by a lack of adequate supply of Vitamin B$_6$, characterized by skin eruptions, gastrointestinal problems, and mental disorders

- *Pellagra* is endemic in certain parts of the world.
- Those who consume a lot of protein-rich foods need not be concerned with contracting *pellagra*.

penurious (pen YOOR ee uhs) *adj.* 1. unwilling to part with money; miserly; stingy; 2. very poor; in poverty

- Mythical King Midas had a well-documented history of being *penurious*.
- Strangely enough, sharecroppers also have a history of being *penurious* but in the second sense of the word.

[-ly *adv.*, -ness *n.*] [Syn. stingy]

perceive (poer SEEV) *vt.* 1. to mentally grasp; observe; take note of; 2. to become aware of through one of the senses

- The ant was able to *perceive* that when the spider invited her to dinner, she was the main course.
- By the odor of food and hickory in the air, Raldo *perceived* that there was a barbecue nearby.

[-d, perceiving*] [Syn. discern]

perception (poer SEP shin) *n.* 1. the act of perceiving or the ability to perceive by means of the senses; 2. insight or intuition or the possession of either of them; 3. the idea, concept, or impression formed as a result of perceiving something

- The nose of the wine gave David the *perception* of ripe cherries and blackberries.
- Despite knowing that they were meeting for the first time, Helene could not shake the *perception* that she knew him from somewhere.

perceptive (poer SEP tiv) *adj.* 1. of or capable of perceiving; 2. having sharp insight or intuition; penetrating

- It was extremely *perceptive* of Frederika to know who the real murderer was before completing even half of Agatha Christie's tale.
- Bruce was *perceptive* enough to tell from the interview that the position had already been filled and that the interviewer was just going through the motions.

[-ly *adv.*]

perfidy (POER fi dee) *n.* a deliberate breaking of trust; faithlessness; treachery

- Susan could not belive Jonathan's *perfidy* in seeing Daphne behind her back.
- General Washington could scarcely believe Benedict Arnold's *perfidy* in giving the British the plans to West Point.

[perfidious* *adj.*, perfidiously *adv.*]

QUICK REVIEW #62

Match the word from column 2 with the word from column 1 that means most nearly the same thing.

1. partisan	a. intuition
2. passive	b. submissive
3. paternal	c. discern
4. pellagra	d. treachery
5. penurious	e. intuitive
6. perceive	f. follower
7. perception	g. fatherly
8. perceptive	h. miserly
9. perfidy	i. illness

performance (poer FAWR mins) *n.* 1. the act of doing something; accomplishment; execution; fullfillment; 2. effectiveness of operation; 3. some deed or feat done; 4. a presentation before an audience

- Jack Nicholson has won the Oscar for best *performance* by an actor on more than one occasion.
- Running on clean oil improves the *performance* of your car's engine.
- The boxer's manager was pleased with his *performance* in his last fight.
- Lois and Barney attended last night's *performance* of *Cats*.

perfunctory (poer FUHNK tir ee) *adj.* 1. done without care; done routinely; superficial; 2. indifferent; lacking in concern

- The mechanic gave a *perfunctory* look at the car before telling its owner that it needed a new muffler.
- When told that she'd need to update her medical insurance coverage, Greta gave a *perfunctory* shrug.

[perfunctorily *adv.*, perfunctoriness *n.*]

periphery (poer IF ir ee) *n.* 1. the edge; an outside boundary line; the perimeter; 2. an outside surface, especially of a spherical object; 3. the immediate surrounding territory; outskirts

- The airport was just at the *periphery* of the pilot's field of vision.
- One can usually tell if a basketball is properly inflated by squeezing its *periphery* and giving it a bounce.
- The new mall is being built just at the *periphery* of the most heavily populated area.

[peripheral *adj.*, peripherally *adv.*] [Syn. circumference]

perishable (PER ish i bl) *adj.* likely to spoil or deteriorate —*n.* something, especially food, that is liable to spoil

- The most *perishable* commodity in the cooler is the ice.
- It is a good idea to refrigerate *perishables,* such as dairy products and meat.

permanence (POER min ins) *n.* the quality or fact of lasting for a very long, if not indefinite, time without changing

- There is a certain *permanence* about a marble statue that long outlasts the person or event it celebrates.
- Some *permanence* is desirable in laundry marks that go on your clothing.

permeate (POER mee ayt) *vt.* to pass into or through and affect every part; infest —*vi.* to penetrate and diffuse

- It took three paper towels to clean up the spill, as the first two became totally *permeated* with liquid.
- Rinna's daughter sent her to college in hope that some learning might *permeate* her thick, yet porous skull.

  [-d, permeating]

perpetrator (poer pi TRAY ter) *n.* 1. one who does something evil; doer of a crime; 2. one who commits a hoax or a blunder

- It is the job of the criminal justice system to lock up the *perpetrators* of criminal activities.
- Mr. Brown hammered a nail between two panels of the chalkboard thereby becoming the *perpetrator* of the infamous skyhook hoax on his physics class.

  [(to) perpetrate *vt.*, perpetrated, perpetrating]

perpetuate (poer PET yoo ayt) *vt.* to cause to continue; make perpetual; preserve from extinction

- The teacher strived to *perpetuate* the myth among her students that she had eyes in the back of her head.
- Regular service intervals and tender care will *perpetuate* the useful life of your automobile.

  [-d, perpetuating]

perplex (poer PLEKS) *vt.* 1. to puzzle; to confuse; to make one doubtful; 2. to make complicated or difficult to understand

- Finding the way to Red Riding Hood's grandma's house using the map *perplexed* the wolf.
- Finding a general cure for cancer continues to *perplex* researchers.

  [-ed, -ing] [Syn. puzzle]

persevere (poer si VEER) *vi.* to continue to make an effort despite opposition; to persist

- The Marines *persevered* in their attempt to climb Mt. Suribachi until they finally prevailed.
- To attain one's life's goals, it is essential to *persevere,* regardless of the obstacles one might encounter.

  [-d, persevering*]

persistent (poer SIST int) *n.* 1. refusing to give up; unrelenting; stubborn; 2. lasting without change; 3. constantly repeated

- The usher was *persistent* in asking the noisy couple to leave the theater.
- Yosemite Park's El Capitan has been *persistent* in resisting the ravages of wind and rain.
- Rote learning is the result of *persistent* repetition of the same information rather than understanding.

[-ly *adv.*]

persnickety (poer SNIK i tee) *adj.* 1. too fussy; too particular or precise; fastidious; 2. showing or needing very careful treatment

- Hazel was very *persnickety* about how her bedding was folded in the linen closet.
- The *persnickety* Nurse Cratchett obsessed about the dressings on her home care patients.

QUICK REVIEW #63

Match the word from column 2 with the word from column 1 that means most nearly the same thing.

1. performance	a. preserve
2. perfunctory	b. fastidious
3. periphery	c. accomplishment
4. perishable	d. constancy
5. permanence	e. persist
6. permeate	f. superficial
7. perpetrator	g. infest
8. perpetuate	h. stubborn
9. perplex	i. outskirts
10. persevere	j. doer
11. persistent	k. puzzle
12. persnickety	l. spoilable

perspective* (poer SPEK tiv) *n.* 1. the artistic picturing of things so as to represent a three-dimensional portrait using two-dimensional drawings by use of lines that converge at a vanishing point; 2. the effect of relative distances on how objects appear; 3. the relationships and proportions of parts to each other and to the whole; 4. a point of view in judging things or events

- The artist's *perspective* makes things disappear in the distance, giving the viewer the feeling of three dimensions.
- *Perspective* makes nearer objects appear larger than distant ones.
- To avoid blowing things out of proportion, we must view them in the *perspective* of how they relate to the whole.

perspicuity (POER spi KYOO i tee) *n.* clear and easily understood; lucidity; clarity in statement and expression

- It is a talent to speak with *perspicuity.*
- *Perspicuity* makes it easy to convey your ideas to others.

  [perspicuous *adj.*, perspicuously *adv.*]

persuasive (per SWAY siv) *adj.* having the power to sway one's opinion or tending to sway one's opinion, beliefs, etc.

- Your argument against a national pickle-spotting hotline was not very *persuasive* to the gherkin lobbyist.
- Over the course of time, the pen has proven to be much more *persuasive* than the sword.

pertinent (PER ti nint) *adj.* to the point; connected to the matter under consideration; relevant

- When seeking a new veterinarian, one's dog's opinion might be quite *pertinent.*
- A list of references and what they have to say could be *pertinent* to the hiring of a housekeeper.

pervasive (poer VAY siv) *adj.* tending to spread throughout something or some group

- Malicious gossip can often be *pervasive* around the workplace, spreading in a matter of minutes.
- The *pervasive* nature of some diseases is the reason for isolating any suspected cases.

  [-ly *adv.*, -ness *n.*]

pessimism (PES i mi zm) *n.* 1. expecting the worst at all times; 2. the philosophy that evil always triumphs over good

- *Pessimism* leads the driver to believe that the bridge is out just around the bend.
- The expectation that bad instincts will win out over good ones is a sign of *pessimism.*
- *Pessimism* makes one see the half-full glass as half empty.

  [pessimistic *adj.*]

phenomenal (fe NAHM in il) *adj.* very unusual; extraordinary; very remarkable

- The medical community has had *phenomenal* success with curing certain cancers.
- *Phenomenal* advances took aviation from the Wright Brothers' flyer to the space shuttle in less than 100 years.

phenomenon (fe NAHM in ahn) *n*. 1. any event, occurrence, or happening that can be determined by the senses and scientifically explained; 2. any of the foregoing, explainable or otherwise

- The *phenomenon* of a total eclipse of the sun is readily explainable with a little knowledge of astronomy.
- It is not so easy to dismiss all the reports of the *phenomenon* of alien abduction by people in many different parts of the world.

  [phenomena *pl.*]

philanthropic (fil in THRAH pik) *adj*. charitable; giving; benign; humanitarian; having a desire to help mankind

- Many of the great robber barrons of the late nineteenth and early twentieth centuries are known today for the *philanthropic* works of the foundations named for them.
- Two such *philanthropic* organizations are the Carnegie and the Rockefeller foundations.

philosophy (fil AHS uh fee) *n*. 1. theoretical or logical analysis of the principles underlying thought, knowledge, conduct, and the nature of the universe—made up of ethics, logic, esthetics, epistimology, metaphysics, etc.; 2. the general or specific principles governing human character and morals

- Many different aspects of *philosophy* concerned the deep thinkers of the seventeenth, eighteenth, and nineteenth centuries.
- The *philosophy* of medical ethicists is ever more taxed in the twenty-first century.
- Because logic is a branch of *philosophy,* it should be no surprise that French philosopher René Descartes gave us the Cartesian coordinates system of naming points by coordinates.

  [philosophic *adj.*, philosophically *adv.*]

phlegmatic (flig MA tik) *adj*. difficult to rouse to action because of sluggishness, dullness, apathy, coolness, calmness, or stolidity

- The United States was very *phlegmatic* in its response to both European wars of the last century.
- The United States was far from *phlegmatic* in getting involved with Iraq in 2003.

  [-ally *adv.*] [Syn. impassive]

physicist (FIZ is ist) *n*. a scientist dealing with the interaction of matter and energy (physics) whose parts are mechanics, optics, heat, light, and most recently quantum physics

- A *physicist* deals with lenses and the laws of refraction and reflection.
- Newton's laws of motion are the province of the *physicist.*
- A *physicist* does not exactly deal with rocket science—er, wait a second; that's exactly what a physicist might deal with.

QUICK REVIEW #64

Match the word from column 2 with the word from column 1 that means most nearly the same thing.

1. perspective	a. principles
2. perspicuity	b. happening
3. persuasive	c. relevant
4. pertinent	d. giving
5. pervasive	e. scientist
6. pessimism	f. extraordinary
7. phenomenal	g. convincing
8. phenomenon	h. impassive
9. philanthropic	i. negativity
10. philosophy	j. lucidity
11. phlegmatic	k. spreading
12. physicist	l. proportionality

physiology (fiz ee AHL i jee) *n.* 1. the branch of medical science dealing with the functions and processes of various bodily organs in relation to the whole organism and each other; 2. the functions and processes of an organism and its vital organs

- It is not earthshaking to conclude that the *physiologies* of men and women are as different as they are alike.
- The *physiology* of most organs must work together for an organism to be truly healthy.

  [physiologies *pl.*, physiological *adj.*, physiologically *adv.*]

pigment (PIG mint) *n.* 1. the coloring matter, usually in the form of a powder or concentrate, that is mixed with a water or oil base to form paint; 2. a coloring matter in the cells of plants and animals —*vi.* to take on color

- Today, more often than not, *pigments* are mixed at the paint counter and added to a base to give thousands of possible shades of paint for your walls.
- Even though it has another function, chlorophyll is the green *pigment* found in many plants.
- A chameleon's skin will *pigment* according to its environs.

  [-ed, -ing] [Syn. tint]

pinion (PIN yin) *n.* 1. a small gear whose teeth fit into a larger rack to accomplish motion; 2. the last bony section of a bird's wing —*vt.* 1. to disable by binding one's arms; 2. to handcuff or shackle; 3. to cut off the pinions of a bird's wing to prevent its flying

- The *pinion* makes possible the rack-and-*pinion* steering so prevalent in today's sportier cars.
- The *pinions* of a bird's wings are often clipped by zoos to prevent the animals from flying the coop, as it were.
- A capturing soldier often *pinions* his captive's arms to prevent resistance.
- A peacock's wings are usually *pinioned* by a zoo's curators, for reasons already mentioned.

[-ed, -ing]

placebo (pli SEE boh) *n.* 1. a harmless unpotent medication given to a patient to humor him or her, or used as a control in a blind test of medications; 2. something said or done to humor or win the favor of another

- Sometimes a *placebo* is given to a patient who would not benefit from a medicine, just to make him think he's on medication.
- Such a pill often makes a psychological difference to the patient, known as the *placebo* effect.
- In tests of medicines, the control group is always given a *placebo* to see whether the medicine being tested has any significant effect.

plagiarize (PLAY jir YZ) *vt.* to take ideas, writings, etc. from someone else and pass them off as one's own

- Copyright laws exist to protect authors from having their intellectual property *plagiarized*.
- Most *plagiarizing* is done by students writing papers, who claim some author's or some encyclopedia's words as their own.

[-d, plagiarizing]

pliable (PLY i bl) *adj.* 1. easily bent or molded; 2. easily persuaded or influenced; 3. adaptable

- Aluminum foil is quite *pliable,* and the heavy-duty kind is suitable for wrapping food for the freezer.
- Some people are *pliable* enough to be easily convinced to buy "wonder products" they see in TV infomercials.
- Some breeds of dog are *pliable* enough to be comfortable living in the Arctic or in mid-latitude climates.

[pliably *adv.*] [Syn. plastic]

pluralism (PLU ril i zm) *n.* 1. existing in more than one form; 2. the holding of more than one office by a single person; 3. a society made up of many diverse ethnic groups or groups from different cultural backgrounds

- Water exhibits a *pluralism* by existing as a liquid, a solid, and a gas, sometimes all at the same time.
- There were times when a president of the United States demonstrated *pluralism* by being his own secretary of state.
- The composition of the population of the United States is about as great an example of ethnic *pluralism* as can be found on earth.

[pluralistic *adj.*, pluralistically *adv.*]

poison (POY zin) *n.* 1. a substance that causes illness or death when eaten, drunk, or otherwise absorbed by the body; 2. anything destructive physically, emotionally, etc. —*vt.* 1. to give poison to; harm or destroy by means of poison; 2. to corrupt

- A cobra's venom is one of the most powerful *poisons* in the animal world.
- Propaganda is a *poison* that the Nazis and the Soviets were adroit at using in the middle of the last century.
- Various pesticides are used to *poison* undesirable rodents.
- Stereotyping certain ethnic groups can *poison* the attitudes of the impressionable toward them.

  [-ed, -ing]

polar (POH lir) *adj.* 1. of, relating to, or near the South or North Pole; 2. of a pole; 3. having polarity; 4. opposite in nature or function

- The earth is not the only planet to have *polar* ice caps.
- Magnets are *polar,* with unlike ones attracting and like ones repelling each other.
- When installing batteries in a radio, you must pay attention to their *polar* alignment.
- Optimists' and pessimists' philosophies are at *polar* extremes of the spectrum.

political (puh LI ti kl) *adj.* 1. of or about, politics, government, country, state; 2. relating to a definite governmental organization; 3. taking sides in political parties

- *Political* leaders are elected in some countries, appointed in others, and seize power by force in still others.
- The secretaries of the cabinet are *political* appointees of the president but must be approved by the Senate.
- Many votes in the legislatures are governed by *political* considerations.

  [-ly *adv.*]

politician (pah li TISH in) *n.* 1. a person actively engaged in politics, often used derisively to mean scheming, after personal gain, etc.; 2. one particularly skilled in politics

- *Politicians* as a group do not enjoy a particularly good reputation, as they're reputed to scheme in the back room.
- Lyndon Johnson was a particularly skilled *politician,* who knew how to play the game to his best advantage.

pollution (puh LOO shin) *n.* 1. the result of defiling; making impure, corrupt, or dirty; 2. contamination with waste materials

- Industrial *pollution* has been considerably abated in California as a result of very strong environmental legislation.
- Air and water *pollution* are probably the two forms of contamination most in the public eye.

  [Syn. contamination]

QUICK REVIEW #65

Match the word from column 2 with the word from column 1 that means most nearly the same thing.

1. physiology	a. sugar pill
2. pigment	b. diverse
3. pinion	c. schemer
4. placebo	d. opposite
5. plagiarize	e. functionality
6. pliable	f. contamination
7. pluralism	g. governmental
8. poison	h. tint
9. polar	i. steal
10. political	j. toxin
11. politician	k. shackle
12. pollution	l. adaptable

ponderous* (PAHN dir is) *adj.* 1. very heavy; 2. difficult to handle because of weight; 3. bulky; massive; seemingly heavy; 4. dull and labored

- Harry and David found that the armoire was a *ponderous* piece of furniture to move.
- Traditionally, and for obvious reasons, the refrigerator is the most *ponderous* appliance to move.
- When not faced with a threat, the gait of the African elephant seems rather *ponderous,* as befits its size.

  [-ly *adv.*] [Syn. heavy]

poorly (POR lee) *adv.* 1. not well; not functioning properly; badly or ineffectively; 2. with a low opinion; disparagingly

- A myopic person sees far things very *poorly.*
- When it comes to exams, Tom tests rather *poorly.*
- Many people thought *poorly* of Ford's Edsel, so the model didn't last on the market for very long.

possessions (puh ZESH inz) *n. pl.* 1. things owned; personal property; 2. property or wealth; 3. any territories ruled by another country

- All Rosanne's *possessions* were destroyed in the fire.
- The Hawaiian Islands and Puerto Rico were among the *possessions* acquired by the United States as a result of the Spanish-American War.
- The territory of Transjordan was a *possession* of the British Crown until 1948.

  [possession *sing.*]

postscript (POHST skript) *n*. 1. a note added after the signature of a letter; 2. an afterthought or supplementary information

- A *postscript* in a letter is usually indicated by the initials P.S. on the line following the signature.
- An epilogue can also be thought of as a *postscript* to a book or play.

potentate (POH tin tayt) *n*. a person who has a great amount of power; ruler; monarch; emperor

- The sultan of Brunei is an Eastern *potentate* of considerable wealth.
- The tsars of Russia were *potentates* until the end; recent British monarchs are not so.

poultry (POHL tree) *n*. domestic fowl raised for eggs and/or meat; chicken, turkeys, ducks, and geese, collectively

- The *poultry* department in most supermarkets is located adjacent to, or in, the meat department.

powwow (POW WOW) *n*. 1. any conference or gathering; 2. among Native North Americans, a ceremony to help cure disease, plan war, etc. characterized by feasting and dancing; a medicine man; a conference —*vi*. to hold a conference; confer

- *Powwows* once conjured up visions of Native Americans and pilgrims smoking a peace pipe in a circle around the fire.
- Any corporate meeting can be refered to as a *powwow,* especially if it is an informal one.

practical (PRAK ti KL) *adj*. 1. gotten by or from practice; 2. usable, workable; sensible; 3. dealing with reality rather than theory; practicable

- A *practical* knowledge of how a car engine works is a good thing to have before attempting to repair one.
- When making home repairs, the rule is to be *practical* about what you can afford to do.
- It is not *practical* to equip an economy car with a V-8 engine.

  [-ly *adv.,* -ity *n.*]

pragmatic (prag MAT ik) *adj*. 1. concerned with everyday practices rather than theory or idealism; practical; 2. opinionated; dogmatic

- A *pragmatic* approach to learning these words means you should study one or two groups of words in one sitting.
- It is not *pragmatic* to try to read through this book in a single sitting; after all, it doesn't have much of a plot.
- An old codger might be quite *pragmatic* in his beliefs about how to make a pot of coffee.

  [pragmatist* *n.,* -ally *adv.*]

praise (PRAYZ) *vt*. 1. to express approval; commend; 2. to glorify; extol

- It is a policy of good management to *praise* employees for good work.
- *Praising* will almost always get better results than criticizing.
- Some congregations exult in *praising* the Lord.

  [-d, praising, -e *n. sing.*] [Syn. laud, acclaim]

preamble (PREE AM bl *or* pre AM bl) *n.* an introduction, especially to a constitution, law, etc. stating what its purpose is

- The *preamble* to the U.S. Constitution sets down its reason for being.
- Wilson's 14 points were his *preamble* to laying out his vision of what the peace treaty ending World War I should look like.

  [Syn. introduction]

precarious (pri KAYR ee is) *adj.* 1. uncertain; insecure; dependent on circumstances; 2. depending on the will or favor of others; 3. depending on chance; risky; uncertain

- Sitting on a flagpole is a *precarious* position to be in.
- One who relies on the goodwill of others has at best a *precarious* chance of success.
- Relying on a lottery to raise the money for your college tuition makes the likelihood of your getting a diploma *precarious* at best.

  [-ly* *adv.*]

QUICK REVIEW #66

Match the word from column 2 with the word from column 1 that means most nearly the same thing.

1. ponderous	a. afterthought
2. poorly	b. sensible
3. possessions	c. confer
4. postscript	d. opinionated
5. potentate	e. heavy
6. poultry	f. commend
7. powwow	g. geese
8. practical	h. insecure
9. pragmatic	i. introduction
10. praise	j. wealth
11. preamble	k. disparagingly
12. precarious	l. emperor

precedence (PRE si DENS) *n.* 1. priority because of superiority in rank, age, seniority, etc.; 2. a ranking of dignitaries in order of importance

- In the succession to the presidency, following the Speaker of the House and the President Pro Tempore of the Senate, the *precedence* is to go through the cabinet secretaries in the order in which their posts were created.
- When seating dignitaries at an event, a prince always takes *precedence* over an earl.
- In poker, a royal flush takes *precedence* over every other hand.

  [precedency *n.*]

precedent (PRE si DINT) *n.* 1. an earlier decision, judgment, act of law, case, etc. that serves as an example for a later one; 2. something done based on earlier events —*adj.* that precedes; preceding

- The right of the Supreme Court to pass on a law's constitutionality was established by *precedent.*
- Many court decisions are based on *precedent.*
- It is chivalrous to give women and children *precedent* over men when abandoning ship.

precept (PREE sept) *n.* 1. a rule of moral conduct; maxim; 2. a commandment or directive meant as a rule of conduct

- Justice for all is a *precept* of American democracy.
- Not watching while a sausage is being made is a *precept* of enjoying eating that sausage.

  [Syn. doctrine]

precipitate* (pri SIP it AYT) *vt.* 1. to cause to happen before expected or desired; to hasten; 2. (chemistry) to make something insoluble so that it separates from a solution —*n.* (chemistry) a solid separated from a solution

- The invasion of Poland *precipitated* England's entry into World War II.
- It took a weight gain of 10 pounds to *precipitate* Melissa's going on a diet.
- Sodium chloride can be *precipitated* out of solution by adding the right chemical, but don't ask me which.
- Silver chloride coming out of solution appears as grayish flakes of *precipitate.*

  [-d, precipitating, precipitation *n.*]

precise (pri CYS) *adj.* 1. accurately said; exactly defined; 2. speaking distinctly; 3. without variation; 4. scrupulous; fastidious

- Be *precise* in what you say, and your words won't be misinterpreted.
- The opposite of *precise* speaking is mumbling.
- An atomic clock is more *precise* than anybody has a practical use for.
- A surgeon must be *precise* in her attention to keeping a sterile field.

  [-ly *adv.*, precision *n.*] [Syn. explicit, correct]

preclude* (pree KLOOD) *vt.* to make impossible; to cut out of the realm of possibilities; to prevent

- Having been scratched from the field of 12 horses in the race *precludes* any possibility of How About That's finishing in the money.
- The drawbridge's being stuck open *precluded* any chance of Iggy's getting to work early yesterday.

  [-d, precluding] [Syn. prevent]

precocious (pri KOH shis) *adj.* 1. matured to a level beyond that which is normal for one of that age (a precocious child); 2. of or demonstrating premature development

- Geoffrey was so *precocious* that he was walking at 8 months of age.
- Mathew was *precocious* enough to be taking college-level math courses while still in junior high school.
- Mozart's *precocious* musical skill is well documented.

  [-ly *adv.*]

predators* (PRED uh TAWRZ) *n.* 1. ones who live by exploiting and robbing others; 2. ones who capture and feed on other animals; 3. birds or creatures of prey

- *Predators* often take advantage of older or disadvantaged people.
- Lions, like most *predators,* are at the top of their food chain.
- *Predators* of the bird family are known as raptors.

predecessor (PRE di CES oer) *n.* 1. a person who held the same office before the one currently occupying it; 2. an ancestor; 3. something that was used before it was replaced by a newer thing

- Lyndon Johnson's *predecessor* as president was John F. Kennedy.
- Cro-Magnon man is believed to have been a *predecessor* of *Homo sapiens.*
- The ice box, which contained a block of ice, was the *predecessor* of the refrigerator.

predict (pri DIKT) *vt.* foretell; to know and state what a future event will be

- If fortune tellers can *predict* the future, why aren't they all rich?
- It is easy to *predict* that the next word you look at after *predict* will be prehensile.

  [-able* *adj.,* -ably *adv.*]

prehensile (pree HEN sil) *adj.* adapted for grabbing, such as the tails of many monkeys; grasping

- If you've ever gone to the monkey house, then you've seen monkeys swinging by their *prehensile* tails.
- Unlike most humans, monkeys and lemurs have *prehensile* feet and can use them to pick things up.

premise* (PREM is) *n.* a prior statement or condition that serves as the basis for an argument or procedure; the underlying assumption

- The *premise* of your asking whether I enjoyed the movie *Gladiator* is in error because I never saw the film.
- When Dawn asked Cathy how she'd enjoyed college chemistry, her *premise* was that Cathy had taken the course, and she was correct.

  [Syn. presumption]

QUICK REVIEW #67

Match the word from column 2 with the word from column 1 that means most nearly the same thing.

1. precedence		a. doctrine
2. precedent		b. prevent
3. precept		c. grasping
4. precipitate		d. ancestor
5. precise		e. foretell
6. preclude		f. earlier event
7. precocious		g. presumption
8. predators		h. ordering
9. predecessor		i. explicit
10. predict		j. advanced
11. prehensile		k. hasten
12. premise		l. exploiters

preoccupy (pree AHK yoo py) *vt.* to occupy one's thoughts to the total exclusion of everything else; to engross or absorb

- Sandy was so *preoccupied* with the book she was reading that she didn't hear her mother call her to dinner.
- It was the job of the point man to *preoccupy* the sentry so that he didn't see the rest of the attacking force.

[preoccupied, -ing, preoccupation* *n.*]

prepossess (pree PUH zes) *vt.* 1. to prejudice or bias, especially favorably; 2. to favorably impress immediately

- Linda loved to *prepossess* a new teacher by showing off her good manners at every opportunity.
- *Prepossessing* one's new employer is not a bad way to start a new business relationship.

[-ed, -ing, prepossessing, *adj.*]

prescribe (pri SKRYB) *vt.* 1. to order or direct; ordain; 2. to order as a medicine or method of treatment (by a medical doctor); 3. (law) to outlaw or invalidate

- The traffic officer *prescribed* a left turn for all traffic at the intersection.
- The doctor *prescribed* a regimen of bed rest and a liquid diet.
- The Constitution *prescribes* cruel and unusual punishment.

[-d, prescribing]

preservation (PREZ ir VAY shin) *n.* 1. protected from harm; 2. kept from spoiling or rotting; 3. maintaining by regulating

- Acid-free sleeves help with the *preservation* of photographs.
- Food *preservation* began with vacuum packaging in the nineteenth century.
- The *preservation* of wildlife is just one assignment of the U.S. Forest Service.

presumptuous (pri ZUMP shoo uhs) *adj.* overconfident or arrogant; taking too much for granted

- How *presumptuous* was the guest at the cocktail party to take a plastic bag from her purse and start filling it with jumbo cocktail shrimp?
- It was rather *presumptuous* of the wedding guest to take a seat at the head table.

  [-ly *adv.*, -ness *n.*]

pretense (PREE tens) *n.* 1. an unsupported claim of having accomplished something; 2. a false claim; 3. a pretending, as in make-believe

- It was quite by accident that a former vice president made a *pretense* to having invented the Internet.
- A major *pretense* of a certain U.S. president is that he can pronounce the word "nuclear."
- Children often learn proper behavior through *pretense* to be adult role models.

pretentious (pree TEN shis) *adj.* 1. claiming some importance or distinction; 2. ostentatious; showing off; self-important

- George of the Jungle was a rather *pretentious* character, considering that Ape was the brains of the outfit.
- The triple loop performed by the roller boarder was a very *pretentious* display of his/her skills.

previous (PREE vee uhs) *adj.* before the present; prior; at an earlier time; preceding

- The *previous* administration enjoyed more popularity than the current one.
- Mary was convinced that she had been a sheep in a *previous* incarnation.

primarily (pry MER i lee) *adv.* at first; originally; principally; mainly

- *Primarily*, vacations seemed more important than school to Ian, but that came to change.
- Alice went to space camp *primarily* to learn more about the solar system.

primary (PRY mer ee) *adj.* 1. first in order or first to have been developed; 2. primitive; fundamental; basic; 3. in the first level of a series or sequence; 4. chief; principal; main

- The *primary* polio vaccine was the Salk vaccine, with Sabin's coming along later.
- *Primary* school is where a child develops fundamental reading and math skills.
- In the *primary* elections, the final candidates are selected.
- The president is the *primary* executive officer in the United States.

primate (PRY mayt) *n.* 1. any of an order of mammals that has soft hands and feet, each terminating in five digits (monkeys, lemurs, apes, humans); 2. the highest-ranking bishop in a province

- Orangutans and gorillas are very different *primates* from your sister Sally.
- A *primate* of the church is so called because he is prime among officials of his region.

principle (PRIN si pil) *n.* 1. a fundamental truth or natural law; 2. the ultimate or underlying cause of something; 3. a rule of conduct or scientific law

- It is a *principle* of Newton's physical discoveries that what goes up must come down.
- The *principle* of jet propulsion might not be obvious from watching a jet plane, but watch a squid propel itself through the water, and you'll get it.
- The *principles* of good manners are not hard to live by and make for a much more civilized existence.

QUICK REVIEW #68

Match the word from column 2 with the word from column 1 that means most nearly the same thing.

1. preoccupy	a. protection
2. prepossess	b. rule
3. prescribe	c. mainly
4. preservation	d. bishop
5. presumptuous	e. preceding
6. pretense	f. engross
7. pretentious	g. fundamental
8. previous	h. prejudice
9. primarily	i. false claim
10. primary	j. outlaw
11. primate	k. ostentatious
12. principle	l. arrogant

pristine* (pris TEEN) *adj.* 1. characteristic of an earlier time or condition; original; 2. as if unopened; unspoiled; still pure

- The *pristine* conditions of the Alaskan forests exist only because humans have interfered with them minimally.
- *Pristine* mountain streams barely exist in the lower 48 states, primarily due to urban and industrial sprawl.

  [-ly *adv.*]

procrastinate (proh CRAS tin AYT) *vi.* to put off doing something to a future time and to do this habitually; to often postpone

- When it comes to doing homework, the better students are generally not the ones who *procrastinate.*
- The motto of the true procrastinator (one who *procrastinates*) is "Never do today what you can put off 'til tomorrow."

  [-d, procrastinating]

procure (proh KYUR mint) *vt.* to get or bring about by some effort; obtain; secure

- It was the sergeant's job to *procure* supplies.
- We must *procure* the right tools for doing the job.

  [-d, procuring, -ment* *n.*] [Syn. get]

profundity (pruh FUHN di tee) *n.* 1. of great depth, especially intellectually; 2. a profound matter, idea, etc.

- Some people find great *profundity* in the works of Salvadore Dali; others just find them funny or clever.
- The works of Gilbert and Sullivan are generally lacking in *profundity,* yet they are very entertaining.
- Do not underestimate the *profundity* of needing to solve the problem of global warming.

profusion (PRUH FYOO zhin) *n.* 1. a pouring forth with great abundance; 2. great liberalness and wastefulness; 3. a rich or lavish amount

- Strawberries, which are scarce throughout the winter, are available in *profusion* come spring.
- Every Congress passes a *profusion* of bills that waste taxpayers' money on local projects.
- Wild blackberries and black raspberries may be found growing in great *profusion* by roadsides throughout the Northeast every summer.

prolific (pruh LIF ik) *adj.* 1. producing an abundance of fruit or offspring; 2. producing many works of the mind (writings, musical compositions, art, etc.)

- Some breeds of cat are very *prolific,* having litters of six to eight kittens at a time.
- Franz Joseph Haydn was *prolific* enough to produce over 150 symphonies during his lifetime, 104 of which still exist in today's repertoire, although only the last 16 are performed frequently.
- Shakespeare has to have been one of the most *prolific* playwrights of the seventeenth century.

  [-ally *adv.*] [Syn. fertile]

protagonist (pruh TAG uhn ist) *n.* 1. the main character in a story, play, drama, etc. around whom the action takes place; 2. the actor who plays that role

- Sam Spade, the *protagonist* created by Dashiell Hammett, first appeared in 1929 and made it big in *The Maltese Falcon.*
- Spade appeared in a few films, with Humphrey Bogart as the *protagonist,* and when the Hammett stories were exhausted, Bogart continued as Raymond Chandler's Philip Marlowe.

provocative* (pruh VAHK uh tiv) *adj.* 1. provoking or tending to provoke to action, thought, feeling, etc.; stimulating; 2. erotic

- Samuel Adams's impassioned writings against the arbitrary actions of the British monarchy were *provocative* enough to be credited with moving the colonists toward revolution.
- The actress wore a very *provocative* gown to the award ceremony.

  [-*ly adv.*]

proximity (prahk SIM i tee) *adj.* the state or property of being near in space or time

- The *proximity* of the Easter and Passover holidays is not a coincidence because the Last Supper was a Passover Seder.
- When driving, it is a good idea to stay out of *proximity* to the car in front of you.

pseudonym (SOO din im) *n.* a false name, especially one assumed by an author so as not to be identified by his readers; pen name

- Mark Twain was the well-known *pseudonym* of Samuel Langhorne Clemens.
- The creator of Perry Mason, Erle Stanley Gardner, wrote other books under the *pseudonym* A. A. Fair.
- The French call a *pseudonym* a nom de plume or pen name.

quandary (KWAHN dree) *n.* a state of uncertainty; a puzzling position or a perplexing situation; a predicament

- Sylvia was in a *quandary* over which dress to wear to her friend Rhiannon's party.
- The *quandary* of whether to accept his friend Randy's invitation to go to the hockey game, or to go to the basketball game with his dad, as previously planned, reduced Howard to tears.

  [Syn. predicament]

quell (KWELL) *vt.* 1. to crush; to put an end to; to subdue; 2. to allay or assuage; to quiet

- It was General Santa Ana's job to *quell* the rebellion of the Texans.
- Bill tried to *quell* Andrea's fears about her upcoming tonsilectomy.
- It should *quell* your concerns about spelling *q* words to know that there's always a *u* following the *q*—as long as it's an English word.

querulous (KWER yoo lis) *adj.* complaining; peevish; inclined to find fault

- Nancy was so *querulous* that no hairstylist wanted to wait on her.
- The gardener finished trimming the roses and was waiting for the *querulous* Mr. Jones to inspect his work, knowing that the latter would find something wrong.

  [-*ly adv.*]

quest (KWEST) *n.* 1. a pursuit; 2. any journey or search in pursuit of a (usually) noble end

- Sir Galahad's *quest* to find the Holy Grail is legendary.
- Frank traveled from ballpark to ballpark around the country in his *quest* to find the perfect frankfurter.

quizzical (KWIZ i kuhl) *adj.* 1. comical; odd; 2. teasing; bantering; 3. perplexing
- The cat had a seemingly *quizzical* expression on its face after it fell off the couch.
- Barry chided Tony about his batting slump in a *quizzical* manner.
- Hailee felt that trying to figure out how this gravity thing worked was rather *quizzical*.

[-ly *adv.*]

QUICK REVIEW #69

Match the word from column 2 with the word from column 1 that means most nearly the same thing.

1. pristine	a. acquire
2. procrastinate	b. fertile
3. procure	c. pen name
4. profundity	d. nearness
5. profusion	e. unspoiled
6. prolific	f. subdue
7. protagonist	g. predicament
8. provocative	h. main character
9. proximity	i. postpone
10. pseudonym	j. abundance
11. quandary	k. stimulating
12. quell	l. depth
13. querulous	m. pursuit
14. quest	n. teasing
15. quizzical	o. complaining

R

radicalism* (RAD i kil IZ im) *n.* 1. the quality or state of being extreme, especially in political matters; 2. extreme in principles, ideas, methods, etc.

- Senator Brown's penchant for *radicalism* brought him the admiration of his friends and the distrust of his enemies.
- The surgeon's reputation for *radicalism* made his patients think twice before assenting to go under the knife.

rancorously (RAN kir uhs lee) *adv.* maliciously; spitefully; with continuous bitter ill will or hatred

- The argument continued *rancorously* as each side showed its contempt for the other.
- Peter treated double-parkers *rancorously* by letting the air out of their tires.

  [rancorous *adj.*]

raucous (RAW kuhs) *adj.* 1. hoarse; rough sounding; 2. loud and bawdy

- The revelers had a *raucous* good time as they partied the night away.
- Gerald had a *raucous* laugh that reminded the average bystander of how a grizzly bear might laugh.

  [-ly *adv.*, -ness *n.*]

reaction* (ree AK shin) *n.* 1. an opposing action or force; 2. a response to a stimulus; 3. a moving backward to an earlier time's condition or way of doing things; extreme conservatism

- Newton's third law of motion states that for every action there is an equal and opposite *reaction*.
- When suddenly poked, it is a natural *reaction* to jump.
- The forces of *reaction* would move the country back to horse-and-buggy times.

reactionary (ree AK shin ER ee) *adj.* characteristic of or advocating definition 3 of *reaction* —*n.* one who advocates same

- *Reactionary* forces wish to return the country's economy to the gold standard.
- The political opposite of a radical is a *reactionary*.

  [reactionaries *pl.*]

rebellious (ri BEL yis) *adj.* 1. resisting authority; engaged in armed resistance against the government; 2. of or like rebels; 3. opposing all control; defiant; 4. difficult to treat

- There is usually one *rebellious* group or another trying to overthrow a government in Central America.
- Teenagers frequently become *rebellious* against parental authority around age 17.
- Dan struggled with a very *rebellious* cowlick of hair.

  [-ly *adv.*, -ness *n.*]

rebuff (ri BUF) *vt.* 1. to snub; bluntly reject; 2. to check or turn back (an advance) —*n.* a snubbing; an abrupt refusal of advice, help, etc.

- Management's offer of a 2% raise was *rebuffed* by the union's representatives.
- Marilyn *rebuffed* Joe's attempt to get back together.
- Liz's attempt to get the floor refinishers back to fix the flaws in their work was met with a *rebuff*.

  [-ed, -ing]

recklessness (REK lis NIS) *n.* 1. foolhardiness; carelessness; 2. rashness; disregard for consequences

- Paul's mom was nervous about his going skiing—especially because he had a history of *recklessness*.
- What appears to be *recklessness* on the part of professional daredevils has usually been very carefully planned out so as to avoid injury.

  [reckless *adj.*, recklessly *adv.*]

reconcile (REK in SYL) *vt.* 1. make consistent; 2. become friendly again; 3. to settle

- At least once a month, everyone should *reconcile* his or her checkbook to make sure that what is in the account jibes with what the book shows.
- Jan and Mary *reconciled* their differences over who should have brought the watermelon to the picnic.
- The divorced couple *reconciled* for the sake of the children.

  [-d*, reconciling, reconciliation *n.*]

QUICK REVIEW #70

Match the word from column 2 with the word from column 1 that means most nearly the same thing.

1. radicalism	a. extremism
2. rancorously	b. response
3. raucous	c. defiant
4. reaction	d. conservative
5. reactionary	e. carelessness
6. rebellious	f. snub
7. rebuff	g. settle
8. recklessness	h. maliciously
9. reconcile	i. noisy

reconnoiter (REE kin OY tir) *vt.* 1. to make a reconnaisance, that is, to seek out information about enemy installations or positions; 2. to make a preliminary survey

- Corporal Smith was sent ahead to *reconnoiter* the lay of the land and look for enemy troops.
- The surveyor was sent to the prospective shopping center to *reconnoiter* the property and the existing traffic patterns and to assess the practicality of the project.

    [-ed, -ing]

recrimination (ree KRIM in AY shin) *n.* the answering of an accusation by accusing the accuser; countercharge

- When Sue threatened to take Jim to court over his dog's digging up her roses, he threatened *recrimination* over her cat's destroying his vegetable garden.
- Barbara threatened *recrimination* if Barry complained to the authorities about her noisy party.

    [(to) recriminate *vi.*]

rectify (REK ti FY) *vt.* 1. to set right; correct; 2. (electricity) to convert alternating current to direct current

- Roberta tried to *rectify* the error that she had made when she omitted Jack's name from the guest list.
- Mr. Jones *rectified* the boundary dispute with his neighbor by moving his fence.

    [rectified, -ing]

redoubtable (ree DOWT ib il) *adj.* 1. formidable; fearsome; 2. commanding respect

- Atilla the Hun's horsemen constituted a *redoubtable* force.
- Heavy machinery is *redoubtable,* and one working with it must exercise care at all times.

reductive (ree DUHK tiv) *adj.* 1. of or characterized by making smaller or lowering in price; 2. tending to making things less complex (usually a disparaging term)

- Certain stores price items so that they may advertise *reductive* pricing schemes.
- Good science teachers take a *reductive* approach to the subject matter so that they can feed the concepts to the students in bite-sized portions.

    [-ly *adv.*]

redundancy* (ree DUHN din see) *n.* 1. the quality of being excessive; superfluity; 2. an overabundance; 3. something that says something already said or does something already done; 4. the part of a redundant statement that is superfluous

- To say that the dirty laundry is not very clean is a *redundancy.*
- Due to a *redundancy* of grain produced most years by U.S. farmers, some of them are paid by the government not to grow certain crops.
- Many commercial airliners have *redundancies* deliberately built into them to back up the main systems.
- "Is not very clean" is the *redundancy* in the first sentence.

    [redundancies *pl.*, redundance *n.*]

refract (rif RAKT) *vt.* 1. to cause a ray of light to bend, as it does when passing obliquely from one medium to another of different density; 2. to measure the degree of bending of a ray of light

- When white light *refracts* through a triangular prism, it separates into the colors of the rainbow.
- An ophthalmologist or optometrist *refracts* one's eyes to determine the proper curvature for corrective lenses.

    [-ed, -ing, -ion, *n.*]

refute (rif YOOT) *vt.* 1. to prove to be wrong; 2. to prove incorrect by argument or evidence

- Mr. Brown's fingerprints and gloves, found at the scene of the crime, *refute* his contention that he was never there.
- It is the defense attorney's job to *refute* the prosecutor's case so that the defendant will be found not guilty.

    [-d, refuting, refutable *adj.*, refutably *adv.*] [Syn. disprove]

regale (ri GAYL) *vt.* 1. to entertain with a great feast; 2. to delight with something enjoyable or amusing

- The opulent party thrower *regaled* his guests with champagne, caviar, and truffled pâté.
- The audience at the Mayfair Theater last night was *regaled* by a confection of music and dance.

    [-d, regaling]

regurgitate (ri GOER ji TAYT) *vt.* 1. to cause to flow backward, notably from the stomach to the mouth; 2. to give back information that has been only partially digested

- Those who go to a party with an upset stomach are likely to *regurgitate* any and all refreshments they partake of.
- Some teachers ask their students to *regurgitate* what they have learned on exams rather than to apply the knowledge in a meaningful way.

    [-d, regurgitating, regurgitation *n.*] [Syn. vomit]

reiterate (ree IT er AYT) *vt.* to say or do again or repeatedly

- If your mother has told you once, she's *reiterated* it 1,000 times: Keep your elbows off the table!
- Those who have not learned the lessons of history are doomed to *reiterate* them.

    [-d, reiterating] [Syn. repeat]

relapse (ree LAPS) *vt.* to slip or fall back into a former condition, disease, or bad habit, especially after improvement —*n.* the act of having a relapse or a recurrence

- After years of successfully fighting her compulsion to gamble, Norma *relapsed* at the Kentucky Derby.
- Just as Carlos seemed ready to be released from intensive care, he suffered a *relapse*.

    [-d, relapsing]

QUICK REVIEW #71

Match the word from column 2 with the word from column 1 that means most nearly the same thing.

1. reconnoiter	a. formidable
2. recrimination	b. disprove
3. rectify	c. bend
4. redoubtable	d. entertain
5. reductive	e. survey
6. redundancy	f. vomit
7. refract	g. superfluity
8. refute	h. recurrence
9. regale	i. repeat
10. regurgitate	j. correct
11. reiterate	k. countercharge
12. relapse	l. lowering

relinquish (ri LIN kwish) *vt.* 1. to abandon (a claim); 2. to surrender (something); 3. to give up

- Carla *relinquished* all claim to part ownership of Ira's cat.
- By the Treaty of Torsedilla, Spain *relinquished* all claims on Brazil to Portugal.
- Mike *relinquished* his sidearm to the palace guard.

  [-ed, -ing] [Syn. abandon, waive, forego]

reluctant (ri LUHK tint) *adj.* 1. unwilling or opposed to participating in; disinclined; 2. marked by unwillingness

- The defendant in most trials is usually a *reluctant* participant.
- Mark seemed *reluctant* to accept Abbie's excuse for not being able to go bowling on Thursday night.

  [-ly *adv.*] [Syn. loath, unwilling]

remiss (ri MISS) *adj.* 1. negligent in; careless about; lax; 2. marked by carelessness or negligence

- Don't be *remiss* in paying your income taxes on time.
- The yard clearly showed that the house's last owner had been *remiss* in performing lawn maintenance.

  [Syn. negligent, neglectful, lax]

remnant (REM nint) *n.* 1. what is left over; remainder; 2. a small remaining part or quantity; 3. last trace; 4. a piece of cloth or carpet left at the end of a roll

- Only a small *remnant* of the turkey remained after the feasters at Bob and Barbara's were finished with it.

- The ice-cream cake disappeared without leaving a *remnant* behind.
- Carpet *remnants* are usually very good buys and, in some cases, can be room size.

  [Syn. scrap, remainder]

remuneration (ri MYOO noer AY shin) *n.* 1. the act of paying for work done; 2. reward; payment; compensation

- A painter usually expects *remuneration* when his job is completed.
- *Remuneration* should be appropriate to the nature of the job performed.

  [Syn. payment]

render (REN dir) *vt.* 1. to deliver, present, or submit for payment (for example, a bill); 2. to give in return; 3. to pay something due or owed; 4. to represent or depict

- The painter will *render* the bill to his customer upon completing the job.
- The Lone Ranger *renders* good in response to evil.
- Ralph *rendered* Phyllis thanks for a job well done.
- The architect *rendered* a drawing of the new kitchen.

  [-ed*, -ing]

renovate (REN uh VAYT) *vt.* 1. to make sound again; to clean up and make like new; 2. to revive; refresh

- Jason enjoyed *renovating* homes so much that he gave up his teaching job to do it full-time.
- When you *renovate* your kitchen, you can expect to improvise and put up with inconveniences until the job is done.
- Wallie felt *renovated* after her plunge in the ocean.

  [-d, renovating] [Syn. renew]

renunciation (ri NUHN see AY shin) *n.* 1. the act of formally giving up, often at the cost of a right, claim, title, etc.; 2. a formal declaration of the foregoing

- His *renunciation* of all claims to the motorcycle came only after receiving a fair amount in compensation.
- The applicant signed the *renunciation* of rights to the deed to the house until the mortgage had been paid off.

  [Syn. disclaimer]

repentance (re PEN tins) *n.* a feeling of sorrow or self-reproach for what one has done or has not done

- Ralph had a deep feeling of *repentance* for not having gotten to know his father better.
- Absolution by *repentance* for indiscretions and sins is one of the attractive qualities of the Catholic Church.

  [Syn. penitence]

reprehensible (REP ri HEN si bl) *adj.* deserving reprimand or rebuke; fault filled; awful

- The judge told the hit-and-run driver that his behavior had been *reprehensible*.
- *Reprehensible* behavior is not permissible under any circumstances—even if you can get away with it.

  [reprehensibly *adv.*]

repudiate* (ri PYOO dee AYT) *vt.* 1. refuse to have anything to do with; disown; 2. to deny the validity or authority of (a charge, a belief, etc.); 3. to refuse to acknowledge (a government)

- Fran *repudiated* any responsibility for the behavior of her ex-husband.
- The ancient Romans typically did not *repudiate* the religious beliefs of their captured subjects, as long as the subjects continued to pay taxes to Rome.
- It is typical of war criminals to *repudiate* the power of the courts that are trying them.

    [-d, repudiating]

resentment* (ri ZENT mint) *n.* feelings of displeasure from having been ignored, snubbed, offended, or injured

- Tom made no attempt to hide his *resentment* of the fact that Mom always liked Dick best.
- A certain former president, who shall go nameless, tried to hide his *resentment* that the Academy of Motion Picture Arts and Sciences never honored him for his movie work.

    [Syn. offense]

QUICK REVIEW #72

Match the word from column 2 with the word from column 1 that means most nearly the same thing.

1. relinquish	a. lax
2. reluctant	b. deliver
3. remiss	c. disown
4. remnant	d. penitence
5. remuneration	e. awful
6. render	f. unwilling
7. renovate	g. offense
8. renunciation	h. surrender
9. repentance	i. payment
10. reprehensible	j. renew
11. repudiate	k. remainder
12. resentment	l. disclaimer

resolute (REZ i loot) *adj.* having or showing a firm resolve; determined; purposeful; unwavering

- We must stay *resolute* in our refusal to give in to terrorists.
- Elaine was *resolute* in her plan to climb Mount Everest.

    [-ly *adv.*] [Syn. faithful]

resolution (rez i LOO shin) *n.* 1. the act or process of breaking something up into its constituent parts; 2. a determining or deciding; 3. the thing determined or decided; 4. a formal statement or opinion adopted by a group; 5. a solution or answering of a question or problem

- A digital picture's *resolution* often depends on how many pixels it is made up of.
- The two parties worked toward the *resolution* of their difficulties.
- The *resolution* to the dispute was to split the baby into two equal parts. (Hmm, where have I heard that before?)
- The General Assembly's *resolution* passed by a unanimous vote.
- To find the *resolution* to a complex math problem, you should first separate the problem into its parts and then solve each of those.

resplendent* (ris PLEN dint) *adj.* brightly shining; dazzling; splendid

- She was *resplendent,* bedecked in her finest jewelry.
- The ship was *resplendent* in the morning sun as she made ready to sail to the Caribbean.

    [-ly *adv.,* resplendence *n.*]

responsibility (ris PAHN si BIL i tee) *n.* 1. condition or quality of being accountable for something's happening; accountability, dependability, obliged, etc.; 2. a thing or person that one holds accountability for

- The *responsibility* for anything that happens on this ship is the captain's alone.
- On a field trip, the teacher takes *responsibility* for all the students' well-being.
- The children are the babysitter's *responsibility.*

restraint (ris TRAYNT) *n.* 1. a holding back or being held back; 2. an influence or action that holds something back; 3. a limitation of liberty; 4. emotional control; impulse control; reserve; constraint

- The patient is confined to her bed by Velcro *restraints.*
- Sometimes we need to use *restraint* to keep from eating that extra dessert treat.
- The Constitution of the United States permits no *restraint* of freedom of speech, which doesn't mean that it doesn't happen.
- *Restraint,* like everything else, should be exercised in moderation.

retain* (ree TAYN) *vt.* 1. to keep; maintain possession of; 2. to continue to have or to hold in; 3. to keep in mind; 4. to hire (as a lawyer)

- One needs to make the monthly mortgage payments to *retain* ownership of a house.
- Walt Disney *retained* his stock in the company long after he had ceased running it.
- It is not easy for all people to *retain* facts in their minds.
- If you intend to pursue your interest in this matter, it might be advisable for you to *retain* an attorney.

    [-ed, -ing] [Syn. keep]

retroactive (RET roh AK tiv) *adj.* 1. affecting things that took place earlier; 2. going into effect at a specified date in the past

- Despite the Constitution's prohibiting ex post facto laws, many tax laws are *retroactive*.
- The congressional budget is always *retroactive* to the beginning of the current fiscal year, even though it is usually approved well after that date.

  [-ly *adv.*]

retrospective (RET roh SPEK tiv) *adj.* 1. looking back on or toward the past; 2. applying to the past; retroactive —*n.* an exhibition of the lifetime work of a person (usually one in the arts); a compendium of one's life's work

- It is often fun to take a *retrospective* look at one's early years.
- Beethoven's work, in *retrospective,* changed classical music for all time.
- The museum is having a *retrospective* on the works of Picasso next month.

  [-ly *adv.*]

reveler (REV il oer) *n.* 1. one who is noisily partying; 2. one delighting in one's freedom; 3. a merrymaker

- Most college students become *revelers* at one time or another.
- Some college students are *revelers* for four years; then they spend the rest of their lives wondering why they did that.
- A *reveler* should always have a designated driver preselected.

  [revel *vi.*, revelry, reveller *n.*]

QUICK REVIEW #73

Match the word from column 2 with the word from column 1 that means most nearly the same thing.

1. resolute	a. accountability
2. resolution	b. constraint
3. resplendent	c. merrymaker
4. responsibility	d. affecting earlier things
5. restraint	e. compendium
6. retain	f. determined
7. retroactive	g. dazzling
8. retrospective	h. answer
9. reveler	i. keep

reverence (REV ir ins) *n.* 1. a feeling of respect, love, and awe (as for something sacred or venerated); 2. a gesture of respect to indicate same; 3. the state of being regarded with deep respect

- Clergymen are often held by their flock in *reverence*.
- *Reverence* is usually the proper attitude to assume during religious services and preparing for SAT exams.

- Great *reverence* permeates the state funeral of a former U.S. president.

  [Syn. honor, awe]

revulsion (riv UHL shin) *n.* extreme shock, disgust, or repugnance; a feeling of great loathing

- *Revulsion* swept through the world at the untimely demise of President Kennedy.
- To avoid causing your *revulsion,* we aver that no animals were harmed in the making of this book.

  [Syn. aversion]

rhetoric (RET oer ik) *n.* 1. the art or skill of using words effectively in speaking or writing; 2. language that is showy or elaborate, but lacking in clarity or originality of ideas or emotions; phony eloquence

- Former President Reagan was extremely good at connecting with the public through use of *rhetoric.*
- Political conventions are always filled with *rhetoric* for the party faithful but unrelated to the real world.

ridicule (RID ik yool) *vt.* the act of making someone or something the object of scorn; to mock; to poke fun at

- Certain political leaders are easier than others to *ridicule* by drawing caricatures of them.
- Political cartoonists are specialists in the art of *ridicule.*

  [-d, ridiculing] [Syn. deride, mock, taunt]

rite (RYT) *n.* 1. a formal ceremony or act associated with a relegious procedure or observance; 2. any customary formal observance, procedure, or practice

- Almost every religion has some sort of *rite* of passage from childhood into adulthood.
- Stravinsky celebrated the pagan *rite* of spring in his tone poem of the same name.

  [Syn. ceremony]

romantic* (roh MAN tik) *adj.* 1. having the nature of or characterized by romance (idealized imagined love and adventure stories); 2. without factual basis; 3. not practical; guided by emotion rather than thought —*n.* a romantic person; romantic literature or music from the Romantic Movement (early to mid-nineteenth century)

- The Arthurian legend is a *romantic* story of the love triangle between Arthur, Guinevere, and Lancelot.
- Many girls have a *romantic* notion about being carried away by Prince Charming to live happily ever after.
- Karl Marx's notion of a society where each person does what he can and receives what he needs was a *romantic* one.
- Beethoven's later works ushered in the *Romantic* Movement in music.

  [-ally *adv.*]

ruffian (RUHF ee in) *n.* a hoodlum; a violent, lawless, brutal person; a tough guy

- Allen's mom did not want him hanging out with *ruffians* after school.
- *Ruffians* are often the bane of an otherwise nice neighborhood.

rural (RUR il) *adj.* 1. not urban or suburban; of the countryside; 2. living in the country; 3. having to do with farming

- *Rural* America is where you'll find the cows grazing.
- Grant Wood's *American Gothic* depicts an imaginary, typical, *rural* couple (who have no relation to a real one).
- A plow and a tractor are necessities of *rural* living.

    [-ly *adv.*] [Syn. bucolic, pastoral, rustic]

QUICK REVIEW #74

Match the word from column 2 with the word from column 1 that means most nearly the same thing.

1. reverence	a. idealized
2. revulsion	b. bucolic
3. rhetoric	c. honor
4. ridicule	d. phony eloquence
5. rite	e. taunt
6. romantic	f. aversion
7. ruffian	g. tough guy
8. rural	h. ceremony

S

sacrosanctity (SAK ri SANKTt i tee) *n.* something very sacred; holiness; inviolability

- The Catholic Church insists on the *sacrosanctity* of the marriage vows.
- To Muslims, the *sacrosanctity* of the Dome of the Rock must not be violated by nonbelievers.

sagacious (suh GAY shis) *adj.* wise; showing keen perception and sound judgment

- A *sagacious* person limits the amount of money he brings to the tables in a casino.
- One who drinks alcoholic beverages and then drives is not *sagacious*.

    [sagaciously *adv.*] [Syn. shrewd]

salvage (SAL vij) *vt.* to save or rescue from a shipwreck, or fire, flood, etc.; to engage in the saving of goods or wrecked ships —*n.* anything so rescued, especially the refloating of lost ships for historical purpose or for monetary compensation, or the recovery of goods from wreckages

- Ken was able to *salvage* few household goods after the tornado had gone.
- Some divers make a living from *salvaging* valuables from shipwrecks.
- The sunken hulks of lost ships are sometimes raised and sold for their *salvage* value.

    [-d, salvaging] [Syn. save, rescue]

sanctimonious (SANK ti MOH nee is) *adj.* pretending to be very holy or pious; feigning righteousness

- A *sanctimonious* person is one with a "holier-than-thou" attitude.
- Fred Flanders was extremely *sanctimonious,* until he was caught one day with his hand in the cookie jar.

    [sanctimoniously *adv.*] [Syn. devout]

sanction (SANK shin) *vt.* 1. authorized approval or empowerment from an authoritative agent or agency; 2. support, encouragement; 3. a coercive measure taken by a group (like a boycott) to bring someone or something into line

- State governments *sanction* marriages within their borders.
- Sue *sanctioned* her daughter's going after her employer in court for failing to pay her in full for her services.
- The United States has imposed economic *sanctions* on Cuba since the early 1960s.

    [sanctioned*, -ing]

sarcastic (sahr KAS tik) *adj.* 1. a taunting remark that has the nature of being caustic, cutting, and/or ironic (usually with the intent to hurt); 2. one who uses such remarks (sarcastic usually implies the intent to hurt)

- When Alice told Phil that his new Mohawk haircut looked awesome, she was being *sarcastic;* she meant awful.
- A *sarcastic* remark often means the opposite of what is said, like irony.

    [sarcastically *adv.*]

207

satire (SAT ah yir) *n.* a literary work, or works, that uses sarcasm, irony, etc. to expose and attack or deride vices, foibles, etc.

- The earliest known *satires* are the plays of Aristophanes.
- In the guise of a travelogue, *Gulliver's Travels* is one of the most famous *satires* of the nineteenth century.
- Mark Twain was especially adept at *satire,* as was Oscar Wilde.

    [satiric *adj.,* satirically *adv.*] [Syn. caricature, wit]

scalpel (SKAL pil) *n.* a small, light knife with a very sharp blade used by surgeons and for dissections

- A *scalpel* was the only way of making surgical incisions before the arrival of the surgical laser.
- Going in for an operation is often referred to as "going under the *scalpel.*"

scapegoat (SKAYP goht) *n.* a person, place, or thing upon which the crimes or misdeeds of others are blamed

- Being a *scapegoat* has a long tradition in history, beginning with an ancient king who kept a goat around to take the blame for everything.
- Killing the messenger who brought the bad news continued the tradition of using a *scapegoat.*

scholar (SKAH lir) *n.* 1. a learned person; 2. the recipient of scholarship assistance; 3. any pupil

- A *scholar* used to refer exclusively to a learned person, or one learned in a particular field, such as a biblical *scholar* or an art *scholar.*
- Former President Bill Clinton was a Rhodes *Scholar,* which means, in essence, that he was paid to study at Oxford.
- My youngest *scholar* just finished kindergarten.

    [Syn. pupil]

scientific (SY in TIF ik) *adj.* 1. of or pertaining to science; 2. based on the principles of science, rather than superstition or conjecture; 3. proven methods

- It is a *scientific* fact that gravity pulls everything toward the center of the earth.
- Many *scientific* principles were discovered and/or stated by Sir Isaac Newton.
- Before a medicine is approved by the FDA for public use, it must be *scientifically* proven to be more helpful than it is harmful.

    [scientifically *adv.*]

scientist (SY in TIST) *n.* a specialist whose profession is one of the physical, earth, or life sciences (that is, biology, geology, astronomy, chemistry, and physics)

- A physician who specializes in research is a *scientist.*
- Social *scientists,* such as sociologists and psychologists, are not considered true *scientists* by the scientific establishment.

- *Scientists* divide their numbers into life *scientists* (botanists and zoologists), physical *scientists* (chemists and physicists), and earth/space *scientists* (geologists, meteorologists, and astronomers).

scrutinize (SKROOT in YZ) *vt.* to look at very carefully; examine closely

- If a deal sounds too good to be true, *scrutinize* it because almost invariably it will prove to be so.
- A jeweler uses a loupe to *scrutinize* diamonds and other gemstones.

    [-d, scrutinizing] [Syn. examine, inspect]

sculpture (SKUHLP chir) *n.* 1. the art of carving wood, chiseling stone, molding metal or clay, etc. into three-dimensional figures, statues, etc.; 2. any figure so made or collection of same —*vt.* 1. to cut, carve, mold, chisel, etc. into figures, statuary, etc.; 2. to change a form by erosion

- *Sculptures* can be as small as cameos that women wear as jewelry or as large as the presidential faces that adorn Mount Rushmore.
- Rodin's "The Thinker" is one of the best-known *sculptures* of nineteenth-century Europe.
- Michelangelo preferred to *sculpture* in marble and insisted that the statue had always been in the marble; he had just removed the excess stone.
- The forces of wind and water have served to *sculpture* the thousands of natural *sculptures* that adorn Utah's Bryce Canyon National Park.

    [-d, sculpturing, sculptural *adj.*, sculpturally *adv.*]

séance (SAY ahns) *n.* a meeting at which a medium or psychic attempts to communicate with the dead

- Morticia went to *séances* to attempt to communicate with her dead uncle Fester.
- After Morticia's sixth unsuccessful try at contacting Uncle Fester at a *séance,* it became clear that he was not going to say "Boo!" to her.

secrecy (SEE kri see) *n.* 1. the condition of being concealed or secret; 2. the practice of keeping things hushed up

- A veil of *secrecy* surrounded the building of the first atomic bomb.
- The *secrecy* surrounding the just-referenced Manhattan Project could not approach the secrecy of the formula for Coca-Cola syrup.
- The government maintains *secrecy* of things it does not want the public to know about by categorizing such events as classified.

QUICK REVIEW #75

Match the word from column 2 with the word from column 1 that means most nearly the same thing.

1. sacrosanctity	a. proven
2. sagacious	b. mold
3. salvage	c. concealment
4. sanctimonious	d. supernatural communication
5. sanction	e. holiness
6. sarcastic	f. knife
7. satire	g. caricature
8. scalpel	h. smug
9. scapegoat	i. physicist
10. scholar	j. fall guy
11. scientific	k. inspect
12. scientist	l. pupil
13. scrutinize	m. rescue
14. sculpture	n. shrewd
15. séance	o. empower
16. secrecy	p. caustic

sedative (SED it iv) *adj.* soothing or quieting; —*n.* medicine that soothes nervousness or excitement

- Many find a warm glass of milk is useful at night as a *sedative* in order to relax before going to bed.
- After observing the car accident, Mema needed a *sedative* to calm her down.

segment (SEG mint) *n.* 1. a division or section of something; 2. (geometry) a part of a line between two named endpoints, one of which has legs on it.

- *Segment* BC is the part of a line with endpoints at *B* and *C*.
- A *segment* is the shortest distance between two points.

  [Syn. part]

selfishness (SEL fish nis) *n.* 1. a condition of being overly concerned with one's own well-being to the exclusion of all others; self-centeredness; 2. prompted by self-interest

- *Selfishness* is the reason for the breakup of most marriages.
- Richard demonstrated his *selfishness* by eating all the strawberries off the top of the strawberry shortcake before anyone had been served.

sentence (SENT ins) *n.* 1. the judgment of a court of law; 2. a group of words that express a complete thought —*vt.* to pronounce judgment; condemn; pronounce punishment

- The court *sentenced* the criminal to a 20-year term.
- In grammar, a phrase is much like a *sentence*, except that a phrase does not convey a complete thought.
- After a jury has found a person guilty, the judge may *sentence* that person to anything from probation to death.

  [-d, sentencing]

sentiment (SENT i mint) *n.* 1. a complex combination of opinions and feelings; 2. an emotional attitude; 3. the meaning behind something

- My *sentiment* tells me that you are a very discriminating person, but I'm usually not a good judge of character.
- The retro look of some automobiles popular in the early part of this century is a blatant appeal to the *sentiment* of cherishing the past.
- Gail told Gil that he could stay, but her tone of voice made it clear that her *sentiment* was far from welcoming.

  [Syn. opinion, feeling]

serendipity (SER in DIP it ee) *n.* 1. an apparent gift for discovering good things by accident; 2. luck or good fortune in accidentally finding something good

- Hershey's chocolate makers had the *serendipity* to discover both peanut butter cups and the shape of the Hershey Kiss.
- Discovering that alloying copper and tin made the hard metal bronze was a case of *serendipity* for early man because the two rarely occurred together in nature.

  [serendipitous *adj.*, serendipitously *adv.*]

shun (SHUHN) *vt.* deliberately stay away from; scrupulously and consistently avoid

- A recovering alcoholic must *shun* all contact with alcoholic beverages.
- It is a healthy idea for everyone to *shun* cigarette smoke, both first- and secondhand.

  [-ned, -ning]

simplicity (sim PLIS it ee) *n.* 1. freedom from complexity or intricacy; simple state; simple quality; 2. plainness; lack of elegance or embellishment; 3. foolishness; lacking sense

- Making a kite is *simplicity* itself and requires only two light sticks, some paper, and some string.
- Jane's wedding dress was elegant by its very *simplicity,* being just a shiny, white, untooled satin.
- Jack demonstrated his *simplicity* when he said, "Nice kitty," just prior to sticking his head into the lion's mouth.

simplistic (sim PLIS tik) *adj.* taking a complicated situation and making it unrealistically simple; oversimplified

- It is *simplistic* to believe that a calculus problem can be solved while standing on one foot.
- Trying to fix an overheating car engine by adding cold water is taking a *simplistic* approach—and is also likely to get you burned.

  [-ally *adv.*]

simply (SIM plee) *adv.* 1. in a simple way; with simplicity; 2. merely; only; just; 3. absolutely; totally

- The dress was made *simply,* in a short time.
- Faith was *simply* trying to be nice by offering her help.
- Will was *simply* furious with the way he had been treated.

sinuate (SIN yoo it *for adj.,* SIN yoo ayt *for v.*) *adj.* 1. *s*-shaped, like a sine curve; sinuous; 2. having an indented, wavy edge, like some leaves —*vi.* to bend or wind in and out

- Some grand-prix automobile race tracks sport *sinuate* sections, unlike American ovals where cars only turn left.
- Some slicing knives have *sinuate* edges for thinly slicing cold cuts and hard cheeses.
- Some of the most dangerous drivers are ones who *sinuate* through traffic.

  [-d, sinuating, -ly, *adv.*]

skeptical* (SKEP ti kl) *adj.* 1. not easily persuaded or convinced; inclined to doubt; questioning; 2. doubting religious doctrine

- In Columbus's day, learned people were not as *skeptical* about the earth's being round as elementary history books would have us believe.
- People from Missouri have a reputation for being *skeptical;* they have to be shown.
- Agnostics are generally *skeptical* about many religious teachings.

  [-ly *adv.*]

skepticism (SKEP ti si zm) *n.* 1. a philosophy that neither truth nor knowledge is attainable by human beings; 2. a doubting attitude, especially pertaining to religious doctrine

- *Skepticism* as a philosophy began in ancient Greece, where its advocates claimed that man did not have the tools to determine what is and what is not true.
- A healthy *skepticism* is a good thing for those who would prefer not to be flimflammed by pie-in-the-sky advertising claims.

  [Syn. uncertainty]

slumber (SLUM bir) *vi.* 1. to sleep; 2. to be inactive or dormant —*n.* 1. sleep; 2. a state of inactivity

- Night watchmen have a reputation—some would say undeserved—for *slumbering* while on the job.
- A volcano that has been inactive for recorded history is more safely regarded as in *slumber* rather than dead.
- A pair of pajamas is usually required for a *slumber* party.

- When Mom or Dad is snoring in the armchair, you might call that a moment of *slumber.*

  [-ed, -ing, -er *n.*]

smugness (SMUG nis) *n.* self-satisfaction to an annoying degree; complacency

- Jackie Robinson never showed any *smugness* for all his accomplishments in major-league baseball.
- A good deal of *smugness* was shown by the mayor of Los Angeles when he lured the Brooklyn Dodgers to the West Coast.

QUICK REVIEW #76

Match the word from column 2 with the word from column 1 that means most nearly the same thing.

1. sedative	a. oversimplified
2. segment	b. complacency
3. selfishness	c. doubting
4. sentence	d. uncertainty
5. sentiment	e. part
6. serendipity	f. wavy edged
7. shun	g. sleep
8. simplicity	h. condemn
9. simplistic	i. self-centeredness
10. simply	j. opinion
11. sinuate	k. plainness
12. skeptical	l. avoid
13. skepticism	m. soothing
14. slumber	n. luck
15. smugness	o. absolutely

society (suh SY it ee) *n.* 1. a group of persons forming a community with a distinct social or economic connection; 2. the system or condition of living together communally; 3. all people collectively, or a particular strata thereof, usually upper crust

- The *society* of the Amish living around Lancaster, Pennsylvania, is distinctly different from the *society* of Chinatown in San Francisco, California.
- Those living on a kibbutz in Israel live in a *society* where every member depends on every other member.
- The *society* we all live in is known as the civilized world.
- Those forming the so-called high *society* live in a world of debutante balls and coming-out parties.

  [societies *pl.*, societal, social *adj.*, socially *adv.*]

solace (SAH lis) *n.* 1. an easing of loneliness, grief, or discomfort; 2. comfort; relief —*vt.* 1. to comfort; console; 2. to give relief

- Company is always a *solace* to someone feeling lonely.
- One who grieves for a loved one often takes *solace* in remembering only the good things about the departed.
- Volunteers often work to *solace* those confined to hospital beds.

[Syn. comfort]

solicitude (suh LIS it ood) *n.* the state of showing care, concern, etc., sometimes to excess

- Marjorie offered her *solicitude* for her neighbor, whose son and daughter had both shipped out with their military units.
- Marjorie accepted Sally's *solicitude* politely, but after Sally left, Marjorie mumbled to herself that she wished everyone would leave her alone so that she could get some rest.

[Syn. care]

solidify (suh LID i fy) *vt.* 1. to unite or firm up (a relationship); 2. to make a liquid into a solid; firm; compact; harden

- Going to the ballpark together often helps to *solidify* a relationship between father and son.
- A mother-daughter relationship is traditionally *solidified* by baking cookies. (Eat your heart out, Murphy Brown!)
- At 0° Celsius, water *solidifies* and becomes ice.
- Tamping down the gravel helps to *solidify* the base for a patio.

[solidified, -ing]

soluble (SAHL yoo bil) *adj.* 1. capable of being dissolved (passed into solution) in water; 2. capable of being solved

- Sugar and salt are both easily *soluble,* while flour is not.
- *New York Times* crossword puzzles are definitely *soluble,* although they get harder as the week goes on, and Saturday's puzzle is a real brainteaser.

[solubly *adv.*] [Syn. dissolvable, solvable]

somber* (SAHM bir) *adj.* 1. dark and gloomy; dull; 2. melancholy; mentally depressed; 3. grave

- When JFK was shot, the mood of the country was very *somber.*
- Veronica was *somber,* reflecting on how much she missed not having been invited to the senior dance.
- A *somber* air pervaded the landing craft's occupants as it approached the beach on D-Day.

[-ly *adv.*]

sonnet (SAHN it) *n.* a poem, usually 14 lines in length in iambic pentameter, generally on a single theme

- Shakespeare was noted for his *sonnets* in addition to his dramatic writings.
- The *sonnets* of Petrarch (1304–1374) are among the earliest known.
- Both Robert Browning and his future wife, Elizabeth Barrett, wrote *sonnets* to each other.

sophisticated (suh FIS ti KAY tid) *adj.* 1. urbane, world wise, knowledgeable, as opposed to naïve or simple; 2. very complex and refined

- City folk tend to be more *sophisticated* than country folk.
- The engines that drive a rocket can be very *sophisticated;* after all, it is rocket science.

  [-ly *adv.*, sophistication *n.*]

spate (SPAYT) *n.* an unusually large outpouring, usually one of words

- Fidel Castro's speeches are often characterized by a *spate* of words that continue for hours.
- When faced with *spates,* the average audience member is prone to fall asleep.

species (SPEE sheez) *n.* 1. a distinct kind; variety; class; 2. (biology) a naturally existing population of organisms that can only breed among themselves; 3. the human race

- Tigers, lions, and leopards are three different *species* of felines.
- Dogs and cats belong to two totally different *species.*
- The human *species* is growing at an alarming rate.

specific (spi SIF ik) *adj.* 1. specifying a precise, limited thing or group of things, characteristics, etc.; 2. of a particular sort or type

- Last week, Mark lost his timepiece—his wristwatch, to be *specific.*
- Bill knew his appointment was between 6 and 7 P.M., but he was not certain of the *specific* time.
- Fran was looking for a folding umbrella with a very *specific* checkerboard pattern.

  [-ally *adv.*] [Syn. explicit, special]

specious (SPEE shis) *adj.* seeming to be correct, without really being so; plausible, but not actual

- Greg's conclusion seemed to be logical, but in reality, his thinking was somewhat *specious.*
- It was her neglecting to account for the difference in time zones that made Laura's calculated arrival time *specious.*

  [-ly *adv.*] [Syn. plausible]

QUICK REVIEW #77

Match the word from column 2 with the word from column 1 that means most nearly the same thing.

1. society	a. harden
2. solace	b. plausible
3. solicitude	c. population
4. solidify	d. outpouring
5. soluble	e. urbane
6. somber	f. explicit
7. sonnet	g. community
8. sophisticated	h. grave
9. spate	i. solvable
10. species	j. comfort
11. specific	k. poem
12. specious	l. care

spectacle (SPEK ti kl) *n.* 1. a strange and/or remarkable sight; 2. a public exhibition on a grand scale —*pl.* a pair of eyeglasses

- The dog balancing on the beach ball was a *spectacle* to behold.
- The parade of the circus performers and animals from the train station to the arena was a *spectacle* worth coming out to watch.
- Willa bought a new pair of *spectacles*.

speculation* (SPEK yoo LAY shin) *n.* 1. the act of thinking about; meditation; 2. gambling in stock or land values

- Whether or not your parents are going to allow you to go away for the weekend is purely a matter of *speculation*.
- Day traders are engaged in stock price *speculation,* and more lose money than gain any.

spontaneous (spahn TAY nee uhs) *adj.* 1. all at once, without advance preparation or premeditation; 2. without apparent outside cause or influence

- Alice's decision to follow the white rabbit was a *spontaneous* one.
- People used to think that maggots appeared on dead bodies by *spontaneous* generation.
- At the pianist's first appearance, the audience erupted in *spontaneous* applause.

  [-ly *adv.*] [Syn. instinctive, impulsive]

spurious (SPYUR ee uhs) *adj.* 1. false; make-believe; not genuine; 2. similar in appearance, but not in structure

- The note asking Linda's teacher to excuse her not having her homework turned out to be *spurious* and was written in Linda's poorly disguised handwriting.

- The bargain diamond ring turned out to be *spurious*, made not of diamond and gold but of glass and gold plate.

    [-ly *adv.*] [Syn. artificial]

squelch (SKWELCH) *vt.* 1. to crush or squash by smashing or stamping on; 2. to suppress or silence fully with a demoralizing effect —*n.* 1. a crushed mass of some-thing; 2. the act of silencing or putting down; 3. the sound made by walking through mud or slush

- Peter tried to *squelch* the invasion of cockroaches by stomping all over them.
- Dictators often try to *squelch* opposition by making massive reprisals after a slight insurrection.
- Suzanne *squelched* a pile of potatoes for tomorrow morning's hash browns.
- Her boots went "*squelch*" as she slogged through the mud.

    [-ed, -ing, -er *n.*]

stemming (STEM ing) *vt.* 1. stopping or checking (especially the flow of a river by damming); 2. closing, plugging, or tamping a hole; 3. removing the stem from a vegetable or piece of fruit

- Damming the river was an attempt at *stemming* its repeated flooding of the town.
- The little Dutch boy's thumb was stuck into the dike in hopes of *stemming* the hole's enlargement by the water eroding it further.
- *Stemming* strawberries before serving them is always a good idea.

stimulant (STIM yoo lint) *n.* any drug, medication, experience, sight, etc. that temporarily stimulates or excites some organ or the central nervous system to increase activity

- Many people can't start the day without a cup of coffee, which acts as a *stimulant* to get them up and running.
- Caffeine, the *stimulant* in coffee, is also in tea, cola, and other soft drinks.

straddle (STRA dil) *vt.* 1. to have one's legs on either side of (a chair, saddle, fence, etc.); 2. to come down on both sides of an issue; to avoid or appear to avoid committing oneself; 3. to walk with one's legs wide apart; 4. to refuse to commit oneself; hedge —*n.* the act or position of straddling

- Tom turned the chair around and *straddled* it while leaning his chin on the chair's back.
- It is customary to *straddle* the saddle when seated on a horse.
- Politicians often find that they risk alienating fewer constituents by *strad-dling* an issue rather than coming down on one side or the other of it.
- Severely bowlegged people walk with a *straddle*, as if they had a saddle between their legs.
- It doesn't pay to *straddle* the question of whether or not to allow the state to infringe on your freedoms.
- *Straddling* is a favorite occupation of many politicians, known as fence sitters.

    [-d, straddling]

straightforward (STRAYT FAWR woerd) *adj.* 1. direct; moving straight ahead; 2. frank; honest; open; 3. clear; unambiguous

- Perry found that the best way to tackle a problem is the *straightforward* one; that is, attack it head on.
- It is best to be *straightforward* in our relationships with others, as that encourages them to be the same way with us.
- Rose has found that when she needs something done, the more *straightforward* she is in her instructions, the more likely it is that the job will be done the way she wants it.

subjective (suhb JEK tiv) *adj.* governed by what is in one's mind, rather than by reality; not objective; personal; introspective

- How to behave in a certain situation is usually a very *subjective* decision, meaning that no two people would act quite the same.
- *Subjective* reactions are normally the product of one's total life experiences.

  [-ly *adv.*]

subtlety (SUHT il tee) *n.* 1. the ability or tendency to be able to make fine distinctions; 2. the quality or condition of being delicately skillful or clever

- *Subtlety* is the difference between clucking your tongue at a child's misbehavior and hitting him or her over the head with a sledgehammer.
- *Subtlety* is an acquired skill, brought about by watching the behavior of your role models over the course of time.

  [subtleties *pl.*, subtleness *n.*, subtle *adj.*, subtly *adv.*]

subvert (suhb VOERT) *vt.* 1. to undermine or corrupt; 2. to overthrow an established power by indirect means

- By reacting to a child's appeal to override the decision of her father, a mother *subverts* the father's authority.
- The Persian emperor's rule was *subverted* by Alexander the Great's invasion, when the emperor's own men killed him.

QUICK REVIEW #78

Match the word from column 2 with the word from column 1 that means most nearly the same thing.

1. spectacle	a. artificial
2. speculation	b. exciter
3. spontaneous	c. fine distinction
4. spurious	d. unambiguous
5. squelch	e. introspective
6. stemming	f. exhibition
7. stimulant	g. smash
8. straddle	h. meditation
9. straightforward	i. undermine
10. subjective	j. impulsive
11. subtlety	k. hedge
12. subvert	l. plugging

sully (SUH lee) *vt.* soil; stain; tarnish or besmirch, especially by disgracing
- Don't try to *sully* my reputation as a legitimate trader of riding and draught horses.
- To *sully* someone's name as an honest businessperson is to ruin their ability to earn a living.

  [sullied, -ing]

superficial* (soo pir FISH il) *adj.* 1. limited to the surface; 2. concerned with the obvious only; 3. cursory and quick; 4. shallow; not profound
- Jackie's wounds from her skateboard accident were only *superficial*, thanks to her having worn protective gear.
- Frank was only interested in *superficial* looks and paid no attention to the inner substance of his dates.
- Barry learned from a terrible experience that the next time he signs a contract, he had better take more than a *superficial* look at it first.
- The president's analysis of the economy was, at best, *superficial*.

  [-ly *adv.*] [Syn. shallow, cursory]

supplant (suh PLANT) *vt.* 1. to replace; supersede; 2. to uproot and replace
- Instructions for operating a light switch dated 03/09/04 are to *supplant* those of 02/18/56 until further notice.
- The white rhododendron in the tub will be used to *supplant* the purple rhododendron next to the driveway.

  [-ed, -ing] [Syn. replace]

suppress (suh PRES) *vt.* 1. to subdue; put down; quell; crush; 2. to keep from appearing; 3. to check or stop; keep back; restrain

- The Chinese government's tanks *suppressed* the protest in Tiananmen Square.
- The plan of the rock group to appear onstage was *suppressed* by the theater's owners who feared a riot.
- When Diane saw the kindergartener take a melted ice-cream bar from her pocket after getting off the school bus, she *suppressed* her urge to laugh.

  [-ed, -ing]

surfeit (SOER fit) *n.* 1. excess; too great a supply; 2. pigging out; 3. nausea or discomfort resulting from overindulgence —*vt.* to feed or supply to fullness or excess; to satiate

- Each year, American farmers produce a *surfeit* of wheat.
- Brad had to loosen his belt, having eaten a *surfeit* of shrimp from the appetizer platters at Rose's wedding.
- Ian felt *surfeit* from having drunk too many beers on an otherwise empty stomach.
- The wedding feast *surfeited* every one of the 103 guests.

  [-ed, -ing] [Syn. satiate]

surreptitious (SOER ep TISH is) *adj.* 1. clandestine; done in a secret or stealthy way; 2. acting in a secret or stealthy way

- The guests to Joanne's birthday celebration all received *surreptitious* invitations so as not to spoil the surprise.
- The concealment of the Greek soldiers inside the Trojan horse had to be *surreptitious* so the Trojans would not suspect anything.
- For those of you planning a prison break, it is a good idea to keep your plans *surreptitious* (wink, wink!).

  [-ly *adv.*] [Syn. secret, clandestine]

susceptible (suh SEP ti bl) *adj.* easily affected or emotionally moved; sensitive in nature; easily influenced

- Some children are very *susceptible* to ear infections.
- Most men are *susceptible* to the appeal of a teary-eyed woman.
- Some people who might not give you the time of day are still *susceptible* to an appeal to their better natures.

  [susceptibly *adv.*, susceptibility* *n.*]

sustain (sus TAYN) *vt.* 1. to keep up; maintain; prolong; 2. to provide food and sustenance to; 3. to carry the weight and/or burden of; 4. to encourage

- The right pedal on a piano is used to *sustain* a note long after the key has been released.
- It takes a lot of puppy chow to *sustain* a growing St. Bernard puppy.

- When two people transport a piano up a hill on a dolly, the person in the rear *sustains* the bulk of the weight.
- The audience's reaction to Sybil's recital was enough to *sustain* her in pursuing her musical career.

[-ed, -ing] [Syn. prolong, support]

symphony* (SIM fi nee) *n.* 1. harmony of sounds, especially of musical instruments; 2. harmony of colors; 3. something noted for harmonious composition; 4. an extensive composition of many parts for a full orchestra

- A well-harmonized quartet produces a *symphony* of sounds to be enjoyed by all.
- Van Gogh's *Sunflowers* is a *symphony* of ochres and shades of yellow.
- The opening four chords of Beethoven's *Fifth Symphony* might be the most recognizable four chords of all time.

synergistic (SIN oer JIS tik) *adj.* the simultaneous working together of several organs or agencies

- Lifting a heavy object without injuring oneself requires a *synergistic* working of muscles in the back, arms, and legs.
- The Department of Homeland Security was a *synergistic* effort to create a more effective agency than the separate agencies that comprised it.

[-ally *adv.*]

synonymous (sin AHN im is) *adj.* equivalent or similar in meaning; having the nature of a synonym; being another word or name for

- For many years, but no longer, the word "Volkswagen" was *synonymous* with inexpensive, economical transportation.
- Cliff'sQuickReviews are *synonymous* with study guides.
- Aspirin, which for many years was *synonymous* with painkiller, was originally a brand name of the Bayer company.

[-ly *adv.*]

synthesize (SIN the SYZ) *vt.* to put together different parts to form a whole; to assemble

- A chemist can *synthesize* salt from sodium and chlorine.
- An electronic instrument can *synthesize* different timbres and frequencies to simulate the sounds made by real musical instruments.

[-d, synthesizing]

QUICK REVIEW #79

Match the word from column 2 with the word from column 1 that means most nearly the same thing.

1. sully	a. equivalent
2. superficial	b. sensitive
3. supplant	c. harmony
4. suppress	d. prolong
5. surfeit	e. satiate
6. surreptitious	f. assemble
7. susceptible	g. correlating
8. sustain	h. tarnish
9. symphony	i. subdue
10. synergistic	j. shallow
11. synonymous	k. clandestine
12. synthesize	l. replace

T

talisman (TAL is min) *n.* 1. something (like a ring, necklace, or bracelet) bearing symbols or engraved figures thought to bring good luck; 2. anything thought to have magic power; something to ward off evil; an amulet

- In many primitive and not-so-primitive cultures, *talismans* are worn to ward off evil spirits.
- Many educated persons have been known to carry a rabbit's foot as a *talisman,* despite the fact that it obviously did not bring much luck to the rabbit.

[-s *pl.*]

tangential (tan JEN shil) *adj.* 1. diverging or digressing; going off at an angle, like a tangent; 2. just touching on a subject, but not dealing with it at length

- The school superintendent started talking about the school budget but soon went off on the *tangential* subject of the breakfast program.
- While examining the world news section of the newspaper, Sandy took a *tangential* glance at the baseball scores.

[-ly *adv.*]

temerity (tim ER it ee) *n.* audacity; recklessness; foolhardiness

- Mark was shocked that only a week into skiing lessons, Allison had the *temerity* to tackle the giant slalom.
- Nobody believed that North Vietnam would have the *temerity* to attack South Vietnam while it was under American protection, but we all know how that turned out.

temperament (TEM per mint) *n.* 1. one's usual state of mind or disposition; nature; natural disposition; 2. excitability; moodiness; capriciousness; volatility

- Collies usually have a very even *temperament* and are very good at herding children who try to stray.
- A Jack Russell terrier's *temperament,* on the other hand, is frenetic or (as some might say) hyper, and it is in perpetual motion.

[Syn. disposition]

temperance (TEM pir INS) *n.* 1. self-restraint; moderation in appetite, expression, indulgence, and so on; 2. totally refraining from drinking alcoholic beverages

- It is a good idea to exercise *temperance* in the amount of fried foods that one eats in a week.
- The *temperance* movement was responsible for the U.S. Prohibition era of the 1930s.

tenacious (ten AY shis) *adj.* 1. holding on firmly; retaining well; retentive; 2. persistent; stubborn

- The British are known for being a very *tenacious* people, which is why they embrace the bulldog as their national mascot.
- When he fell over the cliff, Carl held on to the tree root with a *tenacious* grip until rescuers could reach him.

[-ly *adv.,* tenacity *n.*] [Syn. persistent]

223

tendency (TEN din see) *n.* 1. an inclination, bent, or propensity to move in a certain direction; 2. an apparent moving toward some particular purpose; drift; 3. a purpose or point of view

- Things set in motion have a *tendency* to remain in motion until interfered with by an outside force.
- An object at rest has a *tendency* to remain at rest until acted upon by an outside force.
- Isaac Newton's *tendency* was to state things as laws, such as the two laws of inertia stated above.
- The *tendency* of the American people during the 1980s and 1990s was to move politically toward the right.

[Syn. drift, trend]

tentative (TEN tuh TIV lee) *adj.* 1. proposed, but not definite; uncertain; 2. timid; hesitant

- The *tentative* time for our next meeting is Tuesday at 7 P.M., but check back before putting it on your calendar.
- Joanne wanted to ask Arthur to the dance, but her approach to him was, at best, *tentative*.

[-ly *adv.*, -ness *n.*] [Syn. uncertain]

tenuous (TEN yoo is) *adj.* not substantial; flimsy; inconclusive

- The challenger's lead in the polls is, at best, *tenuous*.
- Nora had a *tenuous* grip on her tennis racket, and it was at risk of flying out of her hand with each swing.

[-ly *adv.*, -ness *n.*]

testimony (TES to MOH nee) *n.* 1. a declaration or statement made under oath, sometimes in response to questioning, before a court of some sort; 2. a public affirmation; any kind of evidence; 3. any sworn statement

- The arresting officer gave *testimony* at the burglary trial.
- The general's *testimony* before Congress was that the army was fully prepared.
- Lynn's *testimony* was given in a letter signed before a notary public.

tether (TE thir) *n.* a rope or cord fastened to something to prevent its escape —*vt.* to tie up or confine something/someone using a tether

- Tetherball is played using a ball attached to a stake by a *tether*.
- It is not unusual to find a dog *tethered* to a lamppost while its owner is in the grocery store.
- Never *tether* your dog for any length of time in the presence of hot sunlight with no recourse to shade and fresh water.

[-ed, -ing]

theoretical (THEE uh RET i kil) *adj.* 1. of or making up an idea or mental concept; 2. limited to theory, but not practical or proven; 3. speculative

- Einstein had a *theoretical* view of the relationship between energy and mass.
- Air travel was purely *theoretical* until the beginning of the twentieth century.
- The existence of life in other galaxies is purely *theoretical*.

[-ly *adv.*]

QUICK REVIEW #80

Match the word from column 2 with the word from column 1 that means most nearly the same thing.

1. talisman	a. disposition
2. tangential	b. evidence
3. temerity	c. stubborn
4. temperament	d. uncertain
5. temperance	e. tie
6. tenacious	f. audacity
7. tendency	g. inconclusive
8. tentative	h. speculative
9. tenuous	i. amulet
10. testimony	j. moderation
11. tether	k. drift
12. theoretical	l. diverging

therapeutic (THE ri PYOO tik) *adj.* working to heal or cure; curative

- Walking is considered to be *therapeutic* for a sore leg, but how that can be beats me.
- Professionals disagree over whether an ice pack or a heat pack is more *therapeutic* for a sore back.

  [-al *adj.*, -ly *adv.*]

thorough (THOER oh) *adj.* 1. complete; omitting nothing; 2. absolute; very exact; accurate; 3. paying careful attention to details

- Yolanda gave a *thorough* accounting of her encounter with the hijacker, taking care to omit no detail.
- The doctor gave Edwin a *thorough* examination, including an electrocardiogram.
- The counterfeiter did a *thorough* job of copying the design for the $50 bill.

  [-ly *adv.*]

throng (THRAHNG) *n.* 1. a great number of people gathered together; a crowd; 2. a mass of things; multitude —*vt.* to crowd together

- The happy *throng* gathered for New Year's Eve in Times Square.
- A *throng* of fruit flies massed around the cut peach, looking to grab a tasty meal.
- The passengers *thronged* together, hoping to get a seat on the next bus.

  [-ed, -ing] [Syn. crowd]

timorous (TIM er is) *adj.* 1. full of fear; subject to fear; timid; 2. caused by timidity

- The most memorable use of the word *timorous* in English literature is in Robert Burns's *To a Mouse,* where he refers to it as a "wee *timorous* beastie."
- It is quite fine for children to be *timorous* about talking to strangers.

    [-ly *adv.*] [Syn. afraid]

tolerate (TAH ler AYT) *vt.* 1. to allow; permit; 2. to respect the beliefs of others, although they differ from one's own; 3. to put up with things or persons who are disliked

- Julie's parents would not *tolerate* her playing after school until her homework was done.
- Though not a believer in the curative powers of chicken soup, Hal *tolerated* a well-meant bowl or two when he was laid up with the flu.
- Karen *tolerated* her in-laws' presence at family gatherings, although she really would have preferred not to see them.

    [-d, tolerating] [Syn. bear]

tome (TOHM) *n.* a book, especially a large, ponderous, and/or scholarly one

- You know Professor Corey; he's the one who wrote the thick *tome* on the eating preferences of different species of termites.
- The writings of J. D. Salinger are not really lengthy enough to call *tomes,* while Leo Tolstoy's works are a different story.

torpid (TAWR pid) *adj.* 1. temporarily having lost all sensation and the ability to move (like a hibernating animal); sluggish; 2. slow and dull; apathetic

- A bear, while *torpid* after just having awakened from hibernation, soon after becomes much livelier.
- A sloth, on the other hand, is always *torpid.*
- Certain members of my family have a tendency to be *torpid* upon the completion of a Thanksgiving feast.

    [-ly *adv.*, -ity, torpor *n.*]

tourniquet (TOER ni kit) *n.* a pressure bandage whose purpose is to temporarily clamp off the flow of blood through a part of the body

- The most commonly seen *tourniquet* among campers is made by tying together two ends of a cloth square, slipping it over a limb, and then twisting a stick through the loop to put pressure on the limb.
- A *tourniquet* is an emergency bandage to prevent excessive loss of blood by a cut trauma subject.

tractable (TRAK ti bl) *adj.* 1. easily managed, controlled, or taught; docile; compliant; 2. easily workable; malleable

- A horse is most *tractable* when it is younger than two years of age.
- Silver is a very *tractable* metal but not as much so as copper.

    [tractability* *n.*] [Syn. obedient]

tradition (truh DISH in) *n.* 1. a custom, belief, proverb, or story handed down orally from generation to generation; 2. the act of handing down same; 3. long established practices; precedent; 4. a historic line of principles, attitudes, or codes of behavior

- The story of the Trojan War had been Greek *tradition* for hundreds of years before Homer wrote it down in *The Iliad.*
- *Tradition* was often entrusted to minstrels, who were singing storytellers and entertainers.
- The Thanksgiving turkey dinner is an American *tradition.*
- Bushido is the Japanese *tradition* of behavior passed down by the samurai warriors.

trait (TRAYT) *n.* 1. a distinguishing characteristic or quality; 2. character; 3. a quality of personality

- A palamino horse is distinguishable from all others by the *trait* of its golden skin color.
- Nose shape is a *trait* that differs less among people than among dogs.
- Honesty is a desirable *trait,* often lacking in used-car salespersons.
  [Syn. quality]

tranquillity* (tran KWIL i tee) *n.* the quality or state of peacefulness; calmness; serenity

- A pastoral scene is one noted for its apparent *tranquillity.*
- Of course, the artist never portrays the cougar waiting behind the rock to disrupt the *tranquillity* of the grazing flock.

QUICK REVIEW #81

Match the word from column 2 with the word from column 1 that means most nearly the same thing.

1. therapeutic	a. peacefulness
2. thorough	b. bear
3. throng	c. precedent
4. timorous	d. pressure bandage
5. tolerate	e. apathetic
6. tome	f. quality
7. torpid	g. obedient
8. tourniquet	h. multitude
9. tractable	i. curative
10. tradition	j. encyclopedia
11. trait	k. accurate
12. tranquillity	l. afraid

transient (TRAN see int) *adj.* 1. temporary; passing with time; 2. passing in a short time; fleeting —*n.* 1. a transient person; 2. a brief electrical surge

- Don't worry, your in-laws' visit is a *transient* one.
- Weather in Texas is very *transient;* if you don't care for it at the moment, just wait five minutes.
- Motels rent their rooms mostly to *transients.*

  [-ly *adv.*, transience *n.*]

transparent* (trans PAR int) *adj.* 1. capable of being seen through; passing light through so as to be able to distinctly see what is on the other side; neither translucent nor opaque; 2. easily understood; very clear; obvious; 3. frank; without guile

- "I wouldn't want to call you *transparent,*" Mabel told Todd, "but I can see your car right behind your belly."
- Will's directions to Doris's place were *transparent.*
- When a child admires a particular toy in the store, his or her motives are usualy *transparent.*

  [-ly *adv.*] [Syn. clear]

trauma (TROW muh *or* TRAW muh) *n.* 1. a bodily shock, wound, or injury; 2. a mental shock or painful emotional experience

- Any cut can be called a *trauma,* but it is the more severe ones that get immediate attention in the emergency room of a hospital.
- Scalding with nearly boiling hot water is one of the most painful forms of physical *trauma.*

  [-tic *adj.*, -tically *adv.*]

travesty (TRA vis tee) *n.* 1. a burlesque or grotesque imitation for purposes of ridicule; 2. a crude, distorted, absurd representation of something

- Political cartoonists love to make a *travesty* of politicians by emphasizing some facial characteristic to a ridiculous extreme.
- A *travesty* was made of Richard Nixon's jowls, for instance.
- Teddy Roosevelt was often portrayed with a monacle, a cigar, and a grotesque shotgun and/or riding crop, making a *travesty* of his avocations.
- The pop diva's remake of a popular 1960s ballad was considered a *travesty* by those who knew and loved the original song.

  [Syn. caricature]

treachery (TRECH ir ee) *n.* 1. a betrayal of trust or faith; treason; 2. an act of disloyalty or treason; perfidy

- Benedict Arnold was known for his *treachery* in delivering the plans of West Point to the redcoats.
- Less well known in the United States is the *treachery* of Vidkund Quisling, whose so-called Fifth Column led to the taking of Norway by Nazi Germany.

tremulous (TREM yoo lis) *adj.* 1. trembling or quivering; 2. marked by trembling or shaking; 3. timid; fearful; timorous

- Maricella's *tremulous* hand made brain surgery an unsuitable occupation for her.
- A good singer often has a *tremulous* voice on a sustained note, known as "tremolo"; bad singers let this *tremulousness* get out of hand.

- It is appropriate to be *tremulous* when unarmed and face to face with an uncaged 600 lb. Siberian tiger.

  [-ly *adv.*, -ness *n.*]

trivialize (TRI vee uh lyz) *vt.* 1. to regard or treat as unimportant or insignificant; 2. to make seem unimportant

- It is easy for an adult to *trivialize* the fears of a child and, by so doing, to traumatize him or her.
- A good teacher will not *trivialize* the questions of students.

  [-d*, trivializing, trivialization *n.*]

truculent (TRUHK yoo lint) *adj.* 1. cruel; fierce; savage; 2. rude; mean; 3. bellicose; warlike; pugnacious

- Genghis Khan took a *truculent* attitude toward nearly everyone but his wife, Sylvia.
- The North Koreans have been *truculent* toward those in the South since shortly after World War II.

  [-ly *adv.*, truculence *n.*]

trustee (TRUS tee) *n.* 1. a person entrusted with the management of someone else's property or money; 2. a country in charge of administering a trust territory; 3. a group of persons or a board appointed to manage the affairs of an institution

- A *trustee* is often appointed by a bankruptcy court to manage the applicant's financial affairs.
- The United Kingdom was made *trustee* over much of the former territory of the Ottoman Empire after World War I.
- Many major instutions' financial affairs are in the hands of a board of *trustees*.

turmoil (TOER moyl) *n.* uproar; confusion; disarray; tumult; commotion

- The floor of the New York Stock Exchange always appears to be in a state of *turmoil*.
- The police do their best to control the *turmoil* as the crowd leaves the racetrack at the end of the Indianapolis 500.
- Fear and *turmoil* gripped the passengers and crew of the *Titanic* in their attempt to leave the stricken ship.

turpitude* (TOER pi TOOD) *n.* 1. depravity or vileness; baseness; 2. any instance of the foregoing

- One of the approved reasons for removing a public official from office is moral *turpitude*.
- The *turpitude* of Adolph Hitler is without parallel in modern times.

tyranny (TIR uh nee) *n.* 1. the government of an absolute ruler; 2. oppressive government; unjust government; 3. cruel and unjust use of authority; harshness; severity; despotism

- The first so-called *tyrannies* took place in ancient Greece, and *tyranny* comes from the Greek word *tyrant*.
- Any modern-day dictatorship is a *tyranny*.
- The Reign of Terror, which followed the French Revolution, was not a *tyranny* in the first sense of the word but was one in the third sense.

  [tyrannies *pl.*]

QUICK REVIEW #82

Match the word from column 2 with the word from column 1 that means most nearly the same thing.

1. transient
2. transparent
3. trauma
4. travesty
5. treachery
6. tremulous
7. trivialize
8. truculent
9. trustee
10. turmoil
11. turpitude
12. tyranny

a. minimize
b. perfidy
c. savage
d. depravity
e. administrator
f. disarray
g. injury
h. quivering
i. severity
j. momentary
k. caricature
l. clear

U – Z

unavailable (UHN uh VAY li bl) *adj.* 1. that which cannot be obtained or had; unreachable; 2. not willing to attend or serve (in a position)

- When Carol tried to get Gerald's address, she found it to be *unavailable*.
- The senator from Arizona was *unavailable* to run as the candidate for vice president.

  [unavailably *adv.*]

unavoidable (UHN uh VOY di bl) *adj.* 1. something that can't be avoided; inevitable; 2. that cannot be nullified or voided

- When the car began to skid, hitting the lamppost was *unavoidable*.
- After the summons had been issued by the officer, the need to respond to it was *unavoidable*.

  [unavoidably *adv.*]

underestimate (UHN doer ES ti mayt) *vt.* to undervalue something; set an estimate that is too low —*n.* too low an evaluation of something's worth

- The appraiser *underestimated* the value of the painting in Diane's living room.
- Victor's conception of how much study time was needed before taking his finals proved to be an *underestimate*.

  [-d, underestimating]

undermine (UHN der myn) *vt.* 1. to dig beneath; tunnel; mine; 2. to wear away and weaken the supports of something; 3. to weaken or impair, especially by stealthy or underhanded means

- The prisoners *undermined* the wall in an attempt to escape.
- The bridge's supports had been *undermined* by the rushing waters of the river below it.
- The authority of the government was *undermined* by the actions of the guerrilla forces.

  [-d, undermining*] [Syn. weaken]

undesirable (UHN diz YR i bl) *adj.* not desirable or pleasing; objectionable —*n.* an undesirable person

- Using television as a babysitter might have an *undesirable* effect on the children's education.
- Speaking loudly in a library is considered *undesirable* behavior.
- Vagrants are often treated by society as *undesirables*.

  [undesirably *adv.*]

unfetter (uhn FET ir) *vt.* to free from restraints of any kind; to liberate

- The coach needs to be *unfettered* so that she can experiment with using different players at different positions.
- *Unfetter* the dog so that he may run about the yard.

  [-ed, -ing] [Syn. liberate]

unheralded (uhn HER ild id) *adj.* uncelebrated in advance; unforetold; not pre-announced; unpredicted

- The circus's arrival in town was completely *unheralded*.
- The president made an *unheralded* trip to the front.

universal (YOO ni VER sil) *adj.* 1. present or occurring everywhere; 2. not limited or restricted; 3. highly adaptable; usable for many different purposes

- Air is *universal* where humans are able to live.
- The Constitution's framers believed in a *universal* right to freedom of speech.
- A hammer is one of the few tools that have *universal* applications.

  [-ly *adv.*] [Syn. general, generic]

unparalleled (uhn PA ruh leld) *adj.* unequaled; unmatched; that has no parallel

- The quality of Geoffrey's cinematography is *unparalleled* in the history of filmmaking.
- Picasso had a grasp of shape relationships that is *unparalleled* in the known art world.

unresolved (UHN riz AHLVD) *adj.* unsettled; undetermined; unexplained; unanalyzed

- The difficulties Ralph and Edna had in understanding one another were *unresolved* by their having a child.
- The chemical composition of the compound remained *unresolved*, even after analysis by spectrograph.

unutterable (uhn UH tir uh bl) *adj.* that can't be described or expressed; inexpressible

- The shock that Sarah felt was *unutterable*.
- Jack found the words needed to describe the horror he felt upon hearing of the fire were *unutterable*.

  [unutterably *adv.*]

upstart (UHP stahrt) *n.* 1. a person who has recently become wealthy, and so is presumptuous or aggressive; 2. one who does not know his/her proper place

- The country club caters to the longtime aristocracy, and its board has always voted to keep *upstarts* out.
- The *upstart* was reprimanded when he tried to cut into the front of the line.

QUICK REVIEW #83

Match the word from column 2 with the word from column 1 that means most nearly the same thing.

1. unavailable	a. objectionable
2. unavoidable	b. unpredicted
3. underestimate	c. presumptuous
4. undermine	d. generic
5. undesirable	e. unequaled
6. unfetter	f. undetermined
7. unheralded	g. unreachable
8. universal	h. inexpressible
9. unparalleled	i. inevitable
10. unresolved	j. weaken
11. unutterable	k. liberate
12. upstart	l. undervalue

urbanized (OER bin YZD) *adj.* changed from countrylike to citylike in character; citified

- The area had only recently become *urbanized,* having been mostly farms less than a generation ago.
- The influx of industry was largely responsible for the *urbanized* character of Allentown.

urge (OERJ) *vt.* 1. to plead, allege, strongly advocate; 2. strongly recommend; compel; 3. to incite or provoke

- Jeannie *urged* Horace to change his mind and visit the zoo.
- Philip of Macedon *urges* his son, Alexander, to go to medical school so that he can become a doctor.
- The rabble-rousers *urged* the crowd to take arms against the government.

  [-d, urging] [Syn. press, exhort]

Utopia (yoo TOH pee uh) *n.* 1. an imaginary island from a book of the same name by Sir Thomas More, 1516; 2. any idealized place; symbol of perfection; paradise

- *Utopia* was the name Sir Thomas More gave to his imaginary island.
- Many believe that Tahiti is as close as one can come to a *utopia* in real life; others would select Hawaii.

  [utopian *adj.*]

vaccine (VAK seen) *n.* a preparation placed into the body to prevent or lessen the effects of a specific infection; disease preventitive; innoculation

- Before Jonas Salk discovered his *vaccine,* polio was the greatest fear of mothers of young children.
- Medical researchers are now seeking a *vaccine* for cancer.

valid (VAL id) *adj.* 1. having legal status; binding under the law; 2. legitimate; in force; effective; 3. capable of withstanding criticism or examination

- To drive, one must have a *valid* driver's license.
- Alternate side of the street parking is *valid* in New York City except on legal holidays.
- No matter how many times something is tried and works, it cannot be proven to be a natural law, yet one case of failure is enough to prove it not *valid.*

valorous (VAL er uhs) *adj.* having or showing courage; bravery; being strong

- Soldiers and sailors are decorated for exhibiting *valorous* behavior.
- The code of chivalry implied an expectation of *valorous* behavior on the part of medieval knights.

vanquish (VAN kwish) *vt.* 1. to beat; to defeat in battle; 2. to force into submission

- In times of war, it is the object of armed forces to *vanquish* the foe.
- In chess, it is customary for the *vanquished* player to concede by upending his or her king.

    [-ed, -ing] [Syn. conquer]

varied (VA reed) *adj.* 1. of different kinds; diverse; 2. of different colors; variegated; 3. altered; changed

- America is unique because of the *varied* cultures of its inhabitants.
- Clothing designs are *varied* in shape, size, and shade.
- Having put on 20 pounds since he bought his suit, Bob thought it advisable to have its size *varied* by a tailor.

    [-ly *adv.*]

variety (vuh RY it ee) *adj.* 1. the state of being diverse; having many choices; 2. a different form or condition from the usual; 3. many different things taken together (like a variety show)

- A *variety* of fresh fruits and vegetables are in season during the summer months.
- Breakfast can be made more interesting by eating a *variety* of cereals rather than eating the same one every day.
- A *variety* show offers an assortment of entertainment.

varnish* (VAHR nish) *n.* 1. a resinous preparation used to give wood a glossy protective finish; 2. the hard, glossy surface produced; 3. a glossy or polished manner —*vt.* 1. to cover with varnish; 2. to make superficially attractive; 3. to polish up; embellish

- *Varnish* may be diluted with turpentine.
- Using coasters on *varnish* helps to prevent its getting discolored by moisture on glass bottoms.

- Cary Grant always appeared well *varnished* in his screen persona.
- A fisherman always *varnishes* his tales about the big one that got away.

    [-ed, -ing]

venerable* (VEN ir uh bl) *adj.* 1. deserving of reverence or respect by virtue of age and dignity or position and character; 2. impressive because of age, history, or religious significance

- Any Bugatti automobile that has survived to this day can certainly be referred to as *venerable.*
- The dowager empress of China, who reigned during the so-called Boxer Rebellion, was a *venerable* woman.

    [venerably *adv.*]

venerate (VEN ir ayt) *vt.* to revere; to regard with great respect; to view as venerable

- Nowadays, teenagers seem to *venerate* very little, with the exception of the pope and Mick Jagger.
- It is customary among Americans to *venerate* our founding fathers and mothers.

    [-d, venerating]

QUICK REVIEW #84

Match the word from column 2 with the word from column 1 that means most nearly the same thing.

1. urbanized	a. diversity
2. urge	b. legitimate
3. Utopia	c. changed
4. vaccine	d. conquer
5. valid	e. impressive
6. valorous	f. citified
7. vanquish	g. embellish
8. varied	h. revere
9. variety	i. innoculation
10. varnish	j. exhort
11. venerable	k. courageous
12. venerate	l. paradise

verifiable (VER i FY i bl) *adj.* capable of being proven true; ascertainible

- For an alibi to be any good, it must be *verifiable.*
- While Jack Benny's age was clearly *verifiable* (he was born in 1894 and died in 1974), he claimed to have been 39 for 41 years.

[verifiably *adv.*]

verisimilitude (ver i si MIL i tood) *n.* 1. the appearance of being true or real; 2. something having the appearance of being true or real

- The best cubic zirconiums have a *verisimilitude* that would fool all but an experienced gem expert into thinking they were diamonds.
- Often, a *verisimilitude* is a truth, but if something appears to be too good to be true, then it probably is.

[Syn. truth]

verity (VER i tee) *n.* 1. conforming to the truth or fact; reality; 2. a principle or belief; a reality

- A skeptic does not believe anything he hears unless he can confirm its *verity.*
- It is a *verity* that men and women are different.

[Syn. truth]

vestige (VES tij) *n.* 1. remaining trace of something no longer used or that no longer exists; 2. a trace; a bit; 3. an atrophied or rudimentary organ more fully developed in earlier forms of a species

- The human appendix is a *vestige,* thought to be from the time when our main source of protein was insects.
- A con man would never succeed in conning his mark, unless the story he told had some *vestige* of truth.
- Apes and humans have *vestiges* of tails, suggesting that some earlier ancestors probably were tailed.

[vestigial *adj.*, vestgially *adv.*]

vex (VEKS) *vt.* 1. to disturb, annoy, irritate, especially in a petty or nagging way; 2. to distress, afflict, or plague

- Ian questioned everything he was asked to do, just to *vex* his parents.
- Melissa found it *vexing* that two-year-old Sebastian listened carefully to what she wanted him to do, smiled at her, and then did whatever he wanted.
- Marge continued to be *vexed* by her rheumatism.

[-ed, -ing] [Syn. annoy]

vicarious (vy KAR ee uhs) *adj.* 1. taking the place of another as a deputy or a stand-in; substituting for another; 2. imagining participation in another's activity

- The deputy sheriff acts with the *vicarious* powers of the sheriff when he forms a posse.
- When Jill told Fran of her exciting ride down the rapids of the Colorado River, Fran experienced a *vicarious* thrill.

[-ly *adv.*]

victory (VIK ter ee) *n.* 1. a final and complete triumph in battle; 2. a specific military battle that ended in triumph for your side; 3. success in any contest requiring the overcoming of obstacles

- Lord Nelson's *victory* at Trafalgar is commemorated by a statue in London's square of the same name.
- L'Arc de Triomphe in Paris has seen *victories* celebrated by armies of several countries.
- Some athletes go to the Olympics to compete, while others go seeking *victory*.

  [victories *pl.*] [Syn. conquest, triumph]

vigilant (VIJ il int) *adj.* staying watchful and alert for danger

- When you are outside your home with a child, you must be *vigilant* at all times.
- Cats appear to be *vigilant* even when they're asleep.

  [-ly *adv.*] [Syn. watchful]

vigor (VIG oer) *n.* 1. active force or strength; 2. active or healthy growth; 3. intensity; force; energy

- A defense attorney's job is to defend his client with *vigor*.
- Rosebushes appear to die in the winter in northern climates, but with the first sign of spring they exhibit new *vigor*.
- It takes the *vigor* of multiple rocket engines to boost a satellite into orbit.

  [-ous *adj.*, -ously *adv.*]

violence (VY uh lins) *n.* 1. physical force that causes damage, destruction, and personal injury; 2. intense force and energy, such as that of a tropical storm, earthquake, tornado, and so on; 3. a violent act or deed

- Gang *violence* has become all too common in certain areas of certain cities.
- Battery is an act of *violence* of one person on another.
- Tornadoes often cause *violence* to people who are caught out in them.

violent (VY uh lint) *adj.* 1. acting with great force so as to injure, damage, or destroy; 2. caused by an act of violence; 3. furious; extreme; intense

- A homicidal maniac has a tendency to be *violent*.
- Video games depicting *violent* acts are not necessarily harmful to children, nor are they necessarily helpful.
- When cold fronts meet warm fronts, *violent* weather conditions often develop.

  [-ly *adv.*]

virtue (VOER choo) *n.* 1. moral excellence and goodness of heart; 2. meritorious in moral quality and rightness of action; 3. effective power or force

- We show *virtue* by the way we live.
- Bill won the day by *virtue* of having four kings.
- The *virtue* of medicine is well known.

QUICK REVIEW #85

Match the word from column 2 with the word from column 1 that means most nearly the same thing.

1. verifiable	a. extreme
2. verisimilitude	b. destruction
3. verity	c. annoy
4. vestige	d. energy
5. vex	e. watchful
6. vicarious	f. goodness
7. victory	g. apparently true
8. vigilant	h. trace
9. vigor	i. ascertainable
10. violence	j. substituted
11. violent	k. truth
12. virtue	l. triumph

viscous (VIS kis) *adj.* 1. having the consistency of a sticky, coherent fluid; viscid; 2. having viscosity

- The *viscous* quality of motor oil is what causes it to adhere to engine parts and protect them against wear.
- How *viscous* a liquid can be expressed scientifically as its coefficient of viscosity, with water's coefficient being 1.

[viscosity *n.*]

vitality* (vy TAL i tee) *adj.* 1. the power to live, or to go on living; 2. life force; 3. mental or physical energy; 4. the power of an institution to flourish

- The question is not how old one is but how much *vitality* one has.
- I've seen 80-year-olds with the *vitality* of 20-somethings, and vice versa.
- A chocolate bar can give one some instant *vitality*.
- The *vitality* of NATO has been open to question since the end of the Cold War.

vitiate (VISH ee ayt) *vt.* 1. to make impure; to spoil; to corrupt; 2. to pervert; weaken morally; 3. to invalidate a contract

- Using any cheese other than parmigiano reggiano *vitiates* the authenticity of an Alfredo sauce.
- The Roman Empire's morality *vitiated* long before the empire crumbled.
- Failure to abide by the limits of the contract will serve to *vitiate* it.

[-d vitiating] [Syn. weaken]

vocalization (VOH kil i ZAY shin) *n.* an utterance; something sung or spoken; an articulation

- The mayor gave *vocalization* to his concern about balancing the budget.
- The *vocalizations* of the tenor at last night's performance were without equal in Mary's experience.

vocation (voh KAY shin) *n.* 1. a calling to enter a certain career; 2. any career, profession, or trade

- Eric's *vocation* as a beachcomber was sealed from the moment his mother bought him the comb.
- Everyone should have some *vocation* or a railroad car full of money.

vociferously (voh SIF oer is lee) *adv.* 1. loudly making one's feelings known; 2. characteristically making a fuss to be sure of being heard

- The crow cawed *vociferously,* as if complaining about the screen separating it from the cherry pie.
- The crowd *vociferously* yelled at the center fielder to throw the ball to home plate.

  [vociferous *adj.*, vociferousness *n.*] [Syn. clamorously, stridently, boisterously]

vulgar (VUHL goer) *adj.* 1. common; popular with the great majority of people; 2. in the vernacular; 3. characterized by lack of culture or refinement; boorish

- Certain computer terms like RAM and ROM have found their way into *vulgar* usage.
- *Vulgar* Latin was quite different from the Latin used in literature.
- Richard's wearing jeans to the opera last Thursday was rather *vulgar,* in Karen's opinion.

  [-ly *adv.*] [Syn. coarse, common]

ward (WAWRD) *vt.* to fend off; parry; push aside or away —*n.* 1. the act of guarding; 2. the state of being under guard; 3. a child or other person placed under the guardianship of another or of a court; 4. each of the parts or divisions of a hospital or a jail; 5. an administrative district of a city or town

- The sun tried to *ward* off the winter cold.
- The guard was *ward* over the second floor.
- The class was the *ward* of the school while in the building.
- By order of the court, Burt Ward was made Bruce Wayne's *ward*.
- The hospital had a maternity *ward* and a prison *ward*, which some would say are one and the same.
- The congressman was elected to represent the third *ward*.

  [-ed, -ing]

whereas (wair AZ) *conj.* 1. it being the case that; because; 2. but, on the other hand; 3. in as much as

- *Whereas* you already have the umbrella, why don't you open it?
- You have the steering wheel, *whereas* I have the car key.
- *Whereas* tomorrow is your birthday, let's party today.

whimsical (WIM zi kil) *adj.* 1. characterized by capriciousness; 2. oddly extraordinary; fanciful; freakish; 3. unpredictable; subject to change

- Artist Peter Max is known for his *whimsical* cartoons.
- Teresa took a *whimsical* notion to jump into the Pacific Ocean.
- We'd love to tell you what the bus schedule is, but as far as we can tell, it's purely *whimsical,* depending on the driver's inclination.

  [-ly *adv.*]

wield (WEELD) *vt.* 1. to handle and use (a weapon or tool, with some skill being implied); 2. to exercise (power, influence, and so on)

- The blacksmith *wields* his hammer very deftly.
- The amount of power the president of the United States *wields* has increased since the drafting of the Constitution.

  [-ed, -ing] [Syn. handle]

wilderness (WIL doer nis) *n.* 1. an uninhabited (by humans), uncultivated region; wild; waste; 2. any open, barren, or empty area, including the ocean; 3. a confused, tangled mass

- Foxes and cougars can thrive only in the *wilderness,* while deer seem to be better able to coexist with people.
- The *wilderness* of the Brazilian rain forest is rapidly disappearing.
- Laura hadn't combed or cut her hair in two years, so when she went to the stylist, he was greeted with a tangled *wilderness* of hair.

  [Syn. waste]

QUICK REVIEW #86

Match the word from column 2 with the word from column 1 that means most nearly the same thing.

1. viscous	a. because
2. vitality	b. common
3. vitiate	c. waste
4. vocalization	d. parry
5. vocation	e. handle
6. vociferously	f. unpredictable
7. vulgar	g. corrupt
8. ward	h. profession
9. whereas	i. energy
10. whimsical	j. articulation
11. wield	k. viscid
12. wilderness	l. stridently

Part II

GRE® Words

Answers to Quick Review questions are found in Part III.

A

abacus (AB i kuhs) *n.* a frame with beads on wires in rows of fives and twos separated by a "reckoning bar," of Chinese origin

- The *abacus* is one of the earliest arithmetic calculators.
- Don't confuse an *abacus* with the very similar Japanese *soroban* that has rows of beads split into fours and ones.

aberration (ab oer AY shin) *n.* 1. a departure from the normal; 2. a deviation from what is right or correct

- Barbara's taking the shortcut home was an *aberration* from her normal driving pattern.
- Jack was prone to mental *aberrations* that caused him to believe he was being persecuted.

abeyance (uh BAY ins) *n.* a temporary suspension or delay of a function or activity

- The rainstorm caused the baseball game to be held in *abeyance*.
- The judge decided to hold sentencing in *abeyance* until the convicted person's counsel could arrange for character witnesses.

abjure (ab JOOR) *vt.* 1. to give up rights, allegiance, and so on under oath; to renounce; 2. to recant

- By his divorce agreement, Ken *abjured* all rights to the family car.
- On cross-examination, Doris *abjured* her previous testimony about having seen the burglar.

  [-d, abjuring] [Syn. renounce]

abrade (uh BRAYD) *vt.* scrape; wear out by rubbing; rub off

- Sally used a pumice stone to *abrade* the dead skin off her right foot.
- Sanding is a good way to *abrade* rough spots off a piece of furniture before applying the finish.
- Grinding wheels are used to *abrade* metal objects.

  [-d, abrading] [Syn. scrape]

abrogate (AB ruh GAYT) *vt.* to repeal or cancel (by authority); annul

- Only a court has the right to *abrogate* a wedding.
- You may not *abrogate* your obligation to support your children unless a court rules so.

  [-d, abrogating] [Syn. abolish]

accretion (uh KREE shin) *n.* 1. growth in size, especially by addition or accumulation of material; 2. accumulated matter

- The *accretion* of sand brought in by the ocean has caused certain beaches to grow in size.
- Regular brushing is needed to remove the *accretion* of plaque on one's teeth.

  [(to) accrete *vi., vt.*]

accumulate (uh KYOOM yoo LAYT) *vt.* to pile up; gather; form a heap

- Over years of saving regularly, wealth *accumulates*.
- Dirty laundry *accumulates* on the floor of any boy's room.
- In the autumn, leaves *accumulate* on the lawn in the temperate climate regions.

[-d, accumulating] [Syn. heap]

adjunct (AD junkt) *n.* 1. an addition; something secondary in importance; 2. a person who is a helper of another —*adj.* an assistant, such as an adjunct teacher, counselor, and so on

- A police officer usually carries a second gun as an *adjunct* to his service weapon.
- A pointer can be a useful *adjunct* at most slide shows.
- An *adjunct* teacher is often found in a primary school classroom in addition to the classroom teacher.

adrenaline (uh DREN uh lin) *n.* first appeared as a trademarked name coined by chemist J. Takamine, who isolated it in 1901; now the nontechnical name for epinephrine, a hormone produced by the inner cortex of the adrenal glands

- *Adrenaline* causes the body's functions to temporarily speed up.
- The body is stimulated to produce *adrenaline* in response to perceived emergency situations.

adroit (uh DROYT) *adj.* skillful either mentally or physically; clever; expert at

- Andy had become quite an *adroit* chess player by the time he was 17.
- Gino was extremely *adroit* with a wheelbarrow full of wet concrete.

[-ly *adv.*] [Syn. dextrous]

adulterate (uh DUHL toer AYT) *vt.* to make impure; water down; to make inferior

- Cream is *adulterated* with milk to make half-and-half.
- Teachers often *adulterate* their criticism of pupils' work so as not to overwhelm them.
- Legislation can be so *adulterated* by amendments that it does not do what it was originally intended to accomplish.

[-d, adulterating] [Syn. dilute]

QUICK REVIEW #87

Match the word from column 2 with the word from column 1 that means most nearly the same thing.

1. abacus	a. renounce
2. aberration	b. abolish
3. abeyance	c. addition
4. abjure	d. dilute
5. abrade	e. heap
6. abrogate	f. dextrous
7. accretion	g. epinephrine
8. accumulate	h. delay
9. adjunct	i. calculator
10. adrenaline	j. scrape
11. adroit	k. oddity
12. adulterate	l. pile

advocate (AD vuh KAYT *for vt.*, AD vuh kit *for n.*) *vt.* to speak or write in favor of something —*n.* a person who pleads the case of another (for example, a lawyer) or who supports a specific action

- Fred wrote to *advocate* tax reform for the state.
- Marsha *advocates* freedom for all to enjoy ice cream without increasing in size or weight.
- Alice is Jose's *advocate* in his suit against the city for overassessing the value of his property.
- Noreen is an *advocate* for the rights of homeless people.
  [-d, advocating] [Syn. support]

affinity (uh FIN i tee) *n.* 1. close relationship; connection; 2. similarity of structure; 3. affection; liking for

- Helen always felt a great *affinity* for Al.
- Tuna and mayonnaise have a close *affinity* to one another.
- Though they are all Romance languages, Italian has a greater *affinity* to Spanish than to French.

affirm (uh FOERM) *vt.* 1. to declare to be true; assert the truth of; 2. to confirm; uphold; ratify

- Jerry came to Ann to *affirm* the validity of Laura's tale.
- The Senate *affirmed* the nomination of the secretary of state.
  [-ed, -ing, -ation *n.*] [Syn. assert]

aggrandize (uh GRAN dyz) *vt.* 1. to make greater, richer, more powerful; 2. to make seem richer

- By certifying the landfill as a suitable building site, the county helped to further *aggrandize* its owner.
- Although not earning a dollar from the transaction, its very happening *aggrandized* Otto's reputation.

[-d, aggrandizing] [Syn. enrich]

agronomy (uh GRAHN uh mee) *n.* management of farmland; the science of producing crops

- For a farmer to get the most from his land, he needs to have some understanding of *agronomy.*
- *Agronomy* teaches that rotating crops allows the land to replenish its essential nutrients after they've been used.

allegory (AL ig AWR ee) *n.* a story in which people, things, and ideas have hidden meanings, often used as a way of teaching values

- Aesop's fables are probably the best-known *allegories* in all literature.
- An *allegory* always has a message apart from its obvious one, which in Aesop's case is provided in the moral at the end.

[allegories *pl.*]

alleviate (uh LEEV ee AYT) *vt.* 1. to lighten; make less hard to bear; 2. to reduce or lessen pain

- Lloyd took one of the boxes of books from Arlene to *alleviate* the load that she was carrying.
- Tears often *alleviate* the burden of emotional stress.

[-d, alleviating] [Syn. reduce]

allocate (AL uh KAYT) *vt.* 1. to earmark or set aside for a specific purpose; 2. to distribute; mete out

- The city *allocated* $200 million to improve mass-transit facilities.
- Having collected hundreds of donated winter coats, it was now up to the lodge to *allocate* them among the less fortunate.

[-d, allocating] [Syn. allot]

alloy (uh LOY *for vt.,* A loy *for n.*) *vt.* 1. to fuse two or more metals to form one that possesses new properties; 2. to reduce the pureness of a rare metal by fusing it with a less precious one —*n.* a metallic substance derived from the chemical fusion of two or more metals

- Wrapping a strip of copper arround tin does not make an *alloy;* the tin and copper must be smelted at high heat to form the new metal, bronze.
- Iron is *alloyed* with carbon and several other metals to produce steel.
- Fourteen-karat gold is produced by *alloying* 24-karat pure gold with other metals.

[-ed, -ing]

amalgamate (uh MAL guh MAYT) *vt.* 1. to join together into one; to unite; to combine; 2. to alloy into an amalgam (an alloy of mercury and another metal, used by dentists in fillings)

- Many smaller companies were *amalgamated* to form some of today's corporate giants, such as General Electric and U.S. Steel.
- Mercury and silver are *amalgamated* to form the amalgam that is losing popularity with dentists as a filling material.

  [-d, amalgamating]

ameliorate (uh MEEL ee uh RAYT) *vt.* to make or become better; to improve

- A visit by a professional cleaning service should *ameliorate* the mess in our living room.
- The automobile company recalled all 2004 model cars to *ameliorate* the problem with the steering pump.

  [-d, ameliorating] [Syn. improve]

QUICK REVIEW #88

Match the word from column 2 with the word from column 1 that means most nearly the same thing.

1. advocate (*vt.*)	a. connection
2. advocate (*n.*)	b. relieve
3. affinity	c. improve
4. affirm	d. symbolism
5. aggrandize	e. distribute
6. agronomy	f. unite
7. allegory	g. enrich
8. alleviate	h. fuse
9. allocate	i. support
10. alloy	j. assert
11. amalgamate	k. farming
12. ameliorate	l. supporter

amenable (uh MEN i bl *or* uh MEEN i bl) *adj.* 1. responsive; answerable to; 2. controllable; submissive

- Would you be *amenable* to someone's making you an offer for your car?
- Pneumonia is *amenable* to treatment with antibiotics.

  [amenably *adv.*] [Syn. obedient]

amortize (uh MAWR tyz) *vt.* 1. to put money aside at intervals to pay off a debt either prior to or at maturity; 2. to prorate an expense over an interval (for tax purposes)

- A mortgage is usually *amortized* over a period of 5 to 30 years, with 30 being the most common term.
- An automobile purchased for business use must be *amortized* over 5 to 7 years rather than taken as a single deduction all at once.

  [-d, -zing]

animosity (an i MAH sit ee) *n.* hostility; a feeling of strong ill will; dislike

- There is a great deal of *animosity* between Boston Red Sox fans and New York Yankee fans.
- Veterans from Germany and America have met each other in the cemeteries of France to show that they have no *animosity* for each other left over from World War II.

  [Syn. enmity]

annul (uh NUHL) *vt.* to nullify; void; cancel; put an end to; invalidate under the law

- Only one amendment to the U.S. Constitution stands out as unique in that it *annuls* another.
- Most contracts contain a paragraph listing the conditions under which it may be *annulled.*

  [annulled, annulling] [Syn. abolish]

anomalous (uh NAM uh lis) *adj.* 1. deviating from the regular rule; strange; abnormal; 2. being or seeming irregular; contradictory

- It was the *anomalous* behavior of the planets Neptune and Uranus that led to astronomers discovering Pluto in 1930.
- Observations of *anomalous* behavior of certain objects in the sky have led to reportings of UFO sightings.

  [-ly *adv.*] [Syn. irregular]

antibody (AN ti BAH dee) *n.* a special protein produced by certain white blood cells to form immunity to certain antigens

- Before the Salk vaccine stimulated the production of *antibodies* against it, polio was the most dreaded disease in the United States.
- Each *antibody* produced by white blood cells is specific to a particular disease.

  [antibodies *pl.*]

antipathy (an TIP ith ee) *n.* 1. a strong or deeply felt dislike; 2. the object of that dislike

- It is rumored that dogs have a great *antipathy* for cats, yet Lois's two dogs and three cats get along famously.
- Jan's new hairdo was the object of Kaj's *antipathy.*

  [Syn. aversion]

apprehension (AP ri HEN shin) *n*. 1. arrest or capture; 2. mental grasp (of); 3. anxiety; dread; 4. judgment; opinion

- The bank robber's *apprehension* was the number one priority of the Boston police.
- Carl had no *apprehension* of the effort that had been put into writing the computer program.
- Harvey looked forward to his day in court with considerable *apprehension*.
- *Apprehension* is a very strange word, in my *apprehension*.

arabesque (a ruh BESK) *n*. 1. a complex decorative design found in Moorish architecture, with intertwined lines suggesting foliage, flowers, and so on; 2. a ballet position in which one leg is extended straight back, one arm is stretched forward, and the other arm is stretched backward; 3. a light musical composition

- Moorish architecture is distinguished by its *arabesques*, which might be carved into the stonework or might be in relief.
- A ballet dancer's *arabesque* is a pose that I would not have attempted even when I was 17 years old.
- Pianists are likely to have encountered the *arabesques* of Robert Schumann.

arboreal (ahr BAW re uhl) *adj*. having to do with trees; living in trees or designed for trees

- Most botanical gardens have their *arboreal* sections.
- Tree sloths are among the *arboreal* creatures that like to just hang out.
  [-ly *adv*.]

archaeology (ahr kee AHL ij ee) *n*. the scientific study of the past (especially of past civilizations and cultures through excavation of their cities, their artifacts, and so on)

- *Archaeology* is responsible for most of what we know about the pharoahs of Egypt.
- *Archaeology* is relatively new in America, and yet it is amazing what it can tell us about the early inhabitants of the western United States.
  [archaeological *adj*.]

archaic (ahr KAY ik) *adj*. 1. belonging to an earlier period; antiquated; 2. old fashioned; 3. no longer in use, except for special occasions

- Oar-powered galleys were in fashion in ancient times, but today would be thought of as *archaic*.
- Some would say that wearing a tie and jacket in the workplace is an *archaic* custom.
- The use of Latin in Catholic Church services has been ruled by Vatican II to be *archaic*.
  [-ly *adv*.] [Syn. old]

QUICK REVIEW #89

Match the word from column 2 with the word from column 1 that means most nearly the same thing.

1. amenable	a. ancient studies
2. amortize	b. design
3. animosity	c. irregular
4. annul	d. obedient
5. anomalous	e. treelike
6. antibody	f. judgment
7. antipathy	g. old
8. apprehension	h. aversion
9. arabesque	i. abolish
10. arboreal	j. pay
11. archaeology	k. protein
12. archaic	l. enmity

ardor (AHR doer) *n.* 1. eagerness; enthusiasm; zeal; 2. warm passion; fire

- Zelda embraced her new job as editor in chief with *ardor*.
- The old-timer spoke with *ardor* as he recounted tales of the good old days in the 1970s.

  [Syn. passion]

articulate (ahr TIK yoo LAYT *for verb*, ar TIK yi lit *for adj.*) *vt.* 1. to annunciate; to speak; to put into spoken or written words; to express clearly; 2. to arrange in connected sequence —*adj.* 1. having parts connected by joints; 2. well spoken; able to speak; 3. clearly presented

- It fell to Abraham Lincoln to *articulate* the needs and wishes of his constituents.
- Many new automobiles have windshield-wiper arms that *articulate* to clean more of the windshield than the older ones.
- Bones of human legs are *articulated* at the knees and at the ankles.
- It is a plus in the business world if you are *articulate*.
- Katherine's presentation to the school board was very *articulate*.

  [-d, articulating, -ness *n.*]

artifact (AHR ti FAKT) *n.* anything man-made (especially a primitive tool, vessel, or weapon)

- *Artifacts* from the wreck of the *Titanic* are making their rounds of American and British museums.
- The earliest *artifacts* to have survived to the present time are from the Old Stone Age.

asperity (uhs PER it ee) *n.* roughness or harshness of surface, weather, sound, or temperament

- The *asperity* of the moon's surface is approximated in Idaho's Craters of the Moon National Monument.
- The area of the United States known as tornado alley is infamous for the *asperity* of its summer weather.

[asperities *pl.*]

aspiration (AS pir AY shin) *n.* 1. a strong desire or ambition; 2. breathing in, as of dust or pollen into the lungs

- It was always Henry's *aspiration* to become a doctor.
- It is essential to wear a mask when sanding to lessen the risk of dust *aspiration*.

assail (uh SAYL) *vt.* 1. to attack physically, or with arguments; assault; 2. to begin working (on a task) with vigor

- Joshua *assailed* the walls of Jericho with trumpets—or so the story goes.
- The opposing party *assailed* the ruling party's budget bill with alacrity.
- Jason *assailed* the job of drywalling the bathroom with an energy his father lacked.
- The sound from the boom box *assailed* Sally's ears.

[-ed, -ing] [Syn. attack]

assimilation (uh SIM il AY shin) *n.* the absorption and incorporation of one thing into another

- It is up to our digestive tracts to perform *assimilation* of the nutrients from the food that we ingest.
- *Assimilation* of diverse cultures is what has made the United States the melting pot of modern civilization.

[(to) assimilate *vt.*]

assuage (uh SWAYJ) *vt.* 1. to lessen; allay (for example, pain); 2. to calm; pacify (for example, anger); 3. to relieve hunger or thirst

- Take two aspirin or acetominophen if you are an adult and are seeking to *assuage* the pain of a headache.
- Checks arriving on time might help to *assuage* the dissatisfaction of the company's laborers.
- Take a canteen full of water with you on a hike to *assuage* the thirst that is bound to come.

[-d, assuaging] [Syn. relieve]

aver (uh VOER) *vt.* to declare to be true; affirm; state positively

- A witness at a trial must *aver* that everything he or she will say will be true.
- Don't *aver* that Bob was where he says he was, unless you witnessed it yourself.
- I *aver* that I am getting a headache.

[averred, averring] [Syn. assert]

QUICK REVIEW #90

Match the word from column 2 with the word from column 1 that means most nearly the same thing.

1. ardor   a. incorporation

2. articulate   b. ambition

3. artifact   c. relieve

4. asperity   d. assert

5. aspiration   e. passion

6. assail   f. primitive tool

7. assimilation   g. harshness

8. assuage   h. enunciate

9. aver   i. assault

B

baste (BAYST) *vt.* 1. to sew with long, loose stitches to keep a garment together prior to the actual final stitching; to tack; 2. to moisten meat while roasting with drippings, melted butter, and so on

- Tailors *baste* a garment together to line everything up before they do the actual stitching of the finished item.
- When cooking a turkey, it is customary to *baste* it every 20 minutes or so to keep it moist.

    [-d, basting]

benevolent (bin EV il int) *adj.* inclined to do good or doing good; kindly; charitable

- John's family had a history of being *benevolent* toward charities.
- The March of Dimes counts on its reputation for contributions from *benevolent* organizations and individuals.

    [-ly *adv.*] [Syn. kind]

benign (bi NYN) *adj.* 1. good natured; favorable; beneficial; 2. noncancerous; nonmalignant

- Beatrice gave Roger a *benign* smile as she passed.
- Vera was relieved to learn from her oncologist that the tumor was *benign*.

bigotry (BIG uh tree) *adj.* the behavior, attitudes, and beliefs of a prejudiced, intolerant person

- Miguel demonstrated his *bigotry* by refusing to sit at a table with anyone who was not from Uruguay.
- Belief in racial stereotypes is characteristic of *bigotry*.

    [bigotries *pl.*, bigot *n.*]

bland (BLAND) *adj.* 1. mild and soothing rather than harsh and grating; 2. without taste; flavorless; insipid; dull

- Milk is a very *bland* drink when compared to orange or grapefruit juice.
- Tex-Mex food is noted for the piquantness of its flavor and is anything but *bland*.

    [-ness *n.*] [Syn. smooth, tasteless]

boggle (BAHG il) *vt.* 1. to confuse or overwhelm; 2. to hesitate at (because of scruples)

- Janice was *boggled* by the huge pile of papers that needed correcting.
- Crossword puzzles often *boggle* the mind.
- Eddie *boggled* at the idea of robbing a grocery store.

    [-d, boggling]

bogus (BOH gis) *adj.* not real or genuine; spurious

- *Bogus* Rolex watches are available on every street corner around Times Square for $50 or less.
- If someone offers you a diamond solitaire for about $100, there's a good chance that it's *bogus*.

  [-ly *adv.*] [Syn. false]

boisterous (BOY stris) *adj.* 1. noisy and unruly; rowdy; 2. rough and stormy

- Football crowds can get somewhat *boisterous*, especially when beer is being consumed.
- Try to keep from being too *boisterous* when you play with your friends.

  [-ly *adv.*] [Syn. vociferous]

bolster (BOHL stir) *vt.* to prop up or support; reinforce —*n.* 1. a long, narrow cushion; 2. any bolsterlike cushion or support

- Diane's family came to *bolster* her during her testimony.
- Please put the *bolsters* back on the sofa.
- *Bolsters* are used to cap the bearing part of a beam and extend its support outward.

  [-ed, -ing]

bombast (BAHM bast) *n.* talk or writing that sounds very important but has no meaning; pompous language

- "You make your bed right now or I'm not going to feed you for the next week" is either an example of *bombast* or an indication of child abuse.
- Nikita Khrushchev's "We shall bury you!" speech is a better-known example of *bombast*.

  [-ic *adj.*, -ically *adv.*]

boor (BOR) *n.* a rude, ill-mannered, or awkward person

- Stop acting like a *boor*.
- When Cindy turned her back on Rita and refused to acknowledge her greeting, she behaved *boorishly*.

  [-ish *adj.*, -ishly *adv.*]

bourgeois (BUR zhwah *or* bur ZHWAH) *adj.* conventional; middle class; ordinary —*n.* 1. a shopkeeper or a businessman; 2. a member of the middle class

- It is often considered an insult to call one's beliefs *bourgeois*.
- The *bourgeois* class, before the French Revolution of 1789, was the group of shopkeepers and self-employed persons between the aristocracy and the workers (or proletariat).

  [-e *fem.*, -ie *n.*]

brazen (BRAY zin) *adj.* 1. showing no shame; bold; impudent; 2. of brass; the color of brass

- Custer's attack at the Little Bighorn was *brazen* if not very smart.
- Trumpets have a very piercing, *brazen* sound.

  [-ly *adv.*]

broach (BROHCH) *vt.* 1. to start a discussion of; bring up; introduce; 2. to drill a hole (in a cask); to tap (a keg) —*n.* a tool for drilling

- Peggy *broached* the subject of going to the movies tomorrow evening.
- Given how hot it had been all day, someone was bound to *broach* the idea of going swimming.
- Tom *broached* the cask of root beer using a tool known (appropriately enough) as a *broach*.

[-ed, -ing] [Syn. utter]

buoyant (BOY int) *adj.* 1. having or showing the ability to float; 2. having the ability to lift one's spirits

- A life vest makes one *buoyant* so that should you accidentally fall from a boat, you would float.
- Spiritual songs are often *buoyant*, lifting one's spirits.

[-ly *adv.*, buoyancy *n.*]

burnish (BOER nish) *vt.* to make or become shiny by rubbing; polish —*n.* a gloss or a polished finish

- Verna *burnished* the silverware in preparation for the big dinner.
- After being polished, the mirror had a nice *burnish*.

[-ed, -ing]

QUICK REVIEW #91

Match the word from column 2 with the word from column 1 that means most nearly the same thing.

1. baste		a. conventional
2. benevolent		b. pomposity
3. benign		c. utter
4. bigotry		d. oaf
5. bland		e. intolerance
6. boggle		f. uplifting
7. bogus		g. impudent
8. boisterous		h. confuse
9. bolster		i. vociferous
10. bombast		j. insipid
11. boor		k. support
12. bourgeois		l. false
13. brazen		m. tack
14. broach		n. polish
15. buoyant		o. kind
16. burnish		p. nonmalignant

C

cacophony (kuh KA fin ee) *n.* harsh, jarring sound; noise

- A *cacophony* of automobile and truck horns greeted the ears of pedestrians walking by the traffic jam.
- When the 35 members of the second-grade band began to play their instruments, the audience was greeted with a *cacophony* of screeches.

  [cacophonous *adj.*, cacophonously *adv.*, cacophonies *pl.*]

cadge (KADZH) *vt.* to beg or to acquire as a result of begging; to sponge

- Most children learn to *cadge* (or not to) at an early age.
- Jason never *cadged;* he just asked for two of anything he wanted, figuring that his parents would compromise and get him one.

  [-d, cadging]

calibrate (CAL ib RAYT) *vt.* to fix, check, or adjust the graduations of an instrument of measurement, such as a meter or scale

- Most bathroom scales need to be *calibrated* by means of a knurled knob.
- Instant-read meat thermometers can be *calibrated* by turning their dials.

  [-d, calibrating]

caliper (KAL ip oer) *n.* 1. an instrument with two curved legs joined at one end by a rivet and used to measure thicknesses and diameters; 2. the part that presses against the spinning wheel in a bicycle brake or on a car's disc brakes

- By swinging the legs of a *caliper* apart and then bringing both tips to the opposite sides of a glass, the glass's outside diameter can be measured.
- Disk brakes bring a car to a stop by the *calipers* pressing their pads against the captive rotors.

camouflage (KAM uh FLAHZH) *vt.* to disguise a person or thing to conceal it (from an enemy) —*n.* any such disguise or disguising

- It is customary to *camouflage* soldiers and weapons to keep them hidden from the enemy.
- *Camouflage* is worn by all U.S. soldiers and Marines under battlefield conditions.

  [-d, camouflaging]

caustic (KAHS tik) *adj.* 1. able to eat away, burn, and destroy living tissue by chemical means; corrosive; 2. biting or sarcastic in wit; cutting type of humor or remark

- Some acids are more *caustic* than others, and you don't want to get them on your skin.
- Sarcasm is *caustic* wit at its most virulent.

  [-ally *adv.*] [Syn. corrosive, sarcastic]

cavalier (KAV uh LEAR) *adj.* 1. casual or unconcerned attitude; an indifference to matters of concern or importance; 2. arrogant and haughty —*n.* 1. a knight or armed horseman; 2. a courteous, gallant gentleman

- Barry had a *cavalier* attitude about his manners, and it would someday come back to haunt him.
- Vaughn was so *cavalier* that most others felt he was looking down his nose at them.
- Part of the outfit of a French *cavalier* was a wide-brimmed felt hat with an ostrich plume sticking out.
- *Cavaliers* made a point of helping damsels in distress.

  [-ly *adv.*]

charisma (kuh RIZ muh) *n.* a special quality or charm that encourages loyalty or devotion

- Joan of Arc's *charisma* is what made her soldiers follow her leadership.
- A rock star or a movie star who has *charisma* attracts a large band of devotees.

  [-tic *adj.*, -tically *adv.*]

chary (CHAI ree) *adj.* 1. careful; cautious; 2. not giving freely; sparing

- Tania was *chary* of hurting anyone's feelings.
- The cafeteria attendant was *chary* of the size of the portions she meted out.

  [charily *adv.*] [Syn. wary]

chemical (KEM ik uhl) *adj.* 1. of or having something to do with chemistry; 2. made by or used by chemistry —*n.* 1. involving the use of alcohol and/or drugs; 2. any of the chemical elements or a compound thereof

- Chemistry studies how *chemicals* interact or fail to interact.
- A *chemical* reaction always occurs when an acid and a base are mixed together, with the resulting compounds being a salt and water.
- It is essential that people avoid developing dependencies on *chemicals*.
- If a *chemical* is an acid, its formula always contains an H (for hydrogen).

  [-ly *adv.*]

churlish (CHOER lish) *adj.* 1. boorish; surly or mean; 2. peasantlike; ill mannered; ill bred

- It was Shirley's *churlish* nature that kept everyone at a distance from her.
- Evan was *churlish,* as if he'd been brought up in a barn.

  [-ly *adv.*] [Syn. boorish]

QUICK REVIEW #92

Match the word from column 2 with the word from column 1 that means most nearly the same thing.

1. cacophony	a. compound
2. cadge	b. charm
3. calibrate	c. measuring device
4. caliper	d. cautious
5. camouflage	e. indifferent
6. caustic	f. boorish
7. cavalier	g. beg
8. charisma	h. concealment
9. chary	i. adjust
10. chemical	j. noise
11. churlish	k. corrosive

circumspect (SIR kuhm SPEKT) *adj.* cautious; careful to consider all aspects before judging, acting, or deciding

- It is a good idea to be *circumspect* in selecting stocks to invest one's money in.
- Being *circumspect* before walking behind a horse is always a worthwhile undertaking.

[-ly *adv.*] [Syn. careful]

circumvent (SIR kuhm VENT) *vt.* 1. to go around; 2. to get the better of by cleverness or craftiness

- Very frequently, people try to *circumvent* the need to pay sales tax by buying online.
- Some landlords incorrectly think that if they lock tenants out, they can *circumvent* the eviction process.

[-ed, -ing]

coagulant (koh AG yoo lint) *n.* something that causes a liquid to coagulate or become solid; solidifier (used especially when referring to blood)

- Thrombin is an element in the blood that acts as a *coagulant,* changing fibrinogen into fibrin—the stuff clots are made of.
- The *coagulants* that turn milk into cheese are bacteria.
- Whipping is the *coagulant* that turns cream into butter.

coagulate (koh AG yoo layt) *vi.* to change from a liquid to a semisolid mass; clot; curdle

- Milk *coagulates* to form cheese.
- Blood *coagulates* to form a scab, protecting the body from invasion by bacteria.
- Cream, when churned enough, *coagulates* to form butter.

[-d, coagulating]

coddle (KAH dil) *vt.* 1. to treat tenderly; pamper; 2. to cook eggs in the shell gently in not-quite-boiling water for two to three minutes

- Babies must be *coddled* while they're at the helpless stage.
- My parents used to enjoy *coddled* eggs, which I could never understand because I found them runny and gross.

  [-d, coddling] [Syn. pamper]

coerce (koh ERS) *vt.* 1. to persuade by use of force; 2. to persuade by use of threats, legal or otherwise; 3. to constrain by use or threat of force

- The U.S. armed forces were used to *coerce* Iraq to leave Kuwait.
- The Internal Revenue Service is expert at *coercing* delinquent taxpayers to part with their funds.
- Police frequently find it necessary to *coerce* prisoners to come along with them.

  [-d, coercing] [Syn. force]

cogent (KOH jint) *adj.* compelling; convincing and to the point (said of verbal means as distinguished from physical)

- Ralph gave Alice several *cogent* reasons they should vacation at a mountain resort rather than at the beach.
- Jackie's arguments for using regular-grade gasoline rather than high test were particularly *cogent,* to the tune of 42 cents per gallon.

  [-ly *adv.*] [Syn. valid]

cognitive (KAHG ni tiv) *adj.* 1. having to do with knowing in the broadest sense; 2. by means of perception, judgment, and conception

- One's *cognitive* skills tend to diminish somewhat with the onset of old age.
- In judging a baking contest, one relies less on one's *cognitive* faculties and more on one's senses.

  [-ly *adv.*]

cognizance (KAHG ni zins) *n.* 1. awareness of something; 2. knowledge perceivable by observation; 3. noticing or perception of

- June had no *cognizance* of the fact that Frank was bringing a guest home to dinner.
- *Cognizance* of the habits of the sperm whale has all been acquired by surveillance.
- Before it jumped into his lap, Omar had had no *cognizance* of the cat's being present in the room.

complement (KAHMP li mint) *n.* 1. that which completes or makes perfect; 2. the full amount; 3. either of two parts that complete each other

- Butter and jam *complement* the flavor of a piece of toasted bread.
- Georgia had a full *complement* of 10 fingers and 10 toes.
- For a proper handshake, another person's right hand is the perfect *complement* to one's own.

  [Syn. completer]

component (kuhm POH nint) *n.* 1. a basic part of something; 2. any part of a high-fidelity system (speaker, tuner, amplifier, and so on); 3. an element or ingredient

- The engine is just one *component* of a complete automobile, albeit a very important one.
- Stereo *component* systems are generally of higher quality than those that come all in one box.
- Egg whites are a major *component* of lemon meringue pie.

  [Syn. element]

conceivable (kuhn SEE vib il) *adj.* that can be imagined, thought of, or understood

- Just a century ago, travel outside of earth's atmosphere was *conceivable* only to science-fiction writers.
- Our reliance on electricity has reached the point where life without it is barely *conceivable*.

  [conceivably *adv.*] [Syn. imaginable]

QUICK REVIEW #93

Match the word from column 2 with the word from column 1 that means most nearly the same thing.

1. circumspect	a. solidify
2. circumvent	b. imaginable
3. coagulant	c. knowing
4. coagulate	d. completer
5. coddle	e. awareness
6. coerce	f. cautious
7. cogent	g. element
8. cognitive	h. bypass
9. cognizance	i. valid
10. complement	j. pamper
11. component	k. force
12. conceivable	l. clotter

concentrate (KAHN sin TRAYT) *vt.* 1. to collect and focus; 2. to increase in strength or density —*vi.* same meanings as 1 and 2 —*n.* a liquid that has been made denser by removing some of its solvent

- *Concentrate* your thoughts on improving your vocabulary.
- *Concentrate* the orange juice for shipping purposes.
- Sometimes it is hard to *concentrate* on a task.

- The intensity of light *concentrates* as you get nearer to the source.
- Grape juice can be made from grape concentrate.

  [-d, concentrating]

concentration (KAHN sin TRAY shin) *n.* 1. fixed attention on some task; 2. the density of something

- After you've graduated from school, you'll want to turn your full *concentration* to landing a job.
- The *concentration* of orange juice in a frozen can is four times that of the juice we drink.

conciliatory (kuhn SIL ee uh TAW ree) *adj.* 1. trying to soothe anger; 2. gaining by friendly acts; making friendly

- When Jack saw how angry the fall had made Jill, he made a *conciliatory* attempt to calm her.
- South Korea has made several *conciliatory* moves toward its neighbor to the north.

  [conciliatorily *adv.*] [Syn. pacifying]

concur (kuhn KOER) *vi.* 1. to occur at the same time; coincide; 2. to act together; 3. to agree; to be in accord

- The phases of the moon and the changes in the oceans' tides have been known to *concur.*
- Two persons must *concur* in the direction of their motion to operate a two-handled tree saw.
- For the Supreme Court to come to a decision, five justices must *concur.*

  [-red, -ring] [Syn. consent]

condone (kuhn DOHN) *vt.* to forgive, pardon, or overlook (a misdeed)

- It is not easy to *condone* one's cheating on an examination in mathematics class.
- Hunting members of endangered species as trophies is a practice that cannot be *condoned.*

  [-d, condoning]

consistent (kuhn SIS tint) *adj.* 1. in accord, agreement, or harmony; compatible; 2. always following the same principles

- It was the Mikado's aim to have the punishment be *consistent* with the crime.
- In raising children, it is very important for parents to be *consistent* in their expectations.

  [-ly *adv.*]

conspirator (kuhn SPEE rit er) *n.* one who conspires; one who acts with others to plan a crime

- Cassius and Brutus were the two most famous *conspirators* in the assassination of Julius Caesar.
- Despite what the Warren Commission report says, most Americans are convinced that there were other *conspirators* beside Oswald in the assassination of President Kennedy.

  [Syn. plotter]

contemplative (kuhn TEM pli tiv) *adj.* 1. inclined to look at intently; inclined to gaze at; 2. tending to study closely 3. being involved in a meditative religious order

- Paul was very *contemplative* of the faces of the men in the lineup, seeking to pick out the killer.
- Olga was *contemplative* of her geometry facts as she prepared for her final exam.
- After joining a *contemplative* order of monks, Tom became known as Brother Jerome.

  [-ly *adv.*] [Syn. pensive]

contentious (kuhn TEN shis) *adj.* 1. always ready for an argument; quarrelsome; 2. likely to provoke a disagreement; provoking controversy

- Defense attorneys tend to be *contentious,* which is what their clients are paying them for.
- As election day approaches, politicians' behavior grows more and more *contentious.*

  [-ly *adv.*] [Syn. belligerent]

contradiction (KAHN truh DIK shin) *n.* 1. in opposition to another position; a denial; 2. a condition in which things are contrary to each other; 3. having elements that appear opposed to one another

- According to Tom, Jerry's account of the accident was a *contradiction* of the facts.
- The history of Germany in the nineteenth and twentieth centuries is a series of *contradictions.*
- Racism is a *contradiction* to the principles expressed in the U.S. Constitution.

  [Syn. denial]

conventional (kuhn VEN shuh nil) *adj.* 1. growing out of custom or normal usage; customary; 2. conforming to accepted standards, rather than natural; 3. non-nuclear

- Saying please and thank you is just part of *conventional,* polite manners.
- It is *conventional* to peel a banana before eating it.
- *Conventional* weapons have become so dangerous that the use of nuclear weapons is overkill.

  [-ly *adv.*] [Syn. customary]

convivial (kuhn VIV ee uhl) *adj.* 1. festive; 2. jovial; fond of having a good time; fond of eating, drinking, and good company

- Most religions have some *convivial* holiday where celebrating is the rule.
- A birthday is usually an occasion for a *convivial* time.

  [-ity *n.*] [Syn. jovial]

QUICK REVIEW #94

Match the word from column 2 with the word from column 1 that means most nearly the same thing.

1. concentrate	a. belligerent
2. concentration	b. customary
3. conciliatory	c. plotter
4. concur	d. denial
5. condone	e. pensive
6. consistent	f. jovial
7. conspirator	g. density
8. contemplative	h. forgive
9. contentious	i. agree
10. contradiction	j. focus
11. conventional	k. compatible
12. convivial	l. pacifying

convoluted (KAHN vuh LOO tid) *adj.* 1. coiled or spiraled; 2. very involved; complicated

- Most hoses are *convoluted* for storage purposes.
- A 20-mile-long *convoluted* unpaved highway climbs from the foot of Pike's Peak to its summit.
- The series of alliances that led to the outbreak of World War I was very *convoluted*.

  [-ly *adv.*] [Syn. complicated]

copious (KO pee uhs) *adj.* 1. abundant; very plentiful; 2. wordy; using language to a great extent; 3. full of information

- Always take *copious* notes during college lectures.
- Fidel Castro's speeches are always *copious*.
- *Copious* information about careers is available in *The Occupational Outlook Handbook,* published by the U.S. Department of Labor.

  [Syn. plentiful, profuse]

corona (kuh ROH nuh) *n.* 1. a crown or tiara, or something resembling same; 2. a ring of light surrounding a bright object (like the sun's corona); 3. an extra whorl of flower parts (as the cuplike shape in daffodils) formed between the inner petals and the stamens

- A *corona* might grace a king's head.
- The sun's *corona* makes a striking display when the sun's disk is in total eclipse.
- The *corona* of a daffodil is what gives this spring flower its unique shape.

correlate (KAW ril AYT) *vt.* to bring things into a mutual relation with each other; to show the relationship between quantities —*adj.* closely related

- One's salary should *correlate* with the hours one works.
- Sometimes it is difficult to *correlate* the amount of good someone does in the world with his or her reward.

  [-d, correlating]

cosmos (KAHZ mohs) *n.* 1. the universe seen as an orderly, harmonious whole; 2. any complete and orderly system

- Earth was once thought to be the center of the *cosmos*.
- The periodic table contains the *cosmos* of chemical elements.

counterpoint (KOWN tir POYNT) *n.* 1. a melody played or sung against a different melody; 2. something set up to contrast with or counteract something else

- *Counterpoint* melodies can be found in classical and popular musical compositions.
- Political-opinion news shows often offer both a point and *counterpoint* format to put forth both sides of an argument.

covert (koh VIRT) *adj.* concealed; disguised; hidden; surrreptitious

- A submarine is a *covert* weapon by design.
- Undercover organizations exist for *covert* operations.

  [-ly *adv.*] [Syn. secret]

covetous (KUH vit uhs) *adj.* longing with envy for something belonging to another person

- Mr. Jones was very *covetous* of Mr. Smith's beautiful green lawn before he discovered it was AstroTurf.
- Ginger was *covetous* of Mary Anne's wavy hair.

  [-ly *adv.*] [Syn. envious, greedy]

cower (KOW ir) *vt.* 1. to huddle up as from fear or cold; 2. to shrink with fear as if avoiding someone's anger or blows

- The Green family *cowered* in the cold, waiting for the furnace to be repaired.
- Lou Costello's *cowering* awaiting Bud Abbott's angry blows was quite a routine, in light of the fact that straight man Abbott was actually Costello's employee.

  [-ed, -ing] [Syn. cringe]

craven (KRAY vin) *adj.* deathly afraid of; very cowardly —*n.* a thorough coward

- Lloyd had a *craven* attitude toward bears.
- Some little children are *craven* about anything with four feet and fur.
- Minnie was *craven* and would not leave her house.

  [-ly *adv.*] [Syn. cowardly]

credence (KREE dins) *n.* belief (especially in the testimony or words of others)

- The evidence gave Willis's words *credence.*
- The district attorney did not give *credence* to the street vendor's words and wanted to see proof.
- Most people do not give *credence* to UFO stories.

critique (kri TEEK) *n.* a critical analysis of something —*vt.* to analyze something, such as a work of art, a book, and so on; to criticize

- TV critics must produce several movie *critiques* per week.
- Literature students are often asked to *critique* a work of poetry or prose.
- Before one *critiques* anything, he or she should have some benchmark by which to judge.

    [-d, critiquing] [Syn. criticize]

QUICK REVIEW #95

Match the word from column 2 with the word from column 1 that means most nearly the same thing.

1. convoluted	a. greedy
2. copious	b. analyze
3. corona	c. contrast
4. correlate	d. cowardly
5. cosmos	e. cringe
6. counterpoint	f. belief
7. covert	g. plentiful
8. covetous	h. mutually link
9. cower	i. secret
10. craven	j. complicated
11. credence	k. universe
12. critique	l. crown

cryptic (KRIP tik) *adj.* having a hidden or disguised meaning; ambiguous; mysterious

- The sphinx was famous in ancient times for asking *cryptic* riddles.
- The oracle at Delphi gave *cryptic* prophecies that could be interpreted many different ways.

    [-ally *adv.*] [Syn. obscure]

crystal (KRIS til) *n.* 1. a transparent mineral, especially quartz; 2. such a mineral with a cut or naturally geometric pattern of facets; 3. the transparent covering of the face of a watch; 4. especially clear and briliant glassware

- *Crystals* of carbon are the hardest known natural substance, also known as diamonds.
- Quartz *crystals* occur in many different colors, with rose quartz being quite common.
- Carlotta took her watch to the jeweler for a new *crystal.*

crystallize (KRIS til YZ) *vt.* 1. to take on a definite form; 2. to form crystals or crystal-like shapes; 3. to coat with sugar

- It took a while for the plan to *crystallize* in Gail's head.
- When water vapor *crystallizes* it forms six-sided snowflakes.
- *Crystallized* ginger is coated with sugar and is delicious but tangy.

  [-d, crystallizing, crystallization *n.*]

culpability (KUHL puh BIL i tee) *n.* the responsibility for something's happening; the blame

- The *culpability* for a rear-end collision always belongs to the rear car's driver.
- Despite having borrowed his father's camera without asking permission, Irwin denied any *culpability.*

  [Syn. blame]

cultivate (KUHL ti VAYT) *vt.* 1. to prepare soil for crop growing; 2. to grow (plants, animals, and so on) from scratch; 3. to improve by training; 4. to develop (a taste for)

- The farmer *cultivates* with a plow before sowing the first seeds.
- Bob *cultivates* flowers every year, starting them in pots in early May.
- In medieval times, monks *cultivated* trees in the shape of candelabras.
- A liking for caviar is a taste one must *cultivate,* as it is not a naturally appealing food.

  [-d, cultivating]

curmudgeon (koer MUHJ in) *n.* an ill-mannered, bad-tempered person; a cantankerous person

- Nobody cared to argue with Mr. Jones because he had a reputation for being a *curmudgeon.*
- Miss Smith was such a *curmudgeon* that it was no wonder she had remained unwed.

cursory (KOER sir ee) *adj.* with little attention to detail; done hastily

- Rita took a *cursory* look at the right front bumper to see whether any damage had been done.
- The doctor gave Ben a *cursory* examination before declaring him fit to return to work.

  [cursorily *adv.*] [Syn. superficial]

QUICK REVIEW #96

Match the word from column 2 with the word from column 1 that means most nearly the same thing.

1. cryptic	a. cantankerous one
2. crystal	b. blame
3. crystallize	c. improve
4. culpability	d. superficial
5. cultivate	e. mineral
6. curmudgeon	f. form
7. cursory	g. obscure

D

debilitating (di BIL i TAYT ing) *adj.* weakening; making weak and feeble; ennervating

- Lou Gehrig was a great baseball player before developing the *debilitating* disease, ALS, which carries his name.
- When Dylan was 2 years old, he developed a *debilitating* temper that caused him to bang his head on things.

[-ly *adv.*] [Syn. weakening]

decimate (DE sim ayt) *vt.* to kill or destroy a large part of the population

- The city officials are hoping that by spraying in swamps they will be able to *decimate* the mosquito population.
- Every seven years or so, locusts *decimate* the crops in some farm areas.

[-d, decimating]

defamation (DEF im AY shin) *n.* an injuring of someone's character by making false statements about him or her; slandering; maligning

- *Defamation* of character is an offense that one can sue for in a civil court.
- The judge ruled that the false statements Girard made about Ruth constituted *defamation.*

[Syn. slander]

deficiency (di FISH in see) *n.* the state of lacking in some essential quality or element; incompleteness; shortage; deficit

- Mark's intellectual *deficiency* leaves him two cans short of a six-pack.
- When Violet bought the car, she found there was a *deficiency* in the rear seat belt.

[Syn. shortage]

degenerate (di JEN er it *for adj. and n.,* di JEN er AYT *for v.*) *adj.* 1. sunken below a former normalcy of condition or character; 2. morally corrupt —*n.* a degenerate person, especially one who is sexually perverse —*vi.* to decline morally, culturally, and so on

- Helen's *degenerate* lifestyle was the result of a difficult childhood.
- Does reading *degenerate* magazines corrupt one, or must one be *degenerate* to buy such magazines?
- Helen, mentioned above, is a *degenerate.*
- As one ages, one's sense of humor tends to *degenerate,* and the jokes get racier.

[-ly *adv.*] [Syn. depraved]

demise (dim YZ) *vt.* 1. to transfer an estate by lease (especially for a fixed amount of time); 2. to transfer sovereignty by abdication or death —*n.* 1. a transfer of an estate by lease (for a fixed term); 2. the transfer of sovereignty by death or abdicating; 3. death

- "*Demising* an apartment" is not a phrase you'll see or hear every day.
- The "*demise* of a monarch" is a much more likely use of the word, even though there are few monarchs left today.
- "Death" is the most commonly used meaning of the term, so let this be the *demise* of this discussion.

[-d, demising] [Syn. death]

demographic (DEM uh GRA fik) *n.* a vital statistic of human population, such as age, income, sex, and so on, used mainly for marketing research
- *Demographics* are a major concern to businesses.
- Before McDonald's picks a location for a restaurant, they need to know that the *demographics* are such that there are many young couples with children that have enough money to eat out a couple times a week.

denigrate (DEN ig RAYT) *vt.* 1. to blacken; 2. to defame; to disparage the character of
- During an election campaign, it has become customary for one candidate to attempt to *denigrate* the other's reputation.
- Negative advertising consists of *denigrating* one's competitor's product.

[-d, denigrating] [Syn. defame, disparage]

derelict (DER il ikt) *adj.* 1. deserted by the owner; forsaken; abandoned; 2. remiss in performance of duty; neglectful of duty; negligent —*n.* 1. an abandoned property; 2. a destitute person with no home or job
- The *derelict* boat bobbed up and down in the waves, just waiting to be swamped.
- The reason the burglars gained access was because the gate guard was *derelict* in his duty.
- The *derelict* building was an eyesore and a haven for a swarm of rats.
- It is not unusual to see a *derelict* sleeping in a cardboard hovel by the side of a building on the Bowery.

[-ion *n.*] [Syn. remiss, negligent]

desiccant (DES ik int) *adj.* drying —*n.* a substance that attracts water and is packed with some goods to prevent water from damaging them
- Silica gel is a *desiccant* often packaged with pills in a plastic, ventilated tube so that water doesn't damage the pills.
- *Desiccants* are sometimes packed with clothing or paper goods in little cloth bags.

[Syn. dryer]

desiccate (DES ik ayt) *vt.* 1. to completely dry; 2. to preserve food by freeze-drying, or just drying it
- Cranberries are completely washed and then *dessicated* before they are packaged for shipping.
- Coffee *dessicated* by freeze-drying is as popular as the brewed type in most homes in the United States.

[-d, desiccating]

desultory (dis UHL ter ee) *adj.* 1. lacking connection; aimless; random; 2. lacking in relevance
- The professor's lecture seemed *desultory,* having no connection to anything the class was studying.
- When Francine went to get her blood drawn for the test, the nurse's asking her to step on the scale seemed to be *desultory.*

[Syn. random]

detest (di TEST) *vt.* to intensely dislike; to abhor; to hate

- President George H. W. Bush shocked many growers when he announced that he *detested* broccoli.
- Most people *detest* having to visit the dentist's office.

  [-ed, -ing] [Syn. hate]

deuterium (doo TEAR ee uhm) *n.* an isotope of hydrogen (atomic weight of 2.014, symbol D) used in nuclear reactors

- *Deuterium* oxide is known as heavy water.
- Regular hydrogen has a single proton in its nucleus; *deuterium's* nucleus has a proton and a neutron.

deviance (DEE vee ins) *n.* a turning away from what is usual or what is accepted as being normal

- Pouring orange juice over your breakfast cereal would definitely be considered a *deviance* from the norm.
- *Deviance* is not necessarily a negative thing, as proven by the Wright brothers at Kitty Hawk in 1903.

  [Syn. variance]

QUICK REVIEW #97

Match the word from column 2 with the word from column 1 that means most nearly the same thing.

1. debilitating	a. hydrogen
2. decimate	b. depraved
3. defamation	c. preserve
4. deficiency	d. hate
5. degenerate	e. slander
6. demise	f. variance
7. demographic	g. statistic
8. denigrate	h. dryer
9. derelict	i. negligent
10. desiccant	j. death
11. desiccate	k. random
12. desultory	l. disparage
13. detest	m. weakening
14. deuterium	n. shortage
15. deviance	o. destroy

diatribe (DY i TRYB) *n.* an abusive, bitter, ranting criticism or denouncing

- Fidel Castro is renowned for his long *diatribes* against the U.S. government.
- *Diatribes* tend to cause the listener to close his or her ears and mind after a short length of time.

[Syn. denunciation]

diffidence (DIF i dins) *n.* lack of self-confidence marked by hesitation in speech

- Stuttering is often an expression of *diffidence*.
- *Diffidence* in speech can often be overcome by overpreparing.

[Syn. shyness]

digress (di GRESS) *vi.* to momentarily or temporarily stray from the main subject

- Max Schulman's Dobie Gillis is famous for straying from his subject and then going back to it with the phrase "but I *digress*."
- While explaining to her class how to find the areas of different quadrilaterals, Mrs. Green *digressed* and told how much she had enjoyed that day's lunch.

[-ed, -ing] [Syn. deviate]

diminutive (di MIN yoo tiv) *adj.* small of stature; much smaller than average; tiny —*n.* 1. a very small person; 2. a word formed from another by adding a suffix indicating smallness

- Gail was *diminutive*, with the top of her head barely reaching Michael's chest.
- The *diminutive* of kitchen is kitchenette.

[-ly *adv.*] [Syn. small]

dirge (DOERJ) *n.* a slow, sad, funereal hymn or poem expressing grief; a lament

- *Dirges* are customary as part of certain religions' funeral ceremonies.
- An elegy is a type of *dirge* without music.

[Syn. lament]

disabuse (dis uh BYOOZ) *vt.* to get rid of false ideas; to set straight; to free from misconception

- Part of growing up is to *disabuse* ourselves of the notion that whatever we need will be given to us.
- It is just as important to *disabuse* ourselves of the idea that good deeds are always rewarded.

[-d, disabusing] [Syn. correct]

disburse (dis BOERS) *vt.* to pay out; to expend (a sum of money)

- Inez *disbursed* $23.47 at the grocery store.
- On payday, your employer *disburses* your salary in the form of a paycheck.

[-d, dispersing] [Syn. expend]

discontent (DIS cuhn TENT) *n.* a dissatisfaction with a person, thing, or state of affairs; a desire for something more or different —*vt.* to make discontent

- Now is the winter of our *discontent* after having shoveled all that snow.
- After 10 days of eating steak and potatoes, one becomes *discontent* with that diet.

disinter (dis in TER) *vt.* 1. to dig up from the grave; to exhume; 2. to bring to light something that had been hidden

- The medical examiner sometimes has to *disinter* a body from the grave in order to perform an autopsy on it.
- It is only with the passage of time that the actual tape recordings of Lyndon Johnson's White House conversations were *disinterred*.

    [-red, -ring] [Syn. exhume]

disinterestedness (dis IN trist id niss) *n.* a lack of caring, involvement, or concern

- When asked whether she would like to go to the Dodgers game, Maria expressed a total *disinterestedness*.
- Joel's *disinterestedness* in getting his schoolwork done on time led to his failing grades.

    [Syn. indifference]

disputatious (DIS pyoo TAY shis) *adj.* fond of arguing; contentious; eager to dispute

- Allen's *disputatious* nature made him a likely candidate for the debating team.
- Whenever Daphne was accused of being *disputatious,* she would retort "That's debatable."

    [-ly *adv.*]

dissonance (DIS uh nins) *n.* 1. inharmonious sounds; chords containing clashing sounds; 2. a lack of harmony or agreement; discord; incongruity

- If you want to learn the true meaning of *dissonance,* go listen to an elementary school band concert.
- The later works of Igor Stravinsky are famous for their deliberate use of *dissonance*.

QUICK REVIEW #98

Match the word from column 2 with the word from column 1 that means most nearly the same thing.

1. diatribe	a. contentious
2. diffidence	b. denunciation
3. digress	c. exhume
4. diminutive	d. shyness
5. dirge	e. indifference
6. disabuse	f. discord
7. disburse	g. deviate
8. discontent	h. correct
9. disinter	i. lament
10. disinterestedness	j. dissatisfaction
11. disputatious	k. small
12. dissonance	l. expend

distillation (DIS til AY shin) *n.* 1. a process by which a liquid is vaporized, and the vapor is cooled to form a purer or more highly concentrated substance; 2. a purifying or refining by distillation

- Alcoholic spirits are removed from fermented mash by means of *distillation.*
- *Distillation* is used to separate gasoline from crude oil.

  [Syn. concentration, purification]

diversity (di VERS i tee) *n.* the quality or state of being different or varied

- The *diversity* of its people is thought to be one of the great strengths of the United States.
- An interesting menu in a restaurant should offer the customers a *diversity* of choices.

  [Syn. variety]

divest (di VEST) *vt.* 1. to strip of clothing or rank; 2. to get rid of unwanted things

- For failing to follow orders, the sergeant was *divested* of his stripes.
- Given the recent performance of the stock market, now seems like a pretty good time to *divest* your portfolio of poor performers.

  [-ed, -ing] [Syn. strip]

divulge (di VULJ) *vt.* to make known, disclose, reveal

- You must promise never to *divulge* the location of the hidden treasure, or else!
- Unless you pay to see my hand, I do not have to *divulge* which cards I was holding when I won that hand.

  [-d, divulging] [Syn. reveal]

dogmatic (dawg MAT ik) *adj.* 1. of or like dogma; 2. accepted without proof; 3. stating an opinion with arrogance

- In the early part of the twentieth century, the story about a young George Washington chopping down a cherry tree was *dogmatic.*
- The scientific community encourages its members to question everything and to avoid being *dogmatic.*
- Dr. Jackson tends to be *dogmatic* when he hands out his diagnoses to the medical students.

  [-ally *adv.*] [Syn. dictatorial]

dolt (DOHLT) *n.* stupid, slow-witted person; blockhead

- The way that man slipped into the bus seat before the pregnant woman could take it marks him as a *dolt.*
- Who but a *dolt* goes out of the house wearing his or her shoes on the wrong feet?

  [-ish *adj.*, -ishly *adv.*, -ishness *n.*]

dormant (DAWR mint) *adj*. 1. asleep; 2. as if asleep; resting; 3. inactive; inoperative

- The night watchman was *dormant* on the job.
- While the cat may appear *dormant,* it is aware of everything going on around it.
- A *dormant* volcano might not have erupted in the last 100 years, yet it is still alive.
- Most of the volcanoes in the Cascades are considered to be *dormant.*

    [-ly *adv.*, dormancy *n.*] [Syn. latent]

dross (DRAWSS) *n*. 1. a scum that forms on the surface of molten metal; 2. waste material; worthless stuff; rubbish

- In a steel mill or foundry, *dross* ends up on the rubbish heap.
- Good garage-sale shoppers learn to separate treasure from *dross.*

dubious (DOO bee is) *adj*. 1. causing doubt; vague; ambiguous; 2. of doubtful value; questionable; shady; 3. skeptical; hesitating

- Valerie was rather *dubious* about whether she was coming to the basketball game.
- That premium-brand watch being offered by the street salesperson for $30 is of *dubious* quality.

dynamo (DY ni MOH) *n*. 1. a forceful, energetic person; 2. an electrical generator

- The chairman of the company was a human *dynamo,* constantly on the go.
- In hydroelectric plants, falling water turns the *dynamo* that generates the electricity.
- That weight lifter is strong as a *dynamo.*

dysfunctional (dis FUNK shi nuhl) *adj*. 1. unable to perform normally or properly; 2. showing impaired or abnormal psychosocial functioning

- A person with *dysfunctional* kidneys has to make use of a dialysis machine.
- Serial killers are among the most *dysfunctional* personalities in the world.

QUICK REVIEW #99

Match the word from column 2 with the word from column 1 that means most nearly the same thing.

1. distillation		a. rubbish
2. diversity		b. purification
3. divest		c. generator
4. divulge		d. variety
5. dogmatic		e. abnormal
6. dolt		f. latent
7. dormant		g. doubtful
8. dross		h. reveal
9. dubious		i. blockhead
10. dynamo		j. strip
11. dysfunctional		k. dictatorial

E – F

edify (ED i FY) *vt.* to instruct so as to enlighten or improve morally, intellectually, or spiritually

- It might *edify* you to know that by the time Mozart was 13, he had been appointed honorary concertmaster at the Court of Salzburg.
- Watching how a building is constructed can be a very *edifying* experience (no pun intended).
- *Edify* means to build, but that usage is pretty much obsolete by now.
  [edified, -ing, edification *n.*]

egalitarian (ee GAL i TER ee in) *adj.* advocating that people should all have equal social, economic, and political rights —*n.* one who so advocates

- The so-called ERA, or Equal Rights Amendment, for women was supported by *egalitarian* groups.
- *Egalitarians* supported the civil rights movement of the late 1960s.

elegy (EL i gee) *n.* 1. a song or poem of praise for the dead; 2. any mournful song or poem

- Gray's "Elegy Written in a Country Churchyard" is an *elegy* that laments the loss of ordinary people.
- Shelly's "Adonais" is an *elegy* mourning the death of John Keats.

elemental (EL im EN til) *adj.* 1. of or like natural forces; typical of the physical universe; 2. basic and powerful rather than subtle or refined; 3. of any of the four traditional elements (earth, air, fire, and water) traditionally thought to comprise all things

- It is *elemental* that satellites orbit their planets.
- The force of an erupting volcano is *elemental* in its power.
- Hunger is an *elemental* drive; the urge to be entertained is not.
  [-ly *adv.*] [Syn. basic]

elucidate (il OO si DAYT) *vt.* to clear up (especially something abstract); to explain

- Please *elucidate* on the subject of why you did not come home last night until after midnight.
- Mrs. Jones would appreciate your *elucidating* on Einstein's theory of relativity so that it is clear to her whether you understand it.
  [-ed, -ing] [Syn. explain]

emaciate (im AY shee AYT) *vt.* to cause to grow excessively thin; to cause to waste away

- Starvation *emaciates* the body.
- People suffering from anorexia *emaciate*.
  [-d, emaciating, emaciation *n.*] [Syn. thin, waste away]

emancipate (im AN si PAYT) *vt.* 1. to set free from bondage, slavery, serfdom, and the like; 2. to free from control or restraint

- Lincoln's Emancipation Proclamation of 1862 did not *emancipate* the slaves living in the Union, only those in the Confederacy, where he had no power.
- At age 18 in most states, a child can be *emancipated* from his or her parents' control.

  [-d, emancipating, emancipation *n.*] [Syn. free]

embezzle (em BEZ il) *vt.* to steal by fraud; to take money from someone on false pretense and then spend it on oneself

- Several corporate executives spent the late 1990s *embezzling* their stockholders' money.
- Con men are skilled in the art of *embezzling*.

  [-d, embezzling, -ment, -r *n.*] [Syn. steal]

emit (ee MIT) *vt.* to send out; send forth; give off; utter; discharge

- A transmitter's antenna *emits* some kind of waves.
- A speaker stands before an audience and *emits* words.
- Old Faithful *emits* hot water at regular intervals.

  [-ted, -ting] [Syn. discharge]

emollient (im AHL yint) *adj.* softening; soothing —*n.* a substance that has a softening effect when applied to the skin

- Many medicinal preparations have an *emollient* effect.
- Proper skin care requires replacing skin moisture every day by using *emollients*.

encomium (in KOHM ee uhm) *n.* a formal expression of praise; a hymn or eulogy

- "America the Beautiful" is an *encomium* to the natural beauty of the country.
- "Adonais" is Shelly's *encomium* to the poet John Keats.

  [Syn. tribute]

enigmatic (EN ig MAT ik) *adj.* like a seemingly inexplicable matter (enigma); perplexing; baffling

- Lightning must have been very *enigmatic* to everyone living prior to the eighteenth century.
- Traveling faster than the speed of light is the stuff of science fiction but is *enigmatic* to today's science.

  [-ally *adv.*] [Syn. obscure]

enunciate (in UHN see AYT) *vt.* 1. to state in a systematic way; 2. to pronounce words clearly; 3. to announce

- Einstein first *enunciated* his theory of relativity in 1905.
- It is important to *enunciate* clearly to make your position understood by others.
- Bob and Carol *enunciated* their engagement to each other.

  [-d, enuciating] [Syn. utter]

enzyme (EN zym) *n.* any one of many proteins developed by plants and animals that act as catalysts in certain chemical reactions

- Chlorophyll acts as an *enzyme* in green plants' process of photosynthesis.
- Pepsin and retsyn are two *enzymes* that aid in human digestion.

epicure (EP ik yur) *n.* a person who has an appreciation of fine food and drink, and enjoys consuming same

- French cuisine has a great appeal to the *epicure*.
- Snails, while a common delicacy in France, are the exclusive domain of the *epicure* in this country.
- Chinese, French, and Italian cuisines are no longer for the enjoyment of American *epicures* only.

[Syn. gourmet, gastronome]

QUICK REVIEW #100

Match the word from column 2 with the word from column 1 that means most nearly the same thing.

1. edify	a. tribute
2. egalitarian	b. gourmet
3. elegy	c. moisturizer
4. elemental	d. utter
5. elucidate	e. obscure
6. emaciate	f. catalyst
7. emancipate	g. waste away
8. embezzle	h. discharge
9. emit	i. basic
10. emollient	j. free
11. encomium	k. steal
12. enigmatic	l. explain
13. enunciate	m. lament
14. enzyme	n. equal rights advocate
15. epicure	o. enlighten

epithet (EP i THET) *n.* 1. an often derogatory word or phrase used to characterize someone; 2. a descriptive name or title (for example, Alexander the Great)

- Egghead is an *epithet* for an intellectual person.
- In King Ethelred the Unready's name, "the Unready" is an *epithet*.

equable (EK wib il) *adj.* not varying very much; even tempered; serene; not readily upset

- Tropical climates are *equable* rather than seasonal.
- It was strange to see George fly off the handle because he is usually quite *equable.*

[equably *adv.*, equability *n.*] [Syn. steady]

equivalence (ik WIV il ens) *n.* equality of value, meaning, force, grade, weight, and so on

- The *equivalence* of 2.54 centimeters and 1 inch is a well-known relationship.
- A generic drug has the chemical *equivalence* of its brand-name cousin at a lower price.

equivocal (ik WIV ik il) *adj.* 1. capable of being interpreted in more than one way; purposely vague; obscure; 2. uncertain; doubtful; 3. suspicious; questionable conduct

- Almost every character in Lewis Carroll's books is *equivocal,* except for Alice.
- The origin of the hamburger is *equivocal,* but everyone attributes the origin of the ice-cream cone to the St. Louis World's Fair.
- The shopkeeper called the police when he considered the behavior of the person hanging around outside his shop to be *equivocal.*

[-ly *adv.*] [Syn. obscure]

equivocate (ik WIV ik AYT) *vi.* mislead; hedge; deceive; be deliberately vague or ambiguous

- Part of a defense attorney's job is to *equivocate,* so as to leave the jury with a reasonable doubt.
- When the police are interviewing a suspect and he or she *equivocates,* they can be pretty sure they've found the right person.

[-d, equivocating] [Syn. lie]

erode (ir OHD) *vt.* 1. to wear away; eat into; disintegrate; 2. to cause to wear away; 3. to form by gradually wearing away

- Anything that is continually rubbed against *erodes.*
- Rain has *eroded* the rocks of Bryce Canyon, Utah, to make all the beautiful, statuesque formations.
- The Grand Canyon is the result of rock being *eroded* over millions of years by the Colorado River.

[-d, eroding] [Syn. wear (away)]

erudition (ER yoo DISH in) *n.* learning acquired through scholarship (by reading and study)

- Everything we know about ancient Greek civilization is the result of archaeology and *erudition.*
- *Erudition* in some form continues throughout life for any intellectually curious person.

[Syn. information]

esoterica (ES oh TER ik uh) *n.* 1. things meant to be understood only by an elite few; 2. confidential things

- The Native American medicine man was responsible for passing down the *esoterica* of his calling to the next generation.
- Every religion has certain persons to whom are entrusted the *esoterica* of the group.

eulogy (YOO li jee) *n.* a speech or writing in praise of a person who has recently died, or a project that has been killed

- It is customary for a *eulogy* to be given by one or more persons at a funeral service.
- Traditionally, any ill traits of the deceased are not mentioned during a *eulogy*.

  [Syn. tribute]

euphemism (YOO fi MIZ im) *n.* 1. a word or phrase that is less expressive substituted for a more expressive one to lessen its impact (*the remains* rather than *the corpse*); 2. the use of such a word

- The "dearly departed" is a *euphemism* for the "dead person."
- Many people speak in *euphemisms,* requiring the listeners to interpret what they are hearing.

  [euphemistic *adj.,* euphemistically *adv.*]

evolve (ee VOLV) *vt., vi.* 1. to develop by gradual change; unfold; 2. to change by evolution

- A winning baseball team *evolves* as all the right players are assembled and become comfortable playing together.
- Modern man is thought to have *evolved* from earlier species, such as Cro-Magnon man.

  [-d, evolving] [Syn. unfold]

excoriate (iks KAW ree ayt) *vt.* 1. to harshly denounce; 2. to rub off the skin of; to abrade; to flay

- Mr. Brown *excoriated* his class for having misbehaved on the class trip.
- Jack *excoriated* his right elbow when he slid into second base.

  [-d, excoriating, excoriation *n.*]

QUICK REVIEW #101

Match the word from column 2 with the word from column 1 that means most nearly the same thing.

1. epithet	a. unfold
2. equable	b. information
3. equivalence	c. tribute
4. equivocal	d. denounce
5. equivocate	e. abstruse things
6. erode	f. expression
7. erudition	g. "the Bald"
8. esoterica	h. lie
9. eulogy	i. equality
10. euphemism	j. wear
11. evolve	k. obscure
12. excoriate	l. steady

exculpate (EKS kil PAYT) *vt.* to prove blameless; to declare guiltless

- The fact that Inez was shown to have been out of town caused the judge to *exculpate* her in the case of the missing bananas.
- Mark was *exculpated* of the charges against him.

  [-d, exculpating, exculpation *n.*] [Syn. to clear (of blame)]

exigent (EKS i jint) *adj.* 1. needing immediate looking into; urgent; critical; 2. needing more than reasonable attention; demanding

- It is *exigent* that Diane return the poorly fitting blouse before the time allowed expires.
- As Melissa found out, raising three small children at the same time is an *exigent* task.

  [-ly *adv.*, exigency *n.*] [Syn. urgent]

extant (EKS tint) *adj.* still existing; not lost or destroyed; not extinct

- Some are hopeful that finding Nessie, the so-called Loch Ness monster, will prove sea monsters *extant.*
- The Cascade Mountains of Washington contain many *extant* volcanoes that are, for the most part, dormant.

  [-ly *adv.*]

extraneous (eks TRAY nee is) *adj.* 1. not pertinent or relevant; 2. coming from the outside; 3. not properly or truly belonging

- When discussing whether something is or is not the right thing to do, the amount you're willing to pay to have it done is *extraneous.*
- The phases of the moon are *extraneous* to the seasons on earth.
- When playing Chopin's piano sonatas, the presence of a flute player is *extraneous.*

[-ly *adv.*] [Syn. extrinsic]

extricable (EKS tri ki bil) *adj.* able to get out from; able to separate from; capable of being disentangled

- An egg yolk is easily *extricable* from a shelled egg—especially after the egg has been hard-boiled.
- The painter's having failed to deliver on his part of the contract made Harvey *extricable* from it.
- A single rubber band is usually quite *extricable* from a ball of rubber bands.

[extricably *adv.*] [Syn. escapable]

extrovert (EKS tra VOERT) *n.* an outgoing person; one who directs her attention away from herself and toward others

- Francesco is quite an *extrovert* for a six-year-old and spends much of his time thinking up ways to get those around him to laugh.
- *Extroverts* are generally a good deal more animated than introverts—their opposites.

[extroversion *n.*] [Syn. outgoing]

facetious (fis EE shis) *adj.* joking or trying to be funny (especially at an inappropriate time)

- Being *facetious* is practically a full-time job for a punster.
- Vicki told Bill, "Don't think I'm being *facetious* when I tell you you're my best friend, but I am."

[-ly *adv.*] [Syn. witty]

facilitate (fa SIL i TAYT) *vt.* to make possible, or to make it easier to do something

- The hardened tips on shoelaces greatly *facilitate* lacing shoes and boots.
- Ramps being installed on most street corners *facilitate* getting on and off sidewalks for the handicapped.

[-d, facilitating] [Syn. ease]

faction (FAK shin) *n.* inside a larger organization, a group of people smaller than the whole working toward or aiming at one specific goal; partisan

- When the school PTA met, one *faction* favored holding a Christmas party, while another was dead set against it.
- Because it is a part of a larger whole, one can properly say that a *faction* is a fraction of a group.

feckless (FEK lis) *adj.* 1. weak; ineffective; 2. careless; irresponsible

- Mary was *feckless* about bringing her umbrella to work, and she paid for it when the skies opened up.

- Allowing a five-year-old to walk alone near a busy street can only be described as *feckless*.

  [-ly *adv.*]

felon (FEL in) *n.* a person guilty of a major crime (guilty of a felony, rather than a misdemeanor); a criminal

- Petty larceny is a misdemeanor, while grand larceny is a felony, and one who commits it is a *felon*.
- The person who wrote the sentence "The boy felon his head" is not necessarily a *felon*.
- Most prison residents in the United States are *felons*.

fidelity (fi DEL i tee) *n.* 1. faithfulness to one's obligations; loyalty; 2. faithful to the story, the truth, the actual sound, and so on

- When two people get married, each should expect the full *fidelity* of the other.
- High *fidelity* is so named because it tries to be faithful to the sound of the concert hall.
- When one reads a news story, it is only right to expect the reporter to show *fidelity* to the actual facts.

  [Syn. allegiance]

QUICK REVIEW #102

Match the word from column 2 with the word from column 1 that means most nearly the same thing.

1. exculpate	a. ineffective
2. exigent	b. escapable
3. extant	c. partisan
4. extraneous	d. clear
5. extricable	e. criminal
6. extrovert	f. irrelevant
7. facetious	g. outgoing person
8. facilitate	h. urgent
9. faction	i. witty
10. feckless	j. faithfulness
11. felon	k. ease
12. fidelity	l. existing

finesse (fin ES) *n.* 1. the ability to handle delicate situations with skill; 2. cunning; artfulness; craftiness —*vt.* 1. to bypass or evade an issue; 2. to manage or deal with using finesse

- Walter handled the customer's complaint with *finesse.*
- Martha tried to *finesse* her way around the requirement that she had to have a driving permit before she could get her license.
- It is a common play in a game of bridge for a player to *finesse* a lower value card past an opponent without losing it.

    [-d, finessing]

fission (FISH in) *n.* a splitting apart; division into two or more parts

- Some cells reproduce asexually by binary *fission.*
- A *fission* of the nucleus of an atom releases considerable energy and is the principle on which the atomic bomb was based.

    [-able *adj.*]

fissure (FISH yer) *n.* 1. a long, narrow, deep crack; 2. a dividing or breaking into parts

- *Fissures* in mountains have been responsible for swallowing up more than one climber.
- Glaciers usually fracture along *fissures,* causing huge icebergs to break off.

    [Syn. crack]

fixate (FIX ayt) *vt., vi.* 1. to focus (the eyes) on an object; 2. to form a persistent attachment to some person or object

- Someone who cannot *fixate* on an object that is distant is said to be myopic, or nearsighted.
- When one person *fixates* on another person so that the attachment becomes excessive, it is time for a psychological expert to be brought in for assistance.

    [-d, fixating]

flag (FLAG) *vi.* 1. to become limp; droop; 2. to lose energy; wane; grow weak or tired

- When a flower does not get enough water, it tends to *flag* but perks up again if watered in time.
- After two hours watching the races, Ida's interest began to *flag.*

    [-ged, -ging]

flaw (FLAW) *n.* 1. a blemish or defect that spoils something's appearance; 2. a defect, fault, or error —*vi., vt.* to make faulty

- The dents in the fender were *flaws* in the automobile's appearance.
- A diamond that does not contain a *flaw* is a very rare (read that expensive) thing.
- Rubbed off patches of gold finish *flawed* the watchband's appearance.

    [-ed, -ing] [Syn. defect]

flora (FLOR uh) *n.* the plants of a region, as distinguished from the animal life (fauna)

- The *flora* of the tropics are varied and colorful.
- The further north one goes, the more bountiful the varieties of *flora* and fauna become, as long as you are south of the equator.

flourish (FLOER ish) *vi.* to grow vigorously; succeed; thrive; prosper —*vt.* to wave a sword, hand, or hat in the air as a mark of; brandish —*n.* a musical fanfare

- Democracy, which had *flourished* for the citizens of ancient Athens, essentially disappeared until the end of the eighteeth century.
- The actor bowed and *flourished* his hat in acknowledgement of the audience's applause.
- Each time the president speaks at a formal event, a trumpet *flourish* precedes his appearance; interestingly that piece is known as "Ruffles and *Flourishes.*"

  [-ed, -ing] [Syn. prosper]

fluctuate (FLUHK tyoo ayt) *vi.* 1. to move back and forth or up and down; 2. to be continuously varying —*vt.* to cause to fluctuate

- The ocean's tides *fluctuate* with the effects from the pull of the sun and the moon.
- The heights of the threads in a shag rug *fluctuate*, often in a discernible pattern.
- Jan *fluctuates* the size of her weekly bank deposit according to the amount of tips she receives that week.

  [-d, fluctuating] [Syn. vary]

flux (FLUHKS) *n.* 1. a continuous moving or change; 2. a material that keeps metals from oxidizing when they are soldered

- Fashion is always in a state of *flux.*
- Public opinion goes through *flux* along with the economy.
- Before soldering copper pipes together, both surfaces to be joined must be roughed up and coated with *flux* paste.

foible (FOY bil) *n.* a small weakness of character; a small frailty

- Being easily tempted is a *foible* many of us share.
- One of Alessandra's *foibles* is an inability to resist fresh whipped cream.

  [Syn. fault]

foment (foh MENT) *vt.* to stir up (trouble); incite (to riot); instigate

- One of President Eisenhower's favorite words was *foment* as he talked of North Korea's *fomenting* a crisis by invading South Korea.
- It has been often debated whether the riots at the Democratic National Convention in Chicago were *fomented* by the demonstrators or by the Chicago Police Department.

  [-ed, -ing] [Syn. incite]

QUICK REVIEW #103

Match the word from column 2 with the word from column 1 that means most nearly the same thing.

1. finesse	a. thrive
2. fission	b. incite
3. fissure	c. artfulness
4. fixate	d. wane
5. flag	e. change
6. flaw	f. separation
7. flora	g. defect
8. flourish	h. fault
9. fluctuate	i. crack
10. flux	j. plant life
11. foible	k. vary
12. foment	l. focus

foreclosure (fawr KLOH zhyoer) *n.* the legal procedure for a mortgager to gain possession of a property when the mortgagee has failed to keep up payments so that the property can be sold to cover the former's expenses

- The bank's attorneys took *foreclosure* action because the borrower was in arrears on the monthly payments.
- *Foreclosure* auctions, in which the *foreclosed*-on properties are sold to repay the mortgage holder, can be a source of real estate bargains.

    [(to) foreclose *vi., vt.*]

foreignness (FAWR in nes) *n.* the quality of not naturally belonging; having the quality of being an outsider; strangeness

- Invading microbes are usually attacked by the body's defenses when their *foreignness* is recognized.
- Westerners' ears have difficulty with the *foreignness* of Asian music.

    [Syn. extrinsicness]

forestall (for STAWL) *vt.* 1. to prevent by performing some action in advance; 2. to hinder; obstruct

- Paying the overdue mortgage *forestalled* the bank's foreclosing on Ms. Green's home.
- Mr. Black obtained a restraining order to *forestall* his neighbor's cutting down the cherry tree.

    [-ed, -ing] [Syn. prevent]

formidable (FAWR mid uh bil) *adj.* 1. causing fear; 2. difficult to overcome; 3. impressive

- Gerald's threat to sue was a *formidable* one as far as Bob was concerned.
- Audrey found the obstacle course a *formidable* barrier.
- Vance's performance on the SAT was *formidable* indeed.

  [formidably *adv.*]

fortuitous (for TOO i tus) *adj.* 1. occurring by accident; by chance; 2. lucky; by good fortune

- Bill's running into his future employer at the ballpark was just a *fortuitous* occurrence.
- How *fortuitous* that Hillary won the state lottery.

  [-ly *adv.*] [Syn. accidental]

forum (FOR uhm) *n.* 1. the ancient Roman open marketplace; 2. a court of law; tribunal; 3. an opportunity for open discussion

- The Roman *forum* was a marketplace in which ideas as well as goods were exchanged.
- A court of law serves as a *forum* in which justice is dispensed (not to be confused with "dispensed with").
- Often a televised debate serves as a *forum* for political candidates to present their ideas and to discuss their plans should they be elected.

fracas (FRAY kuhs) *n.* a noisy fight or loud quarrel; a brawl

- The police had to come break up the *fracas* at the tavern last night.
- When Mr. and Mrs. Unger get into one of their frequent shouting contests, the *fracas* disturbs the whole neighborhood.

frieze (FREEZ) *n.* a series of decorations, painted or sculpted, usually in a horizontal band

- A series of high-relief sculptures forms a *frieze* decorating a fireplace mantle at the Vanderbilt home.

functionary (FUNK shin er ee) *n.* a person who performs a certain function, especially an official

- A server in the cafeteria is a *functionary,* as is a janitor.
- The keeper of public records is a *functionary,* whose function is, obviously, keeping public records.

fusion (FYOO zhin) *n.* 1. joining by melting together; fusing; 2. a joining as if by melting together (for example, two factions of a political party); 3. nuclear fusion

- Welding is a practical form of *fusion* and is used to join the frames of cars and aircraft to their skins.
- In times of war, it has been customary for a *fusion* of the political parties to occur so that the nation acts as one.
- It is the aim of scientists to use nuclear energy formed by *fusion* (the principle of the H-bomb) for peaceful purposes.

QUICK REVIEW #104

Match the word from column 2 with the word from column 1 that means most nearly the same thing.

1. foreclosure	a. union
2. foreignness	b. decoration
3. forestall	c. impressive
4. formidable	d. public official
5. fortuitous	e. brawl
6. forum	f. prevent
7. fracas	g. marketplace
8. frieze	h. extrinsicness
9. functionary	i. accidental
10. fusion	j. legal proceeding

G – H

gainsay (gayn SAY *or* GAYN say) *vt.* 1. to deny; 2. to contradict; 3. to oppose

- Mr. Jones *gainsays* any responsibility for the damage to Miss Wright's automobile.
- "I hate to *gainsay* your story," Paul said, "but it didn't happen like that."
- The loyal opposition *gainsayed* every attempt to get the new budget bill through Parliament.

  [gainsaid, -ing] [Syn. deny]

garrison (GAR is uhn) *n.* 1. troops stationed in a fort; 2. the entire fortified place including troops and weapons —*vt.* to station troops in a place for its defense

- The *garrison* at Fort McHenry withstood bombardment by the British during the War of 1812 while Francis Scott Key wrote the "Star-Spangled Banner."
- During the Vietnam War, *garrisons* were established at so-called strategic hamlets.
- During the Revolutionary War, the British *garrisoned* troops in the homes of the colonists.

garrulous (GAER yoo lis) *adj.* talkative; talking too much about generally insignificant things

- Teenaged girls tend to be more *garrulous* than their male counterparts.
- Most company sales meetings are dominated by *garrulous* persons who love to hear themselves speak.

  [-ness *n.*] [Syn. loquacious, talkative]

genre (ZHAHN ruh) *n.* a kind or type, like literature, music, works of art, and so on —*adj.* designating a class of film, book, or the like by its subject matter—for example, science fiction, comedy

- Henry James was an artist of the literary *genre*.
- The *Star Wars* trilogy gave birth to the *genre* of big-budget sci-fi films.

geyser (GY zoer) *n.* a hot spring from which sprays of steam and or boiling water gush into the air at intervals of time

- Old Faithful in Yellowstone Park is probably the best-known *geyser* in the world.
- Giant, Grotto, Fountain, Castle, and Crested Pool are some other *geysers* in Yellowstone.

gist (JIST) *n.* the main point or essence of an argument, article, and so on

- The *gist* of the thing is the crux of the matter, and that just about says it all.
- Frank did not understand everything the lecturer was saying about calculating the area under a curve, but he did get the *gist* of it.
- Take two hydrogen molecules and one oxygen molecule, and you have the *gist* of water.

  [Syn. essence]

gladiator (GLA dee AYT oer) *n.* 1. any person involved in a public conflict or fight; 2. a swordsman of ancient Rome who fought for the entertainment of the public (not necessarily voluntarily)

- Boxers are often referred to as gloved *gladiators* of the ring.
- The more traditional image of a *gladiator* is of a man in shorts and leather armor, carrying a shield in one hand and a broad sword in the other.

gouge (GOWJ) *vt.* 1. to scoop out; dig out; 2. to overcharge; cheat out of money —*n.* a curved chisel used in woodworking

- Many native people have *gouged* out logs to make dugout canoes—primitive water transports.
- When that restaurant charged $20 for the $7 bottle of wine, they were price *gouging*, and I wouldn't patronize that place again if I were you.

  [-d, gouging]

gregarious (gri GAR ee uhs) *adj.* 1. living in herds or flocks; 2. enjoying the company of others; sociable

- Sheep are *gregarious* animals and never travel alone if they can help it.
- Some dogs are more *gregarious* than others.
- If you're the type of person who enjoys partying, the odds are favorable that you're *gregarious*.

gristle (GRIS il) *n.* cartilage, especially cartilage found in prepared meat

- Karen hates biting into a piece of chicken and finding *gristle*.
- It's not always easy to remove the *gristle* from a roast before cooking it.
- If you really can't stand *gristle,* stick to fish.

gust (GUHST) *n.* 1. a sudden burst of wind; 2. a sudden burst of rain, smoke, fire, and so on; 3. an explosion of laughter or rage

- A *gust* of wind blew Jake's hat off.
- Emily's face was scorched by the sudden *gust* of heat from the burning boat at the amusement park.
- A *gust* of laughter issued forth from the comedian's audience.

  [Syn. wind]

hackneyed (HAK need) *adj.* made trite (meaningless) by overuse

- *Hackneyed* phrases are ones that have been so overused that they have become meaningless, like "a stitch in time saves nine."
- "Right as rain" and "snug as a bug in a rug" are *hackneyed* expressions.

  [Syn. trite]

hamper (HAEM poer) *vt.* to hinder or impede —*n.* a covered basket used for laundry, picnics, or whatever

- Having to slog through knee-deep water certainly *hampers* your getting to work on time.
- The detour *hampered* Blossom from making her scheduled doctor's appointment on time.
- June packed a picnic lunch in a wicker *hamper*.

  [-ed, -ing]

hapless (HAP lis) *adj.* unlucky; unfortunate; prone to mishap

- Jim was so *hapless* that he managed to lose five car keys in one month.
- *Hapless* Harriet was left at the altar by three consecutive fiancés.
  [-ly *adv.*]

QUICK REVIEW #105

Match the word from column 2 with the word from column 1 that means most nearly the same thing.

1. gainsay	a. essence
2. garrison	b. sociable
3. garrulous	c. impede
4. genre	d. wind
5. geyser	e. loquacious
6. gist	f. unlucky
7. gladiator	g. trite
8. gouge	h. military fort
9. gregarious	i. fighter
10. gristle	j. cartilage
11. gust	k. gusher
12. hackneyed	l. cheat
13. hamper	m. class
14. hapless	n. deny

harbinger (HAHR bin joer) *n.* a person or thing that comes before someone or something else to announce the arrival

- The swallows returning to Capistrano is one of the *harbingers* of spring.
- The geese flying south is a *harbinger* of the weather's turning cold.
- The shrill sounding of the Klaxon on a submarine is the *harbinger* of the ship's diving.
  [Syn. herald]

harrow (HAR oh) *vt.* to torment; vex; cause mental distress

- It *harrowed* Connie that her rival had gotten the position she had wanted.
- Studying for the SAT test was a *harrowing* experience for Fred because so much depended on his doing well.
  [-ed, -ing]

haughty (HAW tee) *adj.* having or showing great pride in oneself and disdain for others

- Two of King Lear's daughters were very *haughty*, and it was not until it was too late that he came to appreciate Cordelia.
- Politicians never act *haughty* in public for fear that they'll never be elected again.
- A *haughty* person is a snooty person.

  [haughtily *adv.*] [Syn. arrogant]

herbivore (ER bi VAWR) *n.* plant eater; an animal that eats only plants, as distinguished from a meat-eating carnivore and an omnivore (an animal that eats both plants and meat)

- The largest dinosaurs that ever lived were *herbivores*.
- There must be more *herbivores* than carnivores; think about it.

  [herbivorous *adj.*]

heterogeneous (HET oer oh GEE nee uhs) *adj.* made up of unrelated or dissimilar parts; varied; miscellaneous

- The population of the United States is probably more *heterogeneous* than any other country's.
- Considerably less *heterogeneous* is the population of Japan.
- You'll find *heterogeneous* colors in a bag of jelly beans.

hew (HYOO) *vt.* 1. to chop or cut with an ax or knife; 2. to shape something by chopping pieces away with an ax or knife

- Marcia often *hews* trees to cut up and use for firewood.
- Native Americans *hewed* totem poles from tree trunks.
- Many native cultures make *hewed* pipes and knife handles from wood, bone, and ivory.

  [-ed, -ing, -n *adj.*, -er *n.*] [Syn. hack]

hieroglyphic (HY ruh GLIF ik) *n.* 1. ancient Egyptian picture writing; 2. any picture writing —*adj.* illegible writing

- The Rosetta stone made it possible to translate Egyptian *hieroglyphics*.
- *Hieroglyphics* predate the invention of alphabets.
- Many a teacher has told me that I have *hieroglyphic* writing and need to work on my penmanship.

hormone (HAWR mohn) *n.* 1. a substance (secretion) formed in one organ of the body to cause some kind of action in another part of the body; 2. such a preparation produced artificially

- Adrenaline is a synthetic version of the *hormone* epinephrine, which is secreted by the adrenal glands.
- *Hormones* from the pituitary gland govern our growth rate.

hypothetical (HY pi THE tik il) *adj.* supposing or presuming something although it is unproven

- "What would you do if you were king of the world?" is a *hypothetical* question because we feel safe in assuming that you are not.
- If you ever imagined what type of animal you would be if you could be an animal, you've had *hypothetical* musings.

    [-ly *adv.*] [Syn. theoretical]

QUICK REVIEW #106

Match the word from column 2 with the word from column 1 that means most nearly the same thing.

1. harbinger	a. hack
2. harrow	b. theoretical
3. haughty	c. arrogant
4. herbivore	d. secretion
5. heterogeneous	e. herald
6. hew	f. symbol
7. hieroglyphic	g. vex
8. hormone	h. varied
9. hypothetical	i. plant eater

I

iconoclast (y KON uh KLAST) *n.* someone who attacks and seeks to destroy widely accepted ideas, beliefs, and so on

- Our country's founders could be called *iconoclasts* for attacking the idea of monarchy.
- To evolutionists, creationists can seem to be *iconoclasts* who seek to destroy the theories of evolution; the reverse is seen by the creationists.

  [-ic *adj.*, -ically *adv.*]

idyll (Y dil) *n.* 1. a narrative poem, like a short epic; 2. a pastoral poem or prose work; a work describing a picturesque country scene

- Tennyson's "*Idylls* of the King" falls into the first category as a short epic-type poem.
- Beethoven's "Pastoral Symphony" (No. 6) could be called an *idyll* expressed in music.

  [-ic *adj.*, -ically *adv.*]

igneous (IG nee uhs) *adj.* fiery; formed by heat, especially formed by volcanic action

- Granite is an *igneous* rock.
- Basalt is another *igneous* rock that is formed in sheets.
- Marble is not *igneous* but is a metamorphic rock that began as limestone and had its form changed by volcanic heat.

immaculate (im MAK yoo lit) *adj.* 1. perfectly clean; unsoiled; 2. without flaw; perfectly correct; 3. pure

- The living room carpet looked *immaculate*.
- *Immaculate* diamonds are very rare and very expensive.
- Martha's behavior at the coming-out party was *immaculate*.

  [-ly *adv.*] [Syn. unflawed]

impede (im PEED) *vt.* 1. hinder, block, or delay; 2. to act as an obstacle

- Eating peas by balancing them one at a time on a knife tends to *impede* the progress of dinner.
- An open drawbridge might *impede* one's access to the castle.

  [-d, impeding, impediment *n.*] [Syn. hinder]

impenetrability (im PEN i truh BIL i tee) *n.* 1. something that cannot be passed through; 2. something that cannot be understood; 3. someone unreceptive to ideas

- In the past, a castle's wall was built for its *impenetrability*.
- The *impenetrability* of Germany's code during World War II proved to be a myth.
- Harold's teachers constantly marvel at the *impenetrability* of his thick skull.

imperious (im PIR ee uhs) *adj.* overbearing; domineering; having the qualities of an emperor

- Napoleon was short but had an *imperious* aura about him.
- Often, in times of war, a general needs to be *imperious*.
- Although General George Patton was *imperious,* General Omar Bradley was anything but.

[-ly *adv.,* -ness *n.*] [Syn. masterful]

imperturbable (IM poer TOERB i bl) *adj.* that cannot be disturbed or excited

- Alice listened to all stories with an *imperturbable* calmness.
- Kevin is very excitable and could never be confused with his *imperturbable* brother, Robert.

[imperturbably *adv.*] [Syn. impassive]

impinge (im PINJ) *vt.* 1. to encroach or make inroads (on the rights or property of others); 2. to touch on or have an effect on (someone or something)

- Mary's oak tree has begun to *impinge* on her neighbors' property and is threatening their roof.
- It is not a good idea for a lawyer to make a joke in a courtroom because it *impinges* on the province of the judge.

[-d, impinging] [Syn. encroach]

implacable (im PLAK i bl) *adj.* that cannot be appeased or pacified

- The widow of the soldier was *implacable* with grief.
- When Vic's car broke down 10 miles after he had left the repair shop, his anger was *implacable*.

[implacably *adv.*] [Syn. inflexible]

implausible (im PLAWZ i bl) *adj.* seeming unlikely to be true; not believable

- The excuse, "The dog ate my homework," is at best *implausible*.
- Because Lyle's fingerprints at the scene of the crime were unmistakable, the police felt his alibi was *implausible*.

[implausibly *adv.*] [Syn. unlikely]

implosion (im PLOH zhin) *n.* a bursting inward; collapsing inward

- An old-fashioned television picture tube contains a high degree of vacuum, or absence of air and pressure, so when it breaks, there is an *implosion*.
- You might have seen a film of a building being skillfully destroyed by *implosion* so that it collapses in on itself.

inadvertent (in ad VER tint) *adj.* 1. unattentive; heedless; 2. accidental; unintentional

- Cathy's crashing her car into the wall was *inadvertent*.
- Sam is often troubled by an *inadvertent* urge to scratch his nose.

[-ly *adv.*] [Syn. unintentional]

incessant (in SES int) *adj.* never ceasing; seemingly never ending

- The blaring of boom boxes at certain beaches is *incessant*.
- Rebecca's mom seems to have an *incessant* need to remind her to watch what she eats.

    [-ly *adv.*] [Syn. continual, constant]

inchoate (in KOH it) *adj.* 1. not fully formed; disorganized; 2. in the early stages; incipient

- Julio's term paper is still at the *inchoate* stage, mostly on index cards.
- A six-week-old fetus is *inchoate* in its development.

    [-ly *adv.*] [Syn. rudimentary]

QUICK REVIEW #107

Match the word from column 2 with the word from column 1 that means most nearly the same thing.

1. iconoclast	a. masterful
2. idyll	b. revolutionary
3. igneous	c. unintentional
4. immaculate	d. collapse
5. impede	e. unlikely
6. impenetrability	f. volcanic
7. imperious	g. unflawed
8. imperturbable	h. encroach
9. impinge	i. impassive
10. implacable	j. hinder
11. implausible	k. inflexible
12. implosion	l. denseness
13. inadvertent	m. rudimentary
14. incessant	n. poem
15. inchoate	o. constant

incorrigible (in KAW ri ji bl) *adj.* not capable of being corrected, improved, or reformed (due to bad habits or disregard)

- Lance's *incorrigible* behavior is going to land him in hot water.
- Although her parents have tried again and again to keep Angela from putting on all that makeup, she has remained *incorrigible*.

  [incorrigibly *adv.*]

incursion (in KOER zhin) *n.* 1. an unwanted inroad; 2. a sudden brief invasion or attack; raid

- Egyptian aircraft made a brief *incursion* into Sudanese airspace as they returned from their mission.
- Indonesian troops made an *incursion* into East Timor, seeking to capture a wanted revolutionary.

indefatigable (IN di FAT ig uh bl) *adj.* never growing tired; unyielding to fatigue

- The senator's *indefatigable* efforts have finally succeeded in passing a bill of rights for rabbits.
- The supporters of classifying whipped cream as the all-American treat have been *indefatigable* in their labors.

  [-ly *adv.*]

indelicate (in DEL i kit) *adj.* coarse; crude; improper; gross

- The documentary filmmaker's reference to the president of the United States was, to say the least, *indelicate*.
- It was *indelicate* of Henry to keep referring to his ex-wife as the old battle-ax.

  [-ly *adv.*] [Syn. coarse, improper]

infatuate (in FAT yoo AYT) *vt.* 1. to cause to lose sound judgment; to make foolish; 2. to inspire shallow affection

- The notion of being on the winning side was *infatuating* to Don and caused him to vote for the change in coaches, with dire results.
- Cindy might have completely disagreed with Ned's position on school prayer were she not *infatuated* with him.

  [-d, infatuating, infatuation *n.*]

infiltrate (IN fil TRAYT) *vt.* 1. to pass through weak points in an enemy's line so as to attack from the flank or rear; 2. to pass into a place stealthily so as to attack from the inside or to seize control; 3. to pass through, as in a filter

- It was the job of the platoon of rangers to *infiltrate* the enemy's line to cause havoc in their rear.
- The rebels *infiltrated* the palace guard so as to be in a position to strike when the time was right.
- New coffee-brewing machines use gravity, causing the water to *infiltrate* the grounds and fall into the carafe below.

  [-d, infiltrating, infiltration *n.*]

infirm (in FOERM) *adj.* 1. not strong physically; weak; 2. not strong in one's position; vacillating; shaky

- Certain physically fit senior citizens resent the fact that the elderly and the *infirm* are often referred to in the same sentence.
- Some congresspersons are *infirm* in their voting records on civil rights.
  [-ly *adv.*] [Syn. weak]

inimitable (in IM it uh bl) *adj.* incapable of being imitated; too good to be copied

- Certain products, which we will not name here, have proven to be *inimitable,* although many companies have tried.
- The late Jack Benny was a comedian who influenced many of the comics of today, but as a total package, he remains *inimitable.*
  [inimitably *adv.*] [Syn. unequaled]

insectivore (in SEKT iv AWR) *n.* any of a number of plants or animals (such as shrews, moles, aardvarks, Venus flytraps, and so on) that feed primarily on insects

- It is believed that the human appendix is a vestige left over from an earlier time when humans were *insectivores.*
- One of the best controllers of insect populations is an *insectivore,* which has taken an unfair beating in literature, the vampire bat.

insensible (in SEN si bl) *adj.* 1. lacking in sensation or feeling; unconscious; numb; 2. not recognizing or realizing; unaware

- Perry's five minutes in the freezing water rendered him *insensible* to the temperature of the air.
- Congresswoman Lorraine's self-centeredness caused her to be *insensible* to the wishes of her constituents.
  [insensibly *adv.*]

insincerity (IN sin SER it ee) *n.* the quality of being hypocritical; not to be trusted; not meaning what one says

- Howard's *insincerity* became evident when Diane accidentally scratched the diamond he had given her with her car key.
- When the spider invited the fly to come in and join him for dinner, very few knowledgeable insects would have doubted its *insincerity.*

insinuate (in SIN yoo ayt) *vt.* 1. to gradually and artfully work one's way into; 2. to suggest or imply; to hint

- Joanne wanted the part in the play so much that she continuously *insinuated* her way into the tryouts until she managed to wangle the role.
- Tom's appearing on the platform at the rally for the senator *insinuates* his support for her positions.
  [-d, insinuating] [Syn. imply, suggest]

QUICK REVIEW #108

Match the word from column 2 with the word from column 1 that means most nearly the same thing.

1. incorrigible	a. gross
2. incursion	b. weak
3. indefatigable	c. hypocrisy
4. indelicate	d. unequaled
5. infatuate	e. numb
6. infiltrate	f. uncorrectable
7. infirm	g. make foolish
8. inimitable	h. raid
9. insectivore	i. imply
10. insensible	j. untiring
11. insincerity	k. aardvark
12. insinuate	l. pass through

insufficient (IN suh FISH int) *adj.* not enough; inadequate

- You don't want to write a check if you have *insufficient* funds in your account.
- Never base a conclusion on *insufficient* information.

  [-ly *adv.*] [Syn. inadequate]

insular (IN su loer) *adj.* 1. like an island; detached; isolated; 2. narrow minded; illiberal; provincial in outlook

- The residents of Manhattan live on an island, yet their view of the world is far from *insular.*
- One might expect a resident of a small town in Iowa to have an *insular* view of the world situation, and one would be wrong to think so.

  [-ly *adv.*, -ity *n.*] [Syn. isolated]

insure (in SHUR) *vt.* 1. to contract to receive monetary compensation for loss of property, life, and so on; 2. to guarantee

- Many states require that automobiles be *insured* in case one damages someone else's property.
- By taking the 8:00 A.M. train, Clara *insures* that she will be at work on time.

  [-d, insuring]

intercede (in teor SEED) *vt.* 1. to interfere to help work out an agreement; to mediate; 2. to step in to prevent something from happening

- Bob's mom *interceded* to work out an agreement between him and his brother over which TV show to watch.
- The police *interceded* to keep a gang war from erupting.

[-d, interceding] [Syn. mediate]

interpolate (in TOER puh layt) *vt.* 1. to stick something in amongst others (especially one or more words into a text); 2. to estimate an intermediate value in a table by taking an average of the surrounding values

- One must only *interpolate* a few no's into a text to totally change its meaning.
- To find the value of the sine of 60.5°, *interpolate* from the sines of 60° and 61°.

[-d, interpolating] [Syn. edit]

intractable (in TRAK tuh bl) *adj.* 1. difficult to manage; unruly; stubborn; 2. difficult to manipulate, treat, or cure

- David's cowlick was completely *intractable,* and no hair tonic or mousse seemed able to help.
- The new infection was *intractable,* resisting most known antibiotics.

[intractably *adv.*] [Syn. unruly]

intransigent (in TRAN si jint) *adj.* 1. unreconcilable; 2. refusing to compromise; uncompromising —*n.* a person who is uncompromising

- The governor was *intransigent* in his position against having broccoli as the state vegetable.
- The swimming coach was *intransigent* in his insistence on everyone doing 20 laps in the pool before calling it a day.
- When it came to doing homework before playing after school, Loren's mother was an *intransigent.*

[-ly *adv.*] [Syn. uncompromising]

intricate (IN trik it) *adj.* puzzling because of complicated structure or directions; difficult to follow or understand

- The instructions for assembling the model airplane were extremely *intricate.*
- The *intricate* gingerbread work on the exterior gives a very distinctive character to Victorian-style houses.
- For the beginner, the Japanese game of Go seems simple when, in fact, it is a very *intricate* game.

[-ly *adv.*] [Syn. complex]

introspective (in troh SPEK tiv) *adj.* looking within one's self and analyzing one's inner thoughts and feelings

- Before one commits to a lifetime of doing anything, it is important to be *introspective* and know one's own feelings.
- An *introspective* examination never hurt anybody.

[-ly *adv.*] [Syn. meditative]

invective (in VEK tiv) *n.* 1. an abusive term; insult; curse; 2. strong criticism; violent language

- Using *invective* when speaking of people never won anybody new friends.
- It is not considered appropriate to use *invective* when traveling in polite circles.

irascible (i RAS i bl) *adj.* 1. quick tempered; easily angered; 2. showing or resulting from quick temperedness

- Greg is *irascible* and flies off the handle quite readily.
- The broken front door is a by-product of Max's being *irascible*.

  [irascibly *adv.*] [Syn. irritable]

isotope (Y suh tohp) *n.* any one of two or more elements that share the same atomic number, but have different atomic weights

- Carbon, atomic number 6, has two *isotopes,* C-12 and C-14, with atomic weights shown by their numbers.
- U-235, U-238, and U-239 are three *isotopes* of uranium.

  [isotopic *adj.*]

QUICK REVIEW #109

Match the word from column 2 with the word from column 1 that means most nearly the same thing.

1. insufficient	a. irritable
2. insular	b. uncompromising
3. insure	c. meditative
4. intercede	d. complex
5. interpolate	e. estimate
6. intractable	f. elemental form
7. intransigent	g. curse
8. intricate	h. inadequate
9. introspective	i. mediate
10. invective	j. isolated
11. irascible	k. unruly
12. isotope	l. guarantee

J – L

jamb (JAM) *n.* 1. a side post or any part of a frame for a window or door; 2. a pillar of ore
- When a door is closed, its front and rear edges are in contact with the *jambs*.
- Some metallic ores are found in *jambs*.

jocular (JAHK yoo loer) *adj.* 1. joking; humorous; 2. said as a joke
- It is good to go through life with a *jocular* outlook on things.
- When Jill said you look like a million, she was being *jocular*.
  [-ly *adv.*] [Syn. witty]

laconic (luh KAH nik) *adj.* using few words; brief; to the point
- Calvin Coolidge was a very *laconic* president, rarely wasting words.
- Most people prefer not to be *laconic* for fear of hurting others' feelings.
  [-ally *adv.*] [Syn. concise]

lambaste (lam BAYST) *vt.* 1. to beat soundly; thrash; 2. to scold or denounce
- Killer Kowalski *lambasted* most of his ring opponents.
- Ashley's mother *lambasted* her verbally for getting home after curfew.
  [-d, lambasting] [Syn. thrash]

laudable (LAW duh bl) *adj.* worthy of praise
- Mother Teresa's work with the poor was very *laudable*.
- The rescue workers did a *laudable* job saving the miners after the shaft collapsed.
  [laudably *adv.*] [praiseworthy]

laudatory (LAW duh TAW ree) *adj.* expressing praise or commendation; eulogistic
- The mayor was *laudatory* in his evaluation of the fire department's work.
- The president had nothing but *laudatory* words for the work of the armed forces.
  [lauditorily *adv.*]

ledger (LED joer) *n.* 1. the book for final entry of credits and debits; 2. a long horizontal board that helps support ceiling or floor joists
- A *ledger* is a bookkeeper's best friend, if kept properly.
- All expenses of a business as well as all money taken in must be entered in a *ledger*.
- Every front porch's sides and front are supported by *ledger* boards.

lethargy (LETH er jee) *n.* 1. sleepiness or drowsiness; 2. lack of energy to an abnormal degree
- A feeling of *lethargy* overtook Antoine as he neared the end of the long drive.
- Often, *lethargy* is a sign of the onset of an illness.
  [lethargic *adj.*, lethargically *adv.*]

302

lever (LE vir) *n.* 1. a bar used to pry; 2. a simple machine, consisting of a bar on a pivot (called a fulcrum), used to apply force upward on one end while the other end is pushed downward —*vt.* to pry something up by the use of a lever

- Archimedes said that if he were given a long enough *lever* and a fulcrum to rest it on, he could move the world.
- Probably the *lever* most adult Americans are familiar with today is in voting machines and is used to open and close the curtain.

    [-ed, -ing, -age *n.*]

liberal (LIB oer il) *adj.* 1. freely giving; generous; 2. plentiful; abundant; 3. broadminded; 4. favoring reform; not orthodox

- Children need a *liberal* amount of love from their parents.
- Some people like to put a *liberal* amount of butter or jelly on an English muffin.
- Scandinavian democracies tend to be more *liberal* than the United States when providing medical benefits.
- Martin Luther would have been considered a *liberal* in his day.

    [-ly *adv.*]

QUICK REVIEW #110

Match the word from column 2 with the word from column 1 that means most nearly the same thing.

1. jamb	a. thrash
2. jocular	b. generous
3. laconic	c. commending
4. lambaste	d. drowsiness
5. laudable	e. concise
6. laudatory	f. pry
7. ledger	g. pillar
8. lethargy	h. praiseworthy
9. lever	i. book
10. liberal	j. witty

lien (LEEN) *n.* a claim on someone's property as security for the payment of a debt or loan

- When a car is purchased on a payment plan, a bank usually has a *lien* on it until it is payed off.
- If a house has a mortgage, you can be certain the bank is holding a *lien*.
- An auto mechanic can get a *lien* in lieu of unpaid repair bills.

limn (LIM) *vt.* 1. to paint or draw; 2. to describe (paint a picture) in words

- The expression "I'm *limning* a picture" is not one you hear every day.
- A good radio sportscaster *limns* the action of the game so that listeners feel as if they are there.

  [-ed, -ing]

literati (LIT oer AH tee) *n.* scholarly or learned persons; men or women of letters

- The *literati* are likely to have read the works of William Shakespeare.
- As a general rule, engineers learn their craft but are not counted among the *literati*.

lithium (LITH ee uhm) *n.* a grayish white metallic chemical element; the lightest metallic element

- One of the latest uses of *lithium* is in power cells for watches and cameras.
- *Lithium* batteries, which power laptop computers, are quite expensive.

liturgy (LIT oer jee) *n.* a prescribed ritual for worship in any religious group

- The service in a church, mosque, or synagogue follows a prescribed *liturgy*.
- Needless to say, the *liturgy* in every religion is unique to that religion.

lofty (LAWF tee) *adj.* 1. very high in rank; 2. elevated, like a mountaintop

- The rank of general is a *lofty* one.
- Wanting to be a doctor or other professional is a *lofty* aspiration.
- The *loftiest* peaks in the world are in the Himalayas.

  [loftier, loftiest *adj.*, loftily *adv.*]

loquacity (loh KWA si tee) *n.* talkativeness, especially excessive talkativeness

- Siamese cats are known for their *loquacity*, even though what they say is not said in words.
- A group of hens exhibits *loquacity* by almost constant clucking.

lucidity (loo SID i tee) *n.* 1. clarity of mind; 2. the ability to be easily understood; 3. a period of sanity in a mental disorder

- *Lucidity* should be a requirement for driving a car.
- An author's *lucidity* governs the reader's enjoyment of his or her work.
- Sometimes those in mental institutions experience periods of *lucidity*.

lustrous (LUS tris) *adj.* shining brightly; glorious

- Polished silver has a *lustrous* finish.
- Gold is *lustrous* even without being polished because, unlike silver, it doesn't oxidize.

  [-ly *adv.*, -ness *n.*] [Syn. bright]

QUICK REVIEW #111

Match the word from column 2 with the word from column 1 that means most nearly the same thing.

1. lien		a. gabbiness
2. limn		b. claim
3. literati		c. paint
4. lithium		d. bright
5. liturgy		e. ritual
6. lofty		f. educated
7. loquacity		g. clarity
8. lucidity		h. metal
9. lustrous		i. high

magnitude (MAG ni tood) *adj.* greatness of size, volume, brightness, area, and so on

- The brightness of stars is measured by order of *magnitude,* with white stars being of the highest order.
- Some would argue that the *magnitude* of one's IQ is a measure of how much they know rather than their intelligence.

maladroit (MAL uh DROYT) *adj.* clumsy; inept; klutzy

- A *maladroit* person should not be employed as a waiter or waitress.
- It is very unusual to find a *maladroit* cat, but Karen has had two of them.
  [-ly *adv.,* -ness *n.*] [Syn. awkward]

mammal (MAM uhl) *n.* any of a class of warm-blooded vertebrates, most have hair and all are able to feed their young with milk secreted by the female's mammary glands

- All animals with hair are *mammals.*
- If an animal has feathers or scales, it is not a *mammal.*
- Whales and dolphins are aquatic *mammals.*

manipulate (muh NIP yoo layt) *vt.* 1. to work or operate with the hands; 2. to artfully manage or influence someone in an unfair way; 3. to falsify something for one's own benefit

- One's fingers are used to *manipulate* the keys of a computer keyboard.
- Con artists specialize in *manipulating* people into buying things they don't need or for more money than they can afford to spend.
- *Manipulating* stock prices for one's personal gain is a federal crime.
  [-d, manipulating, manipulation *n.*] [Syn. handle]

marginal (MAHR jin il) *adj.* 1. written in the margin of a page; 2. close to the border or limit, especially a lower limit

- Carol wrote *marginal* notes in all her textbooks, summarizing the content of the page.
- Brad earned just enough money for a *marginal* existence.
- Vinny was diagnosed as a *marginal* schizophrenic.
  [-ly *adv.*]

meadow (ME doh) *n.* 1. a piece of grassland, especially one used as a pasture or for growing grass for hay; 2. a low grassland near a river or lake

- The sheep's in the *meadow,* the cow's in the corn.
- The horses are out grazing in the *meadow.*
- The *meadow* grasses are being cut and baled for hay for animal feed over the winter.

mediator (MEE dee AY toer) *n.* a person who serves as an intermediary for bringing about a peaceful solution to a problem between two or more persons, groups, companies, and so on

- The Taft-Hartley Act calls for strikers to return to work for an 80-day cooling-down period, while *mediators* try to broker a settlement between workers and management.
- A *mediator* is often used to settle disputes between a company and a dissatisfied customer.
- When both sides agree in advance to abide by the *mediator's* decision, it is known as binding arbitration.

membrane (MEM brayn) *n.* 1. a soft, thin, pliable sheet of animal or vegetable tissue that protects an organ, and through which dissolved nutrients can pass; 2. any thin sheet meant to separate or filter

- Every living cell is contained within a *membrane.*
- Modern coffeemakers use a *membrane* called a filter to hold the coffee grounds and keep them out of your cup.

mercenary (MOER sin ER ee) *adj.* 1. working exclusively for money, rather than for an ideal; 2. seeking payment —*n.* 1. a soldier working for pay in the army of another country, or in a paid private military force; 2. a person who will do nearly anything for money

- A *mercenary* worker welcomes the opportunity to work at a dangerous job for high pay.
- High steelworkers are not just *mercenary* but rather have a knack for working in high places.
- Hessian troops were *mercenaries* who fought for the British during the American Revolutionary War.

mercurial (mer KYUR ee il) *adj.* 1. of or containing the element mercury; 2. having qualities attributed to the god Mercury—for example, cleverness, shrewdness, eloquence; 3. quick; quick witted; changeable; fleeting

- Fever thermometers used to be *mercurial,* but now, few are.
- A speedy messenger could be called *mercurial* in the classical sense of the word.
- A good businessman should have *mercurial* qualities.

mettle (MET il) *n.* quality of temperament and character, especially high quality; steadfast; reliable; brave

- Dwight Eisenhower exhibited his *mettle* as a wartime leader in Europe.
- Boeing's B-29 Superfortress showed its *mettle* as a long-range bomber during the war in the Pacific.
- Aluminum has shown its *mettle* as the metal of choice for building airplanes.

milieu (mil YU) *n.* one's surroundings or environment, especially a cultural or social setting

- Fran thrived in the party *milieu.*
- Kenneth was much more comfortable in an intellectual *milieu* than he was in a sporting arena.
- A symphony orchestra's *milieu* is the concert hall.

minatory (MIN uh taw ree) *adj.* menacing or threatening

- Making *minatory* remarks to someone can get one into deep trouble.
- Tigers are known to make *minatory* gestures to warn people or other animals to stay back—unless they are hunting.

[minatorily *adv.*]

mince (MINS) *vt.* 1. to chop or cut into tiny pieces; 2. to weaken or lessen the force of

- One usually *minces* parsley before adding it to recipes.
- Chefs are able to *mince* onion with a chef's knife, but the average home cook is better off using a chopping machine.
- The dean prefers not to *mince* words when pointing out the errors of one of the student's ways.

[-d, mincing]

misanthrope (MIS in throhp) *n.* a person who hates or distrusts everybody else

- Veronica was a *misanthrope* and was absolutely no fun to be around.
- A *misanthrope* might hate or distrust everyone, but he can be the life of the party.

QUICK REVIEW #112

Match the word from column 2 with the word from column 1 that means most nearly the same thing.

1. magnitude	a. surroundings
2. maladroit	b. quick witted
3. mammal	c. menacing
4. manipulate	d. chop up
5. marginal	e. distruster
6. meadow	f. sheet
7. mediator	g. character
8. membrane	h. grassland
9. mercenary	i. money driven
10. mercurial	j. intermediary
11. mettle	k. greatness
12. milieu	l. borderline
13. minatory	m. handle
14. mince	n. awkward
15. misanthrope	o. animal

miscreant (MIS cree int) *n.* an evildoer; criminal; villain —*adj.* villainous; evil

- Comic books are filled with superheroes and super *miscreants*.
- Not all *miscreants* end up in prison, but many people think they should.
  [miscreancy *n.*]

miser (MY zer) *n.* a greedy person who hoards money even at the expense of his or her own comfort

- The classical story of a *miser* is that of King Midas who was granted the ability to turn everything he touched into gold.
- *Misers* are likely to live a shabby life because it is the acquisition of money, rather than the good life, that they crave.
  [-ly *adv.*]

molecular (muh LEK yoo loer) *adj.* consisting of, produced by, or being between molecules

- At the *molecular* level, certain forces hold atoms together.
- *Molecular* study is possible with the electron microscope.

molecule (MAH lik YOOL) *n.* 1. the smallest particle of an element or compound that exists and still retains the properties of that element or compound; 2. a very small particle

- A *molecule* of the element oxygen consists of two oxygen atoms and is represented by the symbol O_2.
- A *molecule* of water contains three atoms, two hydrogen atoms and one oxygen atom, and is represented by the symbol H_2O.
- Flora had a *molecule* of hope that she'd succeed.

mores (maw RAYZ) *n.* traditional behaviors that seem so conducive to the welfare of a group that they come to have the force of law and sometimes even become part of the legal code

- Nomadic tribes live by *mores* alone, having no formal code of laws.
- Often one's *mores* can serve to tell one what is right and what is not right.

mortgage (MAWR gidzh) *n.* 1. the pledging of a property as security for a sum of money; 2. the deed that a mortgager holds —*vt.* 1. to put an advance claim or liability on; 2. to pledge property by a mortgage

- Most homeowners owe banks, with the person who lives in the home making regular *mortgage* payments.
- When a *mortgage* has been paid off, the bank delivers the deed to the new homeowner.
- Charles *mortgaged* his future with college loans.

mute (MYOOT) *vt.* 1. to soften or muffle the sound of a musical instrument; 2. to subdue the intensity of a color —*adj.* softened; subdued —*n.* a person who cannot speak

- Some trumpet players used to play their trumpets into a hat to *mute* the sound.
- A *muted* trumpet does not have the blare of an open-belled one.
- Certain artists are known for their use of *muted* colors.

- Pastel colors are *muted* rather than intense.
- A *mute* is a person without the ability to vocalize sounds.

[-d, muting] [Syn. subdue]

nadir (NAY duhr) *n.* 1. lowest point; 2. the point on a celestial sphere directly opposite the zenith

- The Watergate scandal was the *nadir* of Richard Nixon's career.
- The *nadir* on earth is in the Marianas Trench.
- The moon is at its *nadir* when it is closest to earth.

nascent (NAY sint) *adj.* 1. beginning to form, start, grow; 2. being born

- Compared to the civilizations of Europe and Asia, that of the United States is *nascent*.
- A young child's view of the world is *nascent* and is shaped by parents as well as environment.

[-ly *adv.*] [Syn. starting]

noisome (NOI suhm) *adj.* 1. harmful; dangerous to one's health; 2. having a foul odor

- Cigarette smoking is *noisome* in every sense of the word.
- Playing with explosives can be a very *noisome* pursuit.
- When purchasing fish for dinner, use your nose, and if the fish is *noisome*, reject it.

[-ly *adv.*]

nostalgia (naws TAL juh) *n.* 1. a longing to return to past, happier times; 2. a longing to return home or to familiar things; 3. old things that remind us of the past

- *Nostalgia* for things past is demonstrated by some of the automobiles that have achieved popularity at the start of the twenty-first century.
- There is a big market for old dolls and other *nostalgia* from the childhood of today's older adults as they seek to recapture their past.
- *Nostalgia* was captured by Dorothy in *The Wizard of Oz* with the quote, "There's no place like home!"

[Syn. homesickness]

nourish (NOER ish) *vt.* 1. to feed or sustain a plant or animal with food and water; 2. to foster, develop, or promote a feeling, habit, relationship, and so on

- Parents are responsible for *nourishing* their children physically, emotionally, and—some might add—spiritually.
- A friendship needs to be *nourished* to keep it healthy and thriving.
- Celia does not wish to *nourish* Lou's belief that they have a future together.

novelistic (NAH vil IS tik) *adj.* unique; different; the first of its kind

- Thomas Edison made a fortune from the *novelistic* idea that sounds could be recorded on a wire.
- Truly *novelistic* ideas should be copyrighted or patented to keep them safe from unscrupulous people.

[-ally *adv.*] [Syn. unique]

QUICK REVIEW #113

Match the word from column 2 with the word from column 1 that means most nearly the same thing.

1. miscreant	a. subdue
2. miser	b. starting
3. molecular	c. villain
4. molecule	d. harmful
5. mores	e. homesickness
6. mortgage	f. sustain
7. mute	g. very small
8. nadir	h. unique
9. nascent	i. particle
10. noisome	j. borrow
11. nostalgia	k. bottom
12. nourish	l. traditions
13. novelistic	m. hoarder

O – P

obsolete (AHB sil EET) *adj.* out of fashion; no longer used; no longer current; discarded

- North American Aviation's P-51 Mustang is an *obsolete* fighter plane but was the best fighter of World War II.
- The horse and buggy is an *obsolete* form of transportation.
- The dial telephone has been *obsolete* for years.

[Syn. passé]

occult (uh KULT) *adj.* 1. secret; mysterious; 2. hidden; 3. having powers beyond human understanding

- Some people believe that practitioners of voodoo have *occult* powers.
- Sarah wanted her study of Tae Kwan Do to stay *occult*.
- Rasputin is an *occult* figure in Russian history.

[ly *adv.*] [Syn. esoteric]

odious (OH dee uhs) *adj.* deserving or causing hatred, loathing, and so on

- Stalin, when leading the USSR, was guilty of some very *odious* deeds.
- No one has ever been as *odious* as Adolph Hitler.

[-ly *adv.*] [Syn. hateful]

odium (OH dee uhm) *n.* 1. the condition of being hated; 2. hatred, especially toward a person or despised thing; 3. the disgrace caused by hateful action; opprobrium

- The *odium* of those hurt by the Nazi regime was quite well earned.
- *Odium* toward Saddam Hussein still exists among Iraqis who sought refuge in other countries.

oligarchy (OH li GAHR kee) *n.* a form of government in which power belongs to few; an aristocracy

- An *oligarchy* traditionally consisted of rulers from the aristocratic class of nobles.
- The government of Communist China is (as of this writing) an *oligarchy*, with power in the hands of the Central Committee of the Communist Party.

opaque (oh PAYK) *adj.*1. incapable of allowing light to pass through, as distinct from transparent or translucent; 2. hard to understand; obscure

- Room-darkening shades are *opaque* so that light cannot pass through them.
- To all but a few people, nuclear physics is an *opaque* subject.

[-ly *adv.*] [Syn. obscure]

opprobrium (uh PROH bree uhm) *n.* 1. the disgrace or infamy brought on by association with a very shameful or reproachful act or event; 2. anything bringing shame or disgrace

- *Opprobrium* greeted the regime of Benito Mussolini for its invasion of what is now Ethiopia in the 1930s.
- Any person or country that infringes on the civil rights of any person or group is deserving of *opprobrium*.

orb (AWRB) *n.* 1. a sphere or globe; 2. any of the celestial bodies such as the sun, moon, planets, stars; 3. the eyeball

- An *orb* is round, no matter how you look at it.
- As an *orb,* I'm sure you'll agree, the earth is nice to have around.
- To appreciate that an eyeball is an *orb,* you'll have to see one outside of the skull.

overt (oh VOERT) *adj.* not hidden; open; apparent; public; manifest; observable

- It is against the law in most states to carry a concealed weapon, but the laws governing the carrying of an *overt* weapon differ from state to state.
- Most parents are very *overt* in their love for their children.

[-*ly adv.*] [Syn. open]

parody (PA ruh dee) *n.* 1. a humorous copy of a literary or musical work, often applied to an inappropriate subject; 2. a weak imitation —*vt.* 1. to write or perform a parody; 2. to imitate mockingly

- *Gulliver's Travels* is a *parody* of the travel books that were so popular in Jonathan Swift's day.
- *Parody* is imitation and as such is a form of flattery.
- Certain comedians make a living *parodying* political figures.
- Mel Brooks *parodies* Mary Shelley's book in the motion picture *Young Frankenstein.*

[parodied, -ing, parodies *pl.*] [Syn. caricature]

parse (PARS) *vt.* 1. to separate a sentence into its parts, identifying and explaining the use of each of those parts and their relationship to each other; 2. to describe the preceding

- In times past, it was customary to *parse* sentences in English class, using a diagram.
- When a sentence is *parsed,* it is separated into subject, predicate, and all modifying words (associating them with the words they modify).

[-d, parsing] [Syn. analyze]

pastoral (PAS toer il) *adj.* 1. of shepherds, their work, or their way of life; 2. characteristic of rural life —*n.* a literary or musical work that deals with rural life, usually in an idealized way

- The *pastoral* life is the lifestyle of a shepherd.
- Traditional *pastoral* life is quite different from life in today's rural America.
- Beethoven's *Symphony No. 6* is also known as the *Pastoral* Symphony and depicts country life.

[-*ly adv.*] [Syn. rural]

patron (PAY truhn) *n.* 1. a protector or benefactor; 2. one who uses his or her money to sponsor artists or events

- Classical musicians could not earn a living if it weren't for the support of *patrons.*
- Austrian Prince Esterházy was Haydn's *patron* for much of the musician's adult life.

[Syn. sponsor]

QUICK REVIEW #114

Match the word from column 2 with the word from column 1 that means most nearly the same thing.

1. obsolete	a. caricature
2. occult	b. obscure
3. odious	c. manifest
4. odium	d. sphere
5. oligarchy	e. rural
6. opaque	f. esoteric
7. opprobrium	g. analyze
8. orb	h. sponsor
9. overt	i. aristocracy
10. parody	j. hateful
11. parse	k. infamy
12. pastoral	l. hatred
13. patron	m. passé

peccadillo (PEK uh DIL oh) *n.* a minor or slight sin; a small fault or misdeed

- Mark's roving eye was a *peccadillo* that Noreen did not care to put up with, so she dumped him.
- Treating as a *peccadillo* a child's taking a candy bar from a store without paying is as good as encouraging the child to go on to larger crimes.

pedantry (PED in tree) *n.* 1. petty insistence on exact adherence to minor arbitrary points of learning; 2. ostentatious demonstrations of knowledge

- Mrs. Higgins, true to her *pedantry*, insists that each of her students learn Lincoln's "Gettysburg Address" word for word.
- Bert, in his *pedantry*, never missed an opportunity to use a five-syllable word when a two-syllable one would have done the job.

pedestrian (pi DES tree in) *adj.* 1. walking; done on foot; 2. of or for a walker; 3. lacking interest; ordinary; dull —*n.* a walker

- Special Walk/Don't Walk signs are growing more popular for the benefit of *pedestrian* citizens.
- The UN ambassador's speech was very *pedestrian* and lulled half its listeners into a daze.
- City drivers need to keep an eye out for *pedestrians* crossing the street.

    [-ly *adv.*] [Syn. ordinary]

peripatetic (PER i puh TET ik) *adj.* moving about from place to place; itinerant

- *Peripatetic* movie critics might move from theater to theater and check out the comfort of the seats as well as what's on the screen.
- A nomad lives a *peripatetic* existence.

[-ally *adv.*] [Syn. itinerant]

perish (PER ish) *vt.* 1. to be destroyed or wiped out; 2. to die; disappear

- Many people *perished* in the floods of 2004.
- As it passed over the horizon, the sun *perished* from view.
- Do not *perish* the thought of adding every one of these words to your vocabulary.

[-ed, -ing] [Syn. disappear, die]

perjury (POER joer ee) *n.* lying under oath; failing to tell the truth under formal oath (to a court of law)

- *Perjury* is a crime that is committed more frequently than those who commit it are prosecuted.
- Witnesses who refused to say anything in court cannot be accused of *perjury.*

permeable (POER mee i bl) *adj.* capable of being passed through by fluids (liquids and gases)

- Cell membranes are *permeable* so that dissolved nutrients can pass through them.
- The most common *permeable* item in households today is the coffee filter.

[permeably *adv.*]

perturb (poer TOERB) *vt.* 1. to annoy, alarm, or upset; 2. to cause confusion or disorder; unsettle (Imperturbable means not capable of being disturbed.)

- Francesco is *perturbed* when he thinks someone is hurting an animal.
- Many people are *perturbed* by the sight of blood.
- Shouting fire in a crowded theater might *perturb* the audience enough to cause a riot and so is illegal.

[-ed, -ing] [Syn. disturb]

pervade (poer VAYD) *vt.* to be prevalent or widespread

- A feeling of relief *pervaded* the community after hearing the news that the little girl had been rescued from the shaft.
- A case of blight *pervaded* the Irish potato crop at one time and caused widespread famine.

[-d, pervading]

philistine (FIL is teen) *adj.* 1. uncultured and smugly conventional —*n* 1. small-town people; locals 2. (*P*) the name of the ancient people who often fought with the Israelites of biblical times, and among whose number was Goliath

- The diva's response to a request that she perform a certain number was a *philistine,* "I sang that yesterday."
- Students in a college town often refer to the townspeople as *philistines.*
- Delilah was the *Philistine* woman who was responsible for Samson's haircut.

photosynthesis (foh toh SIN thi sis) *n*. the chemical process by which a green plant combines water and carbon dioxide in the presence of sunlight to form sugars

- *Photosynthesis* is the process by which a green plant manufactures its own food.
- Chloroplasts contain the green substance, chlorophyll, which must be present for *photosynthesis* to occur.

placate (PLAY kayt) *vt*. to stop from being angry; to appease; pacify

- Hailee needed to be *placated* after Sebastian ran off with her toy.
- Neville Chamberlain's big mistake was trying to *placate* Hitler by allowing him to march into Austria.

[-d, placating] [Syn. pacify]

QUICK REVIEW #115

Match the word from column 2 with the word from column 1 that means most nearly the same thing.

1. peccadillo	a process
2. pedantry	b. uncultured
3. pedestrian	c. disappear
4. peripatetic	d. spread
5. perish	e. disturb
6. perjury	f. pacify
7. permeable	g. pettiness
8. perturb	h. itinerant
9. pervade	i. misdeed
10. philistine	j. false testimony
11. photosynthesis	k. ordinary
12. placate	l. passable

placid (PLAS id) *adj*. peaceful; undisturbed; tranquil; calm

- The sea was *placid* following the passage of the violent storm.
- A good businessman always keeps a *placid* demeanor while around customers.

[-ly *adv*.] [Syn. calm]

plaintive (PLAYN tiv) *adj*. sorrowful; mournful; expressing sorrow or melancholy; sad

- Laurie felt very *plaintive* after the loss of her pet parakeet.
- Robbie was *plaintive* after he struck out, making the final out of the game.

[-ly *adv*.] [Syn. sad]

plethora (PLE thir uh) *n.* an overabundance or excess; the state of being too full
- A *plethora* of suds filled the tub to overflowing.
- A *plethora* of customers tried to get World Series tickets, and most of them had to be turned away.

pluck (PLUHK) *n.* courage to meet difficulties or danger; fortitude —*vt.* to pull out or pick (feathers, hairs, and so on)
- Lieutenant Rigers had the *pluck* to lead his platoon into battle at the head of the column.
- Eugine showed his *pluck* by continuing to hunt for survivors in 20-foot surf.
- Butchers used to *pluck* chickens by hand, but today a machine does it better.
  [-ed, -ing] [Syn. fortitude]

plummet (PLUH mit) *vi.* to plunge; to fall straight downward
- When the skydiver jumped from the plane, he *plummeted* some 2,000 feet before his parachute opened.
- An airplane's wings provide lift that keeps it from *plummeting* to the ground.
- A high diver *plummets* from the board until the water breaks his or her fall.
  [-ed, -ing] [Syn. plunge]

plutocratic (PLOO toh KRAT ik) *adj.* of the wealthy, especially those whose wealth carries with it great power and influence (Plutocracy is government by the wealthy.)
- Many *plutocratic* families had acquired their wealth by the 1920s.
- Among America's *plutocratic* family names are Carnegie, Ford, Kennedy, and Rockefeller.
  [-ally *adv.*, plutocracy, plutocrat *n.*]

polarity (puh LAR i tee) *adj.* 1. having the tendency to align along the lines of the earth's magnetic field; 2. having a magnetic attraction; 3. the condition of being divided into two opposing groups; 4. the tendency to have a strong positive or negative attitude toward some reference point (like the positive and negative electrodes of a battery)
- The *polarity* of a magnet can be determined by the way its poles line up when allowed to swing freely.
- Magnetic *polarity* can also be determined by approaching one end with a magnet of known polarity.
- Republicans in the House often show their *polarity* by voting as a block against bills the Democrats support, and vice versa.
- In a closed DC circuit, electrons flow from the cathode (the end with negative *polarity*) toward the anode.
  [polarities *pl.*] [Syn. alignment]

polemic (poh LEM ik) *adj*. 1. of or concerning dispute; controversial; 2. argumentative; disputatious

- *Polemic* persons often enjoy becoming members of a debating team.
- Some of the great *polemics* of the western plains concerned property borders.
- The border *polemics* usually concerned water rights but occasionally dealt with mineral rights.

  [-ally *adv.*]

poseur (poh ZOER) *n*. a person who affects attitudes or manners for the benefit of others; an actor; pretender

- A *poseur* might deliberately affect the manner of another or might do so naturally.
- Impersonators and impressionists are deliberate *poseurs*.
- Sometimes a *poseur* affects an attitude of concern just for the benefit of a judge or jury.

pottery (PAH toer ee) *n*. objects made from clay by a potter; urns, bowls, dishes, and so on made of clay and hardened by heat in a kiln; earthenware

- Some of our best knowledge of ancient civilizations comes from having unearthed their *pottery*.
- Most dishes are made of *pottery*.
- Terra-cotta *pottery* is commonly used for household plants, although plastic is also frequently used.

  [Syn. earthenware]

precipitation (pree SIP i TAY shun) *n*. 1. rash haste; impetuousness; 2. the bringing about of something suddenly; acceleration; 3. snow, rain, sleet, hail, and so on

- The *precipitation* of a conflict is rarely a cause to celebrate.
- Driving too fast might be the *precipitation* for a high-speed accident.
- In the winter, frozen *precipitation* might fall from the sky.

  [precipitate *vt.*]

preempt (pree EMPT) *vt*. 1. to seize before anyone else can; 2. to replace a previously scheduled program (on TV or radio)

- A municipal government can *preempt* someone's property for public use.
- A news bulletin or presidential address sometimes *preempts* scheduled programming.

  [-ed, -ing]

QUICK REVIEW #116

Match the word from column 2 with the word from column 1 that means most nearly the same thing.

1. placid	a. actor
2. plaintive	b. alignment
3. plethora	c. seize first
4. pluck	d. argumentative
5. plummet	e. impetuousness
6. plutocratic	f. earthenware
7. polarity	g. overabundance
8. polemic	h. plunge
9. poseur	i. sad
10. pottery	j. fortitude
11. precipitation	k. calm
12. preempt	l. powerful

prejudice (PREJ uh dis) *vt.* 1. to have or show bias; 2. to cause harm by prejudging —*n.* 1. an opinion or judgment formed before knowing the facts; preconceived idea either favorable or unfavorable; 2. an irrational dislike or hatred, suspicion, or intolerance of a certain race, creed, ethnic group, and so on

- Most children have a *prejudice* for carrots and cucumbers.
- It is wrong to *prejudice* a jury before they fairly try a case.
- One might be *prejudiced* for or against something.
- Racial *prejudice* has been responsible for many hate crimes in the world and in American history.

[-d, prejudicing] [Syn. partiality]

premeditated (pree MED i TAYT id) *adj.* thought out, schemed, or planned beforehand

- First-degree muder is also known as *premeditated* homicide.
- The furnishing of a house should be *premeditated*, or it could turn out to be a disaster.

[-ly *adv.*] [Syn. preplanned]

presage (PRES ij *for n. or v.*, pree SAYJ *or* pri SAYJ *for v.*) *n.* 1. a sign or a warning of an event in the future; augury; omen; 2. a foreboding —*vt.* 1. to give warning of; portend; 2. to have a foreboding or presentiment; 3. to predict

- Many believe that a comet is a *presage* of disaster.
- Most people have an occasional *presage* of something to come.
- Some people consult psychics to *presage* their futures.
- Nostradamus is credited by some as having *presaged* many events, including the huge success of this book.

[-d, presaging] [Syn. omen]

prescience (PREESH uhns) *n.* to have an apparent knowledge of events before they occur; foreknowledge

- *Prescience* is not unlike having a presage, except that it is a complete foreknowledge rather than just a sign.
- Admiral Yamamoto is credited with *prescience* of Japan's defeat if it attacked America.
- Alexander the Great was supposed to have had *prescience* that he would live a glorious but short life.

    [prescient *adj.*, presciently *adv.*] [Syn. foreknowledge]

pressure (PRESH er) *n.* 1. a pressing, squeezing, compressing, or being pressed; 2. compelling influence; demanding force; 3. (physics) force per unit of surface area

- *Pressure* is usually used to squeeze the extra water from a sponge mop.
- Automobile salesmen are infamous for *pressuring* customers to buy right away.
- In physics, one foot-pound is the amount of *pressure* it takes to raise one pound one foot.

prevaricate (pri VAR i kayt) *vi.* to equivocate; to evade the truth; lie

- *Prevaricating* while under oath is a classy definition of perjury.
- Sometimes people *prevaricate* to be polite because nobody asks "How do I look?" expecting to be told "Terrible!"

    [-d, prevaricating, prevarication *n.*] [Syn. lie]

primacy (PRY mi see) *n.* 1. the state of being first in order, time, rank, and so on; 2. the office or authority of a church primate

- A five-star general has *primacy* of rank in the U.S. Army.
- The winner of a race is the contestant with *primacy* reaching the finish line.
- The number one has *primacy* among counting numbers.

proliferate (proh LIF er ayt) *vt.* 1. to reproduce new parts in quick succession; 2. to create or produce in large numbers

- A pair of rabbits tends to *proliferate* at a very rapid pace.
- During a fad, a particular item (such as the Hula Hoop®) *proliferates* in short order and then, just as suddenly, stops.
- The U.S. fighter plane *proliferated* during the Second World War as a result of the strength of American industry.

    [-d, -proliferating]

prolixity (proh LIKS i tee) *n.* tending to use more words than are necessary; long-windedness; verbosity

- Cuba's Fidel Castro has always been known for his *prolixity,* with an average speech running about four hours.
- Brevity is a characteristic of wit; *prolixity* is not.

    [prolix *adj.*, prolixly *adv.*]

propel (pruh PEL) *vt.* to push; drive; impel onward

- Jet engines *propel* most of today's commercial aircraft.
- Propellers *propel* most boats through the water. (Coincidence? We think not!)
- Thomas Edison was *propelled* to fame by his inventions, including the electric lightbulb.

[-led, -ling] [Syn. push]

propitiate (pruh PISH ee ayt) *vt.* to cause to be favorably inclined; to win over; to appease; pacify; regain the goodwill of

- Lincoln planned the Reconstruction to *propitiate* the people of the former Confederacy.
- The clothing store manager gave Gail a partial refund to *propitiate* her and win her furture business.

[-d, propitiating, propitiatory *n.*] [Syn. pacify]

protracted (proh TRAK tid) *adj.* lengthy; drawn out; extended

- The Civil War, which everyone expected to be brief, lasted for a *protracted* period of time.
- Most new car purchases spread payments over a *protracted* number of months.
- When asked why he had not brought home the groceries, Jack gave his wife, Jill, a *protracted* response.

[-ly *adv.*] [Syn. extended]

pundit (PUN dit) *n.* a person who professes to have a great deal of learning on a subject; a supposed or self-supposed authority on something

- Before buying golf clubs, it makes sense to consult a golf club *pundit*.
- Readers of consumer magazines believe themselves to be *pundits* on refrigerators.
- Political commentators profess to be *pundits* on politics.

[Syn. maven]

pungency (PUN jin see) *n.* a strong, sharp taste and/or smell; acridness

- Certain peppers, such as the poblano, are noted for their *pungency*.
- The *pungency* of an onion is enough to bring tears to the eyes of the person slicing it—and not for sentimental reasons.

[pungent *adj.*, pungently *adv.*] [Syn. acridness]

QUICK REVIEW #117

Match the word from column 2 with the word from column 1 that means most nearly the same thing.

1. prejudice	a. foreknowledge
2. premeditated	b. lie
3. presage	c. verbosity
4. prescience	d. extended
5. pressure	e. swarm
6. prevaricate	f. pacify
7. primacy	g. push
8. proliferate	h. maven
9. prolixity	i. partiality
10. propel	j. force
11. propitiate	k. preplanned
12. protracted	l. first
13. pundit	m. omen
14. pungency	n. acridness

quaff (KWAHF) *vt.* to drink deeply with gusto —*n.* 1. the act of quaffing; 2. the drink that is quaffed

- *Quaffing* beer while eating pizza is a well-established sport in some households.
- Harry *quaffed* his brew from a frozen mug.
- Sally stopped into the tavern for a pint of *quaff.*

  [-ed, -ing]

quiescent (kwee ES int) *adj.* quiet and still; inactive

- After hours of standing uncovered, a carbonated drink loses its fizz and becomes *quiescent.*
- A *quiescent* pond is a good place to look for tadpoles.

  [-ly *adv.*] [Syn. latent]

quixotic (kwik SOT ik) *adj.* foolishly idealistic; visionary; impractical

- Tilting at windmills is the ultimate in *quixotic* behavior.
- Some say that draft-card burning is a *quixotic* act, while others call it heroic.

  [-ly *adv.*] [Syn. impractical]

raconteur (RAK ahn TUR) *n.* a person who is very skilled at telling stories

- Aesop was a *raconteur* whose fables always ended in a moral.
- Hans Christian Anderson was a Danish *raconteur* of great skill.

radiate (RAY dee ayt) *vt.* 1. to send out rays of heat, light, and so on; 2. to spread out in rays; 3. to branch out from a center as spokes; 4. to spread happiness and good fortune

- In a hot-water or steam heating system, heat *radiates* outward from a (what else?) radiator.
- As light *radiates* outward from its source, its intensity diminishes.
- Spokes *radiate* outward from the hub of a bicycle wheel.
- It's the job of grandparents to *radiate* love and presents and to shower them on their grandchildren.

  [-d, radiating]

rapacious (ruh PAY shis) *adj.* 1. using force to conquer; looting; 2. taking all one can get; voracious; 3. predacious

- Genghis Khan's Golden Horde had a reputation, well deserved or not, for being *rapacious.*
- Lumbermen have been *rapacious* with the tropical rain forests of South America.
- The cross-country railroad builders were *rapacious* toward the herds of American bison.

  [-ly *adv.*]

rationale (RA shuh NAL) *n*. 1. the fundamental reasons or logical basis for something; 2. a statement of the reasons for something's being done or having been done

- The *rationale* for building a bridge is to ford a stream or river.
- Paying off the bonds that raised the money to build a bridge or road is the *rationale* for charging tolls to use it.
- A modern recasting of the saying "the ends justify the means" might be "Just do it, whatever it is, and come up with your *rationale* later."

reagent (ree AY jint) *n*. a chemical substance used to detect the presence of another or to react so as to change one substance to another

- The *reagent* on a piece of litmus paper turns from blue to red when an acid is present.
- Luminol is a *reagent* that glows when it comes in contact with blood.

recalcitrant (ri KAL si trint) *adj*. 1. refusing to obey authority, custom, and so on; defiant; 2. hard to handle; difficult —*n*. a person with the preceding qualities

- Most of today's criminals started out as yesterday's *recalcitrant* children.
- *Recalcitrant* Israelites rebelled against Rome in A.D. 67.
- Many a *recalcitrant* has been sent to the principal's office.

  [-ly *adv*., recalcitrance *n*.] [Syn. defiant]

recede (ri SEED) *vt*. 1. to move back; draw away from; 2. to distance oneself from; 3. to slope backward; 4. to become less; diminish

- Flood waters almost always *recede*.
- Looking out the rear window of a car, you can watch landmarks *recede* into the distance.
- Most men and women do not appreciate being the owners of a *receding* hairline.
- During the Clinton administration, the national debt *receded* temporarily.

  [-d, receding]

QUICK REVIEW #118

Match the word from column 2 with the word from column 1 that means most nearly the same thing.

1. quaff	a. drink
2. quiescent	b. predatory
3. quixotic	c. withdraw
4. raconteur	d. spread out
5. radiate	e. reasons
6. rapacious	f. defiant
7. rationale	g. impractical
8. reagent	h. chemical
9. recalcitrant	i. latent
10. recede	j. storyteller

receptor (ri SEP toer) *n.* 1. a receiver; 2. a sense organ; a group of nerve endings specializing in receiving impulses

- A radar antenna is both a sender for putting out radio waves and a *receptor* for receiving the signals when they bounce off something.
- The nose contains the *receptors* for smell, while the taste buds are *receptors* on the tongue.
- Rods and cones are light *receptors* on the retina of the eye.

  [Syn. receiver]

recitation (RES i TAY shin) *n.* 1. a public speaking of some memorized verse or prose; 2. a gathering at which this occurs

- Memorization and *recitation* of the works of Homer were the main pillars of a classical Greek education.
- Many tickets were sold for tonight's Keats' *recitation* at the Town Hall.

recluse (rik LOOS) *n.* one who lives a life of solitude and seclusion by choice

- Howard Hughes chose to spend the last years of his life as a *recluse*.
- A *recluse* can be considered an antisocial individual.

  [reclusive *adj.*, reclusively *adv.*] [Syn. hermit]

recondite (REK uhn dyt) *adj.* very profound; beyond the grasp of a normal human mind; obscure; abstruse

- Rocket science is as *recondite* as, well, rocket science.
- Brain surgery is quite *recondite* but less so than rocket science.

  [-ly *adv.*] [Syn. abstruse]

redemptive (ri DEMP tiv) *adj.* 1. serving to redeem or get back, as in trading paper money for silver or gold, or trading stamps; 2. serving to save one's life or soul by the sacrifice of paying a ransom

- Richard made a *redemptive* effort with his silver certificates but was told the time for cashing them in for metal had passed.
- In the biblical narrative of Abraham's sacrifice of his son Isaac, God provides a ram as a *redemptive* substitute for Isaac's life.

  [-ly *adv.*, redemption *n.*]

refractory (ri FRAK toer ee) *adj.* 1. hard to handle; stubborn (said about an animal or person); 2. heat resistant; hard to work or melt (said about metal ore); 3. resistant to disease

- A mule is a very *refractory* animal and must be handled with care.
- The iron age came about rather late in history because of the *refractory* nature of the metal's ore.
- Botanists have worked for decades to produce *refractory* strains of corn and tomatoes.

  [refractorily *adv.*, refractoriness *n.*]

relapse (ri LAPS *for v.,* REE laps *for n.*) *vi.* 1. to fall back into bad habits or evil ways; 2. to have a recurrence of a disease one had recovered from or was in the process of recovering from —*n.* a falling back into

- It is easy for seemingly reformed criminals to *relapse* into their evil ways.
- Just when Gloria seemed to be getting better, she *relapsed* into her illness.
- Ralph was expected to return to work shortly, but that was before his *relapse*.

[-d, relapsing]

relentless (ri LENT lis) *adj.* 1. not easing up or slackening; pitiless; harsh; 2. persistent; unremitting

- Sir Edwin Hillary was *relentless* in his attempt to be the first westerner to reach Mt. Everest's peak.
- The hurricane's winds were *relentless* as they damaged many buildings in the Carolinas.

[-ly *adv.*] [Syn. pitiless]

reparation (REP oer AY shuhn) *n.* 1. a making of amends for some wrong or injury; 2. compensation paid by one country to another to make up for having warred against them; 3. repairing of damage

- The embezzler was ordered by the court to pay *reparations* to the persons he had swindled.
- After World War I, Germany was required to pay *reparations* to her former enemies, which sent her economy into total ruin.
- Barney brought his torn trousers to the tailor for *reparation*.

[Syn. compensation]

repress (ri PRES) *vt.* 1. to hold down or keep back; restrain; 2. to subdue or put down; 3. to control so strictly as to prevent natural development or expression (as a child)

- It is sometimes difficult to *repress* a yawn, especially when someone else yawns first.
- Stalin *repressed* almost all his country's people but especially the minorities.
- By *repressing* a child, one can prevent his or her developing into a healthy individual.

[-ed, -ing] [Syn. subdue]

repulse (ri PULS) *vt.* 1. to repel or drive back; 2. to repel with coldness and lack of courtesy; 3. to disgust and repel; to be disgusting

- The colonel left a rear guard to *repulse* any attempt to surprise his army from behind.
- The new neighbor *repulsed* any attempt on the part of the older residents to welcome him and his family.
- Jennifer was *repulsed* by the bowl of roasted grasshoppers that Allen placed on the picnic table.

[-d, repulsing] [Syn. repel]

resilient (ri ZIL yint) *adj.* 1. bouncing back from adversity; 2. springing back into shape after having been distorted; 3. recovering strength, spirit, and good humor

- Gary showed that he was *resilient* by hitting a home run after striking out three consecutive times.
- Foam rubber is a very *resilient* material, and cushions made from it retain their shape after being sat on hundreds of times.
- Ursala showed that she was *resilient* by joking with the paramedics only moments after they pulled her from the rubble of the collapsed building.

  [-ly *adv.*, resilience *n.*] [Syn. elastic]

QUICK REVIEW #119

Match the word from column 2 with the word from column 1 that means most nearly the same thing.

1. receptor	a. repel
2. recitation	b. compensation
3. recluse	c. rescuing
4. recondite	d. receiver
5. redemptive	e. subdue
6. refractory	f. pitiless
7. relapse	g. elastic
8. relentless	h. fall back
9. reparation	i. abstruse
10. repress	j. gathering
11. repulse	k. difficult
12. resilient	l. hermit

resolve (ri ZOLV) *vt.* 1. to break up into constituent parts; to analyze; 2. to change; 3. to cause; 4. to show the solution —*n.* firmness of purpose; determination

- A prism can *resolve* white light into the colors of a rainbow.
- The two sides tried for weeks to *resolve* their dispute.
- Einstein *resolved* the relationship between energy and matter.
- Edward expressed his *resolve* to find a solution.

  [-d, resolving] [Syn. decide]

rhinestone (RYN stohn) *n.* a piece of colorless glass cut to look like a diamond

- *Rhinestones* were first created in Germany's Rhine Valley.
- Since their creation, *rhinestones* have been popular in costume jewelry.

  [Syn. fake gem, glass]

rigid (RI jid) *adj*. 1. not flexible; unbending; stiff; 2. severe; exacting; strict

- Steel beams are *rigid,* which is why they are used in construction.
- Orthodox religions tend to be *rigid* in their interpretation of the right way to live and worship.
- The rules for raising children should be consistent but not really *rigid*.

  [-ly *adv.*, -ity *n.*] [Syn. unbending]

rivet (RI vit) *n*. 1. a metal bolt with a head on one end (which is heated and put through holes and then flattened on its straight end by hammering), used to fasten metal girders or plates together; 2. something similar used to reinforce seams on work clothes —*vt*. 1. to fasten with rivets; 2. to hold or fix (one's attention, eyes, and so on)

- *Rivets* are used to fasten steel beams together and to fasten an airplane's skin to its frame.
- *Rivets* are often used on blue jeans and coveralls.
- When parts are *riveted* together, they can't be loosened the way they can when screws are used.
- Roxane's eyes were *riveted* by the sight of the jumbo jet coming in for a landing.

  [-ed, -ing]

rudder (RUHD er) *n*. 1. a flat board fixed to the back of a boat or ship and used to steer; 2. a movable attachment to the vertical stabilizer of an aircraft; 3. a guide or control

- A *rudder* seems to be a very effective way to steer a boat; it has been on every watercraft except small, rowed boats since ancient times.
- An airplane's *rudder* is almost always the rearmost part of the craft.
- The White House often tries to act as a *rudder* for public opinion.

ruminate (ROO min ayt) *vt*. 1. to chew cud, like a cow or other ruminant; 2. to think over; consider; meditate

- Cattle, antelope, deer, buffalo, and giraffes all *ruminate*.
- Jerri *ruminated* over the job offer made to her by a competing company.
- Ian *ruminated* over which of the three universities' offers of admission he was going to accept.

  [-d, ruminating] [Syn. meditate]

ruthless (ROOTH lis) *adj*. having no pity; pitiless; cruel

- Atilla the Hun was *ruthless* toward his opponents.
- Neil used to go out with a girl named Ruth, but since she *ruthlessly* left him, he's been Ruthless.
- Organized crime is looking for *ruthless* persons to work as enforcers.

  [-ly *adv.*, -ness *n.*] [Syn. cruel]

QUICK REVIEW #120

Match the word from column 2 with the word from column 1 that means most nearly the same thing.

1. resolve	a. cruel
2. rhinestone	b. guide
3. rigid	c. decide
4. rivet	d. unbending
5. rudder	e. hold
6. ruminate	f. glass
7. ruthless	g. meditate

S

salutary (SAL yoo TER ee) *adj.* 1. conducive to or promoting good health; 2. serving a good purpose in some way; beneficial

- Regular exercise has a *salutary* effect on one's health.
- Over the years, the use of new materials in running shoes has had a *salutary* effect on the speed of sprinters.

  [salutarily *adv.*] [Syn. beneficial]

schematic (ski MAT ik) *n.* a drawing of an architect's plan (blueprint) or a drawing to show the layout of something, such as electrical wiring

- *Schematic* diagrams of a car's wiring are in every automobile's service manual.
- An architect's version of a *schematic* is usually drawn in white on a blue background and is known as a blueprint.

scrutiny (SKROO tin ee) *n.* 1. close examination; close inspection; 2. a long, continuous watch; surveillance

- Legislative bodies should always be under the *scrutiny* of the electorate.
- After extensive *scrutiny* of the pros and cons, the New Jersey Nets' new owners decided to move the team to Brooklyn, New York.
- For decades, U.S. satellites and spy planes kept the Soviet Union under *scrutiny.*

sedulous (SEJ oo lis) *adj.* 1. working steadily and hard; diligent; 2. persistent

- Mack was *sedulous* in his studies of Elizabethan poetry.
- Jeannie was *sedulous* in making sure that she got the best interest rate available.

  [-ly *adv.*] [Syn. busy]

sermon (SOER min) *n.* 1. a speech given as instruction on religious subject matter or morality by a clergyman during a religious service; 2. any speech on behavior, especially a long-winded, boring one

- The subject of many a *sermon* has been that fools rush in where angels fear to tread.
- It is not unusual for the giver of a *sermon* to be referred to as preachy.

sextant (SEKS tint) *n.* a navigational instrument used at sea to find the position of a ship by sighting the horizon and a known star

- Navigators have used *sextants* to guide ships since the second half of the eighteenth century.
- The *sextant* is named for its shape, which is a pie-shaped sixth of a circle.

shard (SHAHRD) *n.* 1. a broken fragment of pottery or glass; 2. (zoology) a hard covering such as a shell, plate, or scale

- *Shards* of broken pottery can be packed into the bottom of a flowerpot to provide drainage for plants.

- While a *shard* is the zoological term for a hard shell or scale, it is not often used in this manner.
- In ancient Greece, *shards* of pottery were known as ostra, and if enough people wrote a man's name on ostra, he was ostracized—made to depart from the city-state.

signatory (SIG nuh TAW ree) *n.* a signer; one who signed an agreement, treaty, contract, and so on

- John Hancock was the first *signatory* of the Declaration of Independence.
- A *signatory* to a contract accepts responsibility for fulfilling that contract.
  [signatories *pl.*] [Syn. endorser]

smelt (SMELT) *vt.* 1. to heat or fuse ore; to refine; 2. to separate impurities from metal by heating it —*n.* small silver-colored food fish found in northern lakes and seas

- When tin and copper are *smelted* together in the proper proportions, bronze is the result.
- Steel is a product of *smelting,* where certain impurities are deliberately added to give the finished product desirable qualities.
- I ate some delicious fried *smelts* with cocktail sauce last night as an appetizer.
  [-ed, -ing] [Syn. refine]

sobriety (suh BRY i tee) *n.* 1. the state of being temperate and not overindulging, especially in alcoholic drinks; soberness; 2. seriousness

- If a car is being driven erratically, it might be pulled over and the driver given a *sobriety* test.
- During the Cuban missile crisis of the early 1960s, the entire world recognized the *sobriety* of the situation.

sordid (SAWR did) *adj.* dirty; filthy; wretched; base; ignoble; mean

- Saddam Hussein's regime in Iraq was *sordid.*
- *Sordid* behavior was customary in the cow towns of the Old West, where debauchery was the norm.
  [-ly *adv.*] [Syn. base]

splice (SPLYS) *vt.* to join pieces together by weaving or intertwining (as with ropes, wires, and so on)

- In a pigtail *splice,* the bare ends of two wires are twisted together, and then hot solder is applied.
- A Western Union *splice* is the most elegant as well as the strongest wire *splice.*
- A square knot is a very effective way to *splice* two ropes together.
  [-d, splicing] [Syn. join]

spontaneity (SPAHN ti NEE i tee) *n.* 1. acting spontaneously; 2. doing things on the spur of the moment without external incitement; acting with self-motivation

- By definition, *spontaneity* is incapable of being planned.
- *Spontaneity* must come from within oneself, and some people have it, while others are afraid of it.

squander (SKWAHN doer) *vt.* to waste; to spend or use wastefully

- Norma *squandered* her money on a CD because she could not wait two days for it to go on sale.
- Jimmy Carter's administration refused to *squander* billions of dollars on the B-1 bomber program.

[-ed, -ing] [Syn. waste]

QUICK REVIEW #121

Match the word from column 2 with the word from column 1 that means most nearly the same thing.

1. salutary		a. waste	
2. schematic		b. join	
3. scrutiny		c. speech	
4. sedulous		d. self-motivated	
5. sermon		e. instrument	
6. sextant		f. surveillance	
7. shard		g. plan	
8. signatory		h. endorser	
9. smelt		i. seriousness	
10. sobriety		j. fragment	
11. sordid		k. base	
12. splice		l. refine	
13. spontaneity		m. busy	
14. squander		n. beneficial	

static (STA tik) *adj.* 1. at rest; not moving; stationary; 2. the opposite of dynamic —*n.* 1. an electrical discharge; 2. the noise produced by an electrical discharge

- The leadership of most dictatorships tends to be *static* because the leader rarely changes.
- *Static* electricity is so named because it does not travel in currents.
- Lightning is a giant discharge of *static* electricity between two clouds or between a cloud and the earth.
- *Static* is an annoyance of AM radio broadcasts but is absent from FM radio.

  [-ally *adv.*] [Syn. stationary]

stimuli (STIM yoo ly) *n.* the plural of stimulus; things that incite or cause reactions; incentives

- Mosquito bites are *stimuli* for scratching (though you shouldn't).
- Special receptors in the nose are affected by the *stimuli* of odors and cause impulses to be sent to the brain.
- Reactions are triggered by *stimuli*.

  [stimulus *sing.*] [Syn. incentives]

stint (STINT) *n.* 1. an assigned task or job; 2. an amount of time spent at a certain task

- Gregory's *stint* was that of a parachute packer.
- Buddy spent an 18-month *stint* on an army base in Alaska.

stockade (stah KAYD) *n.* 1. a barricade or fence, made up of vertical stakes driven into the ground, for the purpose of protection; 2. a fort enclosed in similar walls

- Western frontier forts seen in the movies are *stockades*.
- A *stockade* is also a structure that used to detain prisoners.
- The *stockade* fences of today are not actually stockades because only occasional posts are driven into the ground.

stolid (STAHL id) *adj.* showing little or no emotional reaction; impassive

- A *stolid* expression is essential to being a successful poker player.
- One who is *stolid* all the time is very little fun to be around.

  [-ly *adv.*] [Syn. impassive]

subliminal (suhb LIM in il) *adj.* beneath the level of consciousness, especially suggestions to the unconscious meant to evoke or teach certain behavior

- *Subliminal* suggestions repeated over and over again have long been thought to change someone's overt behavior.
- One of the most insidious uses of such messages is in *subliminal* advertising, where one's unconscious is deliberately bombarded in an effort to make that person buy a certain product.

  [-ly *adv.*]

substantive (SUB stin tiv *or* sub STAN tiv) *adj.* 1. considerable in amount or quantity; 2. having real existence; actual; 3. of or relating to legal rights, as distinguished from procedural matters

- A *substantive* quantity is the same as a substantial quantity.
- For a matter to be *substantive* it must be actual rather than theoretical, for example, an error of commission rather than one of omission.
- A person who has invested money in a company has a *substantive* interest in the success of that organization.

  [-ly *adv.*] [Syn. actual]

subsume (suhb SOOM) *vt.* 1. to include within a larger group or class; 2. to demonstrate or show that something is covered by an existing rule or law

- No law is required to allow you the freedom to speak in a public park because that is *subsumed* by the First Amendment to the Constitution.
- If the Pennsylvania state legislature tried to pass a capital punishment law instituting drawing and quartering, any opposing legislator could prove that such a law is *subsumed* by the Constitution's prohibition of cruel or unusual punishment.

  [-d, subsuming]

summarily (suh MER i lee) *adv.* 1. promptly and without formality; expeditious; 2. hastily and arbitrarily

- The libel case was dismissed by the court *summarily*.
- Randy *summarily* jumped to the conclusion that his brother had damaged his car.

  [summary *adj.*] [Syn. expeditiously]

superimpose (SOO poer im POHZ) *vt.* to place or lay one thing on top of something else; stack; overlay

- Many striking photographic images have been obtained by *superimposing* two or more different images.
- It is a mistake to *superimpose* your moral code on somebody else.

  [-d, superimposing]

sympathetic (SIM puh THET ik) *adj.* 1. of, showing, feeling, or expressing sympathy; 2. in agreement with one's feelings, tastes, and so on; congenial; 3. showing favor, agreement, or approval

- It is never out of style to be *sympathetic* to another person's loss.
- Mary was *sympathetic* toward Joseph's love of red cars.
- Tom's parents were *sympathetic* to his desire to continue his education in graduate school.

  [-ally *adv.*] [Syn. tender, congenial]

QUICK REVIEW #122

Match the word from column 2 with the word from column 1 that means most nearly the same thing.

1. static   a. incentives

2. stimuli   b. overlay

3. stint   c. include

4. stockade   d. stationary

5. stolid   e. tender

6. subliminal   f. task

7. substantive   g. unconscious

8. subsume   h. expeditiously

9. summarily   i. barricade

10. superimpose   j. actual

11. sympathetic   k. impassive

T – U

tacit (TA sit) *adj.* 1. implied; unspoken; 2. not expressed openly, but understood

- *Tacit* reasons are not tangible reasons, and vice versa.
- A second baseman and a shortstop have a *tacit* understanding of who is to cover second base in case of a ground ball.
- It is illegal for a politician to accept money in exchange for a political favor, but it's hard to prove guilt when the agreement is *tacit*.

  [-ly *adv.*] [Syn. implied]

tangible (TAN ji buhl) *adj.* 1. that can be touched; 2. real and able to be valued; perceptible; 3. capable of being understood

- Anything that one can touch is *tangible*.
- One's *tangible* assets are those whose value can be stated.
- If someone is talking but not really saying anything, there is no *tangible* reason to listen.

  [tangibly *adv.*] [Syn. perceptible]

tarnish (TAHR nish) *vt.* 1. to dull the lustre of a metal surface; 2. to besmirch someone's character —*n.* 1. the dullness or oxidation of metal; discoloration; 2. a blemish; a stain

- Silver *tarnishes* in air and always looks dull if left unpolished.
- *Tarnishing* someone's character without valid reason constitutes the crime of libel.
- Polishing metal removes *tarnish* from it.

  [-ed, -ing]

taxonomy (tak SAH nuh mee) *n.* the science of classifying plants and animals by their likenesses to one another, beginning with the most general relationships and getting more and more specific (The classifications, in order, are kingdom, phylum, class, order, family, genus, species.)

- *Taxonomy* was first developed by Carolus Linnaeus, a Swedish botanist of the eighteenth century.
- Linnaeus's *taxonomy* shows humans as genus *Homo,* and species, *sapiens;* hence, all humans are *Homo sapiens.*

  [taxonomic *adj.*, taxonomically *adv.*]

thesis (THEE sis) *n.* 1. a proposition to be argued or defended; 2. a formal and lengthy research paper, usually for a graduate degree; 3. an unproven premise assumed to be true

- The *thesis* of Wilma's argument was that brontosaurus burgers were healthier than tyrannosaurus burgers.
- Bart selected as the topic for his *thesis* the proposition that babies drink more milk than grownups because they don't know any better.
- It is an underlying *thesis* of geometry that a line is infinite in length.

  [theses *pl.*]

336

tiff (TIF) *n.* 1. a slight fit of ill humor; a huff; 2. a petty argument or fight; spat
- When Vicki found that her new MP-3 player didn't work, she had a *tiff*.
- Fred and Ethel had a *tiff* over where they should go on their vacation.
  [Syn. spat]

torpor (TAWR puhr) *n.* 1. a condition of dormancy; sluggishness; temporary (either partial or total) loss of sensation or motion; stupor; 2. dullness or apathy
- After 24 hours of sleeplessness, *torpor* is likely to set in.
- *Torpor* is characteristic among those who spent hours before their TVs in the old days watching the political conventions from gavel to gavel.
  [Syn. stupor]

tranquil (TRAN kwil) *adj.* 1. peaceful; serene; calm; free from agitation; 2. quiet and motionless
- The *tranquil* countryside has been the backdrop to many a violent novel.
- The ocean may be violent on a stormy day but *tranquil* on a calm one.
- Try to maintain a *tranquil* attitude, and you'll have far less heartburn.
  [-ly *adv.*] [Syn. calm]

transgress (trans GRES) *vt.* 1. to overstep one's bounds; 2. to violate the law —*vi.* to sin
- Running a stop sign is a *transgression* of traffic law.
- A sin is a *transgression* against God.
- Eating pork is a *transgression* in some religions but perfectly acceptable in others.
  [-ed, -ing, -ion *n.*] [Syn. sin]

transmutation (TRANS myoo TAY shin) *n.* 1. a changing of one thing into another; 2. (medieval) a changing of lead into gold (believed possible then) by alchemy; 3. (chemistry) a changing of one element into an isotope of itself or another by nuclear bombardment or by decay, for example, changing U_{239} into U_{235} or uranium into plutonium
- The *transmutation* of uranium into plutonium is a by-product of some nuclear reactors.
- We now know, through modern chemistry, that the *transmutation* of lead into gold is impossible.
- A caterpillar's *transmutation* into a butterfly is known as "metamorphosis."
  [Syn. transformation]

tritium (TRI tee uhm) *n.* an isotope of hydrogen with atomic weight 3 and a 12.5-year half-life, used in thermonuclear bombs
- *Tritium* oxide is often referred to as "heavy water."
- Molecules of *tritium* are created by bombarding hydrogen atoms with protons in a particle accelerator.

tyro (TY roh) *n.* a beginner at learning to do something
- Those just learning to play the game of golf are referred to as *tyros*.
- One can be experienced at something and still do it like a *tyro*.
  [Syn. amateur]

unfeigned (uhn FAYND) *adj*. not feigned; not made up; genuine; actual; real

- Martha's disbelief at being found guilty was *unfeigned*.
- Harold's *unfeigned* vision problems were questioned by the Selective Service Board.
- Mary's excuse that the dog ate her homework was *unfeigned*, despite her having deliberately spilled beef gravy on it.

  [-ly *adv.*] [Syn. real]

usury (YOO zhuh ree) *n*. 1. the lending of money at an excessive or illegally high rate of interest; 2. a high rate of interest

- *Usury* is prohibited by law.
- The interest rates that some credit card companies charge is akin to *usury*.

  [usurious *adj.*, usuriously *adv.*]

QUICK REVIEW #123

Match the word from column 2 with the word from column 1 that means most nearly the same thing.

1. tacit	a. peaceful
2. tangible	b. implied
3. tarnish	c. amateur
4. taxonomy	d. interest
5. thesis	e. real
6. tiff	f. proposal
7. torpor	g. besmirch
8. tranquil	h. spat
9. transgress	i. hydrogen
10. transmutation	j. sin
11. tritium	k. transformation
12. tyro	l. stupor
13. unfeigned	m. perceptible
14. usury	n. classification

V – Z

vacillate (VAS i LAYT) *vt.* 1. to waver; to sway back and forth; to fluctuate or oscillate; 2. to waver in attitude; show indecision

- It is not unusual for one's position on an issue to *vacillate* as more and better information becomes available.
- Homer and Marge often *vacillate* on where to go for their summer vacation.

  [-d, vacillating, vacillation *n.*] [Syn. fluctuate]

vagrant (VAY grint) *n.* a person who wanders around without a regular job, supporting him or herself by begging —*adj.* living the life of a vagabond; roaming; nomadic

- *Vagrants* may often be found sleeping on park benches in some of our larger cities.
- In some communities, being a *vagrant* is considered to be a misdemeanor.
- "Beachcomber" is a classy description for one living a *vagrant* existence.

  [-ly *adv.*] [Syn. tramp]

vehement (VEE him int) *adj.* 1. violent; impetuous; moving with considerable force; 2. characterized by strong feeling or passion; impassioned; fervent

- The *vehement* winds brought about by Hurricane Charley laid waste to parts of Florida's Gulf Coast.
- Bess was *vehement* in denying any knowledge of the incident in question.

  [-ly *adv.*] [Syn. fervent]

venal (VEE nil) *adj.* 1. readily bribable or corruptible; 2. characterized by bribery or corruption

- The judge did not appear to be at all *venal,* and this was backed up when Don's under-the-table offer landed Don in jail.
- The mayor and the council struck a *venal* bargain on the award of the contract.

  [-ly *adv.*]

veneer (ven EAR) *vt.* 1. to cover with a thin layer of more costly material; 2. to cause to have a superficially attractive appearance —*n.* 1. a thin layer of wood or other material glued as the outer layer over a base material to give an attractive appearance; 2. a superficial appearance of something positive

- It is customary to *veneer* a piece of wooden furniture with a thin layer of finer wood.
- Kitchen counters frequently are *veneered* with plastic for appearance and washability.
- Mahogany and oak *veneers* are both popular in furniture manufacturing.
- Francine has a *veneer* of culture, despite her lack of formal education.

verbosity (ver BAHS i tee) *n*. wordiness; long-windedness; having an excess of words

- The professor's *verbosity* made it difficult for some of his students to decide what was important and what was not.
- *Verbosity* has been a trait of many politicians, but they wait until after they're elected to exhibit it.

[Syn. wordiness]

veritable (VER i ti bul) *adj*. in effect or practically, although not actually

- Karen had a *veritable* treasure trove of World's Fair memorabilia in her attic and basement.
- Victor prepared a *veritable* smorgasbord of meats and cheeses for his guests.

[veritably *adv*.] [Syn. virtual]

vindictive (vin DIK tiv) *adj*. 1. seeking revenge; in the spirit of revenge; 2. acting to seek vengeance

- The judge tried not to be *vindictive* in deciding the felon's sentence.
- Because Sean had suffered defeat at the hands of his opponent once before, he vowed to be *vindictive* in the rematch.

[-ly *adv*.] [Syn. vengeful]

virtual (VOER tyoo uhl) *adj*. 1. being as if, but not actual (for example, virtual reality or a computer's virtual memory); 2. taking place in cyberspace

- Being able to get bleacher seats at Shea Stadium for a weekday afternoon game is a *virtual* cinch.
- When running a memory-hungry computer program, *virtual* memory makes temporary use of disk space when enough real memory is unavailable.
- E-Bay provides a department-store experience in *virtual* shopping.

[-ly *adv*., -ity *n*.]

viscid (VIS id) *adj*. 1. having a cohesive, sticky, liquid consistency; viscous; 2. covered by a viscid substance

- Chocolate syrup is a *viscid* substance.
- When Jack picked up the jar and felt the *viscid* texture on his hand, it took a moment for him to figure out that the honey had leaked.

[-ly *adv*.] [Syn. viscous]

vituperative (vi TOO per uh tiv) *adj*. berating; speaking abusively to or about

- Walter was *vituperative* in his description of his working conditions and his boss.
- When Harold spoke to Maude, he was very angry and did so in a *vituperative* manner.

[-ly *adv*.] [Syn. scolding]

wistful (WIST ful) *adj*. expressing or showing vague yearnings; longing thoughtfully

- Lloyd was *wistful* for the days when he didn't have to work for a living.
- Liza had *wistful* feelings for her childhood home in Iowa.

[-ly *adv*.] [Syn. yearning]

xenophobe (ZEN uh FOHB) *n.* one who is fearful of strangers and/or foreigners

- Norm was a *xenophobe* and kept a high fence around his house to protect him from strangers.
- *Xenophobes* do not normally excel at parties.

  [xenophobia *n.*, xenophobic *adj.*, xenophobically *adv.*]

zenith (ZEE nith) *n.* 1. the point in the sky that is directly overhead; 2. the highest point; peak

- Getting elected president must be the *zenith* of any politician's career.
- When it comes to mountains, the *zenith* of Everest is the tallest in the world.

  [Syn. summit]

QUICK REVIEW #124

Match the word from column 2 with the word from column 1 that means most nearly the same thing.

1. vacillate	a. scolding
2. vagrant	b. fearful of strangers
3. vehement	c. practical
4. venal	d. yearning
5. veneer	e. viscous
6. verbosity	f. tramp
7. veritable	g. corruptible
8. vindictive	h. cyberspace
9. virtual	i. wordiness
10. viscid	j. fervent
11. vituperative	k. vengeful
12. wistful	l. layer
13. xenophobe	m. summit
14. zenith	n. fluctuate

Part III

ANSWERS TO QUICK REVIEWS

Quick Review Answers

SAT WORDS

Quick Review #1

1. e	5. l	9. d
2. k	6. g	10. f
3. j	7. c	11. i
4. a	8. b	12. h

Quick Review #2

1. h	5. i	9. d
2. f	6. b	10. e
3. a	7. j	11. c
4. k	8. l	12. g

Quick Review #3

1. f	5. l	9. c
2. h	6. i	10. g
3. j	7. k	11. d
4. a	8. e	12. b

Quick Review #4

1. e	5. j	9. d
2. i	6. b	10. c
3. a	7. h	11. g
4. l	8. k	12. f

Quick Review #5

1. f	5. i	9. c
2. j	6. k	10. g
3. l	7. b	11. e
4. a	8. d	12. h

Quick Review #6

1. h	5. k	9. c
2. j	6. a	10. d
3. e	7. i	11. g
4. l	8. f	12. b

Quick Review #7

1. g	5. i	9. d
2. j	6. h	10. c
3. l	7. k	11. f
4. a	8. e	12. b

Note: The answers to 3 and 9 can be used interchangeably.

Quick Review #8

1. f	5. g	9. k
2. h	6. l	10. e
3. j	7. b	11. c
4. a	8. d	12. i

Quick Review #9

1. h	5. k	9. c
2. j	6. e	10. g
3. l	7. b	11. a
4. i	8. d	12. f

Quick Review #10

1. i	5. j	9. g
2. l	6. c	10. b
3. f	7. k	11. e
4. a	8. d	12. h

Quick Review #11

1. g	5. a	9. e
2. i	6. h	10. b
3. f	7. d	
4. j	8. c	

Quick Review #12

1. n	6. k	11. e
2. m	7. b	12. f
3. j	8. h	13. d
4. l	9. a	14. i
5. g	10. c	

Quick Review #13

1. g	7. b	13. m
2. i	8. d	14. o
3. l	9. e	15. n
4. j	10. f	16. p
5. a	11. h	
6. k	12. c	

Quick Review #14

1. b	4. c	7. e
2. h	5. a	8. g
3. d	6. f	

Quick Review #15

1. i	5. c	9. d
2. g	6. j	10. b
3. k	7. l	11. a
4. h	8. e	12. f

Quick Review #16

1. k	5. h	9. a
2. i	6. l	10. f
3. g	7. b	11. e
4. j	8. d	12. c

Quick Review #17

1. i	5. j	9. c
2. k	6. b	10. g
3. h	7. l	11. f
4. a	8. e	12. d

Quick Review #18

1. i	5. g	9. e
2. l	6. k	10. h
3. a	7. d	11. f
4. j	8. b	12. c

Note: Answers to 1 and 9 may be interchanged.

Quick Review #19

1. d	5. c	9. b
2. j	6. k	10. e
3. l	7. h	11. a
4. i	8. f	12. g

Quick Review #20

1. h	5. b	9. g
2. k	6. l	10. f
3. i	7. a	11. d
4. j	8. e	12. c

Quick Review #21

1. e	5. i	9. a
2. j	6. k	10. g
3. h	7. b	11. c
4. l	8. d	12. f

Quick Review #22

1. i	5. c	9. b
2. k	6. h	10. d
3. g	7. l	11. a
4. j	8. e	12. f

Quick Review #23

1. f	6. k	11. g
2. h	7. i	12. b
3. l	8. c	13. m
4. a	9. e	
5. j	10. d	

Quick Review #24

1. g	5. j	9. d
2. k	6. c	10. b
3. i	7. e	11. f
4. h	8. a	

Quick Review #25

1. j	5. k	9. e
2. g	6. c	10. d
3. l	7. i	11. f
4. h	8. a	12. b

Quick Review #26

1. c	5. k	9. d
2. e	6. l	10. a
3. g	7. h	11. f
4. i	8. j	12. b

Quick Review #27

1. j	5. h	9. a
2. g	6. c	10. f
3. l	7. k	11. b
4. i	8. d	12. e

Quick Review #28

1. g	5. l	9. a
2. k	6. j	10. f
3. i	7. c	11. b
4. h	8. e	12. d

Quick Review #29

1. k	5. g	9. e
2. i	6. a	10. b
3. l	7. h	11. f
4. j	8. c	12. d

Quick Review #30

1. g	5. i	9. d
2. j	6. f	10. c
3. e	7. b	
4. h	8. a	

Quick Review #31

1. n	6. k	11. c
2. m	7. h	12. f
3. g	8. j	13. a
4. l	9. b	14. d
5. i	10. e	

Quick Review #32

1. d	5. b	9. c
2. h	6. g	10. a
3. l	7. i	11. e
4. f	8. k	12. j

Quick Review #33

1. c	5. d	9. k
2. f	6. g	10. e
3. i	7. j	11. h
4. l	8. a	12. b

Quick Review #34

1. l	5. k	9. d
2. j	6. i	10. a
3. g	7. f	11. h
4. c	8. b	12. e

Quick Review #35

1. e	5. i	9. d
2. h	6. l	10. g
3. k	7. b	11. c
4. a	8. j	12. f

Quick Review #36

1. h	5. k	9. c
2. j	6. a	10. d
3. e	7. i	11. g
4. l	8. f	12. b

Quick Review #37

1. g	5. i	9. d
2. j	6. h	10. c
3. l	7. k	11. f
4. a	8. e	12. b

Quick Review #38

1. c	4. a	6. g
2. e	5. d	7. b
3. f		

Quick Review #39

1. f	7. d	13. b
2. m	8. q	14. i
3. n	9. l	15. j
4. o	10. a	16. c
5. p	11. e	17. h
6. k	12. g	

Note: Answer choice f works equally well for 1 and 5.

Quick Review #40

1. i	7. k	13. o
2. l	8. d	14. n
3. f	9. g	15. p
4. a	10. b	16. m
5. j	11. e	
6. c	12. h	

Quick Review #41

1. b	4. d	7. f
2. h	5. g	8. a
3. e	6. c	

Quick Review #42

1. j	5. b	9. e
2. l	6. h	10. f
3. g	7. a	11. d
4. k	8. c	12. i

Quick Review #43

1. g	5. a	9. e
2. i	6. k	10. f
3. l	7. b	11. h
4. j	8. d	12. c

Quick Review #44

1. f	5. b	9. a
2. j	6. k	10. g
3. l	7. d	11. e
4. i	8. c	12. h

Quick Review #45

1. i	5. c	9. d
2. g	6. j	10. b
3. k	7. l	11. a
4. h	8. e	12. f

Quick Review #46

1. k	5. h	9. a
2. i	6. l	10. f
3. g	7. b	11. e
4. j	8. d	12. c

Quick Review #47

1. i	5. j	9. c
2. k	6. b	10. g
3. h	7. l	11. f
4. a	8. e	12. d

Quick Review #48

1. i	5. g	9. e
2. l	6. k	10. h
3. a	7. d	11. f
4. j	8. b	12. c

Quick Review #49

1. d	5. c	9. b
2. j	6. k	10. e
3. l	7. h	11. a
4. i	8. f	12. g

Quick Review #50

1. h	6. l	11. d
2. k	7. a	12. c
3. i	8. e	13. n
4. j	9. g	14. m
5. b	10. f	

Quick Review #51

1. e	4. g	7. a
2. h	5. b	8. d
3. f	6. c	

Quick Review #52

1. m	6. j	11. b
2. n	7. c	12. d
3. i	8. h	13. a
4. k	9. l	14. f
5. g	10. e	

Quick Review #53

1. d	4. a	7. f
2. e	5. g	8. b
3. i	6. h	9. c

Quick Review #54

1. o	6. l	11. e
2. m	7. i	12. a
3. n	8. h	13. d
4. j	9. k	14. b
5. g	10. c	15. f

Quick Review #55

1. j	5. k	9. e
2. g	6. c	10. d
3. l	7. i	11. f
4. h	8. a	12. b

Quick Review #56

1. c	5. k	9. d
2. e	6. l	10. a
3. g	7. h	11. f
4. i	8. j	12. b

Quick Review #57

1. j	5. h	9. a
2. g	6. c	10. f
3. l	7. k	11. b
4. i	8. d	12. e

Quick Review #58

1. g	6. j	11. b
2. k	7. c	12. d
3. i	8. e	13. n
4. h	9. a	14. m
5. l	10. f	

Quick Review #59

1. l	5. h	9. f
2. j	6. c	10. d
3. g	7. e	11. i
4. a	8. b	12. k

Quick Review #60

1. g	6. a	11. i
2. j	7. e	12. l
3. k	8. d	13. m
4. h	9. f	14. o
5. c	10. b	15. n

Quick Review #61

1. j	5. f	9. h
2. b	6. a	10. g
3. e	7. d	
4. c	8. i	

Quick Review #62

1. f	4. i	7. a
2. b	5. h	8. e
3. g	6. c	9. d

Quick Review #63

1. c	5. d	9. k
2. f	6. g	10. e
3. i	7. j	11. h
4. l	8. a	12. b

Quick Review #64

1. l	5. k	9. d
2. j	6. i	10. a
3. g	7. f	11. h
4. c	8. b	12. e

Quick Review #65

1. e	5. i	9. d
2. h	6. l	10. g
3. k	7. b	11. c
4. a	8. j	12. f

Quick Review #66

1. e	5. l	9. d
2. k	6. g	10. f
3. j	7. c	11. i
4. a	8. b	12. h

Quick Review #67

1. h	5. i	9. d
2. f	6. b	10. e
3. a	7. j	11. c
4. k	8. l	12. g

Quick Review #68

1. f	5. l	9. c
2. h	6. i	10. g
3. j	7. k	11. d
4. a	8. e	12. b

Quick Review #69

1. e	6. b	11. g
2. i	7. h	12. f
3. a	8. k	13. o
4. l	9. d	14. m
5. j	10. c	15. n

Quick Review #70

1. a	4. b	7. f
2. h	5. d	8. e
3. i	6. c	9. g

Quick Review #71

1. e	5. l	9. d
2. k	6. g	10. f
3. j	7. c	11. i
4. a	8. b	12. h

Quick Review #72

1. h	5. i	9. d
2. f	6. b	10. e
3. a	7. j	11. c
4. k	8. l	12. g

Quick Review #73

1. f	4. a	7. d
2. h	5. b	8. e
3. g	6. i	9. c

Quick Review #74

1. c	4. e	7. g
2. f	5. h	8. b
3. d	6. a	

Quick Review #75

1. e	7. g	13. k
2. n	8. f	14. b
3. m	9. j	15. d
4. h	10. l	16. c
5. o	11. a	
6. p	12. i	

Quick Review #76

1. m	6. n	11. f
2. e	7. l	12. c
3. i	8. k	13. d
4. h	9. a	14. g
5. j	10. o	15. b

Quick Review #77

1. g	5. i	9. d
2. j	6. h	10. c
3. l	7. k	11. f
4. a	8. e	12. b

Quick Review #78

1. f	5. g	9. d
2. h	6. l	10. e
3. j	7. b	11. c
4. a	8. k	12. i

Quick Review #79

1. h	5. e	9. c
2. j	6. k	10. g
3. l	7. b	11. a
4. i	8. d	12. f

Quick Review #80

1. i	5. j	9. g
2. l	6. c	10. b
3. f	7. k	11. e
4. a	8. d	12. h

Quick Review #81

1. i	5. b	9. g
2. k	6. j	10. c
3. h	7. e	11. f
4. l	8. d	12. a

Quick Review #82

1. j	5. b	9. e
2. l	6. h	10. f
3. g	7. a	11. d
4. k	8. c	12. i

Quick Review #83

1. g	5. a	9. e
2. i	6. k	10. f
3. l	7. b	11. h
4. j	8. d	12. c

Quick Review #84

1. f	5. b	9. a
2. j	6. k	10. g
3. l	7. d	11. e
4. i	8. c	12. h

Quick Review #85

1. i	5. c	9. d
2. g	6. j	10. b
3. k	7. l	11. a
4. h	8. e	12. f

Quick Review #86

1. k	5. h	9. a
2. i	6. l	10. f
3. g	7. b	11. e
4. j	8. d	12. c

GRE WORDS

Quick Review #87

1. i	5. j	9. c
2. k	6. b	10. g
3. h	7. l	11. f
4. a	8. e	12. d

Note: The answers to 7 and 8 are interchangeable.

Quick Review #88

1. i	5. g	9. e
2. l	6. k	10. h
3. a	7. d	11. f
4. j	8. b	12. c

Quick Review #89

1. d	5. c	9. b
2. j	6. k	10. e
3. l	7. h	11. a
4. i	8. f	12. g

Quick Review #90

1. e	4. g	7. a
2. h	5. b	8. c
3. f	6. i	9. d

Quick Review #91

1. m	7. l	13. g
2. o	8. i	14. c
3. p	9. k	15. f
4. e	10. b	16. n
5. j	11. d	
6. h	12. a	

Quick Review #92

1. j	5. h	9. d
2. g	6. k	10. a
3. i	7. e	11. f
4. c	8. b	

Quick Review #93

1. f	5. j	9. e
2. h	6. k	10. d
3. l	7. i	11. g
4. a	8. c	12. b

Quick Review #94

1. j	5. h	9. a
2. g	6. k	10. d
3. l	7. c	11. b
4. i	8. e	12. f

Quick Review #95

1. j	5. k	9. e
2. g	6. c	10. d
3. l	7. i	11. f
4. h	8. a	12. b

Quick Review #96

1. g	4. b	7. d
2. e	5. c	
3. f	6. a	

Quick Review #97

1. m	6. j	11. c
2. o	7. g	12. k
3. e	8. l	13. d
4. n	9. i	14. a
5. b	10. h	15. f

Quick Review #98

1. b	5. i	9. c
2. d	6. h	10. e
3. g	7. l	11. a
4. k	8. j	12. f

Quick Review #99

1. b	5. k	9. g
2. d	6. i	10. c
3. j	7. f	11. e
4. h	8. a	

Quick Review #100

1. o	6. g	11. a
2. n	7. j	12. e
3. m	8. k	13. d
4. i	9. h	14. f
5. l	10. c	15. b

Quick Review #101

1. g	5. h	9. c
2. l	6. j	10. f
3. i	7. b	11. a
4. k	8. e	12. d

Quick Review #102

1. d	5. b	9. c
2. h	6. g	10. a
3. l	7. i	11. e
4. f	8. k	12. j

Quick Review #103

1. c	5. d	9. k
2. f	6. g	10. e
3. i	7. j	11. h
4. l	8. a	12. b

Quick Review #104

1. j	5. i	9. d
2. h	6. g	10. a
3. f	7. e	
4. c	8. b	

Quick Review #105

1. n	6. a	11. d
2. h	7. i	12. g
3. e	8. l	13. c
4. m	9. b	14. f
5. k	10. j	

Quick Review #106

1. e	4. i	7. f
2. g	5. h	8. d
3. c	6. a	9. b

Quick Review #107

1. b	6. l	11. e
2. n	7. a	12. d
3. f	8. i	13. c
4. g	9. h	14. o
5. j	10. k	15. m

Quick Review #108

1. f	5. g	9. k
2. h	6. l	10. e
3. j	7. b	11. c
4. a	8. d	12. i

Quick Review #109

1. h	5. e	9. c
2. j	6. k	10. g
3. l	7. b	11. a
4. i	8. d	12. f

Quick Review #110

1. g	5. h	9. f
2. j	6. c	10. b
3. e	7. i	
4. a	8. d	

Quick Review #111

1. b	4. h	7. a
2. c	5. e	8. g
3. f	6. i	9. d

Quick Review #112

1. k	6. h	11. g
2. n	7. j	12. a
3. o	8. f	13. c
4. m	9. i	14. d
5. l	10. b	15. e

Quick Review #113

1. c	6. j	11. e
2. m	7. a	12. f
3. g	8. k	13. h
4. i	9. b	
5. l	10. d	

Quick Review #114

1. m	6. b	11. g
2. f	7. k	12. e
3. j	8. d	13. h
4. l	9. c	
5. i	10. a	

Quick Review #115

1. i	5. c	9. d
2. g	6. j	10. b
3. k	7. l	11. a
4. h	8. e	12. f

Quick Review #116

1. k	5. h	9. a
2. i	6. l	10. f
3. g	7. b	11. e
4. j	8. d	12. c

Quick Review #117

1. i	6. b	11. f
2. k	7. l	12. d
3. m	8. e	13. h
4. a	9. c	14. n
5. j	10. g	

Quick Review #118

1. a	5. d	9. f
2. i	6. b	10. c
3. g	7. e	
4. j	8. h	

Quick Review #119

1. d	5. c	9. b
2. j	6. k	10. e
3. l	7. h	11. a
4. i	8. f	12. g

Quick Review #120

1. c	4. e	7. a
2. f	5. b	
3. d	6. g	

Quick Review #121

1. n	6. e	11. k
2. g	7. j	12. b
3. f	8. h	13. d
4. m	9. l	14. a
5. c	10. i	

Quick Review #122

1. d	5. k	9. h
2. a	6. g	10. b
3. f	7. j	11. e
4. i	8. c	

Quick Review #123

1. b	6. h	11. i
2. m	7. l	12. c
3. g	8. a	13. e
4. n	9. j	14. d
5. f	10. k	

Quick Review #124

1. n	6. i	11. a
2. f	7. c	12. d
3. j	8. k	13. b
4. g	9. h	14. m
5. l	10. e	

Part IV

APPENDICES

Appendix A

Prefixes and Suffixes

Certain beginnings and endings can be affixed to some words or stems of words that change their meanings. These beginnings and endings fall into two categories: Prefixes are tacked onto the beginning of a word, while suffixes are stuck onto the end. Together, these affixed word pieces are called -*fixes*. A -fix can change the meaning of a word altogether, like *un*- undoes something, or it can add a little nuance of meaning, as -*ac* turns a mania (a fad) into a maniac. Watch out!

It is not within the scope of this book to comprehensively examine suffixes and prefixes, but in the following table some of the most common ones are listed, along with a brief sketch of what they do to the words to which they're affixed; many also include examples. I leave it to you to determine whether the -fix is a prefix or suffix from where the hyphen (-) is placed: *fix-(word)* or *(word)-fix*. I'm sure you'll recognize many, if not all, of them.

Prefix/Suffix	Meaning/Usage
a-	same as *ab*- before *m, p,* or *v*
ab-	away; from; off; down (*abhor, abjure*)
abs-	same as *ab*- before *c* or *t*
ac-	same as *ad*- before *p* or *q*
-ac	of, relating to (*maniac*)
ad-	motion toward, nearness to
-ad	forms adverbs, meaning toward, like *cephelad*
af-	same as *ad*- before *f*
al-	means *the* before words of Arabic origin (*algebra*)
-al	forms adjectives meaning like (*personal*) or nouns meaning the act of (*rehearsal*)
-an	belonging to or related to (*Mexican*)

(continued)

Prefix/Suffix	Meaning/Usage
-ance	the act or process of doing (*continuance*), something done (*utterance*)
ap-	same as *ad-* before a vowel
-ar, -ary	forms adjectives meaning relating to (*singular, polar, urinary*)
as-	same as *ad-* before *s*
be-	forms verbs meaning around, thoroughly, excessively, treated as (*beset, bemoan, befriend*)
bi-	two, twice (*biplane, bilateral*)
bio-	life (*biography, biology*)
by-	close by; on the side (*bystander, bypass*)
co-	same as *com-* before *h* or a vowel
col-	same as *com-* before *l*
com-	next to, with, together (*compassion*)
con-	same as *com-* before *c, d, g, j, n, q, s, t, v,* and sometimes *f*
cor-	same as *com-* before *r*
-cy	quality, state, or condition (*lunacy*)
de-	away from; off (*derail*); down (*decline*); reverse action; undo (*decode*)
di-	twice, doubled (*diatomic, dihybrid*)
di-	same as *dis-* before *b, d, g, l, m, n, r,* or *v*
dia-	through; between (*diagonal, diameter*)
dif-	same as *dis-* before *f*
dis-	1. away; apart (*disperse, dismiss*); 2. not or *un-* (*dishonest*); 3. lack of; opposite (*disunion, disease*)
-dom	1. rank; dominion of (*kingdom*); 2. state of being (*officialdom, martyrdom*)
-drome	1. arena (*velodrome*); 2. large field or arena (*airdrome*)
dyn-, dyna-	power (*dynamo, dynameter*)
dys-	bad, impaired, abnormal (*dysfunctional*)

Prefix/Suffix	Meaning/Usage
-eer	a person who makes or does things (*engineer, pamphleteer*)
ef-	same as *ex-* before *f*
em-	same as *en-* before *b*, *m*, or *p* (*emboss, empower*)
en-	1. to cover or wrap (*enrobe*); 2. to cause to be or to make into (*endanger*); in or into (*encase*)
end-	same as *endo-* before a vowel
endo-	within (*endosperm, endocrine*)
epi-	on the outside (*epidermis*)
equi-	equally (*equiangular*)
-er	1. a person having to do with or from somewhere (*hatter, writer, New Yorker*); 2. forming the comparative (*bigger*)
-ery	1. a place for, or a place to be (*eatery, winery*); 2. the act of (*robbery*)
-est	forming the superlative (*greatest, smallest*)
ex-	former (*exwife*)
exo-	outside (*exoskeleton*)
-fy	make; cause to become (*liquefy, putrefy*)
-gamy	marriage (*polygamy*)
geo-	of the earth (*geology*)
-gon	having a certain number of angles (*octagon*)
-gram	to write (*diagram*)
-graph	something that writes, or is written (*telegraph*)
helio-	relating to the sun (*heliotropism*)
hex-	same as *hexa-* before a vowel
hexa-	six (*hexagon*)
holo-	entire, whole (*holograph*)
hom-	same as *homo-* before a vowel
homo-	same, equal, alike (*homonym*)

(continued)

Prefix/Suffix	Meaning/Usage
hydro-	1. water (*hydrometer*); 2. containing hydrogen (*hydrochloric*)
-iatry	treatment (*psychiatry*)
-ic	having to do with (*volcanic*)
-ide	the end of the second name in a compound whose molecule contains exactly two atoms (*sodium chloride*)
idio-	one's own, personal (*idiosyncrasy*)
il-	same as *in-* used before *l*
im-	same as *in-* used before *b, m,* or *p*
in-	in, into, within, (*inside*); toward (*inward*); also used to intensify some words of Latin origin (*inbreed, induct, infer*)
-ine	having the nature of; like (*crystalline*)
inter-	between or among (*interval*); 2. together (*interact*)
intra-	within, inward (*intramural*)
intro-	same as *intra-* (*introvert*)
ir-	same as *in-* used before *r*
-ism	1. condition of being (*pauperism*); 2. devotion to (*nationalism*)
iso-	equal, similar, alike (*isobar*)
-ist	1. one who does or participates in an *-ism* (*satirist*); 2. an expert at something (*scientist*); 3. a believer or adherent to (*atheist*)
-istic, -istical	the former of adjectives relating to an action (*artistic, egotistical*)
-ite	1. inhabitant or native of (*Brooklynite*); 2. a salt of (*halite*); 3. a certain rock (*lignite*); 4. a descendant of (*Israelite*)
-itis	an inflammatory disease (*tonsilitis*)
-lepsy	a fit or attack (*epilepsy*)
-let	1. small, diminutive (*starlet*); 2. small object worn as a band on the body (*anklet*)
lipo-	fatty (*liposuction*)
-lith, -lithic	stone (*batholith, neolithic*)
-logy	study of (*biology*)

Prefix/Suffix	Meaning/Usage
-lysis	destruction; dissolving; loosening; dissolution (*analysis*)
macro-	large or enlarged (*macrobiotic*)
-mania	a mental disorder or a wild enthusiasm for something (*pyromania, hulamania*)
-maniac	a person affected by a mania (*cleptomaniac*)
maxi-	maximum; of larger scope than usual (*maxi-power*), often hyphenated as an attachment to a word
micro-	very small; a millionth of a unit (*microscope, micrometer*)
milli-	one one-thousandth of a unit (*milliliter*)
mini-	miniature (*miniskirt*)
mis-	wrong; wrongly; bad; poorly (*miscue, misfire*)
mult-	same as *multi-* before a vowel
multi-	much; many; more than two (*multichanneled*)
narco-	1. sleep (*narcolepsy*); 2. narcotic (*narcotism*)
neur-	same as *neuro-* before a vowel
neuro-	of the nerves or nervous system (*neurology, neuritis*)
non-	not; the opposite of (*nonagressive*)
nona-	nine (*nonagon, nonet*)
-nym	name (*pseudonym*)
o-	same as *ob-* before *m*
ob-	1. to; for; in front of (*obtrude*); 2. opposed to; against; opposite (*obverse*); 3. upon; over (*obscure*)
oc-	same as *ob-* before *c*
oct(a/o)-	eight (*octagon, octopus*)
of-	same as *ob-* before *f*
-oid	like; resembling (*ovoid*)
op-	same as *ob-* before *p*
-or	1. a person or thing that does something specific (*addressor, incisor*); 2. a quality or condition (*error, savor*)

(continued)

Prefix/Suffix	Meaning/Usage
-otic	1. of or affected with (*neurotic*); 2. producing (*hypnotic*)
oto-	of the ear (*ototic*)
-ous	full of (*beauteous, capacious*)
over-	excessive (*overact, overindulge*)
paleo-	ancient (*paleontology, paleolithic*)
pan-	embracing all (*pantheistic*)
para-	by the side of; subordinate to (*paralegal, paraprofessional*)
-ped	foot (*biped*)
penta-	five (*pentagon*)
peri-	1. beyond; around (*periscope*); 2. near (*perinatal*)
phleb-	same as *phlebo-* before a vowel
phlebo-	vein (*phlebotomy*)
photo-	of or produced by light (*photocopy*)
phyto-	floral; of a plant; vegetation (*phytoplankton*)
plano-	having one side flat (*planoconvex*)
pneumo-	of breathing; the lungs; respiration (*pneumococcal*)
poly-	many (*polygon*)
pre-	before (*prefix*)
pro-	for (*proactive*)
proto-	first in time or importance (*protoplasm*)
pseudo-	false (*pseudonym*)
psych-	same as *psycho-* before a vowel
psycho-	of the mind (*psychotic*)
quadri-	four (*quadrilateral, quadriped*)
re-	again (*rethink*)
retro-	backward (*retrofit*)
rheo-	a flow; current (*rheostat*)
rhino-	nose (*rhinoplasty*)

Prefix/Suffix	Meaning/Usage
self-	of oneself; automatic (*self-interest, self-loading*)
semi-	half; twice in a specified period (*semicircle, semiannually*)
sub-	1. under; beneath; below (*subhuman*); 2. of lower rank than; inferior (*subordinate*); 3. to a lesser degree (*subpar*); 4. near; almost (*substitute*)
suf-	same as *sub-* before *f*
sym-	same as *syn-* before *b, m,* or *p*
syn-	together; at the same time (*synchronize*)
sys-	same as *syn-* before *s, h,* and other aspirate sounds
tele-	at a distance (*telecommute*); of, in, or by (*televise*)
tran-	same as *trans-* before *s*
trans-	across; on the other side of; above and beyond (*transcend, transcontinental*)
tri-	three (*triangle*)
un-	not (*unused, unsupervised*)
vice-	one who acts in place of; second in command (*viceroy, vice president*)

Appendix B

Foreign Phrases

Many phrases and expressions from foreign languages have found a place in everyday English among the better educated. Some of them have been adopted and have found their way into everyone's vocabulary, while some remain foreign yet are used often enough to be worth listing here. A disproportionate number of the words are Latin and French. This should not be a surprise, considering the prominent roles that the French played in our history and literature and that the Romans, whose language was Latin, played in the history of Europe and Britain.

Letters in brackets stand for the language from which the phrase comes, as follows:

Ar., Arabic

Fr., French

Ger., German

Haw., Hawaiian

Heb., Hebrew

Ire., Irish

It., Italian

L., Latin

Sp., Spanish

Foreign Phrase	Definition
adeste fidelis [L.]	always faithful
ad hoc [L.]	temporary
à droite [Fr.]	on the right
affaire d'honneur [Fr.]	a matter of honor
à gauche [Fr.]	on the left
à la rigeur [Fr.]	strictly speaking; if absolutely needed

(continued)

Foreign Phrase	Definition
aloha oe [Haw.]	greetings; love to you; farewell
alter ego [L.]	other self; constant companion
amicus curiae [L.]	friend of the court
amor vincit omnia [L.]	"Love conquers all."—Virgil
anno regni [L.]	year in the reign of
à pied [Fr.]	on foot
ars gratia artis [L.]	art for art's sake
au contraire [Fr.]	to the contrary
autre chose [Fr.]	other thing
aux armes [Fr.]	to arms
avant garde [Fr.]	vanguard; on the cutting edge (esp. in the arts)
avec plaisir [Fr.]	with pleasure
à votre santé [Fr.]	to your taste
ben trovato [It.]	well conceived; ingenious
bien entendu [Fr.]	well understood; of course
bon appétit [Fr.]	good appetite; enjoy
bonjour [Fr.]	good day; hello
bonne chance [Fr.]	good luck
bonsoir [Fr.]	good evening
buenas noches [Sp.]	good night
buenos dias [Sp.]	good day; hello
camino real [Sp.]	royal road; high road
caveat emptor [L.]	Let the buyer beware!
cave canem [L.]	Beware of the dog!
c'est la guerre [Fr.]	That's war!
c'est la vie [Fr.]	That's life!
cherchez la femme [Fr.]	look for the woman

Foreign Phrase	Definition
cogito, ergo sum! [L.]	"I think, therefore I am."—Descartes
comédie noir [Fr.]	black comedy
comme ci, comme ça [Fr.]	like this, like that; so, so
concordia discors [L.]	harmony in discord
coup de grace [Fr.]	deathblow
coup d'etat [Fr.]	*lit.* blow to the state; overthrow the state government
coup de maître [Fr.]	masterstroke
danke schön [Ger.]	thank you very much
danse macabre [Fr.]	dance of death
de facto [L.]	in fact
de gustibus non est disputandum [L.]	one can't argue taste
Dei gratia [L.]	by the grace of God
de nouveau [Fr.]	new
Dominus vobiscum [L.]	may God be with you
en ami [Fr.]	in friendship
en bloc [Fr.]	all together
en clair [Fr.]	clear; not in code
enfant terribile [Fr.]	*lit.* terrible child; child whose behavior causes shock and dismay; mischievous or outrageous one
en garde [Fr.]	on guard
en suite [Fr.]	in succession
entre nous [Fr.]	between us
Erin go bragh [Ire.]	Ireland forever
ex more [L.]	customary
ex post facto [L.]	*lit.* what is done after; retroactive
femme de chambre [Fr.]	chambermaid

(continued)

Foreign Phrase	Definition
fille [Fr.]	daughter
fils [Fr.]	son
garçon [Fr.]	boy; waiter
gendarme [Fr.]	policeman
Gesellschaft [Ger.]	commercial company
Gotterdämmerung [Ger.]	twilight of the gods
gracias [Sp.]	thank you
gravitas [L.]	solemnity
guten Tag [Ger.]	good day
habeas corpus [L.]	*lit.* to have a body
hasta la vista [Sp.]	until next time; so long
haut monde [Fr.]	high society
homme du monde [Fr.]	*lit.* man of the world; sophisticate
id est [L.]	that is
in perpetuum [L.]	forever
inshallah [Ar.]	God willing
in utero [L.]	in the womb
in vino veritas [L.]	in wine there is truth
j'accuse [Fr.]	"I accuse!"—Zola
jeu de mots [Fr.]	play on words
jeune fille [Fr.]	young girl
Kamerad [Ger.]	friend
laissez-faire [Fr.]	let be; leave alone; hands off
le chaim [Heb.]	to life
le monde [Fr.]	the world
l'etat, c'est moi [Fr.]	"I am the state!"—attrib. to Louis XIV
mano a mano [Sp.]	hand in hand

Foreign Phrase	Definition
mea culpa [L.]	my fault
merci beaucoup [Fr.]	thank you very much
mère [Fr.]	mother
Missa solemnis [L.]	High Mass (Roman Catholic)
mitzvah [Heb.]	blessing; commandment
n'est-ce pas? [Fr.]	Isn't it so?
nicht wahr? [Ger.]	Isn't it so?
nil desperandum [L.]	"never desperate"—Horace
noblesse oblige [Fr.]	the inferred obligation of high-ranking people to behave well toward others
nom de plume [Fr.]	pen name
non sequitur [L.]	a remark having no bearing on what was just said; an illogical conclusion from the facts
nouveau riche [Fr.]	newly rich, and hence unschooled in the appropriate behavior of the wealthy
omnia vincit amor [L.]	"Love conquers all!"—Virgil
on dit [Fr.]	*lit.* one says; it is said
o tempora! o mores! [L.]	"Oh times! Oh morals!"—Cicero, meaning "What a time we live in!"
par avion [Fr.]	by airplane; airmail
par exemple [Fr.]	for example
Pax Britannica [L.]	peace imposed by Britain
Pax Romana [L.]	peace imposed by Rome
pax vobiscum [L.]	peace be with you
père [Fr.]	father
peu à peu [Fr.]	little by little
peu de chose [Fr.]	small thing; a trifle

(continued)

Foreign Phrase	Definition
peut être [Fr.]	perhaps
pièce de résistance [Fr.]	the main item
por favor [Sp.]	please
pro bono [L.]	free; without compensation
pro bono publico [L.]	for the public good
pro forma [L.]	according to form
pro patria [L.]	for one's country
quand même [Fr.]	just the same; regardless of consequences
¿qué pasa? [Sp.]	What's happening?
que sera, sera [Fr.]	what will be, will be
quid pro quo [L.]	one thing in return for another
qui va là? [Fr.]	Who goes there?
quod erat demonstrandum [L.]	which is (was) to be demonstrated
quo vadis? [L.]	Where are you going?
raison d'être [Fr.]	reason for being
répondez s'il vous plâit [Fr.]	(*usu.* R.S.V.P.) answer please
salaam [Ar.]	peace (used as general greeting)
salle à manger [Fr.]	dining room
salud [Sp.]	to your health
sans doute [Fr.]	without doubt
sans pareil [Fr.]	without equal
sante [Fr.]	good health
se habla español [Sp.]	Spanish is spoken here.
shalom [Heb.]	peace, well-being (used as general greeting)
s'il vous plâit [Fr.]	please
status quo [L.]	existing condition

Foreign Phrase	Definition
terra firma [L.]	solid ground
terra incognito [L.]	unknown land; unknown ground
tête-à-tête [Fr.]	head-to-head
toujours [Fr.]	always
tour de force [Fr.]	*lit.* feat of strength; an exceptionally skillful production, performance, creation, etc.
tout de suite [Fr.]	at once; immediately
tout le monde [Fr.]	the whole world; everybody
tristesse [Fr.]	melancholy; sadness
Übermensch [Ger.]	superman
und so weiter (usw.) [Ger.]	and so on; etcetera
veni, vidi, vici [L.]	"I came; I saw; I conquered."—Julius Caesar
verbatim [L.]	word for word
vérité [Fr.]	truth; short for cinéma vérité; realism
vice versa [L.]	the other way around; reversed
vive la différence [Fr.]	Long live the difference! [between men and women]
vive la reine [Fr.]	Long live the queen!
vive le roi [Fr.]	Long live the king!
Voila! [Fr.]	There it is!
Wunderbar [Ger.]	wonderful
Wunderkind [Ger.]	child prodigy
Zollverein [Ger.]	customs union